KARI GRIMSTAD is Associate Professor of German in the Department of Language and Literature at the University of Guelph.

'When the name "Hitler" is mentioned, nothing occurs to me' – so said Karl Kraus. For this leading Viennese Jewish critic and intellectual the touchstone of art was ethics. How could he be speechless in the face of a threat to all that ethics means?

To answer this question, the author makes a detailed chronological study of Kraus's intellectual activity as reflected in his work on the theatre. The results are presented in five chapters, each dealing with a different 'mask' adopted by Kraus during the period 1892–1936. Grimstad considers not only theatre and drama criticism in *Die Fackel* and Kraus's dramatic writing, but also biographical data, to help uncover the rationale of his work.

That rationale is the logic of the theatrical mode in which he lived and wrote. The stage was not only his subject matter, it determined what he would see and say. Grimstad argues that when Kraus wrote, his words were the speech of an 'actor' who was often infatuated with himself and obsessed with the need to overwhelm his rival 'actors.' When Hitler's storm-troopers began their march, he could say nothing for the world in which his thought took shape had become a world of theatrics, not 'Realpolitik.'

Kraus criticized plays without reading them and performances without seeing them, obsessed with the belief that his was the voice of all that was true, good, and beautiful. Grimstad observes that he was a prophet who confused the divine inspiration with the Thespian urge, playing to an audience, using a mask for each of his roles, yet thinking he spoke to all mankind, bringing them pure ethos.

This volume will be of particular interest to those working in the fields of theatre criticism, comparative literature, German literature, and Jewish intellectual history.

Karl Kraus

KARI GRIMSTAD

Masks of the Prophet

THE THEATRICAL

WORLD OF

KARL KRAUS

University of Toronto Press

Toronto Buffalo London

© University of Toronto Press 1982
Toronto Buffalo London
Printed in Canada

ISBN 0-8020-5522-2

Canadian Cataloguing in Publication Data

Grimstad, Kari,1937–
Masks of the prophet

Bibliography: p.
Includes index.
ISBN 0-8020-5522-2
1. Kraus, Karl, 1874–1936 – Criticism and interpretation.
2. Kraus, Karl, 1874–1936 – Biography –
Character. I. Title.
PT2621.R27Z62   838'.91209   c81-094800-1

This book has been published
with the help of a grant from
the Canadian Federation for the Humanities,
using funds provided by the
Social Sciences and Humanities Research Council of Canada,
and a grant from the Andrew W. Mellon Foundation to
University of Toronto Press.

All photographs courtesy of
Bildarchiv der Österreichischen Nationalbibliothek

For Hermann Boeschenstein

Alte Liebe rostet nicht.

*Das dramatische Kunstwerk hat auf der Bühne nichts zu su-
chen. Die theatralische Wirkung eines Dramas soll bis zum
Wunsch reichen, es aufgeführt zu sehen: ein Mehr zerstört
die künstlerische Wirkung. Die beste Vorstellung ist jene,
die sich der Leser von der Welt des Dramas macht.*
(F.264/5:31)
The dramatic work of art has no business on the stage. The
theatrical effect of a drama should go as far as arousing
one's wish to see it performed: more than that destroys the
artistic effect. The best performance is that which the reader imagines for himself of the world of the drama.

*Wenn ich vortrage, so ist es nicht gespielte Literatur.
Aber was ich schreibe ist geschriebene Schauspielkunst.*
(F.336/7:41)
When I give a reading, I am not performing literature. But
what I write is written drama.

*Die Masse kann und soll nicht verstehen. Sie leistet genug,
wenn sie sich aus trüben Einzelnen zu jenem Theaterpublikum zusammenschließt, das der unentbehrliche Koeffizient
schauspielerischen Wertes ist.* (F.384/5:28)
The masses cannot and ought not to understand. They accomplish enough when they cease to be dreary individuals and
amalgamate into that theatre audience that is the indispensable coefficient of good acting.

*Ich habe Herrn Moissi Fausts Tod weder spielen gesehen
noch gehört, aber ich bin natürlich dagegen.* (F.577/82:38)
I have neither seen nor heard Moissi portray the dying
Faust, but of course I object to his performance.

❧ Acknowledgments

I would like to thank Professor Hermann Boeschenstein, who originally drew my attention to Karl Kraus, and without whose help and advice this book would never have been written.

My thanks are also due to Professor Hans Eichner, who greatly assisted me in preparing the text of the English translations.

I am grateful to the Österreichische Nationalbibliothek for providing the photographs of Karl Kraus and many of the people he wrote about.

Finally, I owe a debt of gratitude to the Canada Council for a leave fellowship which enabled me to write the first draft, and to the Canadian Federation for the Humanities for a grant in aid of publication.

❧ Contents

~ Preface

Critics and commentators have tried — some more, some less successfully — to put their finger on the unique quality of the character of Karl Kraus. Their problem in its simplest form is this: how can you come to grips with a man who seems to have been able to play so many often contradictory roles? Was Kraus mainly a satirist — or a polemicist? Was he a revolutionary reformer bent on changing society's mores — or an avowed conservative determined to hang on to the old way of life which he saw endangered by progress? Will his devotion to language give us the key? Or will we find it rather in such flamboyant gestures and slogans as his anti-Bekessy battle-cry 'Hinaus aus Wien mit dem Schuft!' [Get that scoundrel out of Vienna!]? Critics who have concentrated on any one of these facets have probably clarified their concept of Kraus to their own satisfaction. For this reader, however, the man was more interesting than any one of these parts. As I examined his works, I began to see that Kraus's mode of thinking and writing was essentially a theatrical one and that it is this phenomenon of theatricality which provides the key to a comprehensive understanding of Kraus both as a man and as a critic. I also saw that it was the theatricality in Kraus's life and works which explains the difficulties faced by students of Kraus who try to pin him down to any one of his roles. Theatricality naturally invites the playing of numerous roles, even though they may conflict with one another.

By theatricality I do not mean merely exhibitionism or affectation, nor is it only a tendency to see and portray life in terms of stark contrasts and antitheses. The essence of theatricality is a management of illusion, in which we take direct aesthetic pleasure from the management itself. Of course, illusion is involved in all art, but often it is merely a way of getting things going and is only in the background. We cannot begin to accept a novel or poem unless we undergo, as Coleridge put it, a 'willing suspension of disbelief.' But once we have suspended our disbelief, we might find our interest occupied by what is immediately being revealed, as in a historical or a naturalistic novel, or in lyric or epic poetry. In the theatrical experience, however, the

consciousness of illusion remains in the foreground of our aesthetic awareness. We want to be fooled. When the show begins, we may gasp at the
setting, not only because of its intrinsic interest but because we see how a
wooden platform has been *transformed*. When the show is over and the
actor takes his bow, we applaud him for having made us almost believe that he
was another person altogether. We do not shout 'Bravo!' at the end of
poems and novels. We do not marvel at the change of the printed page into a
world.

Another way of apprehending the unique importance of theatrical illusion is
to consider the medium of the theatre. Stage scenery, actors, the hall itself,
and the audience around us are physically present. And they are present
realities directly affecting our senses. Words on the printed page, however,
are not in themselves significant. They are not a part of the aesthetic experience: they are only its precondition.

When words are performed, of course, they acquire the present reality of
the theatre. For a performer of words is a real human being shaping thoughts
into sensible sounds and conveying the immediate awareness of human
characteristics. As we shall see later, this possibility of lifting words from the
printed page into the realm of performed experience was one of the great
fascinations of Kraus the man and the critic. So intriguing was the possibility
for Kraus that at times he was led almost into contradiction in his praise of
the Word as the essence of the highest theatrical art.

In short, Brechtian experiments notwithstanding, in good theatre we
must experience illusion qua illusion. But it is important to distinguish at least
three ways in which theatrical illusion functions in our awareness.[1]

The first corresponds to childhood, since it represents the kind of illusion-
making that is appropriate to the fun-loving, playful spirit of children. One
of the first things that children do is to create a world to fulfil their wishes. It is
the world as they would *like* it to be. The child, however, has no intention
of convincing us that this is the way the world actually is. Operetta and farce,
the theatre arts which aim chiefly to play with reality, are works typical of
this kind of illusion.

The second type of theatrical illusion corresponds to maturity. Here we
have a seemingly paradoxical situation. Illusion still remains in the foreground
of our aesthetic awareness, but the artist uses the fabrication of illusion to
illuminate reality, to help us understand reality better. We in the audience
discover in turn what the world really is by virtue of our ability to make
believe. That is to say, our illusion-making powers enable us to step away
from reality to perceive its essential features more clearly and apprehend their
moral significance. Schiller, for example, in his essay 'Die Schaubühne als
eine moralische Anstalt betrachtet,' saw theatrical representation as the quick-
est and most effective method of revealing moral truths:

Welche Verstärkung für Religion und Gesetze, wenn sie mit der Schau-
bühne in Bund treten, wo Anschauung und lebendige Gegenwart ist, wo
Laster und Tugend, Glückseligkeit und Elend, Torheit und Weisheit in tau-
send Gemälden faßlich und wahr an den Menschen vorübergehen ... wo ...
alle Larven fallen, alle Schminke verfliegt und die Wahrheit unbestechlich
wie Rhadamanthys Gericht hält ...

So gewiß sichtbare Darstellung mächtiger wirkt als toter Buchstab und
kalte Erzählung, so gewiß wirkt die Schaubühne tiefer und dauernder als
Moral und Gesetze.[2]

What support for religion and laws when they join forces with the theatre,
where there are concrete examples and a living presence, where vice and
virtue, happiness and misery, folly and wisdom pass before your eyes in a
thousand clear and true images ... where all masks are removed, all make-
up vanishes, and Truth holds court as incorruptible as Rhadamanthus ...

As surely as the effect of visible representation is more powerful than that
of the dead letter and frigid narrative, as surely the effect of the theatre is
more profound and more lasting than that of ethics and laws.

The third stage of illusion in theatre is one of decadence. Here illusion is in
the service of deception and fraud and has become delusion. The artist pretends
to use illusion to discover reality, but in fact he is deluding his audience, since
he is only using the magic of transformation to create a world that he (and
perhaps even they) would wish to be. This is essentially a return to the first
kind of illusion but in a corrupt way, since here pretensions are made not in
the spirit of fun but in the guise of self-deceptive seriousness.

As we shall see, all three kinds of illusion played a role in Kraus's life, both as
objects of his critical attention and as modes of his own behaviour. We shall
also see that Kraus was keenly aware of the enormous ethical significance that
grows out of the relation between illusion and real life. Clearly it is in real
life that our passion for illusion has its genesis. Men come into this world as
natural artificers. The child lives in a state of wonder, constantly creating
worlds that provide room for all the potentialities he contains, which are too
much for ordinary reality. But illusion can also have a sinister genesis. In
modern technological society man is forced to *manage* it. He constantly
changes masks and hats as he changes roles – so much so, in fact, that he often
finds it difficult to know who he really is. Büchner, in *Leonce und Lena*,
allows his fool Valerio to peel off one mask after the other like so many onion
skins. 'Bin ich das? oder das? Wahrhaftig, ich bekomme Angst, ich könnte
mich so ganz auseinanderschälen und -blättern.'[3] [Am I this? or that? You
know, I'm getting scared that I could peel and scale myself absolutely to
pieces.] Here we are offered the possibility that there is *nothing* behind the
last mask – and this is frightening. It is the reductio ad absurdum of man as

a mere player on the world's stage. However, those who recognize the connection between show business and life may adopt an illusion as reality in their own life; accordingly, their philosophy runs: 'What we wish is what is.' But this is a philosophy of unabashed self-deception and is the quintessence of decadence. When we say that 'life is a cabaret, my friend,' we have reached what for Kraus would be the final stage of illusion.

Any observant contemporary of Kraus must have been conscious of his use of the theatrical mode. Obvious examples of his leaning towards the theatrical are his attempts at acting as a young man, his activities as a dramatist in the 1920s, and his very personal use of the theatre in his Theater der Dichtung. But much more in his life was tinged by theatricality: his publication of *Die Fackel*, for example, with its cover (in the beginning, at least) reminiscent of a theatre programme, its contents mini-dramas and maxi-polemics. The 'scenarios' are usually variations on two basic themes: Kraus versus Bahr or Harden or Bekessy, to name but a few, or Kraus in defence of Nestroy or Offenbach or Shakespeare – or Kraus. True, the starring role changed over the years. The youthful gadfly was replaced by the knight in shining armour, the prophet, the Grand Inquisitor, the defeated idealist. The masks were many. Kraus, however, was always guided in his use of theatricality by the belief that his roles were genuine since his intention was true. Others might use illusion to delude people. He would use illusion to unmask this delusion and expose the reality behind it. For him theatricality was as much an ethical as an aesthetic tool; ethics and aesthetics were irrevocably bound together in his concept of life and letters. The tragic paradox is that ultimately his dependence on theatricality and illusion may have caused him to avoid reality and to assume a position of self-deception.

Since I see theatricality as an essential force in Kraus's life, it seemed appropriate to make the main focus of my work a study of his highly individualistic relationship to drama and the theatre. To be true to my subject I have taken a chronological approach to his life and writings in order to let him work out his play from beginning to end.[4]

Ferdinand Raimund

Charlotte Wolter

Above
Zerline Gabillon-Würzburg

Left
Josef Lewinsky

OPPOSITE PAGE
Upper left
Jacques Offenbach

Upper right
Johann Nestroy

Lower
Alexander Girardi

Frank Wedekind

Hermann Bahr

Adalbert Matkowsky

Josef Kainz

Adolf von Sonnenthal

The Burgtheater

Arthur Schnitzler

Bernard Baumeister

Karl Kraus

Opposite
Hugo von Hofmannsthal

Gerhart Hauptmann

Max Reinhardt

Masks of the Prophet:
The Theatrical World of
Karl Kraus

1 The Gadfly
1892 to June 1901

Kraus's interest in the theatre was already evident during his school years. According to his friend Karl Rosner, Kraus as a young boy attended performances of many plays and operettas, both in the Viennese suburban theatres (*Vorstadttheater*) and in the Burgtheater, and was a brilliant speaker and mimic.[1] In the seventh grade, Kraus acted in a performance of Raimund's *Der Verschwender* in a theatre school, and in August 1891 wrote, directed, and acted in a humorous sketch called *In der Burgtheaterkanzlei. Ein humoristisches Imitationsintermezzo*. His first evening of readings before an invited audience was in 1892. Called 'Im Reiche der Kothpoeten' (lit. 'In the Realm of the Dungpoets'), it consisted of selections from modern poets (among them Liliencron and Holz).[2]

His interest in the stage was so intense that he resolved to become an actor. In 1893 he gave a guest performance in the role of Franz Moor in a suburban theatre. Unfortunately, this was a failure (Kraus was outfitted in a costume and wig that were far too large) and he was laughed at by all his literary friends from the Café Griensteidl, whom he had invited to come along. Although he gave two dramatic readings of Hauptmann's *Die Weber*[3] in 1893, he did not go back on stage for many years. As he stated in a very late edition of *Die Fackel,* after his disastrous stage performance as Moor he gave up the idea of achieving dramatic effects with costumes, wigs, and make-up: 'Weshalb ich den Plan, für dramatische Wirkungen dergleichen Utensilien nebst Schminke zu verwenden, sofort aufgab.'[4] The implication of this remark is that Kraus did not, however, give up his intention to produce dramatic effects.

EARLY CRITICISM 1892–8

Before his fiasco on the stage, Kraus had already tried his hand as a critic: from 1892 he wrote articles and reports on the Viennese theatre, both for local publications and for newspapers and periodicals as far away as Breslau,

Leipzig, Bremen, Berlin, and Hamburg. Thus we are well informed of his views on the theatre and on drama during the last seven years before the founding of *Die Fackel* in 1899.

Among Kraus's earliest concerns as a critic were the many pressures that were placed on theatre management. The management of the Burgtheater in particular seemed to have more than its share of problems. Max Burckhard was appointed managing director of this theatre in 1890, a post which he held until 1898. Since the Burgtheater was still a court theatre (officially it was called 'das kaiserlich-königliche Hofburgtheater'), its managing director was under the surveillance of the general manager (*Generalintendant*) of court theatres and was subject to interference from the royal family. The interference of newspaper critics, cliques, and claques who lobbied for certain playwrights was a problem that he shared with other managing directors, as was that of crises involving temperamental actresses; in the early 1890s Kraus especially criticized the leading tragedienne of the Burgtheater, Charlotte Wolter, on this score.[5]

Between 1892 and 1894, Burckhard almost consistently received Kraus's approval for the decisions he made. Commenting on the 1893 Burgtheater production of *Faust I*, Kraus wrote: 'Die großartige Inscenierung war ein neuerlicher Beweis für die Thatkraft und das treffsichere, feinfühlige Kunstverständnis der Direktion.'[6] [This magnificent production was yet another demonstration of the energy and the sure, sensitive expertise of the management.] When faced with the choice whether to make the Burgtheater a 'literary' theatre by introducing plays of literary merit to the repertoire, or to keep it as an actors' theatre with a repertoire based on French melodramas and German farces, Burckhard tried to opt for the first alternative, and this attempt was supported by Kraus.

> *Das Burgtheater überrascht seine Gegner ... nach der langweiligen Kette 'deutscher' 'Lust-' und französischer Schauerspiele durch ein gutes und buntes Repertoire. Interessante Reprisen sollen die furchtbaren Novitäten-schlappen ausbessern. Sophokles, Shakespeare, Calderon, Goethe, Haupt-mann sind allerdings keine schlechte Gesellschaft im Vergleiche zu Wil-brandt, Keim, Davis, Olden, Meyer.[7]*

> The Burgtheater is surprising its opponents ... with a good and varied repertoire. Interesting revivals of older plays are to repair the damages caused by terrible new ones; and indeed Sophocles, Shakespeare, Calderon, Goethe, and Hauptmann are not bad company compared with Wilbrandt, Keim, Davis, Olden, and Meyer.

His only criticism was that Burckhard did not go far enough in this direction, since too few 'literary' dramas were offered and the Burgtheater stage was still dominated by actors and French farces.

Hier eine Serie der Stücke, die seit geraumer Zeit den Spielplan der Burgbühne bilden: 'Der Hüttenbesitzer' von Ohnet ... 'Die Königin von Navarra' von Scribe, 'Eine vornehme Ehe' und 'Ein verarmter Edelmann' von Feuillet, 'Die alten Junggesellen' von Sardou, 'Der Bibliothekar', 'Der Veilchenfresser', 'Fräulein Frau' und 'Der sechste Sinn' von Moser ... 'Der Hexenmeister' von Triesch, auch, aber sehr, sehr selten, einige Klassiker. Das ist die Litteratur unseres Burgtheaters. Theaterstücke, Schauspielerstücke! Und wahrlich, ein Theater soll ja doch vor allem mit seiner Litteratur prunken können, dann erst mit seinen 'Kräften'. Aber wir leben in einer Zeit, in der es keine Schauspielhäuser mehr giebt, sondern Schauspielerhäuser.[8]

Here is a list of the plays which for some time have constituted the repertoire of the Burgtheater: *The Shanty Owner* by Ohnet ... *The Queen of Navarra* by Scribe, *An Aristocratic Marriage* and *An Impoverished Nobleman* by Feuillet, *The Old Bachelors* by Sardou, *The Librarian*, *The Violet-Glutton*, *Miss Woman*, and *The Sixth Sense* by Moser ... *The Sorcerer* by Triesch, also, but very, very seldom, a few classics. This is the literature of our Burgtheater. Plays for the theatre, vehicles for actors! And yet really, a theatre is supposed primarily to be able to boast of its literature, and only secondarily of its performers. But we live in an age in which there are no longer playhouses, but only player-houses.

Kraus commented favourably on Burckhard's choice of modern realistic or naturalistic dramas for his theatre and defended him against the censure of critics such as Ludwig Speidel of the *Neue Freie Presse*, who were for 'tradition' (both in the dramas performed and in styles of acting), as well as against the opposition of a rigid, conservative clique that was influenced in part by that leader of public taste who had 'overcome naturalism' – that is, by Hermann Bahr.[9]

He praised Burckhard's attempts to make the Burgtheater a theatre for 'das Volk.' In 1892, matinée performances at reduced prices were begun, a practice which was greeted enthusiastically by Kraus: 'Durchaus rühmenswert ist der Entschluß ... jeden Sonntag volkstümliche Matineen zu veranstalten. Endlich! Lange hat sich die prüde Vornehmheit der Hofbühne den ärmeren Klassen verschlossen.'[10] [The decision to stage popular matinees each Sunday is absolutely praiseworthy. At last! The prudish refinement of the Burgtheater has long shut out the poorer classes.] He censured the Raimundtheater and the Deutsches Volkstheater (both of which were supposed to produce plays for the education and entertainment of the ordinary people) since these theatres catered to bourgeois tastes.

Das sogenannte 'Deutsche Volkstheater' ... hat sich glücklich und gesund zum Bourgeoistheater entwickelt, zum Theater für die Leute, die ... nach

*des wuchtigen Italieners 'Sündiger Liebe', 'Taub muß er sein' und
nach dem Souper eine gute Verdauung, Ibsen aber überhaupt nicht verlangen ... Deutsches Volkstheater und Raimundtheater ... dienen einer
spießbürgerlichen Kunst.*[11]

The so-called Deutsches Volkstheater [lit., German Popular Theatre]
has happily and healthily turned into the 'Bourgeois Theatre,' the theatre
for people who want to hear 'He must be deaf' after that weighty Italian's
'Sinful Love,' just as they want their digestive juices to flow after supper,
but who never want to see Ibsen ... The Deutsches Volkstheater and the
Raimundtheater are at the service of a philistine art.

However, by 1897 Kraus's opinion of Burckhard had changed. Kraus now
claimed that Burckhard lacked all knowledge of tradition and that he had
instead introduced into the theatre a kind of insipid modernity.[12] No longer
did he praise Burckhard for the realism of his productions; in fact, one of
Kraus's grounds for criticism of Burckhard's 1897 production of Hauptmann's
Versunkene Glocke was that the completely realistic, technically perfect
tone of a sunken bell reproduced in the play was not appropriate. The director
had missed the poetically symbolic significance of the tolling of the bell as
the portrayal of Meister Heinrich's conscience.

*Drei Wochen, heißt es, waren die Bühnentechniker des Hoftheaters an
der Arbeit, den Schall einer versunkenen Glocke – naturgetreu herauszubringen. Das ist einigermaßen grotesk. Schließlich bekam man ein ziemlich
dumpfes und ganz nüchtern gleichmäßiges Gebimmel zu hören. Herr
Burckhard wußte nicht, daß es sich hier um nichts weiter als um die –
naturgetreue Darstellung des menschlichen Gewissens Meister Heinrichs
handelt. Der Glockenton hätte leise anschwellen, dann wachsen und sich
zum furchtbaren, Heinrich tödtenden Schalle fortsetzen müssen. Das
Läuten wird nicht aufhören, der Schall verklingt nie mehr – der Vorhang
fällt. Wie die versunkene Glocke im Burgtheater klang – trotz lang-
wieriger 'technischer' Vorarbeiten: dies mag, da man ja schon im Kom-
mentiren drin ist, als Symbol für die unserem Direktor geläufige Kunst-
auffassung gelten.*[13]

They say that the stage technicians of the Burgtheater were at work for
three weeks producing the – lifelike sound of a sunken bell. This is rather
grotesque. Eventually we were able to hear a rather muffled and quite
uninterestingly steady ding-dong. Mr Burckhard didn't seem to realize that
what was at stake here was nothing more than the – lifelike portrayal of
Master Henry's conscience. The sound of the bell should have at first
swelled gently and then become louder and louder until it killed Henry with
its terrible tolling. The pealing does not stop, the ringing will never die

away – the curtain falls. The way the sunken bell in the Burgtheater rang – in spite of lengthy 'technical' preparations – may serve, since we are already on the subject, as a symbol for our managing director's conception of art.

He now asserted that Burckhard had become managing director of the Burgtheater only by virtue of a bureaucratic error, insinuating that Burckhard was not really suited for the job.[14] This idea was developed at greater length in other articles, in which Kraus's tone became even more sharply sarcastic. In an article in *Die Wage*,[15] Kraus insisted that the appointment of Burckhard as Burgtheater director went against all ethical and artistic considerations. Burckhard, who was a lawyer by profession, had been 'recommended' to the general manager of Austrian theatres, Baron von Bezecny (whose interests were in finanace, not theatre) by a high government official. For the next eight years, Bezecny had taken an active interest in Burckhard's career. The lawyer was first made secretary to the director and, after three months, advanced to the post of director because, Kraus claimed, of 'his artistic incompetence at rehearsals.'

The Burgtheater crisis of 1898 centred around the replacement of Burckhard by Paul Schlenther. Burckhard's dismissal had not been prompted by his artistic ineffectualness, as in Kraus's opinion should have been the case, but rather by the fact that he had become something of an extrovert (he was a cyclist!) and somewhat more liberally inclined. Later in 1898 Kraus reported that the former director had turned up among the theatre critics: 'In achtjähriger Directionsthätigkeit hat er sich allerdings jene Unerfahrenheit in theatralischen Dingen erworben, die in Wien zum kritischen Amte befähigt.'[16] [I must admit that, in his eight years as managing director, he has succeeded in obtaining for himself that inexperience in things theatrical that, in Vienna, qualifies a person for the office of critic.]

The appointment of Burckhard's successor also displeased Kraus. Although Schlenther was a theatre and drama critic, Kraus insisted that he knew nothing about theatre direction. Just as Kraus had played up Burckhard's abilities as a cyclist in order to satirize his inability as a theatre director, so here he focused on Schlenther's interest in beer[17] – on his appointment, Schlenther thought only of the Burgtheater's lucky situation vis-à-vis the 'Löwenbräu,' he was interested only in those plays in which beer was served, he had had the buffet in the theatre equipped to serve beer. Kraus pointed out the ludicrousness of the situation with a somewhat ludicrous pun: 'Man wollte einen Literaten an der Spitze des Burgtheaters haben, und siehe da, Herr Schlenther erweist sich als Doppelliterat.' [They wanted to have a *liter*ary man at the head of the Burgtheater, and behold! Mr. Schlenther shows himself to be a two-*liter*-man (my italics).] In this case, however,

Kraus's satire, although supposedly motivated by an artistic interest in the Burgtheater, remained sharply personal, and, one feels, not quite fair to Schlenther. Kraus seemed to be indulging in satire for the sake of satire, and in this way playing *his* small role in the Burgtheater crisis.

The following appraisals by Kraus of performances by Hugo Thimig and Eleonora Duse best show what his criteria for evaluating actors were in the first three or four years of this period. Both excerpts are taken from an article in *Die Gesellschaft* of February 1893.[18]

Thimigs Schüler [in Faust 1] *[war] eine herrliche, sonnige, natürliche Gestalt. Ja, das ist ein Naturalist, ein echter Menschendarsteller.*

Sie [Eleonora Duse] ist hinausgegangen in die Natur und hat sie begriffen; sie versteht den Schmerz und versteht die Freude, aber eine Freude, hinter der immer der Schmerz lauert. Sie hat kein 'klassisches Profil' und kein schönes, klangvolles Organ und steht doch hoch, hoch über all den in Iamben unkenden Berufstragödinnen diesseits und jenseits des Rheins. Flavio Andó teilte sich mit ihr in die Lorbeeren der naturalistischen Meisterschaft. Die italienischen Veristen haben eine Erneuerung der stockenden Menschendarstellungskunst angebahnt.

Thimig's Student [in *Faust I*] [was] a glorious, sunny, natural figure. Yes, here is a naturalist, an actor who is genuinely able to portray characters convincingly on stage.

She [Eleonora Duse] went out into nature and understood it; she understands sorrow and she understands joy, but it is a joy behind which sorrow always lurks. She doesn't have a 'classical profile' or a beautiful, sonorous voice, and yet she stands far, far above those professional tragediennes who croak blank verse both east and west of the Rhine. Flavio Andó shared with her the laurels for masterful naturalistic acting. The Italian actors of the realist school have initiated a revival of the faltering art of portraying characters convincingly.

Evidently, his usage of the term *Naturalist* and *naturalistisch* has nothing to do with Zolaesque realism and the theories advocated by such 'naturalists' as Arno Holz: he praised Thimig and Eleonora Duse simply for acting naturally and for portraying genuine human beings. In fact during those years he consistently censured all actors who posed and declaimed stiffly in the 'grand style.' He was particularly critical of Charlotte Wolter, the leading Burgtheater tragedienne. In evaluating her interpretation of the 'voice of the Evil Spirit' in *Faust I*, he stated: 'Der böse Geist muß gar nicht sichtbar sein und, wenn er es schon ist, darf er nicht mit so volltönendem Pathos tragieren, wie

es Frau Wolter gethan hat. Muß man denn immer die "Gestalt" und das
"schöne Organ" zeigen?'[19] [The Evil Spirit need not be visible at all, and if it
is, it must not declaim with such sonorous pathos as Mme Wolter. Must
one always show off one's 'figure' and 'beautiful voice'?] The French actress
Sarah Bernhardt was criticized even more sharply: Kraus wrote sarcastically
of 'old Sarah Bernhardt, whose passion is cloaked in stylish robes'[20] and
censured 'the greatest *poseur* of the century' for her inability to appreciate
Ibsen and Antoine's Théâtre libre.[21] In contrast, 'the divine Eleonora Duse'
and the Burgtheater actress Helene Hartmann received Kraus's praise for
the naturalness of their acting. Commenting, for example, on the performances of Frau Hartmann and her colleague, Bernard Baumeister, in Hebbel's
Nibelungen, Kraus wrote: 'Trefflich waren Frau Hartmann (Ute), Baumeister
(Volkert) ... weil sie sehr natürlich waren und den Vers nicht stilvoll behan-
delten.'[22] [Mme Hartmann (Ute) and Baumeister (Volkert) were excellent and
because they were natural did not treat the verse in a declamatory fashion.]

He censured those actors who gave priority to virtuoso 'emoting' and who
changed the text of the drama, thereby falsifying the intention of the
dramatist. In evaluating the actor Barnay's portrayal of Lear, he wrote:

> *Das ist ein überaus verständnisvoller Schauspieler, aber – ein Virtuos. Er*
> *läßt es sich nicht mit Shakespeare genügen, nein, er muß mehr thun, er*
> *will Shakespeare übertrumpfen, verbessert ihn, schmückt ihn mit Sätzen*
> *eigener Erfindung, wenn er mit ihm fertig ist, und zerreißt so die bereits*
> *erzielte Wirkung, zu der ihm der Dichter verholfen hat. Ich denke da an die*
> *'effektvollen Abgänge'. Auch aus dem Leben muß er 'effektvoll abgehen'.*
> *Lear soll schon tot sein, aber Barnay richtet sich noch einmal auf, dreht*
> *'effektvoll' den Kopf und sagt einfach, aber bedeutungsvoll: 'Meine*
> *Tochter! Ich komme, ich komme, ich komme!!'*[23]

Here is an extremely intelligent actor, and yet – a virtuoso. He is not
content with Shakespeare, no, he has to do more, he wants to go Shakespeare one better, he improves on him, embellishes him with sentences of
his own invention when he is finished with him, and thereby destroys the
effect he had produced with the aid of the dramatist. Here I am thinking
of his 'impressive exits.' He even has to make an 'impressive exit' from life.
Lear is supposed already to be dead, but Barnay sits up once again, turns
his head 'impressively,' and says simply but portentously: 'My daughter!
I come, I come, I come!!'

He went on to level similar criticism at Friedrich Mitterwurzer.

> *Der geniale Friedrich Mitterwurzer soll sich ...jüngst in München als*
> *Crampton in Gerhart Hauptmanns prächtigem 'Kollege Crampton'*
> *ähnlich qualifiziert haben. Das Stück schließt mit den zwingenden, für*

Crampton durchaus bezeichnenden Worten: 'So 'n dummer Kerl, Löffler!
So 'n dummer Kerl!' Der Schauspieler ändert. Das ist kein effektvoller
Schluß! Komödiantisch schluchzend und glucksend und vor Rührung
wiehernd umarmt er die Tochter Gertrud: 'Meine Tochter! Meine
Tochter!'[24]

The brilliant Friedrich Mitterwurzer is said to have displayed himself
recently in a similar fashion, in the Munich production of Hauptmann's
magnificent *Kollege Crampton.* The play ends with those compelling
words that are so characteristic of Crampton, 'What a stupid fellow, that
Löffler! What a stupid fellow!' The actor changes this. Sobbing histri-
onically, clucking and snorting with emotion, he embraces his daughter Gertrude: 'My daughter! My daughter!'

Kraus believed that in order to act naturally and to not have to rely on pose
and pathos, an actor not only had to be a great artist but a sincere person
off-stage as well. For example, he wrote about Helene Hartmann and Bernard
Baumeister: 'beide [sind] als Menschen wie als Künstler einfach und
schlicht und warm und natürlich: da gehen beide Begriffe in einander über:
Menschen und Künstler; wie getrennt sind sie bei den andern!'[25] [As human
beings and as artists both [are] simple and unpretentious and warm and
natural: here both notions merge: human being and artist; how separate they
are in the case of the others!] Thus we can trace Kraus's tendency to pursue
ethical judgments into the moral and personal sphere to his very beginnings
as a critic.

In 1894, using naturalness as his criterion, he praised the performance in
Schliersee (Bavaria) of a group of peasant actors under the leadership of
Conrad Dreher. He did, however, caution against Dreher taking this group on
tour, since he felt that the quality of genuineness in their performance of
simple peasant plays would suffer if they lost contact with their peasant
roots.[26]

In the first three or four years of his activity as theatre critic, Kraus was
quite critical of those actors who considered themselves to be stars and who
behaved off-stage accordingly. Charlotte Wolter was particularly guilty in
this respect, and at one point Kraus even suggested that she should be dis-
missed.

Hinter den Coulissen der Hofbühne soll es überhaupt skandalös zugehen.
Frau Wolter regiert: sie kommandiert den Direktor, ... die Regisseure,
alle Schauspieler, das technische Personal. Als sie vor zwei Jahren einiger
Rollen, die eine junge Darstellerin erfordern, enthoben wurde, streikte
sie und drohte mit dem Austritt. Das war die berühmte 'Wolterkrise', die
unbegreiflicherweise alle Welt in Atem hielt. Nun, warum hat man

*damals die Schauspielerin, die solche Ansprüche stellt und sich oft so vor-
schriftswidrig aufführt, nicht in Gottes Namen ziehen lassen? Alle Hoch-
achtung vor den einstigen großen Verdiensten der Dame, aber dem
Burgtheater und – der deutschen Kunst wäre geholfen gewesen.*[27]

Backstage at the Burgtheater matters are apparently quite scandalous.
Mme Wolter reigns: she gives orders to the managing director, ... the
stage-directors, all the actors, the technical personnel. Two years ago,
when she was relieved of roles which demanded a young actress, she went
on strike and threatened to resign. That was the famous 'Wolter crisis,'
which for some unknown reason kept everyone in suspense. Now why
wasn't this actress, who has such pretensions, and who often conducts
herself so irregularly, why for goodness sakes wasn't she let go? With all
due respect for the former achievements of the lady, the Burgtheater and
– German art would profit from such a move.

Such a statement was a far cry from his adulation of this actress in later
years.

Kraus's criticism of actors in 1897 and 1898, however, runs much more
closely parallel to that of the early years of *Die Fackel*. At this point, although
he still used 'natural' and 'naturalistic' as synonyms, they no longer always
were terms of praise. The actor Ermete Zacconi was criticized by him for
depending too heavily on naturalistic detail. He also severely censured the
Berlin actor Emanuel Reicher for his performance in Strindberg's *The Father*.
In the review in *Wiener Rundschau* entitled 'Der Gegenwartsschauspieler,'
Kraus stated: 'Der Naturalismus des Herrn Reicher beschränkt sich auf kleine
technische Neuerungen, die eine durchschnittsmäßige Intelligenz leistet.
Zum unnatürlichen Schauspieler fehlt ihm das Talent.'[28] [Mr Reicher's naturalism is limited to little technical innovations that only require average
intelligence. He lacks the talent to be an unnatural actor.] In an article in the
Breslauer Zeitung on the same topic, his comment was: 'Sein Naturalismus
lebt von dem Mangel an höheren, inneren Qualitäten, und Herr Reicher wäre
herzlich froh, könnte er ein unnatürlicher Schauspieler sein.'[29] [His naturalism feeds on a lack of higher, inner qualities, and Mr Reicher would
be pleased if he could be an unnatural actor.] This last remark is as much a
criticism of Reicher's character ('Mangel an höheren, inneren Qualitäten')
as it is of his artistic abilities. Thus here, too, ethical criteria begin to creep into
Kraus's criticism.

In 'Der Gegenwartsschauspieler' Kraus went on to note: 'Die herrlich
klaren Gedankensätze Strindberg's wurden von Reicher in unverständliche
Interjectionen zerhackt und die Aeußerungen anschwellenden Gefühles
von dieser allesgleichmachenden Spielweise zu nebensächlichen Dialog-
wendungen herabgedrückt.'[30] [The beautifully clear statements of ideas

of Strindberg were chopped up by Reicher into unintelligible interjections and the crescendos of feeling were reduced to trivial turns of phrase by this way of acting, which levels everything.] And in the article in the *Breslauer Zeitung*, Kraus advised Reicher to stay away from plays of literary merit in which both thought and language were important and to stick to plays based on theatrical sensation.[31] This distinction between dramas of literary value and mere stage plays was one which Kraus would develop much more fully in later years.

Although 'naturalism' in the sense of extreme realism seems to have fallen out of favour with Kraus, he still approved of the *naturalness* of some actors. In comparing the performances of the Berlin actor Josef Kainz and the Burgtheater veteran Adolf Sonnenthal in Etchegaray's *Galeotto*, Kraus censured Kainz for underplaying the feelings of the character he was portraying and praised Sonnenthal for the natural tone that he had found to express the emotions of the character he played.

> *Kaum mehr als ein nervöses Spreizen der Finger, ein flüchtiges Grimassiren begleitet seine [Kainz's] 'inneren Vorgänge' ... Sonnenthal ... hat für seine 'inneren Vorgänge' natürliche und herzbewegende Laute gefunden, während Kainz mitten in der leidenschaftlichsten Atktion sich begnügte, die ... Prosa Etchegarays zu skandiren.*[32]

> [With Kainz] hardly more than a nervous spreading of the fingers, a fleeting grimace, accompany the 'events inside him' ... Sonnenthal ... has found natural and moving sounds for those 'inner events,' while Kainz, in the midst of the most passionate action, was content with scanning Etchegaray's prose.

Finally, Kraus began to move closer to the opinion that he was later to express in *Die Fackel* on the subject of the actress Charlotte Wolter. In an article which appeared in the *Breslauer Zeitung* in 1897 (just before the actress's death), Wolter's rendering of the voice of the Evil Spirit in *Faust I*, which he had criticized in 1893,[33] was mentioned favourably: 'Nickelmanns Erzählung von der todten Frau, die unten im See den Finger an den Klöppel der versunkenen Glocke legte, wurde von Lewinsky [a Burgtheater actor] mit einer unheimlichen Größe gebracht, in einem Tonfall, der an den "Bösen Geist" der Frau Wolter erinnerte.'[34] [Nickelmann's story about the dead woman who put her finger on the clapper of the sunken bell down in the lake was spoken by Lewinsky [a Burgtheater actor] with uncanny greatness, in cadences that were reminiscent of Mme Wolter's 'Evil Spirit.'] Whereas previously he had criticized the actress for 'declaiming with pathos' ('der böse Geist ... darf ... nicht mit so volltönendem Pathos tragieren, wie es Frau

Wolter gethan hat'), he now begins to treat 'Pathos' as a positive quality in
an actor's style.

The same peculiar synonymity of 'natural' and 'naturalistic' that we perceived
in Kraus's early criticism of actors is evident in his early drama criticism. In
1892 he wrote of Hofmannsthal's one-act dramatic sketch *Gestern*: 'Naturalistisch ist sie sicher, schon die Studie ist das Naturalistische, und jedes gute
Werk muß naturalistisch, muß natürlich sein.'[35] [It is certainly naturalistic,
the study itself is the most naturalistic [genre], and every good work must
be naturalistic, must be natural.] In the same year, he praised the naturalness
of both dialogue and characters in Gerhart Hauptmann's naturalistic drama,
Die Weber.

> *Hier gibt es keine pathetischen Monologe, keinen Wortschwall; kein
> unnatürliches Wort im Dialog ... keine Drahtpuppen declamiren, sondern
> Menschen sprechen.*
>   *Von verblüffender Naturwahrheit sind die Familien Baumert, Hilse
> und Dreißiger ...*[36]

Here there are no declamatory monologues, no torrent of words: [there
is] not an unnatural word in the dialogue ... rather than puppets
declaiming there are real people speaking.
   The Baumert, Hilse, and Dreißiger families are amazingly true to
nature ...

Gerhart Hauptmann was the dramatist who made the most profound
impression on Kraus in this period. Indeed, to state that he idolized Hauptmann would hardly be an exaggeration. His analysis of *Die Weber* was
particularly sensitive. He pointed out that, although this was not a play in the
traditional sense of the term, it nevertheless fulfilled the requirements of
great (tragic) drama, in that by portraying the development of genuine human
emotion, it awakened fear and pity in the spectator:

> *dieses Drama (ist) kein eigentlich abgeschlossenes und abgezirkeltes, also
> kein eigentliches Schauspiel im streng ästhetischen Sinne ... Und doch
> ein so großartiges Drama, das Furcht und Mitleid erweckt, getreu nach den
> dramatischen Forderungen! Wir haben es wiederum mit einem ... in
> dramatische Form gebrachten Stück Leben, und zwar mit der Vorführung
> einer echt menschlichen Leidenschaft, wie sie wird, ausbricht und ver-
> läuft ... zu tun.*[37]

this is not a really well rounded, precisely defined drama, and so it is not
a play in the strictly aesthetic sense of the word ... And yet it is such a

tremendous drama that awakens fear and pity true to the dramatic rules!
Once again we have to do with a slice of life that has been given dramatic
form, and indeed with the presentation of a genuinely human passion as
it develops, erupts, and disperses.

Hauptmann realistically – and dramatically – depicted the misery of the
weavers. Kraus stated:

> Wie es im menschlichen Innern kocht und gährt, wie das Maß dann voll
> wird, wie es losbricht, das alles ist in dem Drama mit gewaltiger Kraft
> dargestellt. Wir haben hier eine Dichtung vor uns, welche prächtige
> Scenen aus der Wirklichkeit, erschütternde Bilder socialen Elends bietet,
> urkräftig und dabei schlicht und natürlich in der Sprache, mustergil-
> tig in Hinsicht auf dramatische Steigerung, ein echtes Kunstwerk.[38]

How people's feelings boil and ferment, how the measure then becomes
full, how all hell breaks loose, all this is presented in the drama with
powerful force. We have in front of us here a work of fiction that
offers magnificent scenes from reality, deeply moving pictures of social
misery, in a language that has primitive strength and is at once simple
and natural, exemplary as far as the building of suspense is concerned,
a genuine work of art.

In Friedrich Elbogen's play *Dämmerung*, however, the plight of the workers
was not *shown* on stage but was only talked about in a rhetorical manner.
'Das unbeholfene Theaterstück zeigt uns nicht etwa das Elend der Arbeiter,
nein, es bringt nur Worte, hohle Phrasen über das Elend und ist durch-
haucht von einem schülerhaften Pathos.'[39] [This clumsy play does not
show us the misery of the workers, but brings us only words, empty phrases
about their misery, and it is permeated with a callow pathos.] The result
was neither realistic nor dramatic.

In 1897, in his review of a Volkstheater production of Hauptmann's *Der
Biberpelz*, Kraus called the play 'Hauptmann's matchless thieves' comedy,'
and 'the best German comedy since Kleist wrote his *Zerbrochener Krug*.'[40]
He praised the drama's realism and natural simplicity.

> Dieses ... Lustspiel ... zieht seine humoristische Kraft aus den winzigsten
> realen Prämissen: Die Häuslichkeit einer Waschfrau, die Amtsstube
> eines Dorfrichters. Die Handlung beschränkt sich auf den Diebstahl
> eines Klafters Holz, dann eines Biberpelzes ... Aus den unscheinbarsten
> Alltäglichkeiten wachsen die Charaktere in ihrer lebendigsten, voll-
> saftigen Fülle hervor.[41]

This ... comedy ... draws its humorous strength from the tiniest actual
premises: the family life of a washerwoman, the office of a village judge.

The plot is limited to the theft of a cord of wood, then of a beaver coat ...
Out of the most insignificant everyday events grow lively, full-bodied
characters.

Kraus found that the 'activating ingredient of this satirical sketch' was its
lack of plot.

Das treibende Element dieser satirischen Schilderung ist ihre Hand-
lungslosigkeit. Zu ihr gesellt sich der Mangel eines thatsächlichen
Abschlusses ... Die Endlosigkeit dieser Handlungslosigkeit, sie ist es
gerade, was der Hauptmannschen Komödie allen technischen Vorur-
theilen zum Trotz ihren Reiz, ihre kraftvolle Eigenart verleiht.[42]

The activating ingredient of this satirical sketch is its lack of action,
accompanied by its lack of a real ending. The lack of ending of this
lack of action, that is what, in spite of all technical prejudices, gives
Hauptmann's comedy its charm and its powerful individuality.

Even at this early date, one can see that plot was not the prime dramatic
criterion in Kraus's eyes.

Kraus went on to praise Hauptmann's ability as a satirist of society as
evidenced in this comedy, and to chide the audience for not seeing the point
of the satire.

Es ist ein an Gogolsche Karikaturen heranreichendes Bild, wie zum
Schlusse Amtsvorsteher v. Wehrhahn der diebischen Waschfrau, 'der
Wolffen', auf die Schulter klopft und dem Hehler Wulkow sie als ein
Muster der Solidität anpreist. Das Publikum zischt daraufhin, weil es mit
der Aussicht auf neuerliche unentdeckt bleibende Diebstähle der Wasch-
frau entlassen wird, weil es in mißverstandenem Sinne 'die Schaubühne
als moralische Anstalt' betrachtet, auf der, wenn sich schon nicht zwei
Liebende kriegen können, doch zum Mindesten das Gute belohnt und
das Schlechte bestraft wird. Daß ein ganzer Dichter hier die Verkehrt-
heiten dieses dummen Lebens belacht und in einem grotesken Bilde
auffängt, werden die an Schönthans 'Goldene Eva' gewöhnten Leute
wohl kaum gemerkt haben.[43]

It is a scene that comes close to Gogol's caricatures when, at the end of the
play, Judge von Wehrhahn claps the thieving washerwoman, 'die Wolffen,'
on the shoulder and praises her to Wulkow, the receiver of the stolen
goods, as a model of trustworthiness. The theatre audience hissed after
that, because it was left with the prospect of fresh thefts by the washerwoman remaining undiscovered, because it regarded the stage as a 'moral
institution' in a mistaken sense of this phrase – as a place in which, if two
loves cannot get each other, at least goodness should be rewarded and

wickedness punished. That we have here a genuine artist who is laughing at the absurdities of this stupid life and who reflects them in a grotesque picture is hardly noticed by people accustomed to Schönthan's *Goldene Eva*.

In his criticism of both *Die Weber* and *Der Biberpelz*, Kraus shows that he was struck not only by Hauptmann's artistic abilities but also by the ethical stand that the dramatist took, both in his depiction of the plight of the weavers and in his satirical picture of the stupidities of officialdom. That Kraus's admiration for Hauptmann was based on ethical as well as artistic factors can be seen from the following comment on a conversation he had with the dramatist: 'Es war rührend, den bescheidenen, schlichten Mann, der so viel Natur- und so wenig Geschäftsmensch ist, diese Worte sprechen zu hören.'[44] [It was moving to hear that modest, unpretentious man speak these words, that man who is so much interested in nature and so little interested in business.] He was so disappointed in Hauptmann in the 1910s and 1920s because he then felt that the man he had so admired had failed in both an artistic *and* a moral sense.

Hermann Sudermann very early disappointed Kraus, for, although at first he had given promise of being a serious realist, this realism had, in Kraus's opinion, degenerated and become inauthentic. As early as 1893, Kraus wrote about Sudermann: 'Sudermann ist Modeschriftsteller, eben, weil er sich seiner Künstlerwürde begiebt und Handlanger wird, indem er Theaterstücke fabriziert. Er ist nicht einmal mehr der Kompromißler von früher, der Theaterrealist, er ist nur mehr Macher.'[45] [Sudermann is a fashionable writer just because he is sacrificing the dignity of his art and turning into a jobber who manufactures plays. He isn't even the compromiser that he used to be any more, the realist of the stage; he's now only a scribbler.] In his evaluation of the performance of one of the actresses in Sudermann's *Heimat*, Kraus remarked (punning badly): 'Marie Reisenhofer, die Darstellerin der Magda, ist Suder-weibchen durch und durch: Scheinrealistik.'[46] [Marie Reisenhofer, the actress who portrays Magda, is a little Suder-woman through and through: pseudo realism.]

In the early 1890s Schnitzler was among the playwrights Kraus admired, as is evident both in his newspaper articles and in the letters he wrote to the dramatist in 1893. Indeed, the attitude revealed in the letters is very much that of the young, exuberant admirer, who was sometimes even ingratiating in his 'critical' approbation. For example, Kraus wrote to Schnitzler on 22 January 1893: 'Haben Sie zufällig Fr. Bühne Januarheft in die Hand bekommen? Lesen Sie den Artikel von F. Holländer ... Dort finden Sie ... eine *sehr*, *sehr* schmeichelhafte Bemerkung über einen gewissen Arthur Schnitzler.'[47] [Do you happen to have seen the January issue of *Freie Bühne*? Read the article by F. Holländer ... There you will find a *very, very* flattering remark about a certain Arthur Schnitzler.] In the *Magazin für Litteratur*, Kraus in the same year praised Schnitzler's *Anatol*:

> *Arthur Schnitzler gehört gleichfalls in die allererste Reihe der hoffnungs-vollen Jungösterreicher. 'Anatol' ... legitimirt ihn: sieben einak-tige Studien des Fin-de-Siècle-Menschen ... Es sind echt und rechte Komödien ... mit Menschen, die in kurzen, knappen Strichen lebendig gezeichnet sind und wie Menschen sprechen: Décadence, mit gesunder, frischer Realistik dargestellt ...*[48]

Arthur Schnitzler, too, belongs in the very first row of hopeful 'Young Austrians.' *Anatol* ... legitimates him: seven one-act sketches of *fin-de-siècle* man ... These are real, genuine comedies ... with people who are convincingly sketched in short, terse strokes and who speak like real people: decadence, presented with healthy, fresh realism ...

However, shortly after 1893 Kraus's adulation soured. The reasons for this were probably in part of a personal nature. Although Schnitzler's letters to Kraus have been lost, his attitude towards the young critic can be seen in his diaries and in his correspondence with other writers such as Hofmannsthal. In the diaries, for example, Kraus was referred to as 'little K.' and 'K., [the] well-known rascal.'[49] Schnitzler was one of those invited to see Kraus's guest performance as Franz Moor in 1893. His entry in his diary was: '14.1. Theater in Rudolfsheim. Der kleine Kraus fürchterlich als Franz Moor.'[50] [Little Kraus terrible as Franz Moor.] In 1895 he commented: 'Der kleine K., mit dem wir nicht mehr verkehren, der auch noch nach dem neunten ausverkauften Haus ('Liebelei') sagt: "Ja, die Freunde."'[51] [Little K., with whom we don't associate anymore, who, even after nine sold-out perform-ances (of *Liebelei*), says: 'Of course, his friends.']

Schnitzler's remarks make it evident that during this period, in private at any rate, he did not have much use for Kraus either as an actor or as a critic. Kraus's attitude towards Schnitzler changed in a corresponding manner. In his pamphlet *Die demolirte Literatur* (1896), in which he lampooned the Café Griensteidl crowd, of which Schnitzler was a member, Kraus characterized the dramatist as follows:

> *[Er ist] der Dichter, der das Vorstadtmädel burgtheaterfähig machte ... Zu gutmüthig, um einem Problem nahetreten zu können, hat er sich ein-für allemal eine kleine Welt von Lebemännern und Grisetten zurechtge-zimmert, um nur zuweilen aus diesen Niederungen zu falscher Tragik emporzusteigen. Wenn dann so etwas wie Tod vorkommt – bitte nicht zu erschrecken, die Pistolen sind mit Temperamentlosigkeit geladen:* STERBEN *ist nichts, aber leben und nicht sehen!*[52]

[He is] the writer who made the girl from the suburbs presentable for the Burgtheater ... Too good-natured to be able to really tackle a problem, he has rigged up for himself once and for all a little world of bon vivants and *grisettes* in order only occasionally to climb out of these depths to false tragedy. When something like death then does occur – please don't be frightened, the pistols are loaded with spiritlessness: to DIE is nothing, but to live and not to see!

Reporting on a public reading given by Schnitzler of the first act of his *Freiwild*, Kraus wrote: 'Herr Schnitzler verlas den ersten Akt seines 'Frei-wild', einige in der herkömmlichen Weise ganz geschickt gemachte Scenen, in denen er mit seinem oberflächlichen Lebemanns-Humor antiquirte Theater-typen zu zeichnen unternimmt.'[53] [Mr Schnitzler read the first act of his *Freiwild*, a few scenes which were constructed quite cleverly in the customary way. In these he attempts with the superficial humour of a playboy to sketch dated theatrical types.] Although Kraus by no means completely rejected Schnitzler, the predominant impression given by his criticism was that here was a dramatist who was limited, superficial, and old-fashioned, who had a certain talent but lacked true greatness. It is interesting that, in the two instances quoted, Kraus applied his critical comments to both Schnitzler and the characters he portrayed (for example, 'die Pistolen sind mit Temperament-losigkeit geladen,' 'er mit seinem oberflächlichen Lebemanns-Humor'). In the criticism of Schnitzler in later years, Kraus was again unable to distin-guish between his censure of the dramatist and of the characters and failed to see that Schnitzler was being critical of the society he depicted.[54]

Kraus's attitude towards the early works of Hofmannsthal was positive. In his 1892 critique of *Gestern* he wrote: 'Vers und Reim von Meisterhand behandelt, keine Zeile, die gemacht klingen würde, kein Reim, der dem Dichter Schweiß gekostet haben mag. Die Sprache, so schön, so edel, so natür-lich-ungezwungen, wie auf das Kolorit der Scenerie gestimmt, so klassisch-ruhig.'[55] [Verse and rhyme are treated with a masterly touch, there is not a line that would sound contrived, not a rhyme that can have cost the writer effort. The language, so beautiful, so noble, so natural and unaffected, as if harmonizing with the colouring of the scenery, so classically calm.] Kraus drew a parallel between the main character of the play Andrea, who wanted to know nothing of yesterday, and Hermann Bahr, who consistently gave up yesterday's opinions.

Sie [characters such as Andrea] haben jeden Tag eine andere Laune, jeden Tag ein anderes 'Neues', ein anderes fin de siècle, ihnen ist 'morgen Moder, was heute Mode'. Neuidealisten, Symbolisten nennen sie sich, ihr Centrum ist Frankreich, ihr Haupt Maurice Maeterlinck in Brüssel, und nach Deutschland weht ein Zipfel ihres Banners und an diesem hängt Herrmann [sic] Bahr, der echteste Andrea der Litteratur.[56]

They [characters such as Andrea] are subject to different whims every day, every day there is something else that is 'new,' another *fin de siècle*. For them what is modish today is mouldy tomorrow. They call themselves Neo-Idealists, Symbolists, their centre is France, their leader Maurice Maeterlinck in Brussels, a tip of their banner is fluttering towards Germany and hanging on to this is Herrmann [sic] Bahr, the most authentic Andrea of literature.

Shortly before, he had mentioned Bahr's acquaintance with Hofmannsthal, indicating, however, only mild disapproval.

By 1897 Kraus was enthusiastic about a reading by Hofmannsthal of his *Der Thor und der Tod*, written four years previously, but had reservations about the dramatist's later works, which he claimed were written under the influence of Bahr.

> *Hugo von Hofmannsthal (Loris) brachte ... ein seit vier Jahren bekanntes Dramolet 'Der Thor und der Tod' zu Gehör. Mit diesen köstlichen Versen, diesen feinen, wenn auch schon etwas affektirten Gedanken hat damals sein Talent von ihm Abschied genommen. Er tauschte es gegen den Umgang mit Herrn Hermann Bahr ein, der ihn durch seine unaufhörlichen Versicherungen, daß Loris der junge Goethe sei, endlich bethört hat. Seit damals hat Hofmannsthal nichts künstlerisch Nennenswerthes mehr produzirt.*[57]

Hugo von Hofmannsthal (Loris) gave a reading of his playlet *Der Thor und der Tod*, which he published four years ago. With these exquisite verses, these fine, even if somewhat affected thoughts, his talent at that time took leave of him. He exchanged it for the company of Mr Hermann Bahr, who has finally deluded him with his continual assurances that Loris is the young Goethe. Since that time Hofmannsthal has produced nothing artistic that is worth mentioning.

The villain, then, was Bahr rather than Hofmannsthal, which leads us to Kraus's first major confrontation with the Viennese literary establishment.

In the 1890s, Bahr was perhaps the most influential Viennese literary critic, and, with his followers in the Café Griensteidl, he helped set literary trends. Kraus rebelled against this for reasons that seem to have been partly personal (Bahr was a rival critic) and partly idealistic (Kraus disliked Bahr's frequent changes of opinion). His first concerted attack was in 1893, with the article 'Zur Überwindung des Hermann Bahr.' Here, Kraus lampooned the critic's many *Überwindungen* – Bahr had 'overcome' naturalism and now reportedly was ready to 'overcome' symbolism. Kraus's object was to put Bahr in disrepute as a man of letters and as a critic: 'Bahr – der Tagschreiber, der als Litterat überhaupt nicht mehr ernst zu nehmen ist, der im Dienste eines Tagesblattes kritzeln muß, was ihm zum Kritzeln gegeben wird ...'[58] [Bahr

– the journalist, who no longer can be taken seriously as a man of letters, who, at the service of a daily newspaper, has to scribble what he is told to scribble ...] Three years later, he again attacked Bahr in the sharply satirical pamphlet *Die demolirte Literatur.*[59]

It is, however, Kraus's criticism of Bahr as a dramatist and theatre critic that is of specific concern here. In a review of Bahr's *Josephine*, Kraus criticized the play for being boring. Boredom resulted from the coffee-house atmosphere – '*Kaffeehauston*' – of the play: its chatty, everyday dialogue, and its hero's lack of greatness or heroic stature.[60] Similar criticism was levelled at Bahr's *Tschaperl*. The play was 'a completely inconsequential bit of trash, a few silly or at least hackneyed situations'; Bahr had drawn the experiences that went into this play from the 'gossip column of a Monday newspaper.'[61] In addition, the theatrical niveau of the play was extremely low; it was, in Kraus's opinion, as if the last twenty years of German dramaturgy did not exist for Bahr, since he made use of the oldest kind of tricks in his characterization and staging.

In his critique of *Tschaperl*, Kraus also lashed out at what he most basically disliked in Bahr: his pose, his role playing, and therefore what Kraus chose to see as his essential falseness. Bahr posed as both the Austrian man of culture par excellence and the man who had brought culture to Austria. What he actually produced as a contribution to Austrian culture was no more than a string of backstage anecdotes held together by their emptiness of thought and lack of humour, so that in reality he was no more than a hack ('ein Theatertinterl'). This discrepancy between pose or appearance and reality, this lack of honesty (the man *is* not what he would have us think he is), is essentially an ethical criticism and will prove to be one of the main points in Kraus's continuing attacks against Bahr.

Indeed, his dislike of Bahr's 'flexibility' as a critic is but another aspect of his ethical disapproval. For example, in evaluating the performance of Emmanuel Reicher, a Berlin actor in the realistic style, Kraus stated that he felt that Reicher had been made popular as the 'perfect' modern actor by a clique headed by Bahr.[62] Kraus then began to satirize Bahr's subjectivity, his flexibility with regard to critical standards and values, which allowed him to misinterpret and to falsify. His interpretation of an actor's style might fluctuate according to Bahr's reading the previous week. 'Auch auf den zu beurtheilenden Schauspieler überträgt sich dieser ... Subjectivismus; waren Goethes Gespräche mit Eckermann die Lectüre Hermann Bahrs, so erhält der Darsteller eine ganz andere Weltanschauung zugewiesen, als wenn er beispielsweise gerade unter Hebbels Einfluß auf Bahr gespielt hätte.'[63] [This ... subjectivity is transferred to the actor he is reviewing; if Goethe's conversations with Eckermann were Hermann Bahr's reading, then the actor is assigned a completely different philosophy of life than if he, for example, had played when Bahr was under the influence of Hebbel.]

Kraus's censure of Bahr was the first public evidence of his break with the Café Griensteidl crowd and the contemporary Viennese literary scene. The definitive break came with the publication of *Die Fackel*.

DIE FACKEL: THE FIRST TWO YEARS OF PUBLICATION

The first issue of *Die Fackel* (*The Torch*) appeared in April 1899. Its front cover, which looked very much like a theatre programme, proclaimed the theatrical orientation – if not usually of the content, then at least of the style – of the periodical. Against a flaming red background stood the masks of Comedy and Tragedy, with a drawing of the skyline of the city of Vienna forming the backdrop.

The first issue was a programmatic one. Until then, Kraus stated, his fight against the stupidity, ridiculousness, and corruption of contemporary literary life had not been waged by him with as much enthusiasm as he might have liked: he had had to fear censorship, not of the state, but of a chief editor who had to take care not to offend certain cliques (F.1:4). Therefore, the brunt of Kraus's theatre criticism would henceforth be directed against the triangle of the press, the theatres, and the cliques. In the essay 'Die Vertreibung aus dem Paradiese,' Kraus made his programme quite explicit (F.1:12–23). According to him, there existed a capitalist business or market relationship between press and theatre. The press controlled the theatre market in the following manner: the theatres had to pay tribute money to the newspapers in the form of free tickets; the critic who one day sat in a free seat and judged 'freely' would bow before the audience the next day as the thankful playwright, whose play would then be praised by his editorial colleagues. Therefore, the same man not only got free tickets from the theatre as a critic, but also drew royalties as a playwright from the very theatre that was dependent on his critical favour. Such an arrangement was to be deplored on ethical grounds (impartial criticism was impossible if the press had a vested interest in the theatre) as well as on aesthetic grounds – or rather, the aesthetic criticism was part of the ethical criticism. For whereas previously the Viennese theatre had had its roots in the traditions of Vienna (such as the plays of Nestroy and Raimund and the operettas of Offenbach), it was now in the hands of speculators, journalistic jobbers who had sprung up out of the 'garbage of public opinion,' 'operetta usurers' (*Operettenwucherer*) and backstage gossips (*Coulissiers*) (F.1:15).

The meeting places of these taste- and gossip-mongers were the Viennese cafés. Here, they formed cliques that exerted pressure on the two sides they represented – the chief editor and the theatre director. These middlemen who haggled over theatrical standards –' [diese] laut mit Theaterwerten feilschenden Zwischenhändler' (F.1:16) – pressed the 'pure' artist into their mould until he was one of them. The clique which Kraus saw as the most pernicious in its undermining of ethical and aesthetic values was the Concordia, its leading member, Hermann Bahr. However, in the first edition of *Die Fackel*, Kraus chose Julius Bauer as his target, the man who from his chair in the café ruled the theatre world of Vienna and knew how to make the press bow to his wishes (F.1:17).

It was typical of Kraus's technique as a critic to proceed by synecdoche, representing a whole by a part. The parts he chose were often personalities, in keeping with his sharply personal and satirical outlook. Bauer was for Kraus 'the incarnation of literary hucksterism' (F.2:13). Bauer was a theatre critic who also wrote verse and operetta texts. Kraus criticized him as a satirist on the grounds that his wit did not spring from his humorous handling of a situation and, therefore, did not belong on the stage; nor did it come from an emotion such as anger, or from an opinion, so it did not belong on the printed page either. Bauer's humour, Kraus wrote, was satisfied by the sounds of words. But even his puns lacked seriousness and consisted merely of superficial changes of letters, as, for example, the play on the words *Musentempel* and *Busentempel* (lit., 'Temple of Muses' and 'Temple of Bosoms') (F.1:19). In Kraus's opinion, Bauer would be incapable of writing three consecutive lines of prose which would be capable, once freed of puns, of standing on their own. It was, therefore, on artistic or literary grounds that he attacked the choice of such a man as Burgtheater critic.

The second aspect of Kraus's criticism of Bauer was ethical. Bauer's operetta *Adam und Eva* was a failure at its première. Yet, because of the pressure of the newspaper clique on the theatre directors, it was kept in the repertoire for a whole winter (F.1:19–20). Thus, an inferior work was turned into a success, made to earn its creator high royalties, and allowed to corrupt the taste of the public.

According to Kraus, the lack of ethical and aesthetic standards reached ridiculous proportions in the next matter involving Bauer that was discussed in *Die Fackel* (F.4:16–20); here Bahr was implicated as well. The case concerned a production of Oscar Friedmann's play *Das Dreieck* in the Carltheater. Friedmann had been declared of unsound mind by the courts in 1896; he had since become a protégé of Bauer, Bahr, and Karlweis (a minor Viennese playwright), all members of the literary clique. The production of the play resulted in a scandal; the public evidently had been offended by the play's eroticism and had hissed the playwright. Kraus maintained it was Friedmann's three protectors who should have been condemned for their injustice towards the theatre and its public as well as towards a mentally deficient human being (F.1:17). He asserted that Bauer and Bahr had promoted Friedmann's play because they felt flattered by the attention of the young playwright. They enjoyed playing the role of literary protectors and, with the help of Karlweis and the Carltheater, they soon had him 'made' (F.1:19). Bahr worked on the critics so that the reviews were full of praise. Kraus best shows the resultant lack of critical standards by pointing out that in the same newspaper there appeared side by side a violently negative review of Ibsen's *Pillars of Society* and a eulogy of Friedmann's *Dreieck* (F.1:18).

In another issue of *Die Fackel* Kraus stated that he had spoken of the Friedmann case without rancour and without an axe to grind, but only with bitterness (F.5:12). He insisted that the close relationship between the theatre and the press under the guidance of Bahr and Bauer must soon lead to the ruin of both institutions (F.5:3). As a result of this article, Kraus was physically attacked in a café by Friedmann, who was reputedly encouraged by his benefactors (F.9:27). Understandably, perhaps, Kraus's prejudice against Bahr became increasingly obvious after this.

The harm done by the clique behind Bauer and Bahr towards the theatre-going public was only one aspect of the situation that Kraus attacked. The actors, Kraus asserted, were also mistreated, first by the directors of the theatre, then by the newspapers, but ultimately by the cliques themselves, which controlled and were part of both. Applause and critical acclaim in the press meant nothing since they were paid for by the directors (F.20:2) (who then withheld part of the actors' salaries [F.18:28] or demanded favours of the actresses), or by the actor or actress (who otherwise would be called 'untalented' or not be mentioned at all [F.18:27]). Such control amounted to nothing less than blackmail. Since money was the measure, all artistic ability was 'flattened and dried up.' Not even actors who were popular with the audiences and who should not have had to worry about the critics were safe, as Kraus showed in the case of Alexander Girardi, who was praised by the critics for being the best Viennese folk-actor (F.61:16–18). Kraus agreed with this judgment, but despised the people who praised Girardi and accused them of using him: these critic-playwrights pressed their own plays on him, knowing that Girardi's talented acting would make the plays a box-office success.

When at long last a group of actors tried to resist the pressure exerted on them by Bahr and his friends, Kraus came to their defence. In a series of articles and vignettes entitled *Rache des Ballcomités*, he exposed the various ways in which actors were punished for having stayed away from the Concordia Ball. Since all reporters and clique members were there, an appearance was considered mandatory if an actor wanted to be mentioned favourably in theatre critiques. The case of the Burgtheater actor Adolf Sonnenthal showed up the corruption of such a system (F.34:26). When Sonnenthal, who had failed to attend the ball, subsequently gave a performance in Munich, he was reported in the Viennese papers to have been coolly received by the critics and to have played to an empty house. Kraus claimed, however, that the Munich papers had praised him and reported full houses.[64] But the scandal did not stop there. It seems that the critic of the *Münchener*

Neueste Nachrichten must have had some connection with Vienna. For although he had at first praised Sonnenthal's Fabricius, he then found his Nathan inadequate and cited as his authority Hermann Bahr, who, the Munich critic attested, had disapproved of Sonnenthal as far back as 1891. Kraus pointed out the bankruptcy of such criticism by reminding us that Bahr had actually praised Sonnenthal's Nathan.

As had been the case in the pre-*Fackel* years, Kraus's attitude from 1899 to 1901 towards the contemporary Viennese theatrical scene crystallized in his reaction to Hermann Bahr. In the second issue of *Die Fackel*, Kraus called him the 'seducer of our literary youth'; later, he singled out Bahr, Bauer, and Karlweis as the villains in the Friedmann case. Both Bahr and Bauer were leaders in what Kraus termed 'the clannish relationship between theatre and press' that was killing the Viennese theatre.

More specifically, Kraus attacked what he saw as Bahr's lack of critical judgment. As Bahr tended to promote authors indiscriminately (in the Friedmann case, for example) the odds were, of course, that he would have to be right some of the time. His criticism, according to Kraus, was gossipy and personal, and avoided an evaluation of the work of art itself.[65] 'Denn es ist eine Eigenthümlichkeit des Herrn Bahr ... daß er über die Kunstwerke, die er lobt, niemals etwas sagt, wonach man sie von jenen, die er tadelt, unterscheiden könnte; ja, daß er über Kunstwerke überhaupt niemals etwas sagt, sondern nur über die Künstler, die seine Freunde oder Feinde sind' (*F*.56:21). [For it is one of Mr Bahr's peculiarities that he never says anything about the works of art that he praises that could distinguish them from those that he criticizes; indeed, that he never says anything at all about works of art, but only about the artists who are his friends or his foes.]

Kraus insinuated (*F*.68:15–17) that Bahr would never take a critical stand unless it were to benefit him. This lack of objectivity led to inconsistencies in Bahr's criticism, and often to complete changes of opinion: Bahr was like a snake continually shedding its old skin for a new one (*F*.15:14). This was evident in his remarks about political plays; Bahr criticized the performance of Max Dreyer's liberal political comedy *Der Probecandidat* by the Deutsches Theater (Berlin) at the Deutsches Volkstheater (Vienna) on the grounds that the Volkstheater should remain a place for joy and elation for all parties and classes and was, therefore, no place for partisan plays, but his rection to the Burgtheater's performance of Otto Ernst's *Flachsmann als Erzieher* (which, in Kraus's opinion, was but a poor imitation of the Dreyer play) was quite the opposite. This time, while admitting that he hated any political tendency in the theatre, Bahr found the character of Flachsmann, the ideal educator, beautifully detailed. 'Diesmal calculiert er umgekehrt. Er hasse zwar im Theater jede Tendenz, aber er müsse doch sagen, daß die Gestalt des idealen Lehrers "mit einer wahren Pracht geschildert ist; niemals sind unsere Wünsche ehrlicher, inniger und reiner ausgedrückt worden"' (F.67:21). That Bahr's attack on the first play was prompted by self-interest would only be apparent to those who were acquainted with the intricacies of Viennese theatre. The success of the guest performance of the Deutsches Theater at the Volkstheater had not pleased Bukovics (the director of the latter), who had given an exchange guest performance with the Volkstheater troupe in Berlin with little critical acclaim.[66] According to Kraus, Bukovics had then ordered Bahr, his theatre's critic, to be severe in his judgment of the Berlin group.

To demonstrate Bahr's changes of opinion, Kraus devoted many pages of Die Fackel (particularly F.69:37–45) to reprints of Bahr's original theatre critiques from the Deutsche Zeitung and Die Zeit of 1892–8 (particularly the earlier ones) and of the revised version of these critiques in Bahr's collection of essays, Wiener Theater (1899). Kraus showed that passages about the Volkstheater, including some very uncomplimentary remarks about Bukovics, had been left out in the book version. When asked for the reason for these omissions, Bahr had answered that remarks about the stage direction and the players, especially when of a deprecatory nature, were not suited to be preserved for posterity (F.69:37). Kraus then pointed out that even the most petty critical remark about actors and directors of the Raimundtheater and Burgtheater had been preserved for eternity. This reinforced his argument that the more Bahr became involved with the Volkstheater as a playwright, drawing royalties from the performances of his plays, the less critical he became of plays performed in this theatre. This, as far as Kraus was concerned, was the central issue in the Bahr/Bukovics case.'

Before this case is considered in detail, however, it should be pointed out that, as in the pre-Fackel years, what Kraus particularly despised about Bahr was his pose. He posed as the critic who scorned pettiness and concerned himself only with eternal issues, whereas in reality he was just as concerned with royalties and as much of a scandalmonger as most of the other journalists. In the introduction to Wiener Theater Bahr had stated: 'Diese Sammlung von Recensionen ... soll zeigen, wie ich von unsicheren, aber desto heftigeren Forderungen einer recht vagen Schönheit nach und nach doch zu einer reinen Ansicht der dramatischen Kunst gekommen bin' (F.69:37). [This collection of critiques ... is intended to show how, from the tentative but all the more insistent demands of a rather vague concept of beauty, I have gradually arrived at a pure concept of dramatic art.] But behind the pose there was (in Kraus's opinion) self-interest. Kraus claimed that in his critique of Novelli's Shylock in the Neues Wiener Tagblatt Bahr had written in terms of eternal values – '... nach alter Gewohnheit hat er gleich die Sache "ins Ewige gerückt"' (F.40:25) – but had avoided any mention of anti-Semitism in discussing the character of Shylock in order not to remind people of his own anti-Semitic days (ibid). This attack on Bahr is, however, based on innuendo and insinuation, with no concrete proof given that this was the reason Bahr avoided the subject of anti-Semitism, and shows the worst aspect of Kraus's personal type of criticism.

What Kraus called Bahr's Goethean pose was sometimes attacked in a more humorous manner. Kraus introduced a short article on the excesses of Bahr's style with the statement: 'Herr Bahr hat sich kürzlich wieder wie Goethe, der auf der Sonnenhöhe des Lebens steht, benommen' (F.11:28). [Not long ago Mr Bahr behaved again like Goethe standing at life's zenith.] Or: 'Und kennt nicht die ganze Innere Stadt das innige Verhältnis des Hermann Bahr zu dem großen Olympier? ... Ja, er [Bahr] ist der goetheischeste Mensch im heutigen Wien: in diesem Wien, dessen Aristophanes den Namen Karlweis führt und dessen Heine [Bauer] den Text zu "Adam und Eva" geliefert hat ...' (F.15:14–15). [And doesn't the whole Inner City (of Vienna) know the intimate relationship of Hermann Bahr to the great Olympian? ... Yes, he (Bahr) is the most Goethean person in today's Vienna: in this Vienna, whose Aristophanes goes by the name of Karlweis, and whose Heine (Bauer) supplied the text for *Adam and Eve*.]

To return to the Bahr/Bukovics case, let us first consider its background, and then determine its importance for Kraus as a theatre critic. Bahr, who served the Volkstheater as both dramatist and newspaper critic, and Emerich von Bukovics, the theatre's managing director, took Kraus to court on a charge of libel. Kraus was charged with having alleged that Bahr had received a piece of property in St Veit as a gift from Bukovics, whereas a bill of sale produced in court proved that Bahr had purchased the property (admittedly at a price under the market value). Kraus had indeed made such an allegation, although a reader nowadays would miss the point on a first reading, since Kraus operated by insinuation. Having reported that Bahr had given a lecture to the Concordia club on *Bildung*, Kraus stated: 'Hermann Bahr, den man in der letzten Zeit schon der Geschäftsmacherei verfallen wähnte, hat bewiesen, daß es noch eine andere Bildung gibt, als die eines Fonds zur Erbauung einer Villa in Ober-St. Veit ... ' (F.34:29). [Hermann Bahr, whom one believed of late to be preoccupied with business deals, has shown that there is a kind of edification other than that of a fund for the erecting of an edifice in Ober-St Veit.] The next mention of this matter is much less oblique:

Aber Herr Bahr hatte nicht einen, er hatte mehrere unsaubere Gründe für sein kritisches Vorgehen ... Herrn Bukovics ist er nicht nur für Überlassung eines Freiplatzes zu Danke verpflichtet. Andere Journalisten lassen sich durch Freiplätze vom Tadeln nicht abhalten; aber ein Kritiker, dem ein Theaterdirector gleich einen Freiplatz in Unter-St. Veit schenkt, hat guten Grund – zum Bau einer Villa. (F.43:25)

But Mr Bahr did not have just one ground – he had several improper grounds for his critical action … He is indebted to Mr Bukovics not only for letting him have a free ticket [*Freiplatz*]. Free tickets do not prevent other journalists from voicing their criticisms; but a critic who is given a free lot [*Freiplatz*] by a theatre director has good grounds – for building a villa.

Kraus was proven guilty as charged and had to pay a considerable sum of money. However, in his opinion, only some of his facts were wrong, whereas the main part of his argument in his defence was true: that the offices of playwright and critic for the same theatre were incompatible in one person. The villa in Ober- or Unter-St Veit became a symbol for him of the corruption that existed in the Volkstheater in particular and in contemporary Viennese theatre in general.

The second aspect of the Bahr/Bukovics case was the Holzer affair, which was first mentioned in no. 53 of *Die Fackel* (pp. 1–6). Bahr and several other critics had rushed to the defence of Schnitzler, one of whose plays had not been performed by the Burgtheater, although this involved no breach of contract since the play had never really been accepted by Schlenther, the managing director of the Burgtheater. Kraus contrasted this case with that of Holzer, whose play, he claimed, had been contracted by Bukovics to be produced in the Volkstheater. When the play was left unperformed, Holzer was released from his contract, with Bukovics's promise that the play would be put on in the fall of 1899; when Kraus discussed the affair in 1900, the play had still not been produced, and Kraus asserted that Bahr would never protest against this injustice since he was dependent on Bukovics for the production of his own plays.[67] When this aspect of the case came up in court, both Bukovics and Holzer denied that any promise had been made to produce the play in 1899. One can only surmise why Holzer took back what he allegedly had asserted previously. Kraus insisted that his own reasons for mentioning the Holzer affair were completely unselfish, in that he was prompted by a general concern for the rights of authors.[68] But from then on the name Holzer was mentioned only with derision by Kraus and became synonymous with the cowardice of some playwrights in the face of bullying by directors.

Kraus went on, in *Die Fackel* no. 69 (p. 6 ff), to analyse what he considered to be the danger constituted by Bahr: he encouraged untalented people, he was the most obvious representative of all that was killing the Viennese stage, and his criticism was unethical since royalties changed his mind and influenced his critiques. Kraus felt, however, that the libel action he had lost had at least accomplished one thing: the newspapers that reported the trial had had to mention some of the details of the corruption in the theatre which they normally would have passed over in silence. Kraus supported the ethical position he had taken by quoting from other critics (including Maximilian Harden), who had been asked to comment on the topic of objectivity and who agreed that a critic should not write about the theatre that produced his own plays.

Two points are worth noting with regard to Kraus's presentation of the Bahr/Bukovics case. First, the case was important to him because of the question of ethics that it raised. The question of aesthetics (for instance, that Bahr encouraged mediocre playwrights, that Bahr's plays themselves were mediocre) was largely subordinate to the ethical issue. This was typical of Kraus as a critic – and particularly as a theatre critic. Second, his presentation of the case is interesting. In devoting a whole issue of *Die Fackel* to it, Kraus did not simply write an essay defending his stand at the trial. Rather, he proceeded much more theatrically, by dividing *Die Fackel* into several sections, each of which puts the problem of the conflict of interests into a slightly different perspective and adds to the picture of Bahr that Kraus wanted to present. Kraus quoted himself and his court testimony, interjected the opinions and questions of others, and let Bahr, through his juxtaposed critiques, reveal his own lack of scruples. This issue of *Die Fackel* has the air of a well-staged 'production.' The 'producer's' theatrical flair will be much in evidence in later editions of the periodical.

There were other results of the case that are worth noting. As could be predicted, Kraus's relations with Bahr, as both critic and playwright, grew even more strained and Kraus became even more rigid in rejecting all that Bahr advocated. Kraus's isolation as a critic became increasingly pronounced. Ignored (*todtgeschwiegen*) by the influential *Neue Freie Presse* and slandered by other papers, he withdrew more and more from direct contact with the theatre. From the early 1900s on, he rarely attended performances and based his comments on the Viennese theatre largely on his newspaper readings.

Although Kraus was primarily concerned with the ethics of Bahr's behaviour, he also wrote occasionally about Bahr's plays. It is striking, however, that Kraus produced so little drama criticism, and what little there was centred for the most part around the question of authenticity or genuineness and of honesty and scruples. This is particularly astonishing since Kraus was more interested in drama and theatre than in any other form of artistic expression.

According to Kraus, Bahr's plays were not genuine successes – the applause for both *Der Athlet* and *Die Wienerinnen* was dishonestly won, since it was supplied by members of the Concordia, and *Der Athlet* did not last long in the Volkstheater repertoire. Even the subject matter of *Der Athlet* was not authentic. Kraus insinuated that Bahr and Bracco had discussed *Tragödien der Seele*, the play on which the latter was working, and that Bahr had then plagiarized Bracco (F.67:21).[69] Kraus supported this allegation and continued his attack on Bahr's alleged unscrupulousness by quoting in the next issue of *Die Fackel* from Bahr's essay 'Plagiate,' which had appeared in *Die Zeit*. In it, Bahr had defended plagiarism, claiming that 'plagiarism doesn't harm anyone and benefits everyone' (F.68:14). ('Die Plagiate schaden niemandem und nützen allen.')

Kraus devoted only one page to a discussion of Bahr's *Wienerinnen* (F.55: 24–5). He wrote of the boredom produced by this 'silly commercial play,' of Bahr's 'provocative dramatic impotence,' and of 'all that which was disgusting' in the play but which unfortunately was not given dramatic form. However, Kraus made only one specific point: the perspective Bahr had tried to present was untrue. Not only was the picture Bahr gave of Vienna false, Kraus asserted ('das beispiellos verlogene Wienerthum') but so was his pose as a champion of culture, which masked his interest in royalties.

Kraus later again attacked Bahr's *Wienerinnen*, accusing him of not being aware of the basic laws of stage technique (particularly of the use of illusion in the theatre) and of confusing stage actuality with what had been actually experienced: 'Herr Bahr ist also endlich auf dem Punkte dramatischer Weisheit angelangt, Bühnenwahrheit mit dem "wirklich Erlebten" zu verwechseln' (F.72:32). Bahr had complained that the one scene in *Wienerinnen* which people had thought not genuine had been taken exactly from a true life situation.[70] Kraus criticized him for looking at events with the eyes of a local news editor, interested only in presenting events as they had 'really' occurred. This objection is basically the same as that which Kraus levelled at the naturalistic school of acting: stage reality, in order to be genuine, demands something more than facts or real life – it demands illusion, imagination, a touch of the 'unnatural.'

The charges of speculation and swindle and of lack of authenticity were the main points of an important article concerning Bahr's plays in *Die Fackel* no. 68 (pp. 8–13), 'Von der *Mutter* zum *Muederl*.' Kraus opened with the remark that Herr Bahr was a con-man – 'ein Hochstapler.' One would, of course, expect an exposé of one of Bahr's plays or critiques, but instead Kraus played with the theme of the impostor – Bahr was not from Linz, as he had claimed, but from Urfahr, and his early plays, including *Die Mutter* (1891), were not the quintessence of refined culture, as the crowd had been led to believe, but regional art – 'unverfälschte Heimatkunst.' Though French in flavour and touched by *fin de siècle* decadence, these plays were hopelessly provincial, with 'provincial thoughts, provincial psychology, and above all, provincial eroticism' (p. 9) – provincial in the sense that they were gauche and uncultured, although they made a pretence at sophistication. Now, ten years later, after becoming vice-president of the Concordia and a leading member of the big city cliques, Bahr had discovered the provinces and written

Franzl ('Fünf Bilder aus dem Leben eines guten Mannes'). Kraus considered this latest disguise that Bahr had assumed to be the most disgusting and impudent of all ('Wir ... werden die neueste Vermummung als die wider- wärtigste und frechste von allen empfinden ...' – ibid, p. 9). In his opinion, Bahr would have been far more genuine if he had written a play about someone like the newspaperman Wilhelm Singer, who was from the corrupt world which he knew. All he had done in this play was to speculate on natural and pious simplicity. According to Kraus, Bahr was nothing but a literary libertine and all his plays were fraudulent,[71] since all had sprung from speculation (the only difference being a qualitative one – *Franzl* was the worst): '[das] Speculantenthum eines literarischen Libertiners, der seine guten Fähigkeiten um jeden Preis verludern muß ... Der 'Franzl' (scheint) mir in der Reihe der Bühnenbeschmutzungen des Herrn Hermann Bahr auch die ungeschickteste zu sein ... ' (ibid, p. 10). [the speculations of a literary libertine, who must sell off his talents no matter what the price ... In Mr Hermann Bahr's series of stage foulings, *Franzl* (seems) to me to be the clumsiest ...]

Kraus went on to give at least some aesthetic reasons why he considered the play to be so bad. The childlike naturalistic detail to which Bahr devoted so much space (Kraus pointed out that 200 of the 375 pages were given to stage directions[72] and descriptions of scenery) would largely be lost in performance. The extensive use of dialect was objectionable, and Bahr showed bad taste, particularly in his caricature of a Catholic aristocrat. On the whole, however, Kraus did not devote very much attention to aesthetic considerations, but concentrated his attack on the ethics of the playwright. The predominance of ethical considerations in his early criticism was to remain typical of his stance as a critic.

While the quarrel with Bahr was central to these early years of *Die Fackel*, it was not the only instance which revealed Kraus's preoccupation with ethics as a theatre critic. In his reaction to Vienna's allegedly anti-Semitic theatre, Kraus, although, very much to his regret, himself a Jew, was para- doxically much less subjective and personal than in the Bahr case. But here, too, ethics predominated over aesthetics. In his evaluation of the Viennese theatrical scene at the turn of the century, Kraus associated 'corrupt' criti- cism mainly with the bourgeois liberal press, which was for the most part under Jewish control.[73] He strongly criticized its two most powerful repre- sentatives: the newspaper *Neue Freie Presse* and the liberal pressmen's club Concordia (to which, Kraus insisted, Bahr lent a Teutonic aspect).[74] Any theatre which tried to get along without the help of the *Neue Freie Presse* and the Concordia, and with the support of the community, was bound to receive some praise from Kraus, even though the plays it produced might not have been artistically praiseworthy. Such was the case with Adam Müller-

Guttenbrunn's Kaiserjubiläums-Stadttheater. Backed by the municipality
(*die Commune*) and the Christian-Socialist party and dedicated to the performance of German plays, this theatre had, in the first year of its existence,
already achieved some measure of success without the help of the liberal,
Jewish press. However, it had been labelled 'anti-Semitic' by this press.
Kraus had previously made a sarcastic comment (*F*.27) about the fact that
Müller-Guttenbrunn had paid to advertise the repertoire of the theatre in
the *Neue Freie Presse*. In *Die Fackel* no. 28 (pp. 23–9) he printed Müller-
Guttenbrunn's rejoinder, in which the director stated that this had been the
only way in which he could inform people that he had a successful repertory
theatre, since the liberal press had not reported his productions or had given
them bad reviews. Now, as a result of Kraus's criticism, the *Neue Freie Presse*
would not even accept Müller-Guttenbrunn's paid advertisements; therefore, he could not let people know what was being performed. The director
insisted that the label *anti-semitisches Hetztheater* had been pinned on his
enterprise by the *Neue Freie Presse* before the theatre opened and that it was
completely false. In his opinion, this was the liberal press's way of smearing
a theatre that was backed by the Christian-Socialist party and existed without
the help of that press. Three issues later (*F*.31) Kraus corroborated this
opinion by publishing excerpts from a fairly objective brochure by Franz
Joseph Cramer entitled *Das antisemitische Theater*.

In reprinting these two defences of Müller-Guttenbrunn's theatre, Kraus
publicized the injustice done to it and so unveiled one more underhanded
way in which the press controlled the theatre and public taste. The lack of
ethics of the *Neue Freie Presse* and its fellow newspapers was proved once again.
Kraus even played on the theme of anti-Semitism by alleging that the liberal
critic Bernhard Buchbinder and his fellow Jewish journalist-playwrights did
more to promote anti-Semitism than the Jubiläumstheater ever would:
'Wahrlich, der seichte Spott auf jüdische Aeußerlichkeiten, den die aus-
übenden Dramatiker der Wiener Presse ihren Glaubensgenossen im Parkett
oft genug geboten haben, er hat im Sinne christlichsocialer Propaganda erfolg-
reicher gewirkt als die tendenziösen Anläufe des angeblichen Parteitheaters'
(*F*.31:25–6). [Truly, the shallow ridicule of Jewish external appearances to
which the practising dramatists of the Viennese press have often enough
treated their fellow-believers in the stalls has been more successful Christian-
Socialist propaganda than the tendentious charges of the allegedly anti-
Semitic theatre.]

One notes, once more, that it is the ethical question involved in the case
that interested Kraus. Although he admitted that he did not see the success of
the Jubiläumstheater ('Die Teufelsmühle am Wienerberg') as an encouraging symptom of the development of Viennese taste, he made relatively little
comment about the aesthetic merits of the new enterprise. His discussion of

the ensemble and direction was cursory. If they were not the best, they were not the worst either, and as no actor would want to perform in a theatre that the critics of the major newspapers viewed with disfavour, one could hardly expect any more. Kraus singled out two new plays that were worthy of notice – *Liebesheirat* by Frau Baumberg and *Tiberius Gracchus* by Barth – but gave no reasons for this opinion.

Indeed, although the principles of his ethical judgment are not left open to conjecture, one wonders if Kraus's hobby-horse – his attack on the bourgeois liberal press's financial and artistic control of Viennese cultural life – did not blind him to other ethical matters. For, although the question of anti-Semitism was deemed ludicrous by Müller-Guttenbrunn, Cramer, and Kraus, one cannot but notice on reading Müller-Guttenbrunn's letter that he uses *christlich* as a positive term and *jüdisch* as a negative one. 'Aber erfahren soll dieses Publicum [that is, readers of the *Neue Freie Presse*], unter dem sich wohl tausende christliche Familien befinden mögen, in welch' brutaler Weise die *Neue Freie Presse* sich selbst als ein jüdisches Unternehmen in diesem Falle aufgespielt hat'(*F.28:26*). [But this audience (that is, readers of the *Neue Freie Presse*), which probably includes thousands of Christian families, shall find out the brutal way in which the *Neue Freie Presse* has shown itself to be a Jewish enterprise in this case.] Characteristically, Kraus chose to ignore this.

The doubts that Kraus began to have in the few years before the *Fackel* period about the artistic value of the naturalness and realism of the Schlierseer peasant actors[75] now crystallized. In 1899 he referred to his earlier articles (1894) on these players, where he had been relatively positive in his evaluation of their manner of acting, but had warned that, taken from their native province, they would lose the naturalness and sink to the level of circus artists or nine-year-old soubrettes. When this subsequently happened – at least in Kraus's view – there appeared a slightly supercilious note in his critique of the Schlierseer, who had been performing in Vienna for some time (*F.9:19–21*). He now deplored his earlier article in the *Neue Freie Presse*, since he thought it was there that the enthusiasm for such a style of acting had originated.[76] One of his objections was that the critics (including Hermann Bahr) and the audiences saw in the simplicity of the Schlierseers' acting the 'revelation of the highest artistic feeling,' whereas in reality, after having been away so long from their home ground, these players were revealed to be mediocre actors. This kind of naturalness was not art, Kraus argued; the Schlierseers would merely be laughable if they were acting in classical plays, and they could seem to be natural only in dialect plays – '(dem) Dialekt, diesem argen Vorschubleister aller darstellerischen Minderwertigkeit ...[77] (*F.9:20*). [Dialect, that awful abetter of all theatrical inferiority.]

However, by 1900 (*F.48*) what had been mostly artistic criticism of the

Schlierseers had developed into a more typically Krausian attack based on ethical grounds. For along with his aesthetic criticism (he called the players 'these simple and natural people, who have turned into uninteresting routine players'), there was disapprobation of the impresarios, who used these players for their own monetary ends, and of the critics (especially Bahr), who duped audiences into thinking that this was the renaissance promised to the German stage.

The next time Kraus came to grips with extreme realism in the theatre was in his reviews of the Berlin troupe of the Deutsches Theater under the direction of Otto Brahm. Here realism was on a much less naïve level than that of the Schlierseer; that is, some sort of programme for a naturalistic style of acting had been worked out which the actors presumably followed. In the first article in *Die Fackel* on this subject 'Zum Gastspiel des "Deutschen Theaters"' (*F.*10:16–20), Kraus rejected several of the basic assumptions of such a style: the importance of dialect, the emphasis on petty details of speech technique rather than on humour, temperament, and the thought pattern of the lines, and the possibility of applying this style, which was no doubt suitable for exceptional dialect plays such as Hauptmann's *Die Weber*, to plays in the classical repertoire. This was very similar to what Kraus had already written in the *Wiener Rundschau* (15 May 1897) in his review of the Berlin actor Reicher.

In *Die Fackel* no. 43 (pp. 16–25), in the article 'Vom Wechselgastspiel,' Kraus explained in even greater detail why he rejected the style of acting of Brahm's troupe. He repeated sarcastic turns of phrase from previous articles. This was 'eine saubere Regie, die eine Schar von guten Chargenspielern oder Dilettanten zusammenhält, die an schlesischen Dialectübungen gereift sind' and 'eine Art schlesischen Schlierseerthums.' [An inferior direction, which holds together a troop of good character actors or dilettantes who grew up on Silesian dialect exercises; a kind of Silesian Schlierseerness.] But there was one major point of criticism to which all else was subordinate: this style and these artists were anti-artistic (*kunstfeindlich*); in trying to imitate real life exactly, they missed the point that art (in Kraus's opinion) had to surpass life. The naturalistic style lacked a theatrical perspective. It could happen, for example, that a boring actor playing a boring character would be considered a great success by advocates of this style, since he was completely realistic. The Berlin troupe's style amounted to a trivialization of art and nothing more important than a *Milieustück* could be performed successfully in that way. The actors lacked originality and verve, humour, and artistic temperament; this was 'an ensemble ... that owed its only impact to its lack of all instinctive acting skill and drive.'

Kraus contrasted the Berlin troupe with the Viennese tradition, whose actors had individuality, personality, and temperament, and could transform nature into art: 'Diese primäre Natürlichkeit ist hier in Wien bestaunt worden, als ob wir nie große schauspielerische Temperamente erlebt hätten, die die Natur verwandeln und kunstgerecht verarbeiten konnten.' It is interesting to note that Kraus himself had been one of those who, in the early 1890s, had admired the 'primary naturalness' of the naturalistic style of acting and that he had been rather critical when the 'great histrionic temperament' of an actress such as Charlotte Wolter forced her to break the bonds of naturalness and to declaim with pathos.

Lacking the talent to be unnatural or greater than life, and depending only on a few tricks of their trade, the Berlin actors were incapable of making characters in the great classics appear genuine, and their performances of such plays were disastrous. The beauty and even the meaning of the language were disregarded. Theirs was 'the peculiarity of scanning insignificant lines with schoolboy clarity, then taking a dozen of those richest in ideas into their mouth at a single gulp and spitting them nonchalantly into the orchestra ...' Anguish and sorrow were lowered to the level of physical pain: '[Es ist eine] Kunst, die inneres Leid wie Zahnschmerz ausdrückt.' [(It is an) art which expresses inner grief as if it were a toothache.]

Kraus gave the Berlin troupe credit for being well-disciplined and contrasted them in this respect with the sloppy Volkstheater group, which was then giving guest performances in Berlin. He praised those actors who did not quite fit into the naturalistic ensemble, particularly Max Reinhardt, who had trained under Josef Lewinsky in the Burgtheater and in whom one could still hear the *Burgtheaterton*; but such occasional praise was far outweighed by his polemics.

The opposite stylistic extreme prevailed in the Secessionsbühne productions of the symbolist plays of Maeterlinck in the Josefstädter Theater. Kraus devoted a rather lengthy review to these performances (F.48:7-16) but wrote very little about either the plays or the actors. He called what the Secessionsbühne offered 'tired complexities' ('müde Compliciertheiten'). He half-heartedly commended the efforts of Maeterlinck as 'the attempt of a writer to lead ordinary people on extraordinary paths for a few hours' (ibid, p. 10) and ended with praise for the 'fairy-tale atmosphere' that this 'artistic attempt' had managed to produce. This playwright at least did not commit the error of the naturalists, who had tried to make everything realistic. The acting style and the staging received less than one paragraph of comment from Kraus – neither were up to the neo-romantic requirements of the plays, the actors being no more than 'a group of bit players brought up in the style of Berlin naturalness.' The rest of the article became a vehicle for the further disparagement of Bahr as a critic (ibid, pp. 8–10) and for a review of other critics' reactions to the plays. Kraus saw these critics as divided into two camps – the Philistines (*Spießbürger*) and the snobs, that is, those who rejected Maeterlinck out of hand, looking for realism and socio-cultural motivations in his plays, and those who pretended to understand him but really did not: 'Wenn ein Abend, wie der der Darstellung von "Pelleas und Melisande" kein anderes Vergnügen gewährte als das des Anblickes der Rathlosigkeit unserer kritischen Wortführer: – man könnte zufrieden sein.' [If an evening such as that of the performance of *Pelleas and Melisande* offered no other pleasure than than of the sight of the perplexity of our critical spokesmen – one could be content.] Kraus in effect was letting the critics perform on the stage he set up for them, and he pulled the strings. The mode of criticism is again theatrical, and we have another 'performance,' which in his account far overshadows the performances that are supposed to be criticized, and which serves to confirm Kraus's already well-known prejudices.

Kraus's comment that in Reinhardt's speech one could still hear traces of his Burgtheater training (*F*.43:20) reveals his bias towards the Burgtheater style of acting. For Kraus, like the majority of Viennese, still held fast to the mystique of the Burgtheater, although he personally thought that its grandeur was past and the Burgtheater had declined. In the nineteenth century, this theater had been the showplace for Austrian culture. In 1900 it was still called the Hofburgtheater, and was therefore associated with the court: its actors were 'kaiserlich-königliche Hofschauspieler.' There is a certain amount of snobbishness in Kraus's being so appalled at *these* actors – 'Schauspieler des Kaisers!' – putting on a play by the critic-playwright Julius Bauer at a wedding in the house of a Viennese jobber. Kraus admired Lewinsky, one of the actors who performed at this wedding, and refused to believe that Lewinsky had really participated:

> ich erkläre es einfach für eine Verleumdung seitens gewisser, dem
> trefflichen und correcten Mann längst aufsäßiger Notizenschreiber, wenn
> man uns glauben machen will, daß Herr Lewinsky den Shylock in der
> 'Klabriaspartie' des Herrn Bauer gespielt hat. ... [er] ist ... doch einer der
> wenigen Schauspieler, deren feinerer Wesensart es widerstrebt, einem
> Zeitungstyrannen zuliebe ihre Menschen- und Künstlerwürde
> preiszugeben. (F.29:15)

I declare certain newshounds to be guilty of defamation of character if they want to make us believe Lewinsky, this excellent and correct man, whom they have disliked for such a long time, played Shylock in Mr Bauer's *Klabriaspartie* ... [He] is, after all, one of the few actors whose refined character resists sacrificing their dignity as human beings and artists to please a newspaper tycoon.

It will be noted that artistic considerations are secondary in this protest. Kraus seems to be much more concerned with the question of Lewinsky's character.

Lewinsky's manner of delivering speeches had been described by the other critics as being boring, monotonous, and colourless. Kraus defended him against what he called 'the clan of critics' ('die kritische Sippschaft') and claimed that, since the death of Charlotte Wolter, Lewinsky alone had a classical sense of style (F.29:13). In Schreyvogl's book *Das Burgtheater*, special mention is made of Lewinsky for 'der hohle Ton seines Organs [und] sein großer Mund' [the hollow sound of his voice and his large mouth], and he is said to have been an incomparable speaker.[78] Presumably then, when Kraus wrote of a classical style, he meant one that was for the most part declamatory and rhetorical and gave preference to the beauty and meaning of the language. This was an about-face from his censure in the early 1890s of Burgtheater actors and actresses, such as Charlotte Wolter, who still declaimed with pathos and who were not 'natural.'

Although also a Burgtheater actor, Josef Kainz was constantly deprecated by Kraus, whereas the other critics seem to have grown to like him. Kainz represented a new style of acting – according to contemporary reports, he spoke the lines from classical plays as if they had just that moment occurred to him and thereby breathed new life into the classics. His speech technique (every word could be heard) and breath control were supposedly astounding. Schreyvogl notes: 'Er gliederte auch die jedermann geläufigen Monologe anders als alle vor ihm, aber wenn er sprach, schien die neue Auffassung notwendig und richtig.'[79] [He articulated the well-known monologues differently from all the earlier actors, but when he spoke, his interpretation of the lines seemed necessary and correct.]

Obviously we are now at a disadvantage when trying to evaluate an actor of whom we only know at second hand, but whatever Kainz's merits may have been, his new accentuation and interpretation did not appeal to Kraus. He characterized Kainz's speech as 'neurasthenic chattering' ('neurasthenisches Geschnatter') which did not do justice to the text of the play. It particularly angered Kraus that the other critics considered Kainz to be suitable for a 'reform of the classical acting style': 'Es ist einfach bewundernswürdig, wie die Auguren des Berliner und Wiener Theaterparkets in den Defecten des Herrn Kainz allmählich seine Modernität und Eignung für eine innere Reform der classischen Spielweise entdeckt haben' (F.10:19). [It is simply amazing how the augurers in the theatre stalls in Berlin and Vienna have gradually discovered in the defects of Mr Kainz his modernity and his suitability for an inner reform of the classical style of acting.] Kraus wrote ironically of his 'artful cascades of speech' and 'purely phonetic interpretation of Shakespearean thoughts' – that is, according to Kraus, Kainz seemed to like to hear his own voice and, in performing Shakespeare, emphasized secondary lines and threw away important ones, presumably paying greater attention to the sound than to the thoughts expressed by the lines.

It is in Kraus's remarks about the Burgtheater actor Sonnenthal in these two years that the curious mixture of ethical and aesthetic criticism which was noted in his reaction to Bahr, the Schlierseers, Brahm's troupe, and others resurfaces. According to Schreyvogl, Sonnenthal was famous for his abilities as a mime rather than as a speaker; he praised 'his mimicry, his gestures, his bearing.'[80] Certainly if one reads Kraus's eulogy to him in a much later issue of *Die Fackel* ('Das Denkmal eines Schauspielers,' *F*.391/2), one realizes that Kraus considered him to be one of the great actors of the time. In 1900 he also praised Sonnenthal highly, but not on artistic grounds. Sonnenthal had led a group of *Hofschauspieler* who, in defiance of their directors and the theatre reporters, boycotted the Concordia Ball, and 'seiner Anständigkeit gebührt Dank und die Versicherung, daß keiner der rachsüchtigen Händler mit Druckerschwärze sich ungestraft an ihm vergreifen wird' (*F*.33:25) [he deserves praise for his decency, and the assurance that none of the vindictive dealers in printer's ink will attack him unpunished]. One year later he criticized Sonnenthal on artistic grounds, but one suspects that this criticism had other origins. Kraus quoted from Max Kalbeck's account of a new Burgtheater production of *King Lear*, with Sonnenthal as the king. Kraus thought Kalbeck had praised Sonnenthal's performance excessively and had seen a development in the last ten years where Kraus thought there was none. According to Kraus, Sonnenthal still left out important words, as he had done ten years before. One had the impression of a good bourgeois Lear, but (with the exception of his rendering of the Goneril curse) not a great one. In Kraus's opinion, he was not the foremost tragic actor of the Viennese stage, as Kalbeck and others claimed; Bernard Baumeister (another older Burgtheater actor) would have played a much greater Lear. But the real reason for the sharpness of Kraus's criticism is betrayed by one sentence: 'Aber die kritische Phraseologie verlangt für Lieblinge ein unaufhörliches "Wachsen", und ein Lear, der den Concordiaball wiederum besucht hat, muß auch dem unbefangensten Betrachter in besserem Lichte erscheinen' (*F*.78:22). [But critical phraseology demands continual 'growth' for one's favourites, and a Lear who has once again attended the Concordia Ball must appear in a better light to even the most impartial observer.] Unlike the previous year, Sonnenthal had visited the Concordia Ball, and had therefore incurred Kraus's ire. Such criticism by Kraus is really no more objective than that of his opponents, the Buchbinders and Bauers.

Kraus does not seem to have associated a particular style of acting with the Volkstheater. What makes his comments on this theatre interesting is that he reacted very strongly to some of its actors. Alexander Girardi and Annie Kalmar were among his favourites, while he particularly disliked Frau Odilon.

Girardi was the only actor, apart from Lewinsky and Baumeister, who elicited unmitigated praise from Kraus. Describing Girardi as an 'exponent of Viennese popular culture' (F.61:16), Kraus suggested that his achievements as an actor were rooted in his genuine humanity (F.2:28). Girardi used the particular (the Viennese types and characters) to reveal the general (humanity): 'Girardi hatte ... auch schon im Wienerischen immer das allgemein Menschliche zu erfassen gewußt. Und sein Wienerisches war jederzeit wertvoller, als das allgemein Menschliche des Herrn Strakosch [another Volkstheater actor]' (F.61:19). [Girardi had ... always known how to capture the universally human in the typically Viennese, and his typically Viennese was always more valuable than the universally human of Mr Strakosch.] But as Kraus became increasingly involved in his dispute with Bukovics, the director of the Volkstheater, his visits to this theatre must have become far less frequent, and there were surprisingly few references to performances by Girardi.

The only contemporary actress who received his praise was Annie Kalmar, whom he complimented on her natural humour: 'Sie, die Herrlichste von Allen, wird von Publikum und Kritik immerzu noch ... als Ausstattungsgegenstand des Theaters behandelt ... Wenn sie ... eine wirkliche und ungemein natürliche Humorbegabung erweist, so scheinen dies die Leute, geblendet von ihrem Anblick, gar nicht zu merken' (F.2:28 f). [She, the loveliest of all, is still treated by public and critics alike as an object for decorating the theatre. When she shows a real and uncommonly natural gift for humour, the people, dazzled at the sight of her, don't seem to notice at all.] When her contract expired at the Volkstheater, Kraus helped her find employment with the Hamburger Schauspielhaus. Her death in 1901 was a great shock to him; he stopped publishing Die Fackel for several months (from the end of June to October) on the grounds of nervous exhaustion.

Frau Odilon provoked the opposite reaction in Kraus. While he continually attacked her interpretations of roles, his major ground for criticism was that he considered her in league with all the critics (especially Buchbinder) whom he detested. 'Seit es Herrn Buchbinder ... einmal vergönnt war, das Badezimmer der Dame zu beschreiben, ist er der gefügigste Reclamediener der Odilon geworden' (F.77:13). [Since the time that he was granted the privilege of describing the lady's bathroom, Mr Buchbinder has been one of Odilon's most compliant promotion agents.] Once more, ethical and aesthetic reasons for criticism mingled – Kraus considered her interviews given to newspapers for free publicity to be unethical and her constant reports on the trivia of her life to be tasteless. While he criticized other actors as well, the names of Frau Odilon and Kainz became mottos for Kraus, symbolizing bad acting and corrupt critical complicity.

There is some criticism of Schnitzler's plays in the first issue of Die Fackel. This playwright had already been characterized in Die demolirte Literatur

(1896) as 'the writer who has made the girl from the suburbs (*das Vorstadt-mädel*) presentable for the Burgtheater.' In *Die Fackel* no. 1 (pp. 24–5), Kraus called him a playwright of one-acters – he had shown such talent for first acts that he now intended to cultivate his 'dramatic shortness of breath' as a genre. His main criticism of Schnitzler's plays was that their content was petty and their form too complicated. The themes, which in his opinion did not give the audience or reader much to think about, usually developed in a spiral instead of in a straight line (as, for example, in *Die Gefährtin*). Although complimenting Schnitzler on the 'confident and witty' dialogue of *Der grüne Kakadu*, he claimed that the playwright had reduced a potentially great topic (the French Revolution) to the dimensions of a miniature and had then let the curtain fall: 'So sehen wir das Gewaltige zu einem netten Genrebildchen eingefangen. Wo dieses zu jenem sich erweitert, fällt der Vorhang ...'

Kraus's reaction to Hofmannsthal is not so easy to pinpoint. Kraus disliked the comparisons made by other critics (particularly Bahr) between Hofmannsthal and Goethe and insisted that Hofmannsthal had assumed a 'Goethean' pose. In fact, he remarked sarcastically: 'Wer weiß nicht, daß Goethe der Hofmannsthal des 18. Jahrhunderts gewesen ist' (F.15:14). [Who doesn't know that Goethe was the Hofmannsthal of the eighteenth century.]

The main lines of Kraus's criticism of Hofmannsthal's dramas in this period are developed in *Die Fackel* nos 1 and 64. In no. 1, Kraus criticized Schlenther's Burgtheater production of Hofmannsthal's *Der Abenteurer und die Sängerin* and *Die Hochzeit der Sobeïde*. He grudgingly praised Hofmannsthal's aestheticism, since the playwright was at least removed from the corruption of contemporary theatre: '(er ließ) keine Schallwelle von dem eklen Gekreisch unseres Theaterthums an sich herankommen' (F.1:25). [He kept himself insulated from the disgusting screaming coming from our theatrical scene.] He insisted that Hofmannsthal was no poet, although he excelled in reading other poets and had a keen ear for classical rhythms. He was critical of Hofmannsthal's eclecticism (in later articles he insinuated it was not better than plagiarism – see F.60:20–2), maintaining that this had led him lately to depend too much on translations. The playful relationship between form and content that used to exist in Hofmannsthal's works had disappeared, and the spectator was left with costumes and sound that masked a lack of content: '[Er] treibt philologische Lyrik. Nach seiner Weltanschauung zu fragen, nach jenem Etwas, das von seinen Versen übrig bleibt, wenn man sie von Costüm und Anklängen befreit, wäre müßig' (F.1:27). [He cultivates philological lyric poetry. It would be futile to ask for his philosophy of life, for that certain something that is left of his verses when they are stripped of costumes and reminiscences.]

In *Die Fackel* no. 64 Kraus defended Hofmannsthal's *Der Thor und der*

Tod against critics who had rejected the play because it was not realistic enough. Although he still maintained that Hofmannsthal was too eclectic and that his field of interest was limited, he again praised his classical rhythms and his isolation from the market-place. However, Kraus warned that, since Hofmannsthal had made the concession to reality of letting his delicate little play be performed at the Volkstheater in the presence of critics, he would have to learn to live with the stupidity of their criticism. Thus, at this point, Kraus had by no means rejected Hofmannsthal completely, as he was to do later.

While he obviously approved of Raimund and Nestroy, preferring them to Anzengruber, during this period Kraus did not give his reasons in any detail. We see him, however, demanding good performances of plays by Raimund and Nestroy. As long as Alexander Girardi (of the Volkstheater) could play Valentin in Raimund's *Der Verschwender*, no Raimund should be performed at the Burgtheater, and he commented on a planned Burgtheater production of Nestroy's *Lumpazivagabundus*: 'Es ward seltsamer Weise darüber gestritten, ob Nestroy burgtheaterfähig, nicht aber darüber, ob das Burgtheater Nestroyfähig sei' (*F*.75:22). [Oddly enough, they quarrelled over whether Nestroy was suitable for the Burgtheater, and not over whether the Burgtheater was suitable for Nestroy.]

His early attitude towards Shakespeare's plays formed the basis for some of his ideas on the theater he was to develop in the 1910s and 1920s. In his critique of Schlenther's production of *Henry IV* Part 2, he criticized the director for performing Dingelstedt's[81] 'criminal' adaptation of the play ('das Dingelstedt'sche Verbrechen am Dichtergeiste'), in which the ending was changed and much pomp was added. Kraus quoted extensively from Goethe[82] in order to support his own conviction that it was the thought of Shakespeare's dramas and their appeal to the imagination that were important and not the spectacular aspects of the production. Perhaps Shakespeare would be best served if his works were removed from the stage and left to the reader. Kraus stated:

> *Goethe hat gemeint, daß der Brite 'durchaus an unsern innern Sinn spricht: durch diesen belebt sich sogleich die Bilderwelt der Einbildungskraft, und so entspringt eine vollständige Wirkung, von der wir uns keine Rechenschaft zu geben wissen ...' Betrachte man die Shakespeare'schen Stücke genau, 'so enthalten sie viel weniger sinnliche That, als geistiges Wort. Er läßt geschehen, was sich leicht imaginieren läßt, ja, was besser imaginiert als gesehen wird'. Der Spieler Shakespeares befördert die Imagination nicht; aber er darf sie nicht hemmen wollen. Goethe meint, daß es 'kein Unglück wäre', wenn Shakespeare ganz von der deutschen Bühne*

verdrängt würde: 'denn der einsame oder gesellige Leser wird an ihm desto reinere Freude empfinden'. (F.65:27)

Goethe believed that the British dramatist 'definitely appeals to our mind's eye: through it the picture world of the imagination is immediately enlivened, the total impact of which we cannot quite explain.' If we observe Shakespeare's plays carefully, we notice 'that they contain much less perceptible action than intellectual language. He provides actions that can easily be imagined, and indeed can better be imagined than seen.' The performer of Shakespeare does not promote imagination; but he must not intend to restrain it. Goethe thinks that it 'would not be disastrous' if Shakespeare were ousted from the German stage once and for all: 'for the reader, whether lonely or gregarious, will then derive even purer pleasure from his works.'

Apart from the few remarks on naturalistic plays and Maeterlinck discussed earlier, Kraus reviewed only two plays,[83] now forgotten, in the first eighty-one issues of *Die Fackel*. He liked neither of them, but some information on his views can be gathered from his discussion of *critics*. For example, he would quote the theatre or drama criticism of critics whom he did not respect, sometimes commenting sarcastically and obviously taking the opposite side. In *Die Fackel* no. 80 he quoted Max Burckhard (the former managing director of the Burgtheater) from no. 349 of *Die Zeit*: 'Im Burgtheater hat diese Woche Herr Nissen sein Engagement als Major Drosse in *Sudermanns ergreifendem Drama* "Fritzchen" und als Churfürst Friedrich Wilhelm in *Kleists widerlichem, nach Cäsarismus stinkendem Commißkopfstück* "Prinz Friedrich von Homburg" angetreten' (F.80:27). [In the Burgtheater this week, Mr Nissen began his engagement as Major Drosse in *Sudermann's moving drama Fritzchen* and as Prince-Elector Friedrich Wilhelm in *Kleist's Prinz Friedrich von Homburg, that distasteful product of a military mind, which stinks of Caesarism.*] The emphasis is Kraus's. He also cited Buchbinder's derogatory comments about Ibsen's *Brand* (F.49:27-8): 'Dieser Faust im modernen Priesterkleide ... ist kein Bühnenheld ... Ibsens 'Brand' (ist) eines jener Werke ... die absurd und abstract, niemals Heimatsrecht auf der Bühne erlangen werden.' [This Faust in modern priest's clothing is no stage hero ... Ibsen's *Brand* is one of those absurd and abstract works which will never establish themselves on the stage.] Kraus then commented: 'Freuen wir uns, daß zu dieser Sorte von Stücken zwar "Faust" (dieser Brand im unmodernen Priesterkleide), aber nicht der "Kecke Schnabel" [one of Buchbinder's plays] gehört.' [Let us be glad that *Faust* (this Brand in old-fashioned priest's clothing) belongs in this category of plays, but that [Buchbinder's] *Der kecke Schnabel* doesn't.] In this way, we are made aware of Kraus's approval of the Ibsen play, as well as his disdain towards contemporary critic-playwrights such as Buchbinder.

The period from 1892 to June 1901, which saw Kraus take such an active critical interest in the theatre, ended on a slightly more subdued note than it had begun. Kraus's often effusive and brash reaction to plays and the artistry of playwrights and actors of the early 1890s gave way to sharper, more ethically oriented censure of the theatre directors, newspaper critics, and clique members who were, in his opinion, the *real* villains in what he increasingly in the following years saw to be the decline of the theatre. The early importance of Bahr in his criticism is significant, as at the turn of the century he came to see Bahr's relationship to the theatre as critic and playwright in almost symbolic terms. The court case arising out of Kraus's censorious attitude to this relationship, the Bahr/Bukovics case, was perhaps important primarily because it so effectively polarized the critical scene at the beginning of the century: now it was Kraus vs 'the others.' A shift of critical perspective was involved here. From now on, ethical criticism would play a decisive role in Kraus's evaluation of artistic merit. One of the results of this emphasis on ethics in art was that his early criterion of naturalness in acting gave way in the years following 1901 to one of 'greatness of personality' of the actor – to the conviction that an actor could only be a great artist if he were a fine human being. Consequently, in the face of what he increasingly came to view as the *débâcle* of the theatre in the twentieth century, Kraus came to idealize Burgtheater actors such as Charlotte Wolter, Lewinsky, and Sonnenthal, to idealize, in fact, the whole Burgtheater 'tradition' of which he had, as a youthful critic, often been so critical.

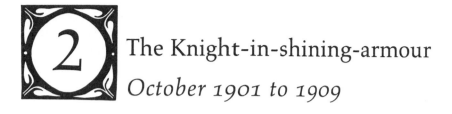

The Knight-in-shining-armour
October 1901 to 1909

Kraus saw the world of the theatre in terms of polarities, dichotomies, sharp contrasts, and wild contradictions. Consequently his theatre criticism reflects the antithetical structure of his vision. His presentation is often theatrical, as he pits player against player (*Spieler* and *Gegenspieler*), hero against villain: Girardi vs Kainz, Baumeister vs Kainz, Offenbach vs Bauer, Wedekind or Wilde or Ibsen or Hauptmann vs Goldmann or Grossmann or st-g (Sternberg) or Schütz – or any number of Viennese critics. The 'plot' of his criticism is in the heroic mould, with Kraus playing the role of the hero in newsprint armour who comes to the rescue of those people, institutions, plays, or styles which he deems ethically and artistically worth championing. As in previous years, he fought for the 'great' Burgtheater style of acting. But with the death of most of the older Burgtheater actors and the continuing infiltration of Berlin naturalism, which was supported by other Viennese critics, he saw no hope for the continuation of that traditon in legitimate theatre. He therefore turned away from this battle and tried to rescue literary drama (*Buchdrama*) from the stage into the safekeeping of the reader, who alone could fully appreciate thought, wit, and ideas. To the stage he left dramas of second-rate literary merit (*Bühnendramen*), which could, in the style of the *commedia dell'arte*, serve as guidelines for actor-improvisers such as Girardi. A subordinate part of his mission was the rescue of such actors from the throes of first-rate literary dramas, since, in Kraus's eyes, it was only in second-rate plays that their improvising genius could find its highest artistic expression. Paradoxically, his turning away from the theatre as a means for effective literary dramatic expression did not prevent him from using the stage to honour Wedekind's *Büchse der Pandora*, in a production in which he himself took part as actor and producer.

If Kraus is the major hero of his writings on drama, the press must still be seen as the great villain. Kraus laid the blame for the sickness of contemporary theatre and drama on the newspaper critics' philistinism and superficiality (his term for this quality was *Feuilletonismus*). The arch-villain in this decade was not Bahr but Maximilian Harden of Berlin. In Kraus's polemics against both these men there was an interaction of ethical and aesthetic criticism, but his basic concerns were no longer quite the same. In the case of Bahr, Kraus had sought to show that his involvement with the same theatre as critic and playwright left the door open for corruption and made him a less than objective critic. The Harden case demonstrates Kraus's growing interest in language, already evidenced in his fight for literary drama. For his battle against Harden is based on that critic's use of language: his aesthetic criticism of Harden's style led Kraus to the conclusion that the man was ethically reprehensible. This view of language as the essential touchstone opens the door to many of the apparent contradictions in Kraus's criticism of the following decades.

There is an important point to watch for. In Kraus's continuing battles for the Burgtheater tradition or literary drama or 'the word,' there is a growing awareness of himself as an artist and creator, and of the other critics as mere critics.

CRITICISM OF ACTORS

How much Kraus's ideal of acting was drawn form the past is revealed by the fact that three of the actors (Lewinsky, Sonnenthal, and Matkowsky) whom he thought great died in this decade, while the fourth (Baumeister) celebrated his eightieth birthday. Lewinsky, Baumeister, and Sonnenthal were all Burgtheater actors, and Matkowsky, although from Berlin, was seen by Kraus as the one hope for the Burgtheater. Therefore, the sum of their acting styles can be called the 'old' or traditional Burgtheater style.

Josef Lewinsky was called by Kraus 'the most learned actor' (F.221:18); the roles he created were the product of long, honest study. For example, Kraus defended Lewinsky's interpretation of the *Dovrealte* (in *Peer Gynt*) in the mask of Ibsen against the criticism of Bahr,[1] among others (F.104:21–2). Although Kraus (for unspecified reasons) had not particularly liked this presentation of the *Dovrealte*, he thought Lewinsky deserved praise for his artistic integrity and honesty, in that he had studied the role seriously and had stuck to his interpretation on the second night rather than let himself be swayed by adverse criticism.

A sequel to this critique appeared just after Lewinsky's death in 1907, when Kraus published four letters he had received from the actor (F.221:6–9). The third of these concerned the *Peer Gynt* performance; Lewinsky admitted that he did *not* know that the Ibsen mask was used in Norway, as Kraus had asserted previously in his defence of the actor. Rather, the thought had forced itself upon him when he was studying the role:

der Gedanke drängte sich mir beim Studium auf, weil mir der Dichter bei dieser Szene so leibhaftig erschien; ich wollte das Publikum nur aufmerksam machen, daß es eigentlich in der Maske des Dovre-Alten den Dichter selber vor sich hat, der ihm so unbequeme Wahrheiten in's Gesicht sagt.

The thought forced itself upon me when I was studying the role, because the author appeared to me so much in person in this scene; I just wanted to make the members of the audience aware of the fact that it was really the playwright himself in the mask of the Old Man from Dovre whom they had in front of them telling them such uncomfortable truths to their face.

That Lewinsky arrived at his interpretation after a long study of the role and of the dramatist's ideas is indicative of the type of actor he was – an actor who rationally thought out and *re*-presented, rather than one who created intuitively. That this was both his and Kraus's view is evident from his fourth letter to Kraus, which referred to a previous article in *Die Fackel*. The letter is dated 1 April 1905, when the actor was recuperating from an illness. Lewinsky's gentleness and decency partly hide the bitterness he felt towards the critics for their lack of understanding of his style of acting.[2] He thanked Kraus for reprinting an essay by Stanislaus von Koźmian,[3] entitled 'Burgtheater 1873' (F.174:13–20). Since Kraus had already called Koźmian 'a genuine connoisseur of the theatre,' the essay warrants examination.

Koźmian concerned himself with two overlapping topics: the undue influence of realism on the acting style of many Burgtheater actors, and an analysis of the acting techniques of Josef Lewinsky and Charlotte Wolter, who were then at the height of their powers. Kraus's editorial comment indicated his agreement with the substance of Koźmian's essay; in fact, he considered it, though written thirty-two years previously, to be of startling actuality since it pinpointed the evils he himself had deplored all these years: 'Burgtheaterverfall, Direktionsjammer und realistischer Stil' [the decline of the Burgtheater, the dreadful state of its management, and a realistic style (of acting)].

The characterization of Lewinsky was, in Kraus's words, excellent. For Koźmian the main criterion of acting was truth, for in keeping with the eternal rules of art and beauty, 'only what is true can be beautiful' (ibid, p. 14). Affectation in speech and gesture had been banned from the best stages and truth, in the form of naturalness, dominated the scene. However, Koźmian warned against excessive realism, which ignored the fact that not everything natural was beautiful. He then went on to consider how the tendency towards realism had lately somewhat weakened the style of Lewinsky, whom he called an 'outstanding, in many ways quite exceptional artist'(ibid,

p. 15). His analysis of how Lewinsky approached his roles is most sensitive. It was Lewinsky's intelligence which gave his creations their distinctive character. He created with his mind or reason rather than with his imagination: 'Er hat mehr Verstand als Phantasie, mehr Forschungstrieb und Reflexionstiefe als poetischen Schwung, er ist schöpferisch, aber nicht die Inspiration und Phantasie, sondern der Verstand bildet seine schöpferische Kraft' (ibid).

Koźmian then contrasted Lewinsky's technique with that of Charlotte Wolter, who represented an entirely different artistic type. Wolter's creative root was her talent, and she worked intuitively, instinctively, from the heart and not the mind. There was no danger of her becoming too realistic (as Koźmian had felt was sometimes the case of Lewinsky, especially in his characterization of Wurm in *Kabale und Liebe*): 'Und trotz ihrer [Charlotte Wolter's] Wahrhaftigkeit und Natürlichkeit wird sie doch niemals in den Realismus verfallen. Davor schüzt sie die überaus originelle und reiche Art ihres Talents, das voll Schwung, überraschend, blitzartig ist ... ' (ibid, p. 18).

Ironically, Koźmian's clarity and critical excellence as an analyst of acting styles heighten the reader's awareness of Kraus's deficiencies in this field. For, although Kraus defended Lewinsky and Charlotte Wolter and often wrote of the Burgtheater tradition, he himself had never really succeeded in analysing these two different aspects of the traditional Burgtheater style so explicitly. Kraus's criticism was often impressionistic (a quality he criticized in the writings of others) or opinionated (particularly when concerned with Kainz), and a well-reasoned, critical yet sensitive analysis of an actor's technique was rare in *Die Fackel*.

In his evaluation of Bernard Baumeister, the Burgtheater veteran, Kraus was consistently and completely positive in this period. In Kraus's opinion, Baumeister was so excellent that he felt other actors should avoid for decades any role on which he had put his personal stamp. For example, Homma, who played the role of Falstaff in the Volkstheater production of *The Merry Wives of Windsor* in 1906, merits only the adjective 'competent' from Kraus:

> *Der tüchtige Herr Homma kann nichts für den bösen Willen der Direction, die ihm den Falstaff zugemutet hat. Die Vorführung des Falstaff in einer Stadt, die Bernard Baumeister, den lieben genialen Naturschwimmer, in dieser Rolle erlebt hat, wird nach Jahrzehnten noch ein parvenühaftes Unterfangen sein. (F.199:23)*

The competent Mr Homma should not be blamed for the ill-will of the management, which entrusted the role of Falstaff to him. The performance of Falstaff in a city which has experienced the brilliant artlessness of their beloved Bernard Baumeister in this role will remain for decades a presumptuous undertaking.

This comment reveals that Kraus's criteria for acting excellence were based very much on the Burgtheater tradition of the 1870s and 1880s, when Baumeister was in his prime. And this tradition, as he continually pointed out in these years, had its roots in good acting, not in the literary excellence of the repertoire – 'Die Schauspielerei, nicht die Literatur war seit jeher die Stärke des Burgtheaters ... '(F.222:15). In fact, Baumeister in a second-rate play would have been far more preferable to a mediocre actor playing a first-rate character such as Falstaff (see F.164:8).

In his ecstatic praise of one of Baumeister's rare performances later in 1906 in the title role of Calderon's *Alcalde of Zalamea*, Kraus was unable to be explicit about these qualities of the actor's performance that impressed him. He stated: 'nie habe ich auf einer deutschen Bühne – die Wolter und Matkowsky nicht ausgenommen – den Eindruck von einem stärkeren Elementarereignis empfangen' (F.222:15). [Never on a German stage – not even with the exception of Mme Wolter and Matkowsky – have I received the impression of an event of greater elemental passion.] This enigmatic *Elementarereignis* no doubt depended on that quality of 'elemental passion' (*das Elementarische*) which Kraus saw and praised in Charlotte Wolter and Matkowsky. But it is rather vague as a critical term. The second quality Kraus praised in Baumeister's performance was clarity of speech: 'Und dieser Achtzigjährige spricht mit einer solchen Klarheit, daß ich auf der vierten Galerie des taubstummen Hauses jedes Wort verstand. Nie kann es ähnliches vorher gegeben haben und nie wird es wiederkehren' (ibid). [And this eighty-year-old speaks with such clarity that I was able to understand every word in the fourth gallery of this house, in spite of its terrible acoustics. Never before can there have been anything like it, and we will never see anything like it again.] Such an effusive and enthusiastic reaction to clear speech must almost seem out of place. And yet the quality of sound was one of the aspects of the traditional Burgtheater style that Kraus remembered most vividly and that he was to seek to emulate in his own readings of plays in the 1902s and 1930s.

Kraus's attitude to Adolf Sonnenthal remained mixed. He published little purely artistic criticism of Sonnenthal; rather, Kraus sharply criticized the press's reaction to him. Kraus complained that Lewinsky was ignored by the liberal press, whereas Sonnenthal was praised excessively by the liberal newspapers and criticized by the anti-Semitic press (F.174:21). However, in the same paragraph Kraus himself praised Sonnenthal, calling him both *ausgezeichnet* and *außerordentlich*. Sonnenthal's death in 1909 was marked in *Die Fackel* primarily by Kraus's disgust with the mixture of sentimentality and commercialism in the lamentations of the liberal press; the *Neue Freie Presse*, for example, seemed to consider the loss of the actor as that of the 'father of a stockbroker [*eines Börsensensals*] of German art' (F.279/80:33).

But a few lines later Kraus did mention the splendid artistry of Sonnenthal and called him 'the most cultured actor' (ibid).

Only once did Kraus try to characterize a particular interpretation of Sonnenthal's, and there it was not speech technique[4] that impressed him, but that other quality of the Burgtheater style: elemental passion, the ability of the actor to appeal to the intuitions and emotions rather than the reason and intelligence of the spectator. He compared various interpretations of Lear that had been given in Vienna in the previous years – by Sonnenthal, Rossi, Barnay, Novelli, and Zacconi. He considered Rossi to have been the most successful in so far as his version gave complete shape to the character. Novelli, Zacconi, and Barnay gave only nuances. Sonnenthal's Lear lacked backbone, but was memorable in certain scenes. However, in Kraus's opinion, the greatness of Sonnenthal in these scenes far outweighed the combined performances of the others. Kraus had attended the first performance by Sonnenthal in this role, had seen this production seven times since, and had particularly praised the scene in which Lear cursed Goneril. It was the elemental rage and passion of which Sonnenthal was capable that impressed him so much. 'Achtmal hat mich – ich hörte ihn schon, als er zum erstenmal das Haus erzittern machte – Sonnenthals Gonerilfluch erschüttert wie kaum eine zweite Temperamentsentladung auf deutscher Bühne (ich müßte denn an Matkowsky-Othello's vulkanische Ausbrüche denken)' (F.191:22). [Eight times – I heard him already the first time he made the house shake – eight times Sonnenthal's curse on Goneril has moved me as scarcely any other outbreak of passion on the German stage has done (I might only find Matkowsky's volcanic eruptions as Othello comparable).]

The mention of Adalbert Matkowsky at this point introduces us to the actor who probably made the most profound impression on Kraus during these years. As in the case of Baumeister and sometimes of Sonnenthal, the quality that Kraus praised most was the actor's passion. Kraus had various expressions for this: 'ein Vulkan' (F.200:20), '[sein] vulkanisches Temperament' F.200:19), '[die] Urkraft dieses Einzigen' (F.200:18), '(ein) Elementarereignis' (F.222:15), 'die Löwenkraft ... die Urgewalt des größten Tragöden' (F.279/80:10), 'Urtöne ... aus seiner Brust' (F.239/40:30), 'solches Toben entfesselter Elemente' (F.200:19). [A volcano; his volcanic temperament; (the) elemental power of this unique perfomer; (an) elemental phenomenon; the lion's strength ... the primeval power of the greatest tragedian; primal sounds from his breast; such raging of unleashed elements.] In Berlin, which was making its name in the theatrical world as the home of the naturalistic style of acting, Matkowsky was the great exception; he was 'der feuerspeiende Matkowsky, dessen Schlacken wertvoller sind als alle Schätze des naturalistischen Flachlands ...' (F.246/7:43) [the fire-spewing Matkowsky, whose dross is more valuable than all the treasures of the naturalistic lowlands ...]. Kraus

raved about this actor's powerful interpretation of Othello: 'sein Othello ...
ist das unerhörteste Erlebnis, das heute auf einer deutschen Bühne geboten
werden kann ... was bedeuten alle Burgtheaterheroen gegenüber der Urkraft dieses Einzigen!' (F.200:18). ([His Othello ... is the most tremendous
experience that can be offered on a German stage today ... of what significance are all the heroes of the Burgtheater compared with the elemental
power of this unique performer!] He regretted only that the last time he had
seen Matkowsky (as the Bastard in *King John* and as Richard II,) he had
found his performance strangely toned down. He assumed that Matkowsky
had let himself be influenced by naturalism (or, as Kraus termed it, by the
'Berliner Natürlichkeitsschwindel' [Berlin naturalistic humbug]) and hoped
that this actor would soon find his own 'natural' (that is, passionate) mode of
acting again. 'Hoffentlich rast er wieder in alter Zügellosigkeit und verachtet
das Urteil jener Theaternivelleure, die dem Löwen vorwerfen, daß er "brülle"'
(F.200:20). [I hope that he will rage unchecked the way he used to and will
scorn the judgment of those levellers of theatrical practices who reproach a
lion for 'roaring.'] Kraus hoped, too, that Matkowsky would be invited to
act at the Burgtheater, for in him lay the one hope of recapturing the great
style of tragic acting which Kraus felt had been lost in the 'democratization'
of this theatre (F.200:21). This hope was to remain unfulfilled, for Matkowsky died three years later.

   If one looks more closely at the article on Matkowsky, it becomes apparent
that Kraus used this actor as an example to highlight problems in the
theatre which had been his hobby-horse for years. Kraus denigrated those
Viennese theatre critics (especially Stefan Großmann) who knew nothing
about Shakespeare productions on German stages; he criticized the naturalistic
style of acting in Berlin, as well as the sad state of the Burgtheater and the
lack of greatness of its Shakespeare interpreters (particularly Kainz and Reimers). If, however, one looks to Kraus for a critical analysis of Matkowsky's
style of acting, one looks in vain. Kraus stated one main quality of Matkowsky – his temperament, his passion. Otherwise, he was able to supply only
very general impressions that do not enlarge the reader's understanding of
the actor (for example 'dieser Einzige' ['this unique (perfomer)'], p. 18; 'der
Unvergleichliche' ['the incomparable one'], p. 20). In order to characterize
the actor, Kraus had to quote from a monograph by the Berlin essayist Julius
Bab: 'Matkowsky ist der Schauspieler Shakespeares ... Es ist eine strö-
mende Harmonie, ein brausendes Ineinandergehen aller Kräfte in diesem Mann,
der, wenn man will, ganz uneigenartig und nichts andres ist als eine unge-
heure Verkörperung des Typus "Mensch". Matkowsky ist unindividuell – wie
Shakespeare' (F.200:19–20). [Matkowsky is *the* Shakespearean actor ...
There is in this man a flowing harmony, a rushing penetration of all forces. He
is, if you will, quite unindividual and nothing other than the incarnation of

the 'human' type. Matkowsky is unindividual – like Shakespeare.] Bab analysed more closely the quality that Kraus called elemental force and dynamic
passion and found, along with this, serenity and sorrow. 'Wie aus dem
Mittelpunkt der Erde schleudert er das Feuer der Leidenschaft hoch und trägt
zugleich mit offenen Händen alle liebliche Heiterkeit und sanft reifende Trauer
der Welt ...' (ibid). [He flings the fire of passion high, as if out of the bowels of
the earth, and at the same time he bears open-handedly all the lovely joyfulness and gently mellowing grief of the world ...] It is curious, however, that
critical analysis once more had to come from a pen other than Kraus's.

The actor to whom Kraus assigned the role of villain in these years was Josef
Kainz of the Burgtheater. Kainz became symbolic of the decay of this
theatre. This was in part because Kraus did not like Kainz's style of acting, but
more particularly because it was this very style which was receiving critical
acclaim from the press. Kraus's criticism was threefold; against the actor
himself, against Schlenther who had hired him, and against the critics for
their acclaim and, in Kraus's opinion, lack of critical discernment.

Kraus's criticism of Kainz had not changed substantially from previous
years; however, the intensity of the attack increased over the years. The main
point was that Kraus thought Kainz lacked genuine talent – genius (Genia-
lität), soul (Seele), or personality (Persönlichkeit). In commenting on Kainz's
performance as Zwirn in Nestroy's Der böse Geist Lumpazivagabundus,
Kraus asserted: 'Sprudelnden Uebermuth und Komik muß man haben, und
kann sie, wenn man sie nicht hat, nicht einmal stehlen. Die Darstellung des
Zwirn ist nicht Sache der "Auffassung" sondern des Talents' (F.88:21). [One
must have bubbling high spirits and humour, and if one doesn't have them,
one cannot steal them. The portrayal of Zwirn is not a matter of 'interpretation' but of talent.] According to Kraus, Kainz's main trick to cover up this
lack of talent was a speech technique in which some lines were tossed off and
others delivered at a slower pace than usual, resulting in what Kraus had
previously termed 'neurasthenic chattering.'[5] In Kraus's opinion, this actor
was no more than a juggler of words – a Zungenjongleur, Zungenequilibrist,
Ekzentrik-Tragiker, der unbeseelte Tonfallkletterer – and belonged on the
vaudeville stage rather than in legitimate theatre. Lacking soul or personality, Kainz was incapable of that quality of elemental passion which Kraus so
admired in Baumeister:

> Echten Schauspielern entströmt die Seele, ob sie wollen oder nicht. Herr
> Kainz bewahrt sie in einem Apothekerfläschchen. Und es ist ein in seiner
> Art rührender Anblick, wenn dort, wo rhetorische Mittel nicht helfen kön-
> nen, wie in plötzlichem Entschluß die Pathetik hervorgeholt und vor dem
> Gebrauch heftig geschüttelt wird ... (F.188:19)

Soul *flows* from genuine actors, whether they wish it or not. Mr Kainz
keeps his in little apothecary jars. And it is a sight which is rather touching
in its own way when, in those places where rhetorical measures cannot
help, with sudden decisiveness pathos is fetched from the shelf and is well
shaken before use.

Kraus claimed that Kainz's peculiar technique of speech not only failed to
make up for this lack of passion, but sometimes also caused him to be
unfaithful to the poet's intention. In *Die Fackel* no. 98, after negative remarks
about Kainz's performance in *Measure for Measure*, Kraus used his typical
technique of contrasting Kainz with actors of whom he approved, this time
with Herr Hartmann and Frau Hohenfels 'who work out the intention of the
author with the most subtle skill' (ibid, p. 14). Faithfulness to the poet's
intention was to remain one of Kraus's most important criteria. In fact, in
this article, he went so far as to state that to leave out one word of Shakespeare
was a crime.

As we have seen, Kraus condemned Kainz's manner of speaking as a cover
for his lack of talent, but he also attacked it as false realism. In 1907 Kraus
reviewed the Burgtheater production of *Julius Caesar*, in which Kainz played
the role of Mark Antony, and commented with unusual detail on the
opening lines of Mark Antony's funeral oration. He claimed that, in trying
to be realistic,[6] Kainz had treated this as a call to order among the masses,
and had drawn out each exhortation. As Kraus transcribed it, it sounded
something like: 'Mit-bür-ger, Freun-de, Röö-määr, hört mich aaan!'
(F.239/40:29). Kraus contrasted this interpretation with that of Emmerich
Robert, one of the great Burgtheater actors of the 1880s, who forced the people
of Rome to become silent and listen to him by the sheer force of his personality, so that in his rendering, the opening words 'Friends, Romans, country-
men ...' belonged to the speech itself rather than forming a preamble to it:
what Robert had done by his personality, Kainz had to do with his vocal cords.
Kraus indicated that performances such as Kainz's were indicative of the
low level to which the Burgtheater had sunk, so that the cries of the carriage
drivers at the end of a performance – *Aus is* – took on the added dimension
of a death knell.

Das Niveau ist tiefer gelegt und man sieht den Leichnam der Burgthea-
terkunst über die Szene tragen, [sic] wenn solch ein Mark Anton seine
spekulative Lungenkraft betätigt ... Und wenn draußen der gewaltige
Ruf 'Aus is' ertönt, so klingt echte Empfindung mit. Denn er bedeutet
längst nicht nur den Schluß der Vorstellung, sondern auch das Ende der
Burgtheaterherrlichkeit. (F.239/40:31)

> The standard is lowered and one can see the corpse of the art of the
> Burgtheater carried across the stage when such a Mark Antony sets into
> motion the speculative power of his lungs ... And when outside the
> theatre the powerful call 'It's over' rings out, then genuine feeling reso-
> nates. For it has long signified not only the end of the performance, but also
> the end of the glory of the Burgtheater.

Kraus's remarks illustrate his extreme dislike of anything he saw as a distortion
of the dramatist's text; but it may well be argued that Kainz's interpretation of the lines as calling the crowd to order is just as faithful to the words
Shakespeare wrote as Robert's interpretation.

In any case, the general acclaim of Kainz continued. In 1908 Kraus de-
nounced a critic who preferred Kainz's interpretation of Valentin in Raimund's
Der Verschwender to that of Girardi. He not only deplored Kainz's lack of
artistry, but he condemned the theatre, the public, and the press, seeing in
their approbation the decline of artistic sensibility in contemporary Vienna.
'Daß Herr Kainz es jetzt wieder wagen konnte, mit seinen Kopftönen in dies
friedlichste Heiligtum gemütvoller Darstellung einzudringen, daß er dazu
eine Bühne, eine Galerie und eine Presse fand, zeigt, wie die Echtheit im
Kunstempfinden dieser Stadt auf dem Krepierstandpunkt angelangt ist'
(*F.*254/5:4–5). [That now Mr Kainz could again dare with his nasal tones to
force his way into this most tranquil sanctuary of warm-hearted acting,
that he found for his purposes a stage, a gallery, and a press, shows how
genuine artistic sensibility in this city is wretchedly dying.]

Thus, from Kraus's criticism, there evolves a concept of a style of acting
largely associated with the ghost of the 'old' Burgtheater tradition.[7] It was a
style which appealed to both sides of man: to his intuition and emotions
through the actor's passion, and to his reason and intellect through the
actor's rhetorical skill. However, when rhetoric became artificial and did not
illuminate the poet's text (as, Kraus felt, was the case with Kainz's interpretations), when the actor had no personality or soul or talent (Kainz again),
then one could neither be instructed intellectually nor moved emotionally,
and the 'grand style,' corrupt and empty now, had no alternative but to die.

THE BURGTHEATER STYLE AND THE BERLIN NATURALIST
SCHOOL

As we have seen, Kraus believed that the old Burgtheater style was dying by
a process of *internal* corruption. Now we must consider a rival school of
acting that, according to Kraus, contributed to the demise of the 'grand style.'
In both instances, he blamed the critics: for their praise of Kainz in the first

case, and for their blind commitment to Berlin naturalism in the second.

Evidently, the naturalism prevalent in Berlin sharply contrasted with the old Burgtheater style Kraus had come to admire so much. He now reduced this contrast to the neat formula *Effektschauspieler/Defektschauspieler*[8] [lit. 'effect actors/defect actors']. Artists of the former kind interpreted or filtered a work of art through their personality, and showed the audience the *essence* of humour, grace, and good taste (see *F.*164:9). Naturalistic actors, in Kraus's opinion, could only display the particular defects that they themselves possessed – lack of personality, spluttering, stuttering – depending as they did on a threefold dialect: '(the) dialects of soul, of costume, and of language' (*F.*138:15). They were bit players (*Episodenspieler*), each specializing in one type of episode, but they were not artists. They lacked not only style, but passion; Kraus called them 'dilettantes without stagefright' (*F.*175:19). Or again, in an aphorism from 1908, he stated that there were two kinds of 'natural' actors: those who had personality and only expressed themselves, and those who *could* express nothing but themselves. The one kind of actor transcended reality with his greatness; the other never managed to get beyond the depths of ugly externals.

Nichts wird von der Schauspielkritik so gern verwechselt wie die Persönlichkeit, die immer sich selbst ausdrückt, und der Mangel, der nichts anderes als sich selbst ausdrücken kann: beides ist Natur. Wir haben einst an jedem Abend das Glück gehabt, ein paar große Menschen vor uns hintreten zu sehen, die sich schauspielerisch nie so ganz verwandeln konnten, daß wir in ihnen die großen Menschen verkannt hätten. Aber nun sagt man uns, die Eigenart habe sich differenziert und Individualitäten seien auch jene, die man sofort daran erkennt, daß sie heiser sind oder stottern oder schielen. Zwei Falstaffs gegenüber ist solche Kritik ratlos: soll sie einer Fülle, die sich selbst spielt, den Vorzug geben, oder einem glaubhaften Bauch? (*F.* 241:23)

Critics of acting like nothing better than to confuse personality, which always expresses itself, and the lack of it, which can express nothing but itself: both are natural. Once upon a time we were lucky enough to have a couple of great people on the stage before us every evening, who, as actors, never could transform themselves so completely that we could have failed to appreciate the great people they were. But now we are told that originality has become refined, and those people are also personalities who are immediately recognizable because they are hoarse or because they stutter or squint. Such critics are at a loss when confronted with two Falstaffs: should they give preference to an abundance that displays itself or to an authentic paunch?

Nor could the naturalistic actor appeal to the intellect of his audience, since his theatre was essentially non-verbal – that is, it depended for its effect on the depiction of a very particular milieu, and not on the presentation of clearly formulated ideas or of characters with style and verbal wit. In fact, taking the production of Gorki's *Nachtasyl* by Reinhardt's Kleines Theater as an example, Kraus found that its only effect stemmed from the melodrama of the misery in the milieu and not from the artistry of any of the actors. 'Es ist nämlich die ausbündigste Narrheit, überhaupt von Schauspielkunst zu sprechen, wo alle Wirkung von der unfehlbaren Melodramatik des Elendmilieus besorgt wird, wo jeder persönliche Mangel wie Charakteristik wirkt ...' (F.138:15).

In naturalistic productions, language, too, became a means to depict a milieu rather than to communicate ideas. Kraus called this '[the] technique of unarticulated speech' (F.175:21) or 'the doctrine of not being able to speak' (F.138:17). This doctrine was even more offensive artistically when it was applied to classical plays. Instead of the actors revealing the essence of the text through language, decorative details such as dialect or 'realistic' stuttering were added to make the play more realistic and thus, supposedly, more convincing. But since such details were not intrinsic or essential, the 'genuineness' which the critics found in the naturalistic style was a misleading artistic criterion. In this case, Kraus blamed the critics' bad judgment on their lack of practical knowledge of the theatre ('ihre Theaterfremdheit') and on their eye for the superficial ('ihr Feuilletongeist'). Kraus reminded his readers that those critics ignored one of the strong sides of the Burgtheater – that is, the ability to portray a milieu. He gave as examples the proletarian milieu of Gerhart Hauptmann's *Hanneles Himmelfahrt* and that of the petty bourgeois in Ludwig Thoma's *Die Localbahn*; both plays were recent Burgtheater productions. But here, it was acting talent and personality that were responsible for the effect produced (F.138:16).

Besides the critics who blindly popularized the naturalistic technique to the detriment of the Burgtheater tradition, Kraus's chief villain in this connection was Max Reinhardt, who propagated naturalism through his acting troupes. At first, Kraus grudgingly praised Reinhardt's enthusiasm and the skill which he had learned at the Burgtheater before going to Berlin (F.138:15). But as time went on, Reinhardt seemed to Kraus to be more and more of a charlatan, trying to hoodwink the critics and the public by appealing to their snobbish instincts with his 'new style' of acting. And, what was even more galling, Reinhardt, '(dieser) nie verlegene Theaterparvenu' [(this) unflappable Johnny-come-lately], was making a lot of money in the process (F.175:20).

In Kraus's opinion, the naturalistic technique of acting had a disastrous effect on art. It led to a levelling of art to the lowest common denominator: episode players who were limited to one trick, a profusion of narrow specialists

(F.175:20) replacing one genuinely talented actor who was capable of por-traying many characters and moods; an emphasis on the low, sordid, and miserable, rather than the great and uplifting, on defects and deficiencies rather than artistic effects and personalities, and on linguistic poverty, rather than on wit, clarity, and beauty of language. Kraus had many terms for this phenomenon – he spoke of '(the) sad bourgeoisification of the Burg-theater'[9] (F.200:21), 'the universal suffrage of art' contrasting it with the 'privileges of personality' of the old Burgtheater tradition (F.239/40:29), and 'the levelling of art.' That such a technique of acting was preferred by the critics to the 'grand style' of the Burgtheater was incomprehensible to Kraus. As his interest in language grew throughout this decade, it became particularly offensive to him when this technique – or any attempt at realism for the sake of realism – was applied on the grounds of 'authenticity' to plays in which language was important. Naturalistic effects were then purely decorative and not necessary. Here can be seen the roots of Kraus's later theories on style and on the essentially structural, non-decorative relationship between form and content, theories which were brought into focus by the Harden polemic in 1908–9.

LITERARY DRAMA AND STAGE DRAMA

Kraus's theories concerning literary and stage drama (Buchdrama and Bühnendrama) stem to a certain extent from the contrast of the Burgtheater style and Berlin naturalism. His concrete statements on the two acting styles date largely from the years prior to 1906, whereas the more theoretical remarks on the two types of drama occur later, between 1907 and 1909. We have seen that he rejected naturalism in part because it emphasized externals, lacked intrinsic greatness, and often undermined the full expressive power of language by the use of dialect. The 'grand style' of the Burgtheater had preserved the intention of the author at least in part by the attention paid by actors of genius to the actual text. Kraus's theories on literary and stage drama take this antithesis one step further. He considered literary drama to be great literature (Dichtung); the dramatist's ideas and the language he used to express them were of primary importance. What Kraus called Bühnendrama, however, is characterized by the German word Schauspiel, which indicates the 'show' or spectacle (and presumes spectators watching) and the 'play' of the actors. Kraus now relegated the actor to such stage plays only and rid what he considered to be literary drama of all externals, including the actors, who, in such dramas, had become mere decoration. Kraus reduced and internalized literary drama to ideas and language only, which could be properly appreci-ated by the reader alone: the reader's mind and imagination were to be the performer and interpreter.

The distinction made by Kraus between *Buchdrama* and *Bühnendrama* was made particularly clear by him in connection with Girardi, whom, as we know, Kraus greatly admired. That his admiration continued is clear from his observation in 1901 that had it been Girardi instead of Kainz who had played Zwirn in Nestroy's *Lumpazivagabundus*, the play would not have been lowered to the level of a 'circus-artist's joke' ('einen Artistenspaß') (*F*.88:22), and from his statement in 1902 that he deplored that Girardi had to perform in Buchbinder's *Er und seine Schwester*, a play which Kraus considered to be an insult to the actor and to the intelligence of the spectators (*F*.100:13).

After 1902 Kraus mentioned Girardi only occasionally, until 1907 when the actor moved to Berlin. This move very much bothered Kraus.[10] Within one year (January 1908 to 1909), he published three essays directly concerning Girardi, as well as shorter notes in the sections entitled 'Tagebuch' and 'Vorurteile.' In the article 'Girardi' (*F*.246/7:38–44), Kraus called him 'one of the most gifted actors.' Those who judged Girardi on the basis of the type or quality of play in which he acted were, in Kraus's opinion, stupid. Girardi had indeed played in inferior plays (by Buchbinder, among others) but this, according to Kraus, did not matter. 'Er [Girardi] läßt sich von einem beliebigen Sudler ein notdürftiges Szenarium liefern und in dieses legt er eine Geniefülle, deren Offenbarung erhebender ist als die Bühnenwirkung eines literarischen Kunstwerks, dessen Weihen doch erst der Leser empfangen kann' (ibid, pp. 41–2). [He (Girardi) takes an inferior scenario from any scribbler you like, and into it he pours a wealth of genius, the revelation of which is more impressive than the effect on stage of a literary work of art, whose solemnities really only a reader can properly appreciate.] Here one can see the beginnings of the distinction Kraus was to make between stage drama and literary drama. Only the actor with his creative energies could bring a stage play alive, whereas the reader was the primary interpreter of literary drama. However, Kraus did not yet go to the extreme of saying that Girardi should *not* act in literary drama. On the contrary, he stated that it was all the better if Girardi 'acted literature.' 'Es ist gleichgiltig, ob Girardi ein Buch oder eine Buchbinderarbeit für seine künstlerischen Zwecke benützt. Spielt er einmal Literatur, umso besser. Sein Valentin ist gewiß das größte Ereignis des Wienerischen Theaters ...' (ibid, p. 42). [It does not matter whether Girardi uses a book or a bookbinder's[11] effort for his artistic purposes. If he occasionally acts in a play that really is literature, so much the better. His Valentin is certainly the biggest event in Viennese theatre ...]

In a 'Tagebuch' entry (*F*.251/2:36), Kraus began with a more general consideration of stage plays and literary drama and ended with praise for Girardi's choosing non-literary opportunities for what Kraus called his 'creative high-handedness' ('seine schöpferische Selbstherrlichkeit'). His position now was more extreme than in the previously cited article. Kraus opened with a concept of the actor's art close to that of the *commedia dell'arte* tradition of theatre.

Die Schauspielkunst sollte sich wieder selbstständig machen. Der Darsteller ist nicht der Diener des Dramatikers, sondern der Dramatiker ist der Diener des Darstellers. Dazu ist freilich Shakespeare zu gut. Wildenbruch würde genügen. Die Bühne gehört dem Schauspieler, und der Dramatiker liefere bloß die Gelegenheit. Tut er mehr, so nimmt er dem Schauspieler, was des Schauspielers ist. Die Dichtung, der das Buch gehört, hat seit Jahrhunderten mit vollem Bewußtsein an der Szene schmarotzt. Sie hat sich vor der Phantasiearmut des Lesers geflüchtet und spekuliert auf die des Zuschauers. Sie sollte sich endlich der populären Wirkungen schämen, zu denen sie sich herbeiläßt. Kein Theaterpublikum hat noch einen Shakespeare-Gedanken erfaßt , sondern es hat sich stets nur vom Rhythmus, der auch Unsinn tragen könnte, oder vom stofflichen Gefallen betäuben lassen. 'Des Lebens Unverstand mit Wehmut zu genießen, ist Tugend und Begriff':[12] damit kann ein Tragöde so das Haus erschüttern, daß jeder glaubt, es sei von Sophokles und nicht von Wenzel Scholz. Heil Alexander Girardi, der in der Wahl unliterarischer Gelegenheiten seine schöpferische Selbstherrlichkeit betont! (F.251/2:36)

The art of acting should make itself independent again. The actor is not the servant of the dramatist, but rather the dramatist is the servant of the actor. Shakespeare, of course, is too good for that. Wildenbruch would be good enough. The stage belongs to the actor, and the dramatist should merely provide the opportunity. If he does more, then he takes from the actor what belongs to the actor. Literature, to which the book belongs, has knowingly sponged on the theatre for centuries. It fled there from the lack of imagination of the reader and speculates on that of the audience. It should at long last become ashamed of the popular effects to which it condescends. There hasn't been a theatre public which has grasped a single thought of Shakespeare's. Rather, people always let themselves be drugged by the rhythm, which could also convey nonsense, or by a liking for the subject of the play. 'To enjoy life's folly with a wistful smile/Is virtue and a concept': with these words a tragic actor can so move an audience that everyone believes they are by Sophocles and not by Wenzel Scholz. All hail Alexander Girardi, who, by his choice of non-literary texts, emphasizes his creative independence!

In the next article on Girardi ('Girardi und Kainz,' F.254/5:4–7), Kraus developed his theory on theatre and drama further. He stressed Girardi's uniqueness and creativity, defending him against the critics who deplored the literary level of the plays he acted in. Kraus called him 'the richest theatrical creator,' '(a) creative actor,' and '(an) actor of (unique) individuality.' He praised Girardi for picking plays by Buchbinder rather than Nestroy, since this gave him the chance to create naturally by extemporizing.

> *Wenn er sich von einem Buchbinder einen Pappendeckel liefern läßt, so bleibt er ungebunden; nie vermöchte ein großer Künstler sich selbst auszuschöpfen, wenn er zugleich einer anderen künstlerischen Persönlichkeit diente. (Ibid, p. 5)*

> *Da er nicht Possen schriebt, muß er sie sich liefern lassen. Notwendig hätte er es nicht; er schafft ja doch aus dem Stegreif. (Ibid, p. 7)*

If he has a cheap work delivered to him from a man such as Buchbinder [lit.: 'bookbinder'], then he can remain free [lit.: 'unbound']; a great artist could never use his creative potential to its full extent if he were at the same time to serve another artistic personality.

Since he doesn't write farces, he has to have them written for him. In fact, he doesn't have to, as he creates ex tempore.

Kraus felt that Girardi could neither tackle the long chain of aphorisms spoken by the comical *raisonneur* in Nestroy's plays nor handle the broad comedy of the second figure of the Nestroy world, the type that Wenzel Scholz used to play in Nestroy's day (ibid, pp. 6–7). And, what is perhaps even more surprising, Kraus insisted that, if a literary drama was to be performed on stage, the interests of the poet-dramatist would best be served by either a mediocre ensemble or a routine actor.

> *Soll die Literatur auf die Bühne gehören, dann dient ihr im besten Fall der Regisseur, der ein mittelmäßiges Ensemble in der Hand hält, aber nie die darstellerische Individualität. (Ibid, p. 5)*

> *Ein vollkommener Routinier wie Herr Thaller, der die überkommene Form des dünnen Sprechkomikers beherrscht, ist als Weinberl, Kampl, Ultra, Titus Feuerfuchs durchaus glaubhaft. (Ibid, p. 7)*

If literary works are to be performed on the stage, then they are best served by the theatre director who is in charge of a mediocre ensemble, but never by an actor who has his own individuality.

A completely routine actor such Mr Thaller, who has mastered the traditional form of the tall and skinny comic character, is absolutely believable as Weinberl, Kampl, Ultra, Titus Feuerfuchs.[13]

Looking back over Kraus's attitude towards Girardi in this decade, one can see in miniature the development of his theory on literary drama and stage drama. In 1901 he had stated that Girardi, not Kainz, should play roles such as Zwirn in Nestroy's *Lumpazivagabundus* (F.88:22), and had considered it shameful that Girardi had had to act in a second-rate play by Buchbinder (F.100:12–13). Now, in 1908, Girardi was not a Nestroy actor and was preferable in a Buchbinder play. The closest Kraus came to a compromise in his new theories was in the statement that, in a very few exceptional cases, both the acting and the poetic personality merge, as, for example, in Girardi's Valentin (F.254/5:7). But in its broadest terms, Kraus's new theory distinguished between the function of drama and that of the theatre. Drama, he asserted, was literature (*Dichtung*), the theatre was entertainment. The primary function of *Buchdrama* was to communicate the ideas of the poet to the reader, whereas the theatre was to provide the opportunity for the actor to create, using the schema provided by a usually second-rate *Bühnendrama*, and thereby to entertain an audience. 'Die wahren Schauspieler lassen sich vom Autor bloß das Stichwort bringen, nicht die Rede. Ihnen ist das Theaterstück keine Dichtung, sondern ein Spielraum' (F.272/3:44). [Real actors only let the authors supply them with their cues and not their speeches. For them, the play is not literature, but an opportunity for play-acting.]

This antithetical view of drama and the theatre was incompatible with some of the views Kraus expressed on the Burgtheater. In 1904 he did not separate the classics of literary drama from the Burgtheater acting tradition. Although he insisted that the Burgtheater had always been a training ground for acting talent and had never been the leader in discovering, influencing, or advancing new literary trends, he at that time still considered the neglect of the classical repertoire to be a major offence (F.156:2–3). The great actors of that theatre had created some of the most memorable moments for him in plays by Shakespeare and other 'literary' dramatists. One has only to recall his remarks in 1906 about Matkowsky (who, although not of the Burgtheater, was the one actor Kraus believed could have saved that theatre): 'His Othello, I know, is the most incredible experience that can be offered on a German stage today' (F.200:18). According to his theory, however, Kraus did not think that Shakespeare should be played by even the greatest actors: 'Neunzehntel Shakespeare wird an dem größten Schauspieler zuschanden' (F.254/5:5).

If the Burgtheater were no more than a training-ground for acting talent, then, in the light of his theories, second-rate plays should provide a better opportunity for the actors' creative abilities than the classics. But throughout this period Kraus continually complained about the low quality of plays in the repertoires of *all* Viennese theatres. So again, fact and theory do not coincide. Probably one of the *real* reasons behind Kraus's separating the functions of drama and the theatre was his disappointment at the lack of talent or personality in the new actors of the Burgtheater, at their over-dependence on realistic effect and decorative detail, and at the complete absence of 'greatness.' Kraus tried to rescue Shakespeare and all literary dramatists from the clutches of untalented actors into the care of the reader. The shift in this case was from great play/great actor/spectator (of the Burgtheater of the 1870s and 1880s) to poet-dramatist/great play/reader (of the new theories). Not only did the reader replace the passive spectator, but, to a certain extent, his imagination took on the creative process that had been left to the actor in the stage production. This, in Kraus's opinion in 1909, was the only valid 'presentation' of literary drama.

> Das dramatische Kunstwerk hat auf der Bühne nichts zu suchen. Die thea-
> tralische Wirkung eines Dramas soll bis zum Wunsch reichen, es aufge-
> führt zu sehen: ein Mehr zerstört die künstlerische Wirkung. Die beste
> Vorstellung ist jene, die sich der Leser von der Welt des Dramas macht.
> (F.264/5:31)

The dramatic work of art has no business on the stage. The theatrical effect of a drama should go as far as arousing one's wish to see it performed: more than that destroys the artistic effect. The best performance is that which the reader imagines for himself of the world of the drama.

However, Kraus later came to realize that most people cannot read well enough, that they need help, but not from the actor, who depends heavily on spectacle and stage business. The help they need can only come from a better reader than they are, a reader who is concerned with the text, understands it, and 'performs' it by voice only, thus focusing attention on the text instead of diluting the effects of the words with rival effects of gesture and décor. Such a reader then becomes another kind of actor – the kind of actor Kraus himself became in the following decade, in his Theater der Dichtung.

Kraus's interest in literary drama paralleled his increasing preoccupation with language: his early aphorisms on language (F.241) are almost contemporaneous with his earliest specific comments on literary and stage drama (F. 246/7). In these aphorisms, Kraus displays a certain élitist streak. For example, he lamented that the word was everyone's tool and not the exclusive property of the writer, unlike musical notes and paint, the tools of the musician and the artist. Therefore, writing (Schriftstellerei) could be judged by anyone who could read or write, that is, by anyone who had the tools. They could criticize a written work if they did not recognize in it the expression of their own opinions, whereas they would never condemn a piece of music or a painting for this reason (F.241:14).

In another aphorism, Kraus rejected the notion that an idea was best
served by reaching the masses in a straightforward way: 'Einer Idee ist weit
mehr gedient, wenn sie nicht so gefaßt wird, daß sie den geraden Weg in die
Massen nehmen kann.' In fact ideas should not be easy to understand: 'Eine
Idee muß von sich sagen können, sie komme gar wenig unter Leute' (F.241:25).
Similarly in the following maxim (which, for all its pessimism, did not keep
Kraus from publishing), he expressed his concern as to what could happen to
the word once it had left the writer's care: 'Ich traue der Druckmaschine
nicht, wenn ich ihr mein geschriebenes Wort überliefere. Wie kann ein Dramatiker sich auf den Mund eines Schauspielers verlassen!' (F. 272/3:45). [I
don't trust the printing press when I deliver my written word to it. How can
the dramatist rely on the mouth of an actor!]

In the theatre, the actor could falsify the poet-dramatist's idea or thought
for the sake of a stage effect. Thus Sonnenthal could move an audience to
tears but often went against the idea of the text.

> Wenn ein Väterspieler [Sonnenthal] als Heinrich IV. in dem Satz: 'Dein
> Wunsch war des Gedankens Vater, Heinrich' den Vater betont, kann er
> das Publikum zu Tränen rühren. Der andere, der sinngemäß den 'Wunsch'
> betont, wird vom Publikum bloß nicht verstanden. Dieses Beispiel zeigt,
> wie aussichtslos das Dichterische auf dem Theater gegen das Schauspieleri-
> sche kämpft, um schließlich von dessen Siegen zu leben. Das Drama behaup-
> tet seine Bühnenhaftigkeit immer nur trotz oder entgegen dem Gedanken.
> (F.272/3:44–5)

> When an actor [Sonnenthal] playing the role of a father – Henry IV –
> stresses the word 'father' in the line 'Thy wish was father, Harry, to the
> thought,' he can move an audience to tears. Another actor, who, in
> keeping with the meaning of the text, stresses 'wish,' is simply not under-
> stood by the audience. This example demonstrates how hopelessly the
> poetic fights against the theatrical in the theatre and finally lives on by dint
> of the latter's victory. Drama always asserts its stageworthiness only in
> spite of or in opposition to its thought.

Furthermore, the public could grasp situation comedy but not 'witty,' intellectual humour. What was successful on stage was, therefore, plot or situation
and content, but not subtleties of language.

> Auch am Witz schmeckt ein Theaterpublikum bloß den stofflichen Reiz. Je
> mehr Körperlichkeit der Witz hat, je mehr er dem Publikum etwas zum
> Anhalten bietet, um so leichter hat er es. Deshalb ist Nestroys gedanklicher
> Humor weniger wirksam als etwa die gleichgültige Situation, die ihm ein
> französisches Muster liefert. Das Wort, daß 'in einem Luftschloß selbst die

Hausmeisterwohnung eine paradiesische Aussicht hat', versinkt. Wenn ihm nicht die vertraute Vorstellung des Hausmeisters zu einiger Heiterkeit verhilft. (Ibid)

In the case of wit as well, the theatre public appreciates only the thrill of the subject matter. The more physical substance wit has, the more it offers the audience something to hang on to, the easier at time it has of it. Therefore, Nestroy's intellectual humour works less well than, for example, an indifferent (comic) situation furnished him by his French source. The line 'In a castle built in the air even the caretaker's apartment has a heavenly view' flounders –unless the familiar notion of the caretaker provides some amusement.

In an essay entitled 'Schauspielerkultus' (*F*.164:5–11), Kraus analysed the attraction and power of the actor, as well as the instinctive reaction of the audience. Kraus preferred the spectator who could get so involved in a performance that he thought it was real life to the cool observer who was ready to scratch off the greasepaint and expose reality (ibid, p. 6). Again using the example of Sonnenthal as Henry IV, he pointed out that spectators usually were inspired by the sound of what was said rather than its meaning. A good actor could move an audience with a speech from a good or a bad play. 'Auf den Rhythmus kommt es an, nicht auf die Bedeutung. Dies ist, seitdem "des Lebens Unverstand mit Wehmut zu genießen Tugend und Begriff" ist, trotz dem Naturalismus das Wesen aller Theaterkunst' (ibid, p. 7). [It is the rhythm that matters, not the meaning. In spite of naturalism, this has been the essence of all stage craft ever since 'enjoying life's folly wistfully' has become 'virtue and concept' (that is, ever since rubbish like this quotation has caught on simply because it is couched in verse).] Kraus's basically élitist bent is again evident here, for he denied the possibility of spreading intellectual culture by means of the theatre. 'Die Möglichkeit einer Verbreitung geistiger Kultur wird fast so sehr überschätzt wie ihre Dringlichkeit ... Und das Theater? Als Surrogat, nicht als Maßstab kulturellen Strebens wollen wir es betrachten' (ibid). [The possibility of the dissemination of intellectual culture is almost as greatly overrated as the urgency of this dissemination ... And the theatre? Let us look at it as a surrogate, and not as the measure of cultural endeavours.]

In addition to legitimate theatre, Kraus was also interested in vaudeville and operettas. In the types of vaudeville considered by him, the importance of the word was minimal, so that this kind of theatre is farthest removed from literary drama. In *Die Fackel* no. 279/80 (pp. 12–13) he distinguished between the comedy of the clown, which was merely that of unexpected misfortune, and that of vaudeville, which, being the reductio ad absurdum of a life in which man had become a machine, was the only kind of humour nowadays

that had philosophical relevance – 'der einzige Humor von Weltanschauung.'
In a world that had become far too complicated, the knockabout magnified
these complications to the point where they revealed their ludicrousness.

The kind of slapstick Kraus had in mind when he discussed vaudeville in
these terms can be judged from his description of a scene worthy of a Chaplin
movie. Kraus pointed out the comedy of life versus the machine. Life in its
most absurd conditions is more powerful than all the massive machinery that
we have invented to control it.

> Nur ein Papierschnitzel will auf einmal nicht parieren. Es bleibt nicht liegen,
> wenn man es der Bequemlichkeit halber hingeworfen hat, es geht immer
> wieder in die Höhe. Das ist ärgerlich, und man sieht sich gezwungen, es
> mit dem Hammer zu bearbeiten. Noch immer zuckt es. Man will es er-
> schießen. Man sprengt es mit Dynamit. Ein unerhörter Apparat wird
> aufgeboten, um es zu beruhigen. Das Leben ist furchtbar kompliziert gewor-
> den. Schließlich geht alles drunter und drüber, weil irgend ein Ding in
> der Natur sich dem System nicht fügen wollte ...

Only a scrap of paper suddenly does not want to obey. It does not remain
on the ground when you have lazily thrown it away, it keeps on floating
upwards. This is annoying, and you see yourself forced to go at it with
a hammer. But it still quivers. You want to shoot it. You blast it with dyna-
mite. The machinery invoked to quiet it is monstrous. Life has become
terribly complicated. Finally everything is turned topsy-turvy because something or other in nature refused to conform to the system ...

Kraus analysed the attraction of vaudeville at greater length in an article
'Bekannte aus dem Variété' (F.289:17–22).[14] Unlike legitimate theatre, which
soothed its audiences by giving them plot and opinion which they could
rationally cope with, vaudeville theatre tended to unsettle its audience by
mirroring 'the great peculiarities of life.' In a drama, the action is presented
in jest – in Hamlet's words, 'They do but jest, poison in jest, no offence i' the
world' (Act III, scene 2). As long as a lot of words are spoken, one has time
to distinguish between real action and make-believe, but acrobats and clowns
'play beyond the bounds of our possibilities and therefore give offence even
while they are jesting.' Their humour represents everything we are, that is,
everything we do not know. A troupe of acrobats represents the essence of
kinship (Sippschaft); their artistry is identical with the concept of family.[15]
The knockabout shows us 'the man who stands in the way of man,' the man
who goes on to greater and greater victories over life until he stumbles over a
toothpick. He is the Schlemihl type, who embodies the absurdity of life.

> Der Knockabout – das ist der Triumph der maschinellen Kultur ... Der
> Knockabout stellt uns alle zusammen dar. Sein Humor ist grundlos, wie

*wir selbst es sind. Er hat Wirkung ohne Ursache, wie wir selbst von nirgend-
wo kommen, um fortzuschreiten. Sein gewalttätiger Humor umfaßt die
ganze Tragik unserer Zweckbeflissenheit, und das Riesenmaß seiner Gesten
hat kein Vorbild in einem einzelnen Lebenstypus.*

The knockabout is the triumph of the machine age ... The knockabout
represents us all. His humour is without foundation, just as we ourselves
are. He has effects without a cause, just as we ourselves come from nowhere
in order to move on again. His violent humour covers the whole tragedy
of our enslavement to purposes, and the gigantic dimensions of his gestures
have no model in a single human type.

And when the knockabout has shown that life is coarse nonsense that cannot
be punished severely enough by death, a philosopher – the juggler –appears on
the scene. He has learned to cope with the absurdity of life by playing
with things (or ideas). 'Er keucht keinem Zweck entgegen und spielt mit
den Dingen. Er lebt im sichern Port der Skepsis, hantiert mit zehn Bällen und
weiß, daß einer wie der andere ist ... Die Erfahrungen der Liebe haben ihm
die Nase abgefressen, aber sein Verstand ist ganz geblieben.' [He does not
labour breathlessly for a purpose and plays with things. He lives in the safe
harbour of scepticism, juggles ten balls, and knows that the one is like the
other ... Experiences in love have eaten away his nose, but his intelligence
has remained whole.] Kraus concluded that in the mirror of vaudeville we
become frightened by our human image as we recognize the absurdity of
life. Therefore, since man tries to avoid this fright, vaudeville was losing
ground to trained animals (*boxende Känguruhs*) and verbal wits (such as
the funny man and straight man of the British music halls of the 1920s).
For Kraus, this last type of show business act was not essentially vaudeville.
For, with the use of verbal wit, our intelligence can take over and dominate
what had been a primarily *intuitive* reaction when we viewed the acrobats,
clowns, and jugglers.

These remarks by Kraus on vaudeville theatre, especially those on the knockabout, are extremely perceptive, particularly where he presents this theatrical
mode as a mirror of human absurdity and sees its effect on the audience not
only as one of entertainment, but also as one of recognition and fright.
Today's reader can recognize the theme of alienation that so concerned the
'theatre of the absurd' of the 1950s and 1960s. In fact, many of the roots of
absurd theatre can be seen in vaudeville theatre. In order to expose theatrically the absurdity of life and man's alienation from man, dramatists such
as Ionesco and Pinter have had to use quite similar slapstick effects (for example, the early plays of Pinter, especially *Act without Words*, and Ionesco's
The Chairs and *The Bald Soprano*). But in spite of his love of it, it was not
vaudeville but the operetta that Kraus regarded as the perfect stage vehicle.
In the essay, 'Grimassen über Kultur und Bühne' (*F.*270/1:1–18), Kraus

studied the function of the operetta and contrasted its effectiveness on stage with the essential shortcomings of the drama and the opera. For Kraus, the operetta presented the perfect union of words and music on stage. The dramatic and theatrical elements were in harmony; the nonsensical, chaotic gaiety of the operetta's content united perfectly with the relaxing effect of the music, which gave it form. In this chaos, we could catch a glimpse of the absurdities of the real world, and be the better for this experience. 'Vereinigt sich die lösende Wirkung der Musik mit einer verantwortungslosen Heiterkeit, die in diesem Wirrsal ein Bild unserer realen Verkehrtheiten ahnen läßt, so erweist sich die Operette als die einzige dramatische Form, die den theatralischen Möglichkeiten vollkommen ebenmäßig ist' (ibid, p. 8). [If the relaxing effect of the music is combined with an irresponsible gaiety that allows us to glimpse in this chaos a picture of our real follies, then the operetta proves to be the only dramatic form which is in complete harmony with the potentialities of the theatre.] In Kraus's opinion, the stage play was an imperfect form since the stage or theatrical aspect triumphed over and spoiled the poetry and the thought. The opera was imperfect since an incongruity existed between the seriousness of the theatrical action and the strange custom of singing; the musical element made fun of the theatrical and a natural parody resulted. The only successful *Gesamtkunstwerk* was the operetta. 'Zu einem Gesamtkunstwerk im harmonischesten Geiste aber vermögen Aktion und Gesang in der Operette zu verschmelzen, die eine Welt als gegeben nimmt, in der sich der Unsinn von selbst versteht und in der er nie die Reaktion der Vernunft herausfordert' (ibid, p. 9). [In the operetta, however, action and singing can unite and form a composite work of art in the most harmonious sense, for in the operetta a world is accepted in which nonsense is the normal state of affairs and never challenges reason to react against it.]

The last part of the above quotation is important in considering what Kraus thought the ideal effect of the operetta to be. The nonsense of the operetta was not rationalized but was accepted on its own terms. The emotions of the spectator were appealed to, and out of an emotional reaction there arose thought: 'Der Gedanke der Operette ist Rausch, aus dem Gedanken geboren werden ...' (ibid, p. 10). In assigning considerable educational value to the nonsense of operettas, Kraus gave the example of their influence on him as a youth, which was greater, he claimed, than that of the classical works that the school system had pressed on him. By being given a distorted picture or caricature (*ein Zerrbild*) of classical beauty in an operetta, a young person's imagination could be spurred on to seek it in the real classics. 'Vielleicht wird seine Phantasie zu der Bewältigung jener Fleißaufgabe gespornt, sich aus der "Schönen Helena" das Bild jener Heroen zu formen, das ihm die Ilias noch vorenthält' (ibid, p. 10). [Perhaps his imagination will be spurred to the mastery of the task of creating for himself on the basis of *Die schöne Helena* an image of those heroes he does not know as yet from reading the *Iliad*.]

Kraus saw the age of Offenbach and Strauß as the golden age of operetta. Contemporary operetta, however, had broken the spell of nonsense and upset the balance between the dramatic and the theatrical. Composers and librettists such as Victor Leon, Buchbinder, and Bauer had abandoned humour, charm, grace, and gaiety and introduced seriousness, reason, modern psychology, and a false folksiness, since more money could be earned from life's seriousness than from life's nonsense. Ironically, the result was that the nonsense from which formerly art had been born now turned into absolute nonsense. The operetta form was kept, but the content of the *Salonoperette* was changed and stuffed with logic – nonsense taken seriously, presented as truth, deprived of costume and fantasy and the exotic. The clerk type became the new hero. It was the democratizing effect signalled by such a hero that bothered Kraus most deeply. One of the results of this development was the incredible banality of the lyrics (such as Leon's 'So eine Depesche ist oft fatal – o Elektrizität! – Es gibt Zeiten, wo man wünschte – daß man dich nicht erfunden hätt!' [Such a telegram is often awkward – oh electricity! – There are times when one wishes – that you hadn't been discovered!]). The curiosity even of people of the upper classes about the private life of the clerks as shown on the stage carried over to the personal life of the performer, resulting in personality cults fostered by the theatre columnists. Kraus saw this as one of the bad effects of naturalism. 'The naturalism of the singing clerk makes it easier for one to identify with the private life of the performer' (ibid, p. 15).

The state of the modern operetta was seen by Kraus as a sign of a cultural, as well as theatrical, decline, a sign of the lack of greatness, of the levelling and democratization that he deplored in contemporary culture. His objections were essentially the same as those he raised against legitimate theatre: the predominance of business interests, the preponderance of realism, which killed fantasy and made the actor a slave of banality. Kraus's 'rehabilitation' of the works of Offenbach in his Theater der Dichtung in the 1920s and 1930s was an effort to revive 'genuine' operettas and to restore to the imagination its 'creative' function, so as to cure, in some small way, a cultural as well as a theatrical ill.[16]

FEUILLETONISMUS

In an essay entitled 'Feuilleton und Bühne' (*F*.114:1–6), Kraus defined *Feuilletonismus* as the superficial, chatty approach that the feuilleton writer brought to any question that he tackled.[17] This attitude plagued all the arts, and particularly the theatre. 'Der Theaterkritiker sieht und denkt die Dinge nicht bühnenhaft, sondern feuilletonistisch ...' [The theatre critic doesn't see things from a theatrical point of view, but rather from that of the *feuilleton*

...] Under the general heading of 'Feuilletonismus,' I shall include several auxiliary points of criticism that Kraus made: the critics' lack of knowledge of the theatre (*Theaterfremdheit* or *Bühnenfremdheit*), their philistinism (that is, their material interests and their lack of culture), snobbishness (particularly their false literary aspirations), and stupidity. Kraus's comments in this connection can be grouped in three categories, concerning critics who also wrote plays, critics who 'doubled' as directors, and finally critics who were content to be critics.

Among the critics who were also playwrights, Bahr was still his prime target, although less frequently than before. In *Die Fackel* no. 85 (pp. 11–15), using good taste as a criterion, he censured Schlenther for subjecting the Burgtheater audience to Bahr's 'terrible' play *Der Apostel*. He then condemned Bahr for including scenes which were sensational but superficial. Kraus proceeded by innuendo, a quality of his criticism that is less than admirable. For example, he put two 'facts' together (Bahr's attack on Weisse's direction of a Volkstheater production and the story that Bahr had a personal grudge against Weisse, who had wanted to pay him only 500 Gulden for *Tschaperl*), thereby suggesting a causal relationship, but at the same time stating that he did not think this was so (*F.*144:26–7).

Stylistically, too, Kraus's criticism of Bahr is often inferior in that it lacks clarity. His comment on Bahr's play *Die Andere* consisted of an overdrawn metaphor (the play was compared to wine which had started to ferment), which tends to obscure rather than enlighten the present-day reader (*F.*189:26). The sharpness of Kraus's earlier attacks against Bahr is missing. What was perhaps clear enough to a contemporary reader is not so to someone reading Kraus now, and one must reread the passage in order to receive the simple message that the play was bad and that the critics did not like it; but *why* Kraus thought the play bad is more than he cared to or could tell us.

However, on one occasion at least, Kraus did better. In one of his most effective lampoons against Bahr, he simply reprinted the following poem by Lenau, underlined a few words, and dedicated it to Bahr (*F.*112:18):

AN HERMANN BAHR
  EINEM FORCIERTEN

Zu besiegen deine schwere
Ungelenkigkeit,
Bist du tanzen in die Lehre
Gangen zu Sankt Veit.

Und der wackre Meister bläute
In den Leib dir ganz
Seinen Rhythmus, und die Leute
Lobten deinen Tanz.

Schief ist all dein Hirn gebeutelt,
Jedes Glied verdreht;
Drum wer tanzend nicht sanctveitelt
Dünkt dir kein Poet.

TO HERMANN BAHR
   SOMEONE WHO TRIES TOO HARD

To master your heavy clumsiness you took dancing lessons in *St Veit.*

And the worthy master completely hammered into your body his rhythm, and the people praised your dance.

Awry has all your brain been shaken, each limb distorted; *therefore whoever doesn't do St Vitus's dance you will not think a poet.*

This is an effective satirical technique, since the poem can be read at several levels. The title 'Einem Forcierten' suggests that Bahr's poetry was an artificial hothouse product. The mention of St Veit reminds one of the villa in the Bahr/Bukovics affair and the corruption in the theatre that this affair symbolized, but at the same time Bahr's excessive mannerisms are satirized: if he is a good writer, a person suffering from St Vitus's dance is a good dancer; his writing is the symptom of a disease. The last stanza extends the satire to Bahr's criticism: the only writers who appeal to him are those who 'dance' as he does. Moreover, the suggestion that Bahr's 'master' was a saint introduces a pseudo-religious note that makes fun of Bahr's setting himself up as the prophet of a new literary age.

In general, however, Bahr no longer had for Kraus the symbolic significance he used to have. There were probably several reasons for this: there were many other critic-playwrights to vent his criticism on, many of whom were probably worse or potentially more dangerous than Bahr, or even more enlightening as far as Kraus's critical cause was concerned; Kraus's centre of criticism shifted from the somewhat petty theatre corruption with which Bahr was involved to corruption of the language, which in turn revealed other aspects of artistic and social decay. His polemical prototype here was Maximilian Harden.

Other journalist-playwrights mentioned by Kraus were Lothar, Buchbinder, Schütz, and Großmann. Schütz (*F.*189:26) and Großmann (*F.*199:21–3) were both criticized on ethical grounds for forcing the production of their plays on theatres (especially the Volkstheater) which were dependent on them for critical approval. Lothar was a mediocre dramatist in Kraus's opinion. Both characters and setting in his *König Harlekin* were superficial.[18] He was also accused of fraud, since he had 'translated' the dramatic works of a certain Italian, Battistini, who, as it turned out, was none other than Lothar himself. Buchbinder was criticized for his lack of talent and bad taste (F.100:12–13). All of the critic-playwrights mentioned were said to be bad dramatists and to have no idea of the demands of the stage (F.114:5). They were uncultured, narrow-minded, and primarily concerned with business. Thus Kraus characterized both Julius Bauer (of the *Extrablatt*) and Buchbinder (of the *Neuer Wiener Journal*):[19]

> *So soll der Nachfolger Heinrich Heines [Bauer] dem Mann [Buchbinder] zugeredet haben, an dessen Schicksal er mit der leicht verständlichen Zärtlichkeit des Collegen und Landsmannes Antheil nimmt: die gleiche Unbildung und die gleiche Enge des mit Theaterbrettern vernagelten Horizonts und die gleiche Entwicklung, die aus dem Talent eines ungarischen Pferdehändlers einen Wiener Humoristen und Beherrscher des Wiener Theatermarktes macht. (F.107:21)*

This is the way the successor of Heinrich Heine [Bauer] is said to have advised the man [Buchbinder], in whose fate he takes an interest with the easily understandable fondness of a colleague and fellow countryman: the same lack of culture and the same narrowness of a horizon nailed shut with boards from the stage, and the same development which makes a Viennese humorist and ruler of the Viennese theatre market out of a Hungarian horse-trader.

As Kraus remarked in the essay 'Feuilleton und Bühne': 'Die Frage, ob hier künstlerische oder ethische Interessen schwerer verletzt werden, wird sich so bald nicht entscheiden lassen' (F.114:6). [The question whether artistic or ethical interests are more deeply hurt here cannot so easily be decided.]

As for critic-directors, Kraus completely discounted the efforts of the critic Felix Salten, who produced and directed a music-hall venture called the *Jung-Wiener Theater zum lieben Augustin* (F.86:12–23). Kraus pointed out the corruption of this enterprise, for although the audience largely rejected the show (which closed not long after it opened), it was praised by Siegfried Löwy (one of the backers) in an article in the *Berliner Börsencourier*, and in Salten's own newspaper, the *Wiener Allgemeine Zeitung*, in a feuilleton by Frau Zuckerkandl. In Kraus's opinion, Salten was a con-artist who had hoodwinked his audience with a heavily publicized show that amounted to nothing. Kraus criticized the production for its lack of artistry and for its bad taste. Salten's choice of actors was poor; even Wedekind's talent as a ballad singer was wasted, for although he would have been good in an intimate cabaret show, he was lost performing before two thousand spectators. Kraus called the staging of the Uhland-Schumann ballad 'Des Sängers Fluch' a scandal and a shame (F.86:22; F.91:15). Salten was also inconsistent as a

critic, for two years before he had criticized the director of the Burgtheater
for having had the unfortunate idea of producing a dramatic version of Schiller's ballad 'Die Glocke.'

Kraus pointed out Salten's lack of knowledge of the stage, his *Bühnenfremdheit*: 'Mich wollte es längst dünken, daß das Theaterverständnis dieses
kritischen Scharfrichters keiner praktischen Belastungsprobe ausgesetzt werden darf,' (F.86:22). [I have long been of the opinion that this critical
executioner's knowledge of the theatre cannot stand up to a practical test.]
Kraus contrasted this with Salten's pretensions of expertise, and by quoting
some of Salten's statements, he effectively satirized his snobbishness.

> *Herr Salten hat in Paris das Cabaret studiert, und er brachte uns Herrn
> Streitmann [a mediocre tenor]. Herr Salten fand, daß 'zwischen Drama,
> Epos und der Lyrik sich Formen eingeschoben haben, welche Krystal-
> lisationen sind aller vibrierenden, sensitiven, erregenden, scheinbar flüch-
> tigen und doch perspectivisch tief wirkenden Empfindungsmomente
> der Zeitpsyche', und er entdeckte Herrn Natzler [a mediocre vaudeville
> actor]. (Ibid, p. 21)*

> Mr Salten studied the cabaret in Paris, and he brought us Mr Streitmann
> [a mediocre tenor]. Mr Salten found that 'amongst dramatic, epic, and
> lyric poetry, forms have interpolated themselves which are crystallizations
> of all vibrant, sensitive, exciting, seemingly ephemeral and yet, in
> their effects, far-reaching moments of the psyche of the age,' and he
> discovered Mr Natzler [a mediocre vaudeville actor].

And Kraus did not miss the opportunity to remark that Salten's critical sense
had failed not only in this production, where he had not even been capable
of choosing and arranging the various acts successfully, but also previously,
when, for example, he had advised naturalistic actors to take on classical
roles. Kraus ended with an example of Salten's bad style; here, language was
reduced to decoration and did not mean anything. After giving us this
picture of Salten's ethical and artistic emptiness, Kraus summed the man up in
one sentence: 'Herr Salten *kann* manches, aber er *ist* nichts' (ibid, p. 23).
[Mr Salten *can do* a lot, but he *is* nothing.]

Kraus's criticism of the journalists as theatre critics was quite extensive
in this decade. That Kraus considered the press critics to be no better than
gangsters is indicated by his names for them: *das Pressmaffia, die Revolver-
presse*, and the portmanteau word made up from 'Journalist' and 'canaille,'
which is one of his favourite terms of abuse, *die Journaille*. To illustrate the
insolence of their threats and their hold over theatres, Kraus quoted Schütz of
the *Neue Freie Presse*, who reportedly had stated that, if he were a theatre-

director in Vienna, he would never produce a play by a dramatist who had publicly criticized Viennese critics. For Kraus the swamp of corruption, which was the meeting ground of the 'press-maffia' and its subservient theatre directors, was revealed by this remark (F.101:14).[20]

Kraus had long complained that theatre critics were not trained for their job, and he had advocated an apprenticeship or *Studienreise* similar to that of an art critic. Some critics knew nothing outside of the theatre they wrote about – Stefan Grossmann, who wrote about the Volkstheater for the *Arbeiterzeitung*, had badly misrepresented the facts about German Shakespeare productions (F.200:17–21). Others did not understand the plays they criticized. Such a one was Herzl, who could see only triviality in Nestroy's plays (F.88:11–18), or Sternberg of the *Neue Freie Presse*, who saw Hauptmann's *Die Weber* as a 'social democratic' play (F.162:18), or Paul Goldmann, who misinterpreted the 'Vermummter Herr' in Wedekind's *Frühlings Erwachen* as the devil (F.217:24). Factual inaccuracies in their critiques demonstrated that many of them did not even know the plays they were discussing (for example, Goldmann's review of *Erdgeist*, F.188:22), or at most had read commentaries but not the text of the play (for example, Bahr, F.91:19–22, who had read Wilamowitz's twenty-page introduction to the translation of Euripides' *Herakles* but who, to judge from his comments, had obviously not read the play).

Trivial, superficial criticism by critics who knew nothing about the theatre could only do harm. It could not possibly help an actor to improve his performance. One of the most absurd examples of the worthlessness of such criticism was given in *Die Fackel* no. 123 (pp. 26–7). Here, Kraus cited two different critiques of the same performance by the same critic, one printed on 1 December in the *Sonn- und Montagszeitung* and the other on 2 December in the *Wiener Allgemeine Zeitung*. Not only did the critic have to make his opinion suit the styles of these papers, but it appeared that the facts differed in the two reports. Kraus pointed out that the criticism the actor received might depend on the critic's lack of understanding, his malice, his attempts to be witty, or his need for stylistic variety, all of which were quite irrelevant to the task. But an actor's existence might depend on whether he received good or bad reviews and this, Kraus insisted, should not be left to the whim of an untalented and untrained journalist. Nor could actors be guided by critics who could not see beyond the surface of a performance, who could not distinguish between the dramatic means used and the effect produced by an actor. This was especially evident in the critics' warm reception given to naturalist actors and dialect players because they were so real. The even more disastrous result that occurred – according to Kraus – when these actors were advised to try classical roles has already been alluded to.

The critics' opinion won out over fact, and 'mood criticism' (*Stimmungs-*

kritik) resulted. In an article entitled 'Die neue Zeitung' (*F.*118:1 ff), Kraus had declared that his mission was to free the press from opinion-making and to give it the fact-finding job that it had in other countries. In order to do so, the press would have to be purged of literature (and as well literature of the press). By 'literature' in the press, Kraus meant a literary style that was flowery, metaphorical, decorative, impressionistic, and, in his opinion, completely superficial and pretentious. It was the snobbishness of the philistine that was revealed by such a style. A case in point was Kalbeck's critique of a play by Gustav Triesch, a playwright whom Kraus had called 'one of the dreariest spirits of our indigenous literature' (*F.*95:20–1): even such a dramatist could not keep Kalbeck from aesthetic pretension and gossip. 'Herr Kalbeck läßt sich selbst von Herrn Triesch die Freude am Aesthetisieren und Feuilletonschwätzen nicht trüben' (ibid). Kalbeck's critique of the Triesch play *Das Complot* consisted of a long drawn-out metaphor on watered-down wine (its making, serving, and drinking) which Kraus found both hackneyed and dreary.

Salten, in his criticism of Wilde's *Salome*, was also a snob who tried to divert attention from the fact that he was a philistine. Not ony did he miss the point that the foreground of this play was erotic, he also covered his thoughtlessness with clichés and slogans. In such criticism, language had lost touch with its original meaning and, therefore, with reality, just as literature had lost touch with life and life with literature.

> *'Hier sind tiefere Bezüge', meint Herr Salten geheimnisvoll, 'verzweigtere Zusammenhänge, und wir lieben in unserer Zeit den farbig dunklen Schimmer tiefer Bezüge, den feinen Pulsschlag, der durch verzweigte Zusammenhänge klopft.' Ein Satz, für den man Herrn Salten aus innerstem Herzen dankbar sein muß. Denn hier ist jener farbig dunkle Schimmer tiefer Bezüge zwischen der Gedankenlosigkeit und dem Schlagwort, hier ist jener feine Pulsschlag der Phrase, der immer zu klopfen beginnt, so oft das Wort 'Zusammenhänge' in der modernen Kritik genannt wird. Es ist merkwürdig. Seitdem in die Literatur die Sehnsüchte eingeführt und die Zusammenhänge mit dem Leben entdeckt wurden, hat die Literatur den Zusammenhang mit dem Leben und das Leben die Sehnsucht nach der Literaur verloren.* (F.227/8:6)

'Here are most profound links,' Mr Salten suggests mysteriously, 'more complex connections, and in our age we love the colourfully dark shimmer of profound links, the delicate pulse-beat which throbs through complex connections.' A sentence for which one must be most heartily thankful to Mr Salten. For here is that colourfully dark shimmer of profound links between thoughtlessness and catchphrase, here is that delicate pulse-beat of the cliché which always begins to throb when the word 'connections' is used in modern criticism. It's remarkable. Ever since yearnings were introduced into literature and connections with life were discovered, literature has lost its connection with life and life has lost its yearning for literature.

In his theories on language, Kraus tried to restore the connection between the word and its essence. He thought that he could then destroy the power of the cliché and expose the sham he saw around him in all areas, whether cultural, political, aesthetic, or economic.

Two other points must be made with regard to Kraus's criticism of the critics. First, he never lets us forget their 'stupidity' and their 'ignorance of the ways of the world.' This was demonstrated, for example, in their criticisms of Otto Ernst's play *Die Gerechtigkeit*, which had as its theme the abuses of the press. In writing about this play, each critic, according to Kraus, unwittingly selected abuses that were the regular practice of his own newspaper (*F.*122:7–8). As another example of stupidity, he cited Goldmann's criticism of Hauptmann's play *Rose Bernd* (*F.*155:19–20). Goldmann had not liked the lack of action in the drama; he had complained that the events happen before the play or between acts, so that there is no action, but only talk on stage. Kraus commented sarcastically that Goldmann found it strange that seduction, rape, and infanticide were not shown on the stage; for Goldmann, it was the events themselves that mattered rather than the poet's 'imaginative reworking' of these events. By harping on his opponents' 'stupidity,' Kraus of course constantly played up his own image of critical superiority.

Second, one must not lose sight of the cultural aspect of Kraus's criticism both of the theatre and of the critics. Kraus deplored what he considered to be the loss of true Viennese culture. The art of the suburban stage (*die Vorstadtbühne*) died when Girardi left for Berlin. Kraus blamed the critics for this, since they never truly appreciated Girardi's talent. They were also blamed for welcoming to Vienna people like Jarno and Karczag (of the Theater an der Wien), whose sentimental nationalism and *Wienerthum*, Kraus alleged was false. In the first place, he argued, they were not from Vienna – Karczag and Jarno were both 'old-time Viennese from western Hungary' ('Altwiener aus dem westlichen Ungarn'). In the second place, theatre was strictly business for them (as, for example, the *Jung-Wiener Theater zum lieben Augustin*, with which Karczag was involved). Consequently, in this way, too, the genuine Viennese *Vorstadtbühne*, built up by people like Nestroy, was being ruined. It is important to note, however, that this was Kraus's very personal pessimistic view of Viennese culture. According to Hofmannsthal and Stefan Zweig, to name but a few, these were quite splendid times.

SPECIFIC DRAMA CRITICISM

There were few non-contemporary dramatists to whom Kraus gave the title *Dichter* in this period; Shakespeare, Raimund, and Nestroy are the only ones that can be named with any degree of certainty.[21] Direct comments on even these playwrights are scarce.

Any attempts to 'adapt' Shakespeare were severely criticized.[22] As early as 1902 Kraus asserted that it was a sacrilege to leave out a single word Shakespeare had written (F.98:15). And in 1903 he protested against Müller-Guttenbrunn's 'adaptations' of Shakespeare for the partisan purposes of the Jubiläumstheater: 'zu seinen Ungunsten (spricht), daß er [Müller-Guttenbrunn], der Literat ... eine Schaubühne politischer Propaganda dienstbar gemacht, Shakespeare als antisemitischen Hausdichter verwendet und die Parteifessel als Schmuck getragen hat' (F.146:11). [It is to his discredit that he (Müller-Guttenbrunn), the man of literature ... has made a stage serve the purposes of political propaganda, has used Shakespeare for anti-Semitic purposes, and has worn his party shackles like an ornament.]

Kraus had surprisingly little to say about Raimund, other than that he regarded him as the greatest Austrian writer (F.232/3:27). Nestroy received very much more attention, although from 1908 onwards, Kraus tended not to emphasize his achievement as a dramatist but rather as an intellectual wit and satirical thinker who, while having to use the stage as his medium, was much better appreciated by a reader than by a spectator.[23] In 1901, however, although Kraus stressed Nestroy's wit and drew comparisons linking his genius with that of Swift and Shakespeare, he was also aware of Nestroy's importance in the theatre. He spoke of his ability to analyse human nature and of the theatrical cleverness of the plot of *Die Eisenbahnheiraten* (F.88:15). Thus, considerations of plot and of character portrayal as well as of wit and linguistic skill were important criteria at this early date. But Nestroy's real importance for Kraus was not evident until the publication of the essay 'Nestroy und die Nachwelt' in the next decade.

Ibsen's death in 1906 offered Kraus an occasion to make fun of the critics, who eulogized him with the same words (*schrecklich, fürchterlich*) they had used years before to damn performances of his *Wild Duck*. Kraus's technique was simply to quote the critics; particularly bad passages were printed spaced by him. He also tried to present a relatively objective view of Ibsen's contribution to the theatre by printing an essay in praise of the dramatist by Egon Friedell (F.204), as well as two essays, one in the form of a letter by Karl Hauer and one by Wedekind, critical of at least part of Ibsen's work (F.205). Kraus's own remarks were limited to a one-page answer to Hauer's letter, in which he agreed with Hauer's basic thesis – his 'unmasking' of Ibsen. Hauer's letter, in turn, had been in answer to Friedell's article, which he felt was too positive. In Hauer's opinion, the later Ibsen presented only 'a pale charade art.' There were no significant ideas, no real passions; as Hauer stated:

Ich finde im ganzen Ibsen keinen Gedanken, der für die Menschheit bedeutungsvoll wäre, wohl aber spüre ich hinter dem formaltechnischen 'Revolutionär' überall einen zugeknöpften Reaktionär mit Gehrock, Zylinder, Glacés und Ordensband, der mit seinen 'großen Zweifeln' überall dort einsetzt, wo bei Geradegewachsenen der ungebrochene gesunde Instinkt entscheidet. (F.205:3)

In all of Ibsen, I don't find one thought which would be meaningful for mankind; I do, however, detect at all times behind the man who is formally and technically a 'revolutionary' an uptight reactionary with frock-coat, top-hat, kid gloves, and order-of-merit, whose 'great doubts' always set in precisely where with healthy people unreflected, sound instinct decides.

Quoting Nietzsche, Hauer pronounced the cure: 'Il faut méditerraniser l'art.'

In his answer to this letter, Kraus stated that he himself had been a champion of the earlier Ibsen, the dramatist of *Peer Gynt* and *Brand*, that is, of the period roughly before 1873, when he began to write prose plays with modern settings. Ibsen had then become 'a rationalist of the marvellous,' and his criticism of society developed into a 'dramatic abracadabra.' His writing lost its greatness – the echo of the cliffs of Ibsen's native fjords, as Kraus put it – and his earlier verbal magic that had excited the spectator's imagination gave way to bald intellectual prose (ibid, p. 4).

Kraus furthermore disagreed with Ibsen's handling of the theme of woman in his bourgeois realist dramas (especially in *A Doll's House*). Ibsen's mistake, in Kraus's opinion, lay in his treating man and woman as one and the same, and therefore in seeing the problem of woman in her being compelled to be a doll, rather than in her *right* to be a doll (as, for example, Wedekind had done in the 'Lulu' plays). Paradoxically, Ibsen was just as old-fashioned a dramatist as Hebbel (in *Maria Magdalena*), in that he still saw the essence of dramatic conflict in the loss of virginity. 'Er steht am Ende einer langen Reihe von Dramatikern, für die "Mann und Weib eins" sind und die, wenn sich ein Konflikt ergibt, den dramatischen Knoten aus einem verlorenen Jungfernhäutchen knüpfen,' (ibid, p. 5). Evidently, Kraus failed to appreciate the immense achievement of Ibsen's later plays and his remarks on the great Norwegian are both inappropriate and inadequate.

As in the case of Ibsen, the important feature of Kraus's evaluation of Hauptmann was his preference for those of his works in which he saw the dramatist's poetic imagination at work, and his almost complete rejection of those that were realistic or naturalistic. The major exceptions here were *Der Biberpelz* and particularly *Die Weber*,[24] which, as we have seen, Kraus greatly admired. Kraus called the 1904 production of *Die Weber* the 'greatest dramatic event that Vienna has seen in years' (F.162:16). In this social drama, the naturalistic mode was appropriate to illustrate the misery and poverty of the weavers and so to pillory the social ills that allowed this situation to exist. When the play was passed by the censors provided that the words *Fabrikant* and *Gendarm* were omitted, Kraus protested that Hauptmann was not against factory-owners and policemen in general, but only wanted to characterize the mood of the weavers. In the weavers' dialogues, every word belonged in its place; the text was so perfect that any change could only harm it. Because of this textual perfection, Kraus considered this play to be literary drama rather than stage drama.

However, in 1904, Kraus deplored that Hauptmann was on the decline (F.155:19). A year later he regretted that for years the development of Hauptmann's enormous ability had seemed blocked. But even this criticism is offset by a jibe at some of Hauptmann's Austrian contemporaries: 'Trotzdem halt ich die Impotenz eines Gerhart Hauptmann noch immer für zeugungsfähiger als die Fruchtbarkeit eines österreichischen "Heimatkünstlers"' (F.178:15). [Nevertheless I still consider the impotence of Gerhart Hauptmann to be more fertile than the fecundity of an Austrian *Heimatkünstler*.][25]

Kraus had neither seen nor read *Und Pippa tanzt!* (1906) when he wrote that the play impressed him as being extremely poetic and sensitive. His reaction was based solely on his reading of negative remarks about the drama by the critic Paul Goldmann.

> *Ich kenne Gerhart Hauptmann's Glashüttenmärchen 'Und Pippa tanzt!'
> noch nicht, aber hoffentlich wird die Lektüre des Buches nicht völlig
> den schönen Eindruck verwischen, den das Werk nach der verhöhnenden
> Feuilletonkritik des entsetzlichen Paul Goldmann auf mich gemacht
> hat. Daß es eine besonders feine und dichterische Sache sein muß, geht so
> ziemlich aus jeder Zeile des besonders gemeinen Geschmieres hervor.*
> (F.195:24)

> *Ich kenne 'Pippa' nicht, möchte mir mein Urteil über die Dichtung, das
> ich mir nach dem Feuilleton gebildet habe, vorläufig nicht durch ihre Lektüre erschüttern lassen.* (Ibid, p. 25)

I am not yet acquainted with Gerhart Hauptmann's fairy-tale about a glass works *Und Pippa tanzt!*, but I hope that when I read the book, this will not completely eradicate the lovely impression that the work has made

on me after reading the derisive feuilleton criticism of the appalling Paul
Goldmann. That it must be a particularly sensitive and poetic play can
be inferred from nearly every line of this particularly vulgar piece of scrib-
bling.

I don't know *Pippa*; however, for the time being I don't want to read the
play and thereby shake the judgment I have made of it through my
readings in the feuilleton.

Once more, we can see that Kraus was probably more interested in the
critics than in the plays being criticized. Goldmann had not liked the
play's lack of logic or 'meaning.' Kraus's reaction was predictably extreme.
Perhaps, he stated, a fairy-tale did not have to 'mean' anything. Besides, it was no concern of the critics whether the poet meant anything. The
playwright could consider himself to have succeeded if he made them
think at all (ibid, p. 26). The result of such a radically non-intentionalist
critical position (if it were taken completely seriously) would have serious
consequences for criticism and comes as a surprise from someone like Kraus,
who on countless other occasions had shown great interest in the intentions of authors. However, Kraus was obviously justified in rescuing the
magic of poetry from such rational dullards as Goldmann. They were
clearly not predisposed to enjoy poetry on an intuitive level but had to try
and see everything through their reason, and the results were absurd.
Kraus strengthened his argument with examples of the irrational in stories
by Strindberg,[26] Edgar Allan Poe, and E.T.A. Hoffmann, as well as with
an 'illogical' quotation from Goethe's 'West-östlicher Divan' (*Lied und
Gebilde*).[27] And in *Die Fackel* no. 200 (pp. 9–13), he allowed a poet,
Thaddäus Rittner, to give a purely poetic interpretation of *Pippa*, stating in
an editorial note: 'Ich freue mich, dieser von einem Dichter besorgten
Ehrenrettung einer Dichtung Raum geben zu können, an der die Rationali-
sten der deutschen Kritik – von Harden bis Goldmann – den Zorn der
eigenen Ratlosigkeit ausgelassen haben' (ibid, p. 9). [I am delighted to be able
to print this rehabilitation by a poet of a poetic work on which the
rationalists of German criticism – from Harden to Goldmann – have vented
the anger of their own perplexity.]
With the possible exception of Nestroy, the playwright who made the
greatest impression on Kraus during these years was Frank Wedekind.
Kraus's admiration for him as a dramatist and revolutionary ethical thinker
lasted throughout this period, in spite of Wedekind's unsuccessful performance in Salten's *Jung-Wiener Theater zum lieben Augustin* (Kraus
blamed everything on Salten) and of Wedekind's defence of Maximilian
Harden.[28] In 1905 Kraus even produced and acted in Wedekind's *Büchse*

der Pandora during two performances held in the Nestroyhof of the
Trianontheater.[29] It was attended by invited guests only and was pre-
ceded by a long introduction by Kraus. But there is evidence in *Die Fackel*
that he took Wedekind seriously well before this. In 1904 he had called
Wedekind 'Germany's most fascinating dramatist' (*F.*152:21). In 1903 he
quoted other Viennese critics' opinions of *Erdgeist* and *Büchse der
Pandora* in order to show how they had misunderstood the many-sidedness
of Lulu by trying to make her confrom to the one aspect each individual
liked, and had set themselves up as ethical judges of woman. Kraus completely agreed with the 'message' of the plays,[30] that is, with their exposé of
the sham of 'normal' morality and their defence of aesthetic perfection
in woman as her highest morality.

> *[Wedekinds] Standpunkt einer Weltbetrachtung ... die die höchste 'Sitt-
> lichkeit' der Frau in ihrer höchsten ästhetischen Vollendung erblickt und
> die ethischen Maßstäbe an den Schädeldecken heuchlerischer Herren
> der Schöpfung zerbricht; die das Virginitätsideal von den Wünschen jener,
> die entjungfern wollen, ableitet und muthig erklärt, daß in diesem freu-
> denarmen Dasein die 'Dirne' den Absichten des Schöpfers näher
> kommen könne als – das Dirndl ... (F.*142:18)

[Wedekind's] way of looking at the world ... which sees the highest
'morality' of woman in her highest aesthetic perfection, and which breaks
ethical yardsticks on the skulls of the hypocritical lords of creation;
which models its ideal of virginity on the wishes of those who want to
deflower, and which boldly declares that in this existence where joys
are few the prostitute could come closer to the intentions of the creator
than a straitlaced girl.[31]

Kraus outlined more fully what he considered to be the aesthetic merits of
Büchse der Pandora in his introduction (subsequently published in *Die
Fackel* no. 182) delivered on the night of the performance of his production of
the play. The play did not so much centre on a character, as was perhaps
the case in *Erdgeist*, but rather in an idea or thought – for example, that the
evil in Pandora's Box is unleashed when woman's 'pure' sexuality is used
by men; the immorality of this 'use' contrasts with the basic morality of Lulu,
who always remains true to her many-sided self. The playwright presented his characters in ideal or general terms; Lulu[32] was the ideal of sexuality;
the Marquis Casti Piani '[is] presented on stage not as a white-slave trader,
but rather as the personification of the cult of white-slavery' (ibid, p. 8).
Lulu was not active, as she had been in *Erdgeist*, but passive – in fact, it was
not she herself, but her charm (*Anmut*, that is, her sexual attractiveness),
which was the heroine of the drama.

*Lulu, die Trägerin der Handlung im 'Erdgeist', ist jetzt die Getragene.
Mehr denn früher zeigt sich, daß ihre Anmut die eigentliche leidende
Heldin des Dramas ist; ihr Porträt spielt eine größere Rolle als sie
selbst, und waren es früher ihre aktiven Reize, die die Handlung scho-
ben, so ist jetzt auf jeder Station des Leidensweges der Abstand zwischen einstiger Pracht und heutigem Jammer der Gefühlserreger.*
(Ibid, pp. 4–5)

Lulu, who carries the action in *Erdgeist*, is now the one who is
carried. More than previously it is evident that her sexual attractiveness
is the real, passive heroine of the drama; her portrait plays a greater role
than she herself does, and, whereas previously her active charms had
moved the plot forward, now at every station of her life of suffering it is the
gap between previous splendour and present misery that arouses our
feelings.

The drama did not depend on the depiction of a milieu or on ensemble acting
for its effect. Wedekind was not interested in realism but in reality.

*Daß Frank Wedekind ein Menschenschilderer ist, wäre schon ein Lob, das
ihn über die Milieuschilderer himmelhoch emporhöbe. Aber er ist auch
der erste deutsche Dramatiker, der wieder dem Gedanken den langentbehr-
ten Zutritt auf das Theater verschafft hat. Alle Natürlichkeitsschrullen
sind wie weggeblasen. Was in und hinter den Menschen liegt, ist wieder
wichtiger, als was für einen Sprachfehler sie haben.* (Ibid, p. 7)

[To say] that Frank Wedekind depicts people would already be praise enough to lift him miles over the heads of those who depict a milieu. But
he is also the first German dramatist who put thought back on the stage,
where it has been missed for so long. All the fads of naturalness have
suddenly vanished. What lies in and behind human beings is again more
important than the kind of speech defect they have.

It can, however, be argued that the very qualities Kraus esteemed highly
are in fact weaknesses of *Büchse der Pandora*. The aspects of characterization that Kraus praised, such as idealization and passivity, contribute to extremely undramatic drama. In Act I, Lulu appears only briefly at the end
of the act; otherwise, we are merely told what has happened to her and what
reactions she has provoked in those around her. This is the least dramatically effective method of presenting a character; the audience can identify only
with difficulty with a character who is only talked about. The result is not
tragedy or drama but, at most, pathos and, at worst, bathos (as in the recounting of the superheroism of Geschwitz and the young student in Act I).[33]
In Kraus's estimation it was the idea or thought that was most important in

drama, and characters and plot must be subordinate to it and serve it. Essentially the idea of this play is criticism of contemporary morality. However the two-dimensionality of the characters and the lack of action short-circuit the dramatist's purpose of ethical criticism, of putting forth an idea which involves moral recognition on the part of the spectator. In a drama of this kind we should be able to recognize that a character is making a moral decision,[34] for or against which we react. Lulu never decides. Here the criticism can be made that not only is the play undramatic but also it suffers from a curious lack of moral dimension.

Several statements in Kraus's introduction cast a peculiar light on his stand as a critic. He stated, for example, that it was ridiculous to think that a writer could *choose* his material: 'Als ob der Dichter "Stoffe" "wählen" könnte ...' But one can only ask: 'Why not?' He asserted that, in his opinion, Wedekind had brought into absolute congruence his view of the world and his view of the theatre – that is, his ethical and his aesthetic position: '[Wedekind ist ein] Dramatiker, der keine Zeile geschrieben hat, die nicht Weltanschauung und Theateranschauung zu absoluter Kongruenz brächte ...' (p. 11). But Kraus neglected to mention that, although the morality of the play might have been new and startling, the drama's form was not innovative or revolutionary. And finally Kraus risked appearing absurd as a critic when he stated that anyone can read or put anything into the true work of art, in which the poet has formed his world: 'Aber in das wahre Kunstwerk, in dem ein Dichter seine Welt gestaltet hat, können eben alle alles hineintun' p. 12. And he continued: 'Die Frage, ob es dem Dichter mehr um die Freude an ihrem Blühen [d.h., der Frau] oder mehr um die Betrachtung ihres ruinösen Wirkens zu tun ist, kann jeder wie er will beantworten.' [The question whether the dramatist (Wedekind) is more concerned with the joy of her (Lulu's) blossoming or with the observation of her ruinous effect (on others) can be answered by anyone in any way he likes.] If Wedekind's intentions were really that unfathomable, it is difficult to see on what grounds Kraus praised his ethics and his *Weltanschauung*.

Kraus later also defended Wedekind's first major play, *Frühlings Erwachen*, which was completed in 1891 but not performed until 1906, when Reinhardt dared to produce it in Berlin. Kraus was as much interested in showing the critics to be fools as in championing the play. He was particularly incensed by Goldmann, whom he challenged to define his terms instead of smearing the play with moral opinions.[35] In his defence of this play, Kraus is on firmer ground than he was with *Büchse der Pandora*, for here we do have plot and character, which are reinforced by the thought of the play. Characters such as Moritz, Melchior, and Wendla struggle to make moral decisions. The audience can identify with or reject these people and the decisions they make. But it is interesting that Kraus did not go into a detailed analysis of this tragedy; rather, he settled for more general terms, such as 'Wedekinds wundervolle Kindertragödie, dieses dichterischeste Werk der modernen Kunst und stärkste Bekenntnis modernen Geistes, das die deutsche Dramaturgie fünfzehn Jahre liegen ließ ...' (F.217:24). [Wedekind's marvellous children's tragedy, this most poetic work of modern art and the strongest affirmation of the modern spirit, left lying for fifteen years by the German stage ...]

Kraus's reasons for defending Wedekind's plays, and particularly *Büchse der Pandora*, give the reader some insight into his criteria for an effective drama. What is interesting is that Kraus paid so little attention to plot and character development and assigned the greatest importance to the *thought*. In the years following, most of the plays that he praised highly had to conform to the criterion of what he considered to be excellence of thought. And all of Kraus's own dramas were obviously written with this in mind. Ironically, the result (as in the case of *Büchse der Pandora*) was curiously undramatic drama.

Whereas in Wedekind's plays Kraus defended the author's ethical position as presented in his work and embodied in the main character, the ethical issue immediately became a personal one with Oscar Wilde, and Kraus continually had to defend the author's right to be a homosexual against critics who insidiously brought this fact to bear on their literary evaluation of Wilde's works.[36]

Two dramatic works of Wilde were of special concern during this period: a dramatization of *A Portrait of Dorian Gray* and *Salome*. In *Die Fackel* no. 151, before any attempt had been made at dramatizing *Dorian Gray*, Kraus published two quotations from the book and commented on the beauty of these passages, which he found poetic and profound. In the same article, he also attacked the ethics of the press (especially the *Neue Freie Presse*), which made money off the 'business' of homosexuality by accepting want ads advertising homosexual availability, but which employed critics like Friedrich Schütz, who were morally outraged over the homosexuality of Oscar Wilde and who then applied their outrage to Wilde's works. But Kraus's rage exploded four years later, in 1907. Jarno, the director of the Theater in der Josefstadt, feigned concern for Wilde when in reality he was worried because several theatres were trying to beat him to a premiere of the dramatization of *Dorian Gray*. Kraus was angered by the paradox that the beauty of art could be used by unethical 'theatrical usurers,' whom he compared to hyenas.

Oskar Wilde, vom Auswurf der Menschheit zum Liebling der Wiener Gesellschaftskreise herabgesunken, nach seiner Ermordung seiner künstlerischen Habe beraubt, ein Kunstwerk vom Theaterwucher ausge-

*beutet, zur schäbigsten Sensation mißbraucht, der schöne Jüngling
Dorian von vier Theaterkassierern abgeknutscht – man möchte Karl
Moorisch durch die ganze Natur das Horn des Aufruhrs blasen, Luft,
Erde und Meer wider das Hyänengezücht ins Treffen führen! ... Nichts
macht und nichts ist in Wien unmöglich. Man kann das reine Kunst-
werk der 'Sünde', um deren Willen sein Schöpfer in der Tretmühle
siechen mußte, auf der Hausbühne des päderastisch unbescholtenen
Herrn Buchbinder zu Ehren kommen lassen (F.232/3:6–7)*

Oscar Wilde, who has sunk from being the outcast of humanity to
becoming the favourite of Viennese social circles, who, after being murdered, was robbed of his artistic effects; a work of art exploited by
profiteering in the theatre, misused for the sake of the shabbiest sensation; the lovely youth Dorian cuddled by four theatre cashiers – like
Karl Moor one would like to blow the horn of rebellion through the
whole of nature, to rally air, earth, and sea against this pack of
hyenas! ... In Vienna, nothing makes you impossible and nothing is
impossible. This pure artistic work of 'sin,' for the sake of which its
creator had to waste away on the treadmill, can be praised on the stage
patronized by the impeccably heterosexual Mr Buchbinder.

The theatrical tone of such criticism is unmistakable, particularly in the
dramatic gesture conjured up by the wish: 'Man möchte Karl Moorisch
durch die ganze Natur das Horn des Aufruhrs blasen, Luft, Erde und Meer
wider das Hyänengezücht ins Treffen führen!' Indeed, although this is a
point that will be discussed more fully later, we should always be aware that
most of Kraus's criticism was as well staged and produced as any play.
Many of the rhetorical devices that he used – especially sharp contrasts and
seeming paradoxes such as, 'this pure artistic work of sin' – are based on the
principle of dramatic conflict.

In his article on *Salome*, Kraus again tried to show the critics to be fools
and to defend Wilde against them. He also reported on the relative merit of
different productions of the play and evaluated it as a literary work of art.

His evaluation of the play was completely positive. Kraus praised its intensity of mood and the rhythmic harmony of plot and language: 'ein Meisterstück, das an kondensierter Stimmung und rhythmischem Einklang von
Handlung und Sprache kaum seinesgleichen in der Weltliteratur hat ...'
(F.150:6). There is a very fine appreciation of the lustful undercurrents and
the atmosphere of foreboding in the play – of the clashing of two worlds:
the 'Christian' and the 'natural,' the spiritual and the sensual, heaven and
earth, Jochanaan and Salome.

*Die somnambule Stimmung einer aus Wollust und Grauen bereiteten Vi-
sion; das rhythmisierte Tempo des aus schwüler Ruhe zur Katastrophe*

eines Zeitalters hastenden Fiebertraums; die aus dumpfen Seelen, aus einer
Zisterne und aus dem Himmel dräuende Wende zweier Welten, der
unsichtbare Galiläer und ein stilisierter Mond, der vom blanken Rund zum
scharlachfleckigen Ungetüm alle Phasen irdischen Unheils begleitet ...
(F.150:11)

The somnambulent mood of a vision born of lust and foreboding; the
rhythmical tempo of a feverish dream hastening from sultry calm to the
catastrophe of an age; the turning-point of two worlds arising threaten-
ingly from dull souls, a cistern, and the heavens; the invisible Galilean and a
stylized moon that, changing from an unblemished circle into a purple-
flecked monster, accompanies all the phases of sublunar disaster ...

Or, as he stated more cryptically: 'Das Große an Wildes Dichtung ... ist eben
die Umfassung des Ewig-Niedrigen mit den welthistorischen Kulissen des
Zeitlich-Großen' (F.227/8:7). [The greatness of Wilde's play ... resides
precisely in the fact that eternal baseness is set against a world-historical
backdrop of time-bound greatness.]

At that time (December 1903), Kraus was acquainted with three interpretations of the play, in Berlin, Vienna, and Hamburg. It is quite possible that he
saw the Hamburg production early in 1901, when he visited the dying
actress Annie Kalmar in that city. Kraus, however, made no specific statement
to this effect. Although he admitted that he had not seen Gertrude Eysoldt
in the role of Salome in Berlin, he did not say that he had not seen the
production,[37] and was no more explicit about his attendance at the performance of the play in Vienna. The reader can perhaps surmise from the more
detailed nature of his comments that he at least saw the Hamburg production.

In evaluating the three attempts at staging the drama, Kraus stated that
he was looking for the director who could best bring out the unearthly and
unnatural elements of the play. The director of the Berlin production turned
the drama into a 'family idyll in the house of Herod' (F.150:10), written
in a language that had scarcely been purified of the slang of the streets of
Berlin. In it the unnatural had been humanized and naturalized. In the Volkstheater in Vienna, loud theatricality and stale pathos had spoiled the play.
In both cases, the director was at fault, for, in Kraus's opinion, such a play
needed strong direction, since the main effect was rooted in the mood
produced by the ensemble.

Was vermag die blendendste Einzelleistung in einem Stücke, dessen
Wirkung ausschließlich in der Ensemblestimmung wurzelt? ... Beide
Richtungen entspringen derselben geistigen Dürftigkeit deutscher Thea-
terregie und führen zum Verderben einer Dichtung, bei der Regie
alles ist ... (F.150:10)

What can the most splendid individual performance achieve in a play
whose effect is rooted entirely in the mood produced by the ensemble? ...
These tendencies spring from the same spiritual poverty of German
theatre direction and lead to the ruin of a work in which (theatre) direction is everything ...

It was the third production, that of Berger[38] at the Deutsches Schauspielhaus
in Hamburg, that best gave to the drama the theatrical form which the poet
would have wished. This director had inspired a group of actors, not many of
whom would individually have been Burgtheater material, to act together
and achieve much greater effects than one was accustomed to in either Vienna
or Berlin.

Having spent approximately three pages on his discussion of *Salome* and
the three productions of it, Kraus now devoted nine pages to Schütz, who
had reviewed the play in the *Neue Freie Presse*, and the remaining two pages
of his article to an attack on two other critics. This disproportion speaks for
itself: evidently, Kraus was at least as much concerned with polemics against
Viennese theatre criticism as with the theatre itself – or, to put matters
differently, he was less concerned with Oscar Wilde's drama than with the
dramatization of himself as Wilde's defender. The critics were the villains,
and Kraus staged himself as the hero who was to rescue Wilde from their
clutches. Kraus played his role with great gusto. He labelled all the critics
'philistines'; the only exceptions were those who were snobs as well as philistines. He observed sarcastically that one of the great joys that the play
provided was the spectacle of critics of both the Left (for example, the Jewish
liberal press) and the Right (the anti-Semitic press) united in their attacks
against the play, thus revealing the essence of philistinism in all its purity and
unity.

> *Das Schauspiel, die Kritiker der 'Neuen Freien Presse' und des 'Vaterland'*
> *Arm in Arm zu sehen, kehrt nicht oft wieder. Welche suggestive Kraft*
> *muß einem Kunstwerk innewohnen, das es vermocht hat, den Philistersinn,*
> *von den verschiedenen Parteischlacken ... erlöst, sich in Reinheit und*
> *Einheit offenbaren zu lassen.* (F.150:13–14)

> The spectacle of seeing the critics of the *Neue Freie Presse* [the Left] and
> of the *Vaterland* [the Right] arm in arm doesn't recur often. What sugges-
> tive power must a work of art possess that enables it to reveal the essence
> of philistinism in all its purity and unity, cleansed of the dross of factious-
> ness.

From Kraus's remarks about the standards used by others, we can deduce
what some of his criteria and opinions were. First of all, evaluation had to
be relevant to the aesthetic merits of the play. Schütz's criticism of the drama

on the grounds of historical veracity was not relevant, nor was Nordau's damnation of *Salome* on moral grounds (because of Wilde's 'perversity'). The critic must not falsify the intention of the dramatist. Schütz, for example, claimed to have discovered some anti-Semitic intent on the part of Wilde: he objected to the quintet of Jews talking Yiddish, but had failed to notice that this detail was the invention of the director of the Volkstheater production and had not been intended by the author. And finally, although Kraus admitted that it was not everyday fare, he preferred the exoticism of Wilde's play to the Austrian regionalism (specifically, Medelsky's play *Liebessünden*) acclaimed by Schütz (*F.*150:13).

Kraus's polemics against corruption in and around the theatre rubbed shoulders in *Die Fackel* with his fight against corruption in other walks of life, and his different preoccupations could not always be kept distinct. In the first two years of publication of his periodical, Kraus had frequently attacked the operation of one of the major Austrian railway lines, the Südbahn, and in 1901 the Volkstheater produced a play – *Der neue Simson* – by an official of this railway, one Karl Weiß, who wrote under the pseudonym of C. Karlweis. Kraus attended the premiere and discovered to his surprise that the 'new Samson' was no one else but himself. In *Die Fackel* no. 83 (pp. 14–16), he reported his reaction when in a 'new play by C. Karlweis' – Kraus did not mention the title – an actress in men's trousers, portraying a high-school student named Alfred Ackermann, entered the scene and promised to found a newspaper, which would be against everything and everybody and which would carry the title *Der Gestank*. Kraus found the play dull – he called it a 'concoction prompted by revenge and completely lacking in wit' – and suggested that it was in better taste to write a newspaper against everyone than a play against one individual.

By an odd coincidence, Karlweis died shortly after the publication of this issue of *Die Fackel*; the next issue reverted to the topic none the less. Kraus now published a letter that he had intended to send to the censorship department, asking them to ban Karlweis's play on the grounds that it was illegal to represent on the stage people who were still alive. The stage was not the place for private quarrels, since the person attacked could not answer back from the balcony, and anything he printed in response afterward did not have the resonance of a speech from the stage. With regard to this particular play, he claimed that it was not even drama but only a dramatized polemic, with auxiliary scenes which were meant to disguise this main purpose from the censors. It was therefore a bad play, but its author was also culpable on ethical grounds; he had in effect bought the success of the play, since all critics who were against Kraus (and this included most in Vienna) would automatically praise it. Kraus was also repelled by what he assumed to be the author's intention of earning royalties on a sensation based on him. Finally, the play demonstrated a perverse morality in that it was acclaimed for attacking a man who attacked corruption.

> *Welche verdammenswerthen Tendenzen aber läßt sie [die Behörde]*
> *durch Verhöhnung des Kampfes gegen die Unmoral Popularität*
> *gewinnen! ... Ich muß mich entschieden dagegen auflehnen, daß man*
> *den zum Genusse des 'Neuen Simson' nachrückenden Bevölkerungs-*
> *schichten falsche Meinungen über den Corruptionshaß beibringt, der*
> *heute die einzige ehrlich positive Aufgabe aller wahren Patrioten*
> *bildet ... (F.84:8–9)*

What damnable trends do they [the authorities] permit to gain popularity by deriding the fight against immorality! ... I must emphatically protest against their teaching false opinions about hatred of corruption to the masses who come flocking to enjoy *Der neue Simson*. This hatred nowadays constitutes the only honestly positive responsibility of all true patriots.

Kraus appended a one-page commentary to this letter, in which he evaluated Karlweis. He considered him to have been overestimated by the press critics, who saw in him a Viennese Aristophanes and a folk-poet ('wieder einmal droht ein für die Innere Stadt präpariertes Wienerthum mit dem urthümlichen verwechselt zu werden' – F.84:10). But Kraus placed more blame for this on the press, especially the *Neue Freie Presse*, than on Karlweis, and sarcastically stated that their overestimation would stop now that the playwright was dead: 'Indes, die Bereitwilligkeit, einen Autor zu überschätzen, hält bei der Clique nicht länger vor, als es ihr das *Interesse* gebietet, und unsterblich pflegen ihre Günstlinge nur solang zu sein, als sie nicht gestorben sind' (ibid). [However, the willingness of that clique to overestimate an author lasts only as long as it *benefits* by this, and its minions tend to be immortal only so long as they haven't died.]

Der neue Simson was only one example of the poor quality of drama on the Viennese stage at the turn of the century. One of Kraus's most eloquent statements on the impoverishment of contemporary theatre and drama was probably a three-line paragraph entitled 'Repertoire' (F.85:21), in which he listed the names of the dramatists being performed in Vienna on 25 October 1901: 'Doczi, Mosenthal, Blumenthal, Kadelburg, Karlweis, Landesberg, Stein, Buchbinder, Weinberger.' Not one of these names is still remembered; most had connections with the Jewish liberal clique, which Kraus insisted was ruining the cultural scene; not one classical or first-rate contemporary playwright is on the list.

In 1901 Kraus mused on the advantages of putting theatres under state control, since the stage was an educational institution. Such a measure could reacquaint the public with such 'unknown' authors as Shakespeare,

Goethe, and Hebbel and wean the spectators from the influence of Victor
Leon, Buchbinder, and Bahr. He went on to state that all artistic activity could
then be regulated by two considerations, its suitability to its purpose
(*Zweckmäßigkeit*) and necessity:

> *Alles künstlerische Schaffen wird in gesünderen Tagen von den Erwä-*
> *gungen der Zweckmäßigkeit und vor allem der* Nothwendigkeit *gezügelt*
> *werden. Die Cardinalfrage ... mag etwa lauten: Würde der Besitzstand*
> *deutscher Dichtung, den so viele reiche Geister mehren halfen, der*
> *tausendmal Ausgesprochenes in tausend Formen birgt, eine Bereiche-*
> *rung erfahren?* (F.83:2)

In healthier days, all artistic activity will be regulated by considerations
of its suitability to its purpose and above all by *necessity*. The main
question ... will perhaps read: Would the assets of German literature,
which so many creative minds have helped to increase, which contain
things said a thousand times in a thousand forms – would these assets be
enriched?

One practical purpose that a play could have would be a didactic one. This
quality was found and praised by Kraus in some contemporary plays, most
of which were artistically not first-rate.[39] All of them would be classified as
Bühnendramen rather than *Buchdramen*. An educational purpose could be
found in Madjera's *Helden der Feder* and Otto Ernst's *Die Gerechtigkeit*, both
of which were *Tendenzstücke* and had the abuses of the press as their
theme. The didactic power of these plays was for the most part based on the
relevance of the subject or the cause they advocated. In Kraus's opinion,
because of the power of the press, criticism of this power would soon be the
only subject that an artist could work with (F.122:2). He also stated that
the stage was a better place for exposing this problem than *Die Fackel*: 'Was
bedeutet ein Jahr der "Fackel" neben dem Versuch, im Rampenlicht dem
Volk die Verheerungen am künstlerischen und materiellen Besitzstande zu
zeigen, die das Walten der Journaille verübt ...' (F.122:3). [How can a year
of *Die Fackel* compare to an attempt to show the people on stage the devasta-
tion of artistic and material assets that the rule of the newspaper rabble
brings about ...]

In defending Madjera's *Helden der Feder*, Kraus argued that the conventionality of this production should not have been criticized: the suicide of
Antonie Baumberg, who had been a victim of the press,[40] was still fresh in
one's mind, and the theatre could not be expected to cope adequately with a
play that dealt with such a topical issue.

> *Die kritischen Besserkönner haben ... das 'Conventionelle' der Bühnenge-*
> *staltung getadelt. Der Vorwurf lag nahe, trifft aber den Autor nicht ...*
> *Der ehrlichen Lehrhaftigkeit seiner Absicht* konnte *die künstlerische Aus-*

führung nicht gewachsen sein. Der Conflict, den er zu meistern suchte,
der Kampf der Persönlichkeit gegen die papierne Tyrannis, hat eben erst im
Falle Baumberg zu einem tragischen Abschluß geführt. Er brennt wohl
schon da und dort in den Gemüthern, ist aber noch nicht über die Schwelle
des Zeitbewußtseins hinausgelangt. In die Bühnensphäre verpflanzt, kann
er keinen andern als einen conventionellen Ausdruck empfangen ... Hier
galt es, einer Tendenz die Bühne erst als Tribüne zu gewinnen ... (F.102:17)

The smart aleck critics disapproved of the 'conventionality' of the production.
The reproach is obvious, but does not affect the author ... The artistic
execution *could not* have been equal to his honest didactic intention. The
conflict that he tried to master, the battle of a personality against the
tyranny of the press, has not led to a tragic conclusion before the Baumberg
case. This conflict is doubtless already smouldering in some minds; it
has, however, not yet crossed the threshold of the consciousness of the
times. Transplanted into the sphere of the stage, it cannot but be expressed
in a conventional manner ... Here the question was to win the stage as a
rostrum for a [new] trend ...

Concerning Otto Ernst's *Die Gerechtigkeit*, Kraus wrote:

es (ist) [dem Autor] um die Popularisierung einer neuen Tendenz zu
thun ... Nach fünfzig Jahren wird sie, wenn sie nur bis dahin program-
matisch der Menge eingebläut ist, ihre Dichter finden. Sie heute bloß
auszusprechen, ist ein Verdienst, ihr die Bühne, und die erste des
Reiches, zu erschließen, eine culturelle That, deren aufklärende Wirkung
die kunstlose Form nicht schwächen, die didaktische Gewandung nur
fördern kann ... Darum ist das Unternehmen, zu dem sich zufällig ein
schwächlicher Dramatiker und ein planloser Director einigten, nicht hoch
genug zu preisen, trotz allen Halbheiten, die dem Werke anhaften ...
(F.122:2–3)

[the author] (is) concerned with popularizing a new trend ... After fifty
years, if this trend has been drummed into the people's mind, it will find its
poets. Just to give expression to it today is of merit; to open up to it the
stage, and indeed the most important stage in the country, is a cultural deed,
the enlightening effect of which its artless form cannot weaken and its
didactic manner can only promote ... Therefore, this undertaking, in which
a rather weak dramatist and a haphazard director have happened to join
forces, cannot be praised highly enough, in spite of all the imperfections
that the work has ...

Further evidence of Kraus's preoccupation with the ethical rather than aesthetic merit of this play can be seen in the fact that most[41] of the article on

Die Gerechtigkeit in *Die Fackel* no. 122 consisted of a report on the other critics' adverse reaction to the play, as well as quotations of Richard Wagner's remarks on the terrible power of the press and the fear generated by this power.

In two plays dealing with politics, it was again the authors' didactic intent that received praise from Kraus. Ludwig Thoma's *Localbahn* was the better of the two; Kraus called it 'the only modern peasant comedy' and praised Thoma for proposing to discourage liberal philistines from politicking (*F.*129:1–4). Hawel's play *Politiker* was 'a play of indisputable educational value.' However, its didactic success did not result from the dramatist's artistry[42] but rather from the play's message: 'die gesunde Moral des Stückes lautet: "Politische Parteien – a Bund Hadern wie der andere!"' (*F.*153:24). [The healthy moral of the play runs: 'Political parties – the one's as much a bunch of rags as the other!'] Kraus ended with the remark that the novelty of the material overrode artistic considerations: 'in der Freude über stoffliches Neuland schweigt der Kunstrichter ...'

In a sense, these plays were a kind of popular art, and it sufficed that they were useful and educational for the time. In waiving artistic considerations, Kraus was able to concentrate on the ethical argument of the plays and to use them in his fight against the corruption of the times.

The last group of playwrights to be considered here is distinguished by the fact that they enjoyed general esteem – as at least two of the three still do today – while Kraus thought very little of them. Unfortunately, his discussions of Hofmannsthal, Schnitzler, and Sudermann tend to be somewhat general and to lack the incisiveness of detailed critical analysis. Thus, for example, his evaluation of Schnitzler occurred within the more general framework of a report on Schnitzler's having been awarded the Bauernfeldpreis for literature. For Kraus, this dramatist was no revolutionary in art (as other critics had asserted) and often did not measure up to the psychological burden he had taken upon himself. Even so, and although he was an unfashionable person treating modern material, his work was gracious and in good taste: 'Kein Revolutionär, keiner, der auf den Pfad künstlerischer Seelenerkenntnis ein neues Licht gestellt hat. Ein unmoderner Mensch, der moderne Stoffe trägt und dabei – ein Wunder – doch nicht protzig, nicht ungraziös wird' (*F.*133:6). [Not a revolutionary, not a person who has placed a new light on the path of the artistic reconnaissance of the mind. An old-fashioned person who treats modern subjects and who, to one's amazement, does not become snobbish or ungracious in doing so.] But in Kraus's opinion, his dramas were not great literature.

Kraus was no more enthusiastic about Hofmannsthal than he had been in 1899, when he insisted that Hofmannsthal was not a poet (*F.*1). He was still quite unable to appreciate him as a dramatist. There is very little mention of this playwright in these years, partly, to be sure, because he did not produce and publish much drama. The only quality that Kraus could appreciate in Hofmannsthal was his good taste.[43] In his fleeting allusions to Hofmannsthal's art, one of Kraus's major objections was still that it was derivative – '[Hofmannsthal is] an artist who derives from art and not an artist who creates out of himself' (F.242/3:24) – and he complained that this dramatist's work was all brocaded style with nothing behind it. In this respect, Kraus compared him to Harden: 'Both write brocade, but Hofmannsthal's verse is less ceremonious' (ibid). This was the same criticism Kraus had made when he mentioned Hofmannsthal's *Fragment eines Puppendramas* as an example of Viennese aestheticism being introduced to Berliners by Alfred Kerr ('the impotence of Viennese aestheticism striding along in splendid garments' – F.216:24).

Sudermann, whom critics like Goldmann and Kalbeck praised, was always referred to in negative terms by Kraus – 'a bad poet' (F.186:25), 'a speculator in back-buildings' ('ein Hinterhäuserspekulant') (F.188:17–18). The slickness of his plays and their philistinism repelled Kraus. Sudermann thought, or had been led to think by the critics, that he was an avant-garde dramatist ('ein kühner Neuerer') and a literary playwright, but in Kraus's opinion he was neither, and it was this pretence that he criticized most severely. But it was the critics who were most to blame for foisting a second-rate playwright on the theatre audiences. Thus, drama criticism again brings us back to criticism of the critics.

THE POLEMIC WITH MAXIMILIAN HARDEN

Just as the Bahr/Bukovics case crystallized Kraus's stand vis-à-vis theatre and press in the early years, the Harden case can be considered the landmark for the years 1901–9. Exception could perhaps be taken to including Kraus's polemic with Harden in a work that deals with Kraus and the theatre. Although Harden was a theatre critic, Kraus's definitive break with him did not occur on the basis of theatre criticism but as the result of two morality trials in which Harden involved himself.[44] But to take such a narrow view would be to miss Kraus's point. For Kraus, aesthetic and ethical criticisms were often intertwined. It was aesthetic criticism of Harden's misuse of the German language that proved Kraus's adverse judgment of his ethical stand. In fact, Kraus's standard of language and of style and the relation between form and content is so all-pervasive that all these factors must be considered an integral part of his criticism of the theatre.

Kraus's literary relations with Maximilian Harden had started off well.[45] As late as 1903, Kraus was pro-Harden, and some of his early remarks, seen in the light of events four years later, seem very ironic. Harden had published an article in the *Neue Freie Presse* (Kraus's *bête noire*), and the Viennese public naturally expected Kraus to feel hurt or at least annoyed. However, Kraus stated that he did not take this as a personal insult – indeed, he was glad to see good German style for once in the *Neue Freie Presse*!

> *Keine andere Empfindung, als das Vergnügen, in der 'Neuen Freien Presse' einmal Deutsch zu lesen, war hier natürlich, keine andere habe ich selbst ... gefühlt. (F.136:14–15)*
> *Ich selbst erfreute mich harmlos an dem seltenen Anblick tadellos deutscher Sätze in der 'Neuen Freien Presse'. (Ibid, p. 18)*

No other feeling than the pleasure of reading [good] German, for once, in the *Neue Freie Presse* was called for here, and this was just what I felt.
I myself took harmless pleasure at the unusual sight of impeccable German sentences in the *Neue Freie Presse*.

Kraus admitted to differences between himself and Harden, but stated that these differences were already evident in *Die Fackel* no. 2. Harden had asserted that the Viennese press was superior to that of Berlin, and Kraus had replied in this issue of *Die Fackel* that in Berlin journalism was separated from literature, whereas its Viennese counterpart was linked with literature and controlled it (*F.* 2:6). In Berlin, the press reported facts; in Vienna, it cloaked its opinions in style. Harden wanted to improve the press stylistically; Kraus wanted to worsen it so that it could not hide its 'shameful intentions' behind intellectual pretensions.

> *Harden, der an das Zeitungswesen den Maßstab einer relativen Ethik anlegt, will die Presse verbessern. Ich will sie verschlechtern, will es ihr erschweren, ihre schändlichen Absichten hinter geistigen Prätentionen wirken zu lassen, und halte die stilistisch bessere Presse für die gefährlichere ... Eine vorläufige Amerikanisierung der Presse, eine Annoncierung der Käuflichkeit, die jeden Zweifel ausschließt und das Offenbarungsmysterium der Druckerschwärze verscheucht, ist uns Culturbedürfnis. Ich klebe an der Zeitung, weil sie sich zwischen Welt und Betrachtung geschoben hat und weil es gilt, die Menschen wieder zu den Dingen zu führen, ich habe soviel Sorgfalt an die 'Neue Freie Presse' verschwendet, weil sie die literarischeste der deutschen Zeitungen ist ... (F.136:18)[46]*

Harden, who applies the standard of relative ethics to journalism, wants to improve the press. I want to worsen it, I want to make it more difficult for it to carry out its shameful intentions behind intellectual pretensions, and I consider a stylistically improved press to be a more dangerous press ... A temporary Americanization of the press, an advertisement of venality, which expels all doubt and banishes the illusion that printer's ink is a source of miraculous revelation, is for us a cultural necessity. I stick to newspapers because they have thrust themselves between the world and one's view of it, and because it is necessary to lead people back to things again; I have lavished so much attention on the *Neue Freie Presse* *because* it is the most literary of German newspapers ...

By 1907[47] Kraus's attitude towards Harden had changed radically. In *Die Fackel* no. 229, Kraus alluded to a report published by Harden of an interview Harden had had with Bismarck:

Ich wünschte ... daß ich einmal so viel Muße wie Lust hätte, zu zeigen, mit welcher Gesinnung, in welchem Stile und auf welchem Zettelkasten der Mann [Harden], dessen Intimität mit Bismarck mit der zeitlichen Entfernung von dessen Todestage zunimmt, das deutsche Geistesleben bedient. (F.229:24)

I wish ... I could have the leisure one day to match my desire to show in what spirit, in what style, and by means of what card index German intellectual life is served by this man, whose intimacy with Bismarck is increasing in direct proportion to the time that has passed since Bismarck's death.

In the same year, a complete double issue (*Die Fackel* no. 234/5) was devoted to 'Maximilian Harden: Eine Erledigung,' while in early 1908 most of another double issue contained an essay entitled 'Maximilian Harden: Ein Nachruf' (F.242/3:4–52). The exact details of the background of these articles are not always easy to ferret out, but all one really needs to know is that Harden, as editor and publisher of the Berlin periodical *Die Zukunft*, led a kind of witch-hunt against some members of the aristocracy (including Graf Moltke) who were accused of homosexuality, and that Kraus disapproved of Harden's tactics on ethical grounds. Kraus proceeded to demonstrate Harden's lack of ethics by showing that Harden's style was terrible.

Ich gehe in der Schätzung stilistischer Vorzüge weiter und nehme sie zum Maßstab ethischer Werte. Daß einer ein Mörder ist, muß nichts gegen seinen Stil beweisen. Aber der Stil kann beweisen, daß er ein Mörder ist ... (Das) Charakterbild des Herrn Harden aus dem Briefwechsel zwischen Moritz und Rina sich entwickeln zu lassen, muß jeden Stilkenner locken. (F.234/5:6)

I go further in my appreciation of stylistic merits and take them as the measure of ethical values. To say that someone is a murderer does not necessarily prove anything against his style. But the style can prove that he is a murderer ... To construct a picture of Mr Harden's character from the correspondence between Moritz and Rina must be tempting to any stylistic expert.

He claimed that, in Harden's writings, form and thought were not fused:

In der literarischen Persönlichkeit lebt der Gedanke von der Form, und die Form vom Gedanken. In Herrn Harden vegetieren sie armselig nebeneinander, der Gedanke fristet sein Dasein von der kläglichen Gewißheit, daß ihn die Anderen nicht hatten, und die unbestreitbare Eigenart des Ausdrucks besteht von Gnaden der Indolenz, mit der die deutsche Sprache im Zeitungsdienst jegliche Notzucht zu ertragen gelernt hat. Wäre Herr Harden nicht durchaus originell, er wäre überhaupt nicht. (Ibid, p. 9)

In the literary personality, the thought lives from the form and the form from the thought. In Mr Harden they vegetate in an impover- ished manner next to each other. The thought ekes out an existence from the wretched certainty that the others didn't have it, and the indisputable individuality of the expression exists by grace of the indolence with which the German language at the service of the press has learned to endure every kind of rape. If Mr Harden were not completely original, he would not exist at all.

In order to be noticed, Harden had to 'use' language in a novel way. As Kraus described it: 'Language mounts stilts, in order to raise itself above the average. ... Bombast is a crutch' (ibid). Harden had become the modern *précieux ridicule*. But his supposed erudition and culture only weighed him and his readers down.

Schon das Bildungsgepäck, das er mitschleppt, wenn seine Gedanken von Berlin nach Potsdam reisen, verwehrt ihm die freie Bewegung ... Aber mythologische Koffer, theologische Hutschachteln und Zitatenkisten – mehr, als auf preußischen Staatsbahnen erlaubt ist – liegen durcheinander, belästigen die Mitreisenden und zwingen sie zum Mitleid mit dem schwitzenden Passagier. (Ibid, p. 11)

The luggage of erudition that he drags along with him when his thoughts travel from Berlin to Potsdam already impede his free movement ... But mythological suitcases, theological hatboxes, and trunks of quotations – more than are allowed on Prussian state railways – lie higgledly-piggledy, inconvenience his fellow-travellers, and force them to take pity on the sweating passenger.

His quotations reflected the speaker not the topic. Kraus proceeded to debunk the literary legend of Maximilian Harden and to show that the stir caused by such a *littérateur* could unmask German intellectual life far better than Harden himself could ever have done in his critiques[48] (ibid, p. 22).

Probably Kraus's most effective method of criticizing Harden's style and deflating him as a literary personality was his publishing 'Übersetzungen aus Harden' (sometimes entitled 'Desperanto') in two columns printed side by side, one with a phrase or sentence written by Harden, and the second (usually much shorter and less picturesque) a rephrasing in ordinary German.[49] Here, Kraus demonstrated most graphically that the mountain had indeed brought forth a mouse – that the thought or idea was puny and the language purely decorative and designed to hide rather than reveal the idea.

Differentiating between his style and Harden's, he claimed for himself a way of writing in which thought had become language and language thought. In *Die Fackel* no. 279/80 (p. 12), Kraus compared his own style to architecture, in that everything was integrated and necessary, whereas a reader coming to Harden's works would have to be a specialist in all fields or thumb through ten volumes of an encyclopaedia in order to understand one sentence. In his own style, content and form stood in a structural relationship; in Harden's, they stood in an ornamental relationship. There was, in his opinion, no character or personality behind such a florid style as Harden's; rather, it was based on a learnable trick (see F.242/3:39). Kraus had made a similar criticism of the puns of Bauer and Heine. By extension, of course, he insinuated that he himself *did* have character and personality. He also criticized Harden for being unaware of the effects his words could produce in a reader. In Kraus's opinion, a writer should be aware of all the interrelations and associations his work could evoke; otherwise, he should not write.

> *Nun gibt es aber nichts, was das schriftstellerische Können empfind-licher bloßstellt, als im Leser Vorstellungen zu erzeugen, die man nicht beabsichtigt hat. Lieber nicht zum Ausdruck bringen, was man meint, als zum Ausdruck bringen, was man nicht meint. Der Schriftsteller muß sämtliche Gedankengänge kennen, die sein Wort eröffnen könnte, und sich jenen aussuchen, der ihm paßt. Er muß wissen, was mit seinem Wort geschieht. Je mehr Beziehungen dieses eingeht, umso größer die Kunst; aber es darf nicht Beziehungen eingehen, die seinem Künstler ver-borgen bleiben. (F. 256:27)*

Now there is nothing that can more painfully expose literary ability than producing in the reader ideas which one had not intended. Better not to express what one means than to express what one does not mean. The writer must be aware of all the trains of thought that his word can evoke and must seek out the one that suits him. He must know what

happens to his word. The more associations it makes, the greater the
art; but it must not create associations which remain hidden to its artist.

Kraus's theories on language and the word have their roots in the question
of language and style posed in the Harden case. Kraus's stipulation that a
sentence (particularly if he himself had written it) should be read twice
before its intrinsic meaning and beauty could be evident went completely
against the journalistic mode, which demanded that one wrote *about*
something, that one expressed a superficial opinion rather than revealed the
truth.

*Das Verlangen, daß ein Satz zweimal gelesen werde, weil ers dann Sinn und
Schönheit aufgehen, gilt für anmaßend oder hirnverbrannt. So weit
hat der Journalismus das Publikum gebracht. Es kann sich unter der Kunst
des Wortes nichts anderes vorstellen, als die Fähigkeit, eine Meinung
deutlich zu machen. Man schreibt 'über' etwas.* (F.279/80:6)

*Das größte Kompliment, das mir je gemacht wurde, war es, als mir ein
Leser gestand, er komme meinen Sachen erst bei der zweiten Lesung auf
den Geschmack.* (F.256:28)

The desire that a sentence be read twice in order that its intrinsic meaning and beauty may become evident is considered to be presumptuous or
crazy. It is to this point that journalism has brought its public. The only
thing it can imagine by the art of the word is the ability to clearly express an
opinion. One writes 'about' something.

The greatest compliment I was ever paid was when a reader admitted to me
that he acquired the taste for my work only on the second reading.

Or again, and here Kraus uses theatre imagery to clarify his case:

*Die Feuilletonisten, die in deutscher Sprache schreiben, haben vor den
Schriftstellern, die aus der deutschen Sprache schreiben, einen gewaltigen
Vorsprung. Sie gewinnen auf den ersten Blick und enttäuschen den
zweiten: es ist, als ob man plötzlich hinter den Kulissen stünde und sähe,
daß alles von Pappe ist. Bei den anderen aber wirkt die erste Lektüre,
als ob ein Schleier die Szene verhüllte. Wer sollte da schon applaudieren?
Wer aber ist so theaterfremd, sich vor der Vorstellung zu entfernen
oder zu zischen, ehe die Szene sichtbar wird? So benehmen sich die meisten; denn sie haben keine Zeit.* (F.256:29)

The feuilleton writers who write in the German language have a huge
advantage over the writers who create out of the German language.

They win on the first glance and disappoint on the second: it is as if one were suddenly to stand backstage and to see that everything is made of cardboard. With the others, however, the first reading produces an effect as if a veil were covering the scene. Who would applaud at that point already? But who is such a stranger to the theatre as to leave the performance or to hiss before the scene becomes visible? Most people behave in this manner, because they have no time.

Kraus pointed out all the trouble he took with his own essays in order to get exactly the right word or expression. This led him not to 'die Phrase als Ornament' as was the case with journalists in general and with Harden in particular, but to 'das Innerste der Sprache.'

> *Diese Jagd nach den letzten Ausdrucksmöglichkeiten führt ins Innerste der Sprache. Nur so wird jenes Ineinander geschaffen, bei dem die Grenze des Was und des Wie nachträglich nicht mehr feststellbar ist, und in welchem gewiß oft vor dem Gedanken der Ausdruck war ...* (F.256:31)

This hunt for the final possibilities of expression leads to the innermost depths of language. Only in this way can that union be created in which the boundary between 'what' and 'how' can no longer be detected in retrospect and where certainly often the expression was there before the thought.

And in a short aphorism (F.277/8:61), it is again language that is to seek out thought, and not the reverse: 'Die Sprache sei die Wünschelrute, die gedankliche Quellen findet.' [Let language be the divining rod that finds springs of thought.]

And from all these remarks it is evident that, for Kraus, good style was not just a matter of the right mixture of proper grammar and 'pure' language. In fact, he stated that he was not a purist and that he used local idioms for artistic purposes.

> *die Verwendung unreinen Materials kann einem künstlerischen Zweck dienen. Ich vermeide Lokalismen nicht, wenn sie einer satirischen Absicht dienen, der Witz, der mit gegebenen Vorstellungen arbeitet und eine geläufige Terminologie voraussetzt, zieht die Sprachgebräuchlichkeit der Sprachrichtigkeit vor, und nichts liegt mir ferner, als der Ehrgeiz eines puristischen Strebens. Es handelt sich um Stil.* (F.256:29)

The use of impure material can serve an artistic purpose. I do not avoid local expressions if they can serve a satirical end. Wit, which works with given conceptions and assumes a common terminology, prefers [actual] linguistic usage to linguistic correctness, and nothing is further from my mind than the ambition of purism. It is a question of style.

The antithetical basis of Kraus's criticism became increasingly obvious in the years 1901 to 1909. At times he took an 'intentionalist' stand as, for example, in his insistence that the dramatist's literary intention be preserved and not perverted by propaganda or business, or in his excessively rigid criterion that a writer should be aware of every reaction he could provoke in a reader. But at other times his critical arguments were so 'non-intentionalist' as to come close to absurdity, as, for instance, when he asserted that a fairy-tale did not have to have a meaning and that the meaning did not concern the critics (in his evaluation of *Pippa*) or that one could interpret Lulu (in *Büchse der Pandora*) in whatever way one liked. Sometimes he was objective in his criticism; he wanted the newspapers to discover and present facts rather than to create public opinion.[50] But just as often his criticism was subjective and even opinionated. He would insist, of course, that his opinions were based on the truth and on fact; however, it did not matter if one or two facts were wrong as long as his main argument was true. His comments on his artistic reworking of material (*das Stoffliche*) in his essays[51] lead the readers to think that they do not need to be acquainted with the subject matter, since style was all-important. But many of his essays cannot be properly understood without some knowledge of the subject matter.[52] And finally, concerning the two main principles in his criticism of theatre and drama, the ethical, didactic principle, although often intertwined with the aesthetic, was sometimes widely separated from it – the didactic being concerned with stage plays, and the aesthetic or *das Dichterische* with literary dramas, which Kraus wanted to be removed from the stage. However, he also associated the stage with a third factor, the entertainment principle – great actors amused their audiences with mediocre plays. His attempt to fuse the didactic, the aesthetic, and the entertaining was seen in his consideration of the old style of operetta, particularly the operettas of Offenbach.

Thus, although the reader must be aware of antitheses in Kraus's criticism, his attempts at synthesis of these contradictions are equally important. It is through his use of the theatrical mode that he best demonstrated antithesis and synthesis, for this allowed him to take an antithetical stand with regard to a problem, as well as to synthesize the functions of ethics, poetry, and entertainment. Until 1909, with the exception of his production of *Die Büchse der Pandora* and his involvement with the cabaret, he had confined his theatricality to the 'drama' of the essay and the 'stage' of *Die Fackel*. In the next decade, he was to venture on to the platform to give readings from his works, and in the 1920s his involvement with the stage itself became important, since he wrote and produced plays of his own as well as gave platform readings in his Theater der Dichtung.

The Prophet
1910–18

What is perhaps most surprising about Kraus's remarks on Nestroy during these years is that he considered this dramatist's works to be *Buchdrama* rather than *Bühnendrama*. Kraus admired Nestroy's ability to reveal, through his wit and with aphoristic clarity, the essence of man. When reading Kraus's praise of Nestroy's use of language[1] and of the depth of his humour, one soon notices that Kraus saw in the great Austrian dramatist a kindred spirit, since many of the qualities he praised in Nestroy were those that, on other occasions, he claimed as his own.

Although Kraus rarely went to the theatre during this period[2] and received most of his information from newspaper critiques, he lost interest in neither theatre nor drama. He dwelt on what he thought to be the decay of the Burgtheater, contrasting this theatre in the 1910s with its former glory or with the only group which he deemed to constitute a geniune actors' theatre, the Budapester Orpheumgesellschaft. Kraus's play readings, which he began in 1916 but which flourished particularly after the war, were in part an attempt to revive the attention to the dramatic text that he felt had been an essential part of the 'old' Burgtheater tradition, and in part an effort to 'rescue' dramas of literary excellence from contemporary productions (particularly those by Reinhardt), which he considered unworthy of them. In this Theater der Dichtung, Kraus placed the main emphasis on the language and thought of the dramas, rather than on considerations of character and plot.

The mixture of ethical and aesthetic criteria seen previously in Kraus's works was strongly evident in the period from 1910 to 1918 in his criticism of actors, contemporary playwrights, and theatre producers. In his revelation of the (unethical) reality behind appearances, he usually employed a very theatrical style. This was particularly true in his censure of war propaganda plays.

After the outbreak of the First World War, long pauses occurred in the publication of *Die Fackel* (10 July to 5 December 1914, and 23 February to 5 October 1915), and the size of the issues was reduced. Although he never ceased using *Die Fackel* as an instrument with which to damn the war, his most effective exposé of both war and the society which spawned it was not there but in the drama *Die letzten Tage der Menschheit*, composed mainly during the summers of 1915 to 1917. The play, which was not published until after the war, was an extreme form of *Buchdrama* and was never meant for the stage. In it, as will be seen in chapter 4, Kraus's theatricality and his preoccupation with language effectively complement each other.

NESTROY

In 1912, in the essay 'Nestroy und die Nachwelt' (*F*.349/50:1–23), Kraus discussed his evaluation of Nestroy as a satirist at great length and tried to 'rescue' the dramatist from his reputation as a writer of farces. By pursuing Kraus's arguments to a logical conclusion, one arrives at a somewhat unexpected view of Nestroy as a writer, not of stage vehicles, but of satirical literary dramas whose merit would best be appreciated by a reader.

Kraus opened by describing 'posterity' – the *Nachwelt* – as an age in which catch words and phrases had taken over, reason and spirit were separated, the machine dominated, and which lacked a transcendental dimension. The machine which had caused the most damage was the printing press.

> *Fünfzig Jahre läuft schon die Maschine, in die vorn der Geist hineingetan wird, um hinten als Druck herauszukommen, verdünnend, verbreitend, vernichtend. Der Geber verliert, die Beschenkten verarmen, und die Vermittler haben zu leben. Ein Zwischending hat sich eingebürgert ...*
> (Ibid, pp. 2–3)

For fifty years now the machine has been running, into the front of which spirit is put in order to come out at the back as printed matter, diluting, diffusing, destroying. Those who give lose, those who receive are impoverished, and the middle-men make a living. An interloper has become established.

He later described the age as one which had no ear for language and could only appreciate facts. 'Denn eine Zeit, die die Sprache nicht hört, kann nur den Wert der Information beurteilen. Sie kann noch über Witze lachen, wenn sie selbst dem Anlaß beigewohnt hat' (ibid, p. 22). [For an age that has no ear for language can only judge the value of information. It can still laugh at jokes if it has itself witnessed the incident which provoked the joke.] Everyone had talent, but no character; ethical decay permeated everything. 'Morgenblattfroh krähen sie auf dem zivilisierten Misthaufen, den zur Welt zu formen nicht mehr Sache der Kunst ist. Talent haben sie selbst. Wer ein Lump ist, braucht keine Ehre, wer ein Feigling ist, braucht sich nicht zu fürchten, und wer Geld hat, braucht keine Ehrfurcht zu haben' (ibid, p. 22–3). [Delighted with their morning newspaper, they crow on the civilized dung-heap, which art can no longer shape into a cosmos. They themselves have talent. The scoundrel doesn't need honour, the coward doesn't·need to be afraid, and whoever has money doesn't need to have any respect.]

Satire was the only art that could cope with such an age, for with satire, the more desperate the battle, the stronger the art (ibid, p. 23). It was here that Nestroy fitted in. For if art is that which outlasts its occasion (ibid, p. 22), then, Kraus felt, Nestroy's art had passed the test: 'er hat die Hinfälligkeit der Menschennatur so sicher vorgemerkt, daß sich auch die Nachwelt von ihm beobachtet fühlen könnte ...' (ibid, p. 18). [He so reliably anticipated the frailty of human nature that posterity, too, could feel observed by him ...] In fact, his satire was even more applicable to Kraus's contemporary world than to the Austria of the 'Vormärz' period. 'Was hat Nestroy gegen seine Zeitgenossen? ... Er geht antizipierend seine kleine Umwelt mit einer Schärfe an, die einer späteren Sache würdig wäre ... er wittert die Morgenluft der Verwesung' (ibid, pp. 20–1). [What does Nestroy have against his contemporaries? ... Anticipatively, he tackles the little world around him with an aggressiveness worthy of a later subject ... He sniffs the morning air of decay.]

Nestroy saw the world in the particular, on a small scale, and from there inferred the general; his art was the shortest connection between the real and the ideal.

Nestroy hat aus dem Stand in die Welt gedacht, Heine von der Welt in den Staat. (Ibid, p. 4)

Wenn Kunst nicht das ist, was sie glauben und erlauben, sondern die Wegweite ist zwischen einem Geschauten und einem Gedachten, von einem Rinnsal zur Milchstrasse die kürzeste Verbindung, so hat es nie unter deutschem Himmel einen Läufer gegeben wie Nestroy. (Ibid)

Nestroy took as his starting point a certain class or profession and ended up in the world; Heine took the world and ended up in the state.

If art is not what they believe and permit, but rather the path between what is seen and what is thought, the shortest connection between a rivulet and the Milky Way, then never under German sky has there been a runner like Nestroy.

Unlike Heine and the feuilleton writers, Nestroy did not seek to inform; at his best, his works spiritualized even the most recalcitrant material.

Bei Nestroy, der nur holperige Coupletstrophen gemacht hat, lassen sich in jeder Posse Stellen nachweisen, wo die rein dichterische Führung des

Gedankens durch den dicksten Stoff, wo mehr als der Geist: die Vergeistigung sichtbar wird. (Ibid, p. 10)

With Nestroy, who has only written rough-hewn verses for comic songs, passages can be found in every farce where it can be seen that the way in which the thought is made to penetrate the most solid substance is pure poetry and that there is more than spirit – spiritualization.

It was in Nestroy's use of language that, Kraus felt, his genius lay. In Nestroy's humour, meaning and form were one. Problem and content were interwoven and thought was discovered through language.

Dieser völlig sprachverbuhlte Humor, bei dem Sinn und Wort sich fangen, umfangen und bis zur Untrennbarkeit, ja bis zur Unkenntlichkeit umschlungen halten ... (Ibid, p. 7)

Nestroy ist der erste deutsche Satiriker, in dem sich die Sprache Gedanken macht über die Dinge. Er erlöst die Sprache vom Starrkrampf, und sie wirft ihm für jede Redensart einen Gedanken ab. (Ibid, p. 12)

This humour, which is totally in love with language and in which sense and word catch one another, embrace, and remain embraced inseparably, until they cannot be told apart.

Nestroy is the first German satirist with whom language wonders about things. He delivers language from its torpor, and it bears him a thought for every phrase.

When Nestroy used clichés, he manipulated them until they revealed their true origin. As Kraus stated:

Die Phrase wird bis in die heuchlerische Konvention zurückgetrieben, die sie erschaffen hat:
'Also heraus mit dem Entschluß, meine Holde!' 'Aber Herr v. Lips, ich muß ja doch erst ...' 'Ich versteh', vom Neinsagen keine Rede, aber zum Jasagen finden Sie eine Bedenkzeit schicklich.'
Die Phrase dreht sich zur Wahrheit um:
'Ich hab die Not mit Ihnen geteilt, es ist jetzt meine heiligste Pflicht, auch in die guten Tag' Sie nicht zu verlassen!' (Ibid, p. 13)

The hackneyed phrase is driven back into the hypocritical social convention that created it:
'Alright, out with your decision, my dear!' 'But Mr von Lips, I really must first ...' 'I understand. There's no thought of saying no, but to say yes you find it proper to have time for reflection.'

The cliché is twisted into the truth:
'I have shared need with you, and now it is my most sacred duty not to leave you when times are good, too.'

Nestroy's most characteristic trait was his wit, and this, in Kraus's opinion, lessened the effectiveness of his plays on stage (ibid, p. 6). Kraus set out to show that the theatrical form of Nestroy's dramas was only a disguise for their spiritual and intellectual richness; that, in effect, *no* theatre production could do justice to the plays. This is the same argument encountered in the preceding chapter when Kraus discussed the suitability of Girardi as a Nestroy actor. Girardi is now mentioned again, in much the same connection as previously: Kraus was still of the opinion that Girardi's creative powers were greater than the *theatrical* worth of Nestroy's plays. But Kraus reiterated that the theatricality of the plays was merely a disguise.

> *Aber als Ursprung und Vollendung eines volkstümlichen Typus dürfte ein Girardi ... ein schauspielerische Schöpfer ... über den theatralischen Wert der Nestroyschen Kunst hinausragen, welche ihre eigene Geistesfülle nur zu bekleiden hatte ... In Girardi wächst die Gestalt an der Armut der textlichen Unterstützung, bei Nestroy schrumpft sie am Reichtum des Wortes zusammen. In Nestroy ist so viel Literatur, daß sich das Theater sträubt ...* (Ibid, p. 8)

> *Er [Nestroy] nahm die Schablone [for example, from French farces], die als Schablone geboren war, um seinen Inhalt zu verstecken, der nicht Schablone werden konnte.* (Ibid, p. 5)

But Girardi, the original, perfect folk type ... an actor who creates characters ... could tower above the theatrical worth of Nestroy's art, which was only there to disguise its own intellectual richness ... With Girardi, the character grows with the lack of textual support; with Nestroy, it shrivels up with the richness of language. In Nestroy there is so much literature that the theatre protests ...

He [Nestroy] took the stereotype [for example, from French farces] that was born as a stereotype, in order to conceal a content that could not become stereotyped.

The playwright's wit and satire were conveyed by the main character of each drama, whom Nestroy himself used to act. But even on the stage Kraus saw Nestroy not so much as an actor but rather as a 'costumed attorney for his own satirical licence' (ibid, p. 8). The roles he created were only an excuse for speaking his mind: 'Der höhere Nestroy ... ist einer, der nur Kopf hat und

nicht Gestalt, dem die Rolle nur eine Ausrede ist, um sich auszureden ...'
(ibid). [The higher Nestroy ... is someone who has only a head and no definite
form, for whom the role is only an excuse for having his say ...] After his
death, the roles became mere costumes, waiting for someone with the same
satirical spirit as Nestroy to take them over. 'Mit Nestroys Leib mußte die
Theaterform seines Geistes absterben ... In seinen Possen bleibt die Haupt-
rolle unbesetzt, solange nicht dem Adepten seiner Schminke auch das Erbe
seines satirischen Geistes zufällt' (ibid). [When Nestroy died, the theatrical
form of his spirit had to die, too ... In his farces the lead role remains open
so long as the actor who inherits his make-up does not also inherit his satirical
spirit.]

However, Kraus did not seem to wish to say that Nestroy was incapable of
creating for the theatre. In fact, he did say that Nestroy's creative strength
was so great that he could fill the stage with characters and theatrical effects.

*Noch sonderbarer, daß der in die Dialoge getragene Sprach- und Sprech-
witz Nestroys die Gestaltungskraft nicht hemmt, von der genug übrig
ist, um ein ganzes Personenverzeichnis auszustatten und ... den
Schauplatz mit gegenständlicher Laune, Plastik, Spannung und Bewegung zu füllen.* (Ibid, p. 7)

It is even stranger that Nestroy's linguistic wit, which is carried into the
dialogues, does not hamper his ability to create characters. There is
enough of it left over to outfit a complete cast and ... to fill the stage with
graphic and visual humour, as well as suspense and action.

In both Nestroy and his stage characters, reason and feeling, wit and
pathos accompanied each other.[3] The reader was always aware of two stylistic
levels: that of the clown and that of the tragic figure.

*Der Raisonneur Nestroy ist der raisonnierende Katalog aller Weltgefühle.
Der vertriebene Hanswurst, der im Abschied von der Bühne noch hinter der
tragischen Figur seine Späße machte, scheint für ein Zeitalter mit ihr
verschmolzen, und lebt sich in einem Stil aus, der sich ins eigene Herz greift
und in einem eigentümlichen Schwebeton, fast auf Jean Paulisch, den Scherz
hält, der da mit Entsetzen getrieben wird.* (Ibid, p. 12)

*Oft aber ist es, als wäre einmal die tragische Figur hinter dem Hanswurst
gestanden, denn das Pathos scheint dem Witz beizustehen.* (Ibid, p. 13)

Nestroy, the *raisonneur*, is a *catalogue raisonné* of all universal feelings.
The clown, expelled from the stage, who, as he takes his leave, still stands
behind the tragic figure and plays tricks, seems for that era to be fused
with the tragic figure. He enjoys life to the full in a style that plucks its own

heart-strings and that, in a peculiarly suspended tone, almost à la Jean Paul, turns its own horror into a jest.

However, it is often as if the tragic figure had been standing behind the clown, for its pathos seems to make the jests even funnier.

Nestroy's witty juggling of these two levels led the dramatist-satirist to a position of irony – completely non-partisan, he could only see and present the contradictions of both sides of a problem.

> *Wie verwirrend gesinnungslos die Kunst ist, zeigt der Satiriker durch die Fähigkeit, Worte zu setzen, die die scheinbare Tendenz seiner Handlung sprengen, so daß der Historiker nicht weiß, ob er sich an die gelobte Revolution halten soll oder an die verhöhnten Krähwinkler, an die Verspottung der Teufelsfurcht oder an ein fanatisches Glaubensbekenntnis ... Der Künstler aber nimmt so wenig Partei, daß er Partei nimmt für die Lüge der Tradition gegen die Wahrheit des Schwindels.* (Ibid, p. 17)

The satirist shows how confusingly unprincipled art is by his ability to use words that go beyond the apparent argument of his plot, so that the historian does not know whether he is supposed to stick to the much praised revolution or to the much mocked citizens of Krähwinkel, to the ridicule of fear of the devil or to a fanatical confession of faith ... The artist, however, is so impartial that he takes the part of the lie of tradition against the truth of swindle.

Kraus went on to state that the satirical artist stood at the end of a development that had relinquished art. Ironically, he was both the product of this development and its hopeless opposite (ibid, p. 23). At the end of the essay, he reaffirmed the relevance of Nestroy's satirical wit in contemporary times by stressing what he (Kraus) termed the metaphysical dimension of the dramatist's humour. 'In den fünfzig Jahren nach seinem Tode hat der Geist Nestroy Dinge erlebt, die ihn zum Weiterleben ermutigen. Er steht eingekeilt zwischen den Dickwänsten aller Berufe, hält Monologe und lacht metaphysisch' (ibid). [In the fifty years since his death, Nestroy's ghost has experienced things that give him courage to go on living. He stands wedged in between the paunches of all professions, holds monologues, and laughs metaphysically.]

There are two reasons why Kraus's essay on Nestroy is important for our purposes. In the first place, Kraus laid greatest emphasis on Nestroy's use of language (his wit and satire) and particularly on his use of language to reveal the thought of the plays (ibid, p. 12). Kraus had almost nothing to say about character and action in the dramas. Although Kraus did not use the term *Buchdrama* at this point, it is obvious that he considered Nestroy's plays to be literary dramas rather than stage plays. They would, therefore, be perfect material for what was to be Kraus's Theater der Dichtung. Kraus's statement that Nestroy's main roles were waiting not for an actor but for a satirist to take them over also seems to indicate that he, as a satirist, had inherited Nestroy's plays.

This brings us to the second point of interest, which is the very clear parallel that Kraus drew between Nestroy and himself. The qualities that he praised in Nestroy's works were those which he either saw in himself or considered to be his goals. The intimate relationship between language and thought (which Kraus had found in Nestroy's plays; ibid, pp. 7, 12) was often mentioned by him. For example, the 'essential,' non-decorative role of the word is indicated in an aphorism from 1911: 'Der Gedankenlose denkt, man habe nur dann einen Gedanken, wenn man ihn hat und in Worte kleidet. Er versteht nicht, daß in Wahrheit nur der ihn hat, der das Wort hat, in das der Gedanke hineinwächst' (F.323:18). [The thoughtless person thinks that you have a thought only when you have it and (then) clothe it in words. He does not understand that in reality only that person has it who has the word into which the thought grows.] His remark that Nestroy worked from the particular to the general in his plays (F.349/50:4) echoes a comment that he had already made about himself: 'Ich kann nun von dem kleinsten Schmierfink aus die prinzipiellsten Dinge erörtern ...' (F.296/7:47). [By using the most insignificant scribbler as my starting-point I can now discuss the most fundamental things ...] Kraus claimed that Nestroy's most characteristic quality, his wit, would probably, if he had lived in the twentieth century, have found expression in the aphorism or the gloss rather than in the dramatic form of farce and comedy (F.349/50:6). At that time, Kraus himself was producing many aphorisms and glosses, most of which were based on paradox and antithesis – that is, on the same dialectical principle that he saw in Nestroy's wit (ibid). And finally, Kraus used the same phrase to describe what he (F.336/7:40) and what Nestroy (F.349/50:8) wrote: '[Es] ist geschriebene Schauspielkunst.' [(It) is the written art of the actor.] The remark, although ambiguous, points to theatricality of mode, if not to theatrical practicability.[4] In fact, the rather theatrical pose in which he pictured Nestroy in the last sentence of the essay might well have been one that he saw for himself: 'Er steht eingekeilt zwischen den Dickwänsten aller Berufe, hält Monologe und lacht metaphysisch' (ibid, p. 23). [He stands wedged in between the paunches of all professions, hold monologues, and laughs metaphysically.]

Kraus evidently felt that Nestroy, the satirist who happened to be an actor-playwright, was a kindred soul. For many years, Nestroy was to be the writer whose works would most intensely occupy Kraus, in his capacity both as adapter and as reciter (in his Theater der Dichtung), and who was thus to satisfy Kraus's two main interests: language and the theatre.

THE BURGTHEATER

From 1910 to 1918, in Kraus's writings the decay of the Burgtheater became
symbolic of the decay of the times. His approach was again based on
contrasts and antitheses. The present scarcity of great actors was contrasted
with the former period of glory when actors not only had talent, but were
great human beings as well. The present artistic mismanagement and confusion of purpose of the Burgtheater, as well as its lack of acting talent, was
compared unfavourably with the excellence within well-defined, albeit narrow,
limits of the Budapester Orpheumgesellschaft, a Viennese company which
received some rare praise from Kraus in 1912.

But throughout these essays, articles, and quoted reports, what remains
constant is Kraus's evident concern for the traditions of the Burgtheater
and his dismay at the passing of dignity, honesty, and artistry, of a comple-
mentary union of aesthetic and ethical purpose which he feared he would
perhaps never see again.

In the essay 'Das Denkmal eines Schauspielers' (F.391/2:31–40) Kraus
paid eloquent tribute to the actor Adolf Sonnenthal. The essay also expressed
Kraus's tribute to the era that had produced such a great actor (the 1850s
to 1880s) and his indictment of contemporary times. For, as he stated elsewhere, it is really not the actor who deserves a monument, but his era,
since his art is completely dependent on the reception that it receives in time:
'die Schauspielkunst (ist) die einzige ... die ohne den Empfänger nicht leben
kann und mit ihm stirbt ...' (F.339/40:29). [The actor's art is the only one ...
which cannot live without an audience and which dies with the artist ...]

The essay was prompted by the publication of Sonnenthal's correspondence.
The humanity revealed in his letters impressed Kraus;[5] he saw in this
actor the most perfect representative of a bourgeois culture that in Kraus's
own times had disintegrated.

> Ich habe den wahrsten Menschen kennen gelernt, und es war ein Schau-
> spieler. Adolf Ritter von Sonnenthals Briefwechsel – ... welch eine
> Dichtung aus Milde und Männlichkeit, Anmut und Adel, Güte und Größe,
> die die Natur zustandegebracht hat ... Nie hat es einen ritterlicheren
> Ritter gegeben als diesen vollkommensten Darsteller einer bügerlichen Kul-
> tur, deren kläglicher Zerfall noch durch die Harmonie dieser Licht-
> gestalt geadelt wird. (F.391/2:32)

> Wenn je eine schauspielerische Begabung würdig war, durch ein Denk-
> mal vor dem Gesicht der Taubheit geehrt zu werden, so war es diese,
> die sicher wie keine zuvor den Umfang des von der Bühne zu umfangenden
> Lebens hatte und die vollkommenste Sprache einer Gesellschaft führte,
> wie Girardi die eines Volks. (Ibid, pp. 37–8)

I have got to know the most genuine human being, and he was an actor. Sir Adolf von Sonnenthal's correspondence – … what a work of art, composed of gentleness and manliness, gracefulness and nobility, goodness and greatness, which nature brought about … Never was there a more gallant knight than this most accomplished portrayer of a bourgeois culture, whose lamentable disintegration can still be ennobled by the harmony of this singular figure.

If ever an actor's talent was worthy of being honoured with a monument in the face of deafness, then it was Sonnenthal's, which surely like no one else's before him extended to the full spectrum of life that can be shown on the stage and which mastered the perfect language of the society, as Girardi had mastered that of the people.

The unity and harmony of this man were contrasted with the disharmony and decay of both contemporary theatre and society, in which everything that could make life more beautiful was destroyed by doubt (*zerzweifelt*, ibid, p. 33). The society of Sonnenthal's time was superior in that it had shown itself receptive and alive; it was here that Kraus drew the parallel between theatre and era.

Die Höherwertigkeit eines Zeitalters beweist sich … nicht an dem höheren Niveau literarischer und sonst gewerblicher Fertigkeit; nicht einmal an dem Dasein vereinzelter schöpferischer Mächte, die nur Boten sind des kommenden Chaos. Sondern sie hat sich an der höheren Aufnahmsfähigkeit bewiesen und an der größeren Bewegtheit der Masse, und die Kultur des Theaters zeigt den Wärmegrad des Lebens an. (Ibid, p. 33)

The superiority of an era is not demonstrated … by the higher level of literary or any other professional skill or even by the existence of individual creative powers, which are merely messengers of the coming chaos. Rather, superiority evidences itself in finer receptivity and in the greater empathy of the masses, and the art of the theatre is an indicator of the temperature of life.

Kraus claimed that in Sonnenthal's time there were social norms that revealed themselves in the ethical boundaries of politeness, customs, and manners, and, on the artistic level, in pathos and the use of clichés – qualities that, to modern tastes, would seem mannered and unnatural. Within these boundaries, the 'elemental forces' of the actor's art could be unleashed on the stage, where they belonged: 'eben in solcher Zeit werden die Urkräfte auf der Bühne entfesselt … die Sitten der Vorzeit waren der Spielraum für die Kraft' (ibid, p. 36). [Even in such an era elemental forces were released on stage … the customs and manners of olden times gave full scope to strength.] *Kraft* und *Urkraft* are rather general terms of critical evaluation. In this context, they seem to refer to the strength of personality that distinguished the representative actors of the 'old' Burgtheater tradition and that Kraus missed in most contemporary actors, who were used to subjecting themselves to the will of the director within the confines of the ensemble. Kraus ended the essay with a eulogy to the great Burgtheater actors of the past, in which he characterized the distinct quality of sound with which each actor as an individual had impressed him. Two years, later, he reprinted this praise almost verbatim in the form of the following poem:

SONNENTHAL

Faßt Mut zum Schmerz, daß seine Thräne nicht mehr fließt
und dieser große Chor der Jugendbühne stumm ist:
Die Glocke, die Charlotte Wolter hieß;
der Hammer, der mit Lewinskys Rede das Gewissen schlug;
und einer Brandung gleich die Stimme des Zyklopen Gabillon;
Zerlinens Flüstern; und Mitterwurzers Wildstroms Gurgellaute;
eine Tanne im Wintersturm jedoch war Baumeisters Ruf;
und schwebend, eine Lerche, stieg des jungen Hartmann Ton,
vermählt dem warmen Entenmutterlaut Helenens;
und Hagel, der durch schwülen Sommer prasselt, Krastels Sang;
und edlen Herbstes Röcheln Roberts Stimme;
und Sonnenthals: die große Orgel, die das harte Leben löst.
Und all der Sänger Stimme und Manier,
die noch verstimmt, von solchem Geiste war,
daß sie bewahrt sei gegen alles Gleichmaß,
womit die Narren der Szene und der Zeit
die lauten Schellen schlagen. (F.418/22:60)

SONNENTHAL

Take courage to bear the hurt that his tears no longer flow
and that this great chorus of the stage of our youth is mute:
The bell whose name was Charlotte Wolter;
The hammer which with Lewinsky's speech struck the conscience;
and like the surf the voice of the Cyclops Gabillon;
Zerline's whispering; and Mitterwurzer's gurgling torrent sounds;
a fir-tree in a winter storm, this was Baumeister's call;
and soaring, a lark, rose young Hartmann's voice,
united with the warm duck-mother-sound of Helene;
and hail, rattling through sultry summer, Krastel's singing;
and noble autumn's rattle Robert's voice:

and Sonnenthal's: the great organ that dissolves hard life.
And voice and style of all the singers,
which, even when out of tune, was of such a spirit
that it might be preserved against all uniformity
with which the fools of the stage and (our) time
jangle their bells.

What Kraus considered to have happened to the great tradition of the Burgtheater under the corrupting influence of journalism was most vividly illustrated by an article entitled 'Pikanterien eines 87-jährigen' (F.400/3:22– 6).
It concerned the publication in the *Neues Wiener Journal* of the memoirs
of the 87-year-old Burgtheater actor Bernard Baumeister. Unlike the Sonnenthal correspondence, which was published after the actor's death and therefore not aimed at self-aggrandizement, these memoirs were no more than
gossipy anecdotes, some from the 1850s, with Baumeister as the hero. Remembering the respect Kraus had had for this actor[6] and the disdain he always
showed towards disreputable theatre gossip, we can appreciate his anger
and disappointment. He stated that he was not revolted by the incidents themselves, but by Baumeister's recounting and publishing them, with names,
dates, and colourful details.

Particularly galling to Kraus was a report of Baumeister's meeting Charlotte Wolter in Berlin, when she had invited him to a private supper. The
actor peppered his account of the incident with such phrases as 'the volcanic
tragedienne, *a volcano in life* as on the stage …' (ibid, p. 25), insinuating
that 'die Wolter' had intended the invitation to include more than supper.
Kraus sarcastically stated that Charlotte Wolter had never mentioned the
incident because it had been of no consequence to her and she had forgotten it.
But Baumeister's bad taste was unforgivable. Predictably, the ethical flaw
that Kraus picked out was Baumeister's friendship of sixty years' standing
with the journalist to whom he had recounted these memories.

Die höchste Achtung vor den großen Augenblicken der Bühne, zu denen in
all dieser Zeit, episodistisch, die Männlichkeit dieses Mannes sich em-
porgerafft hat – vor der memoirenreinen Einheit der Gestalten eines
Sonnenthal und eines Lewinsky verschwinden sie zur Episode …
(Ibid, p. 26)

The great moments on stage to which from time to time in all these years
the virility of this man had raised him deserve the highest respect – but
compared with the consistency of figures like Sonnenthal and Lewinsky,
whose characters have not been sullied by memoirs, they shrink to a
mere episode …

As so often before, Kraus's admiration of a man's artistic achievements vanished when he discovered what he thought was an ethical flaw.

Since Kraus, possibly with two exceptions,[7] did not visit the Burgtheater during this period, he depended on his usual source of information about the theatre, the reports in Viennese newspapers. It would not be profitable to discuss all the Burgtheater actors mentioned in *Die Fackel* on the basis of these reports, since they do not emerge as individuals. We might look for an actor who seemed to represent for Kraus the decay of the Burgtheater. However, Kainz, who had been his favourite scapegoat in his earlier criticism and might have continued to play this role, died in 1910, so that Kraus only rarely found an occasion to mention him. He quoted both from an ebullient letter written by Kainz in his youth to his father and from Salten's positive remarks about it. In Kraus's opinion, Salten had done Kainz a disservice in publishing this letter, since he showed the actor to be a bad poet, and therefore – Kraus argued – an inferior personality.

> *Daß ein Schauspieler kein Dichter ist, beweist wohl mehr für als gegen den Schauspieler, aber daß er ein schlechter Dichter ist, beweist etwas gegen ihn, und die geistige Persönlichkeit sinkt auf jenes epigonische Maß einer schöngeistigen, welches so oft mittlere Heldenväter befähigt, sich zum klassischen Tonfall selber etwas hinzuzudichten* (F.354/6:44)

> That an actor is no poet probably speaks for rather than against his quality as an actor, but that he is a bad poet speaks against him, and the stature of his mind is (thereby) reduced to the merely imitatory stature of a *bel esprit* which so often enables second-string actors of average ability to add something of their own to the classical cadence.

Here was yet another example of the critic trying to read more into the lines than was there: 'Salten: "Und was für eine Herrschernatur richtet sich da auf"' (ibid, p. 43); 'Kraus: "Wie wenig Humor braucht ein Schauspieler und wie viel Psychologie ein Feuilletonist, damit eine Herrschernatur herauskommt ..."' (ibid, p. 44). [Salten: 'And what a sovereign nature arises there.' Kraus: 'How little humour an actor needs and how much psychology a *feuilleton* writer must have in order for a sovereign nature to emerge ...']

The second occasion on which Kraus mentioned the actor was the unveiling of a bust of Kainz in the Burgtheater in 1914. Under the heading 'Wie schön wäre das Leben,' Kraus tried to imagine how beautiful life would be if the ceremony had been mentioned in the newspapers in a factual four-line report, as would have been the case in Nestroy's time. Now, in an era infected by 'newspaper sickness,' every inconsequential event assumed gigantic proportions: 'Aber die Zeit hat die Zeitung bekommen und das ist die große Krankheit. Es gab Mückenstiche und es entstand Elephantiasis' (F.399:32).

[But our era has the newspaper, and this is a serious illness. There were
mosquito bites, and they resulted in elephantiasis.]

With Kainz dead, no single Burgtheater actor could quite replace him in
the role of scapegoat. No actor now living was as uncritically and uncompro-
misingly acclaimed by the journalists as Kainz had been and, therefore, no one
could be such an effective foil for Kraus's attacks on the critics. For a time,
however, Kraus seemed to consider Georg Reimers an acceptable substitute.
Reimers had started his career playing heralds in the Burgtheater, had
then gone through a naturalistic phase,[8] and had subsequently advanced to
major roles as a result, in Kraus's opinion, of his talent, not for acting, but
for advertising himself (F.307/8:27). Kraus criticized Reimers for his lack of
greatness as an actor and as a human being, the critics for glossing over
this deficiency and trying to make Reimers seem great, and the audiences for
blindly accepting the critics' verdict. As in his attacks on Kainz, his criticism of Reimers was merely one way of showing the contemporary artistic and
spiritual poverty and moral decay.

Reimers, in Kraus's opinion, should have continued playing heralds, a role
for which he was equipped by nature (F.307/8:26) although, even in a
walk-on part, he was convincing in armour only if he kept the visor of his
helmet closed (F.345/6:51). But Reimers had what Kraus considered to be
a false reputation for being thoughtful, honest, and upright, and therefore the
public and the critics assumed he had great character, overlooked his lack
of talent, and proclaimed him a great actor. The illusion that such a congruence between art and life always existed was, as Kraus explained on the
occasion of Reimers' twenty-fifth anniversary as an actor at the Burgtheater,
typical of Viennese aesthetics.

> *Man sieht in Wien überhaupt weniger auf den Zweck als auf die schönen
> Mittel ... Die Schauspieler dieser Stadt gehören zu den Erscheinungen,
> die ihrer Beliebtheit ihre Popularität verdanken und umgekehrt ... Daß
> einer, um eine deutsche Eiche auf der Bühne zu sein, im Leben aus
> Pappe sein könnte, und daß einer auf der Bühne aus Pappe sein kann und
> im Leben eine deutsche Eiche, das geht der Wiener Ästhetik, die eine
> weibliche Wissenschaft ist, nicht ein, und sie feiert immer die fünfund-
> zwanzigjährige Identität von Kunst und Leben (F.307/8:26)*

In Vienna, people are generally less concerned with the end than with
the lovely means ... Actors in this city are among those people who are liked
because they are popular and vice versa ... The fact that someone can be
as solid as a German oak on the stage and of cardboard in real life, and that
someone can be of cardboard on the stage and as solid as a German oak
in real life – this fact is not admitted in Viennese aesthetics, which is a
feminine science that always celebrates the twenty-fifth anniversary of
the identity of art and life.

Kraus then tried to demolish Reimers' 'great character' with a quotation from an interview the actor had given, in which he told in detail what he usually ate for supper.

In his opinion, Reimers was just a petty bourgeois, who should have gone into business instead of becoming an actor; for now, with Reimers playing heroes, the Burgtheater style lacked any heroic dimension and might as well be declared defunct; in fact, the best way to preserve the classical tragedies would be to take them off the Burgtheater repertoire (F.418/22:56). But with critics such as Wittmann still in control of public taste, this would be too much to expect. Kraus then pointed out that critic's bad judgment. For example, paraphrasing Wittmann's critique of Reimers's interpretation of Othello, he stated: 'Herr Reimers ist seinen Vorgängern zum mindesten ebenbürtig, weil Krastel und Sonnenthal besser waren, aber Hallenstein schlechter. (Wiewohl natürlich selbst Hallenstein nicht schlechter, sondern besser war)' (F.398:13). [Mr Reimers is at least equal to his predecessors because Krastel and Sonnethal were better, but Hallenstein was worse. (Although, of course, even Hallenstein was not worse, but better.)]

Thus, with Reimers cast by the Burgtheater directors in the role of great heroes, Kraus could deliver the ultimate critical blow – matters were now even worse than in Kainz's time: 'Man muß kein Bewunderer des armen Kainz sein, um zu fühlen, welcher Entgeistigung jetzt das arme Burgtheater entgegengeht.' (F.307/8:28). [You don't have to be an admirer of poor Kainz to feel what spiritual void the poor Burgtheater is now moving towards.]

It should be pointed out that in two of the statements Kraus made in connection with Reimers, he flagrantly contradicted himself. The whole tenor of his criticism had been that there *was* a link between a man's ethics and his artistic abilities, and now he expressly denied this:

> *Daß einer, um eine deutsche Eiche auf der Bühne zu sein, im Leben aus Pappe sein könnte ... das geht der Wiener Ästhetik ... nicht ein ...*
> (F.307/8:26)

> *Ich würde es nämlich ertragen, daß ein Schauspieler ein Fallot wäre, wenn er sich nur verpflichtet, anständig zu spielen.* (Ibid, p. 28)

The fact that someone can be as solid as a German oak on the stage and of cardboard in real life ... is not admitted in Viennese aesthetics ...

I could really put up with an actor being a scoundrel as long as he contracted to act decently.

If it were indeed true that a man's ethics and his artistic abilities were interconnected, it would be impossible for an actor to be 'of cardboard' or a 'scoundrel' in his private life and to be 'as solid as an oak' on the stage.

If Reimers was relatively conspicuous in the years before the war as a representative – that is, bad – Burgtheater actor, then this dubious honour would have to go to Tressler in the later war years. Tressler, in Kraus's eyes, was no more than a superficial bit player, who could copy all styles of acting.

Herr Tressler ist ein durchschnittlicher Maskenschauspieler, der den Charakter bei der Nase nimmt, ein Chargenspieler von der Art, die auf den Provinzbühnen in einer dem Bühnengenius und allem echten Theaterwesen abholden Epoche noch immer massenhaft produziert wird.
... [ein] äußerlicher, leerer, technisch beflissener Kopist aller Stile ... (F.457/61:41)

Mr Tressler is an average fancy-dress actor, who takes the character he plays by the nose, a bit player of the kind still produced in masses on the provincial stages in an era which is averse to acting genius and everything that is genuine in the theatre.
... a superficial, empty, technically zealous copyist of all styles ...

In 1917 Kraus published an article entitled 'Schweizer Idylle' (F.457/61: 40–6), concerning Tressler's newspaper account of the Burgtheater guest performances in Zürich. The tour itself, as well as Tressler's detailed, chatty report of it (with himself as the centre of attraction), the public's interest in such irrelevant, frivolous gossip, and the 'journalistic shamelessness' which allowed such rubbish to be printed while war raged and soldiers died – all this, in Kraus's opinion, was typical of such mean, low times.

Die journalistische Schamlosigkeit, die dem Herrn Tressler erlaubt, uns spaltenweise den Nachtisch zu servieren und an Tagen, wo das Blut in Tonnen fließt und sinkt, sich zum Mittelpunkt der Betrachtung zu machen, gehört zu den undenkbaren und dennoch körperhaften Erlebnissen dieses allerschuftigsten Zeitalters ...
Da nun die Bevölkerung dieser Stadt in Dingen des Theaters zwar ihren Geschmack überwunden, aber ihr Interesse für die Privatangelegenheiten der Schauspieler gesteigert hat, so läßt sie sich, während ihre Angehörigen in Schützengräbern liegen, gern und willig von Herrn Tressler erzählen, wie er sichs im Schlafwagen, Bett Nr. 10, auf der Fahrt nach Innsbruck bequem gemacht hat. (F.457/61:41)

The journalistic shamelessness that permits Mr Tressler to serve us up columns full of dessert and on days where blood flows and sinks by the barrel allows him to make himself the centre of interest, this shamelessness belongs to the unthinkable and yet actual physical experiences of this meanest of ages ...
Since the people of this city have overcome their good taste as far as matters of the theatre are concerned, but since on the other hand their

interest in the private lives of the actors has grown, they freely and willingly allow themselves to be told by Mr Tressler how he made himself comfortable in the sleeping-car in bed no. 10 on the trip to Innsbruck, and in the meantime their relatives are lying in the trenches.

Kraus pointed out the vulgarization of social life by citing Tressler's account of a dinner given by the Austrian embassy in Switzerland for the actors, at which many aristocrats were present. Kraus saw the dinner as an advertising device, to which the aristocrats, however unwittingly, were party; supposedly representing tradition, they lent an air of respectability to propaganda for the Burgtheater. The mediocre actors who were their table companions were not worthy of them, whereas this had not been the case in the 'good old days' of the Burgtheater when it was a part of a *genuine* tradition (F.457/61: 45–6). And, of course, the chief culprit responsible for this levelling, dishonour, and shamelessness was the press, which was both the motivating force and the medium. '[Man] überläßt es meiner, immer nur meiner Ohnmacht, die inneren Grenzen gegen den Feind zu schützen, der sie längst überschritten hat: gegen die Zeitung, die durch ihr bloßes Dasein der Zeit, der sie dient, die Ehre geraubt hat und die Scham, es zu fühlen' (ibid, p. 46). [(They) leave it to my weakness, always only to my weakness to defend the inner boundaries against the enemy, who has long since overstepped them: against the press, which, by its mere presence, has robbed the age it serves of its honour and of the sense of shame to feel that it has been robbed.] Thus Tressler typified the Burgtheater decline of the war years, which not only paralleled the decay of the times, but also, in its frivolity, presented a terrible contrast to the tragedy of the war.[9]

In 1917 Alexander Girardi was at long last invited to perform at the Burgtheater. In view of the degenerate state of that theatre, the move could only be considered by Kraus as a curse and not an honour.

GIRARDI IM BURGTHEATER

Hat man deiner Kunst den Palast erschlossen,
o fliehe den Fluch der unseligen Erben!
Es glückt ihnen, deine Natur zu verderben.
Spiel ihnen, ebendort, einen Possen! (F.472/3:11)

Die Zeitgenossenschaft geriet ... auf den kindischen Einfall, einem Girardi
das Burgtheater zu eröffnen, anstatt es ihm zu Ehren zuzusperren.
(F.474/83:121)

GIRARDI IN THE BURGTHEATER

Have they opened the palace to your art? Then flee the curse of the wretched heirs! They will succeed in destroying your nature. Play them a trick even there!

Our contemporaries fell upon the childish idea of opening the Burgtheater to a Girardi instead of closing it in his honour.

The actor's death a few months later prompted not only sorrow on Kraus's part, but also anger at 'the unauthorized mourners' – the same people whose lack of appreciation had driven Girardi to leave Vienna and go to Berlin: 'he (went) to Berlin out of disgust at a Berlinized Vienna ...' (F.474/83:21). In the essay Kraus wrote to mark the great actor's death, 'Am Sarg Alexander Girardis' (F.474/83:120–2), Kraus contrasted Girardi's humanity with the inhumanity of the times: if Sonnenthal and the Vienna of the 1870s and 1880s had typified a positive parallel between the times and the art they produced, Baumeister the corrupting influence of a mediocre era on a talented artist, and Kainz, Reimers, and Tressler the negative side of the slogan which claims that an age gets the art it deserves ('der Zeit ihre Kunst'), Girardi was the exception that proved the rule. In such an era, he had never been more than an outsider, a constant reminder of the excellence that had been lost: 'denn dieses Bühnenleben war das Maß des Unermeßlichen, das uns verloren ist. Da stand durch drei Jahrzehnte ein Gast der Zeit in ihrem unsäglichen Ensemble, und es war von tragischer Wirkung, wie die Natur zur letzten Aussprache mit einer Entmenschtheit kam ...' [For this actor's life was the measure for the immeasurable excellence we have lost. For three decades a guest of time stood in its unspeakable ensemble, and it was tragic to watch how Nature had its last dialogue with inhumanity ...]

Since the managing director formulated the artistic policy of the theatre, hired the actors, and chose the plays to be performed, he, too, had to accept the blame for what Kraus considered to be the decline of the Burgtheater. The position changed hands many times during this period. In 1910 Schlenther returned to Berlin. From 1910 to 1912 the post was held by Alfred Freiherr von Berger, a Viennese who had been the managing director of the Hamburger Schauspielhaus. On his death, he was replaced by the Burgtheater actor Hugo Thimig, who, in turn, resigned in 1917 and was followed by Max von Millenkovich. Meanwhile, in 1918, the position of general manager (*Generalintendant*) of all Austrian court theatres (the Burgtheater was still officially the Hofburgtheater) was taken over by Baron Leopold Andrian-Werburg. When Millenkovich resigned as managing director of the Burgtheater, also in 1918, Andrian appointed a triumvirate to manage and direct it: the writer and critic Hermann Bahr, the actor and director Max Devrient, and Major Robert Michel. 'Bahr was supposed to be responsible for the programme, Devrient for casting and all questions of personnel, and Michel was to function as the extended arm of the general manager in the Burgtheater.'[10] However, this arrangement lasted only until the capitulation of Austria-Hungary in November 1918. From then until 1921 the actor and director Albert Heine held the post of managing director.

Up to 1910, Kraus's attitude towards Berger had been favourable. It was Berger who had coined the word *Journaille*, and it was his production of Wilde's *Salome* that Kraus had praised so highly.[11] In 1910, however, Kraus changed his mind about him, and in an article in no. 311/12 of *Die Fackel*, 'Der Freiherr,' he explained why. His reasons were mainly of an ethical nature.[12] Berger lacked character and tried to jump on too many bandwagons.

Nicht von der Parteien Gunst und Haß verwirrt, sondern im Gegenteil, weil er jedem einzelnen sich anzubiedern sucht, schwankt sein Charakterbild in der Geschichte. (F.311/12:1)

Dieser Mangel an Persönlichkeit aber tritt mit den Jahren so sehr in Erscheinung, daß ... überhaupt nichts anderes übrig bleibt als der Mangel an Persönlichkeit. (Ibid, p. 3)

The way he is seen varies from time to time, not because his image is blurred by the love and hatred of the factions but, on the contrary, because he tries to hobnob with everybody.

This lack of character, however, has become so much more prominent over the years that ... there is nothing at all left but lack of character.

This weakness had led Berger into the camp he had formerly criticized – the *Journaille* – and allowed him to write articles for the *Neue Freie Presse*. Here, he committed two more 'ethical' errors: he downgraded the late Ludwig Speidel (the only critic whom Kraus had ever admired) to the same low level as that of the other critics (ibid, p. 6) and he praised Maximilian Harden (ibid, pp. 7 ff).

Thus, we can assume that Kraus would not now be predisposed to like Berger's efforts as managing director of the Burgtheater. That this was indeed true is made clear in the same article. Kraus felt that Berger's innovations were of a decorative rather than an essential nature: 'ich habe mit Wehmut die welken Blätter betrachtet, die zur Totenklage der Königinnen in "Richard III." von den Soffitten fielen. Dieser Erneuerer [Berger], dachte ich, ist ein Restaurateur, der weniger auf das gute Fleisch sieht als auf die schlechte Garnierung' (ibid, p. 4). [I have with melancholy watched the withered leaves fall from the soffits during the dirge of the queens in *Richard III*. This innovator (Berger), I thought, is a restaurateur who pays less attention to the good meat than to the bad garnish.] This superficiality was, of course, entirely in keeping with the spirit of the times as Kraus saw it. So, too, was another aspect of Berger's management. In Kraus's opinion, he contributed to mediocrity by de-emphasizing the Burgtheater tradition of great acting personalities and, instead, placing the accent on ensemble playing – but without any talented actors to make up the ensemble.

Wenn Herrn v. Berger ein Schauspieler stirbt, so sagt er, daß mit Rücksicht auf dessen Unersetzlichkeit kein Nachfolger engagiert werde, und daß das Publikum von den Persönlichkeiten entwöhnt und zur Würdigung des Ensembles erzogen werden müsse. Solcher Aufschrei der geplagten Mittelmäßigkeit, die keinen größeren Ehrgeiz kennt, als den Gymnasiasten die Lektüre der Klassiker zu ersparen, mag rührend sein; aber durch die Entschuldigung, daß er für den Tod nichts könne, wird Herr v. Berger der Verantwortung dafür, daß er das Leben nicht ruft, kaum entgehen. (Ibid, p. 12)

If an actor dies on Mr von Berger, then he says that since the deceased is irreplaceable he will not engage a successor and that the public must be weaned from the cult of personality and taught to appreciate the ensemble. Such an outcry of tormented mediocrity that knows no greater ambition than sparing high-school students the reading of the classics may be touching; but the excuse that he cannot be blamed for someone's death will not absolve Mr von Berger from his inability to create [new] life.

In *Die Fackel* no. 331/2, Kraus again emphasized Berger's superficiality. He quoted from Berger's announcement of the 'restoration' of the Burgtheater, which consisted of repairs done to the auditorium. Portraits of the late great actors of that theatre were hanging on the walls, but, as Kraus pointed out, the stage was filled with mediocrity. Moreover, Berger's style was terrible, so that the decline of the theatre he directed was only to be expected: 'Der Kanzleistil des Burgtheaters ist heute der beredteste Führer durch seine Katastrophen' (*F.*331/2:38). [The officialese of the Burgtheater is the most eloquent guide through its catastrophes today.]

Kraus had little to say about Thimig as managing director of the Burgtheater. However, no great actors were hired during Thimig's time; rather, the proliferation of 'non-talent' continued, and actors such as Walden and Wüllner[13] were contracted. According to Schreyvogl's chronicle of the Burgtheater, Thimig judged each play according to its literary importance[14] – a trait which could not endear him to Kraus, who felt that plays of *literary* merit should not be performed. Some of the plays that he added to the repertoire (such as Shaw's *Pygmalion*, Schnitzler's *Der einsame Weg*, Ibsen's *Rosmersholm*) would also not win him Kraus's favour, to say nothing of two plays introduced during the war years: Hans Müller's patriotic play *Könige*,[15] and Meyer-Förster's comedy *Alt-Heidelberg*. And, in 1914, Thimig was instrumental in hiring the first non-actor director (*Regisseur*) Artur Holz, on whose name Kraus made many a bad pun (*Holz* = wood), and who was the director of the 1917 production of *King Lear* that Kraus criticized so severely.[16]

BURGTHEATER-TRADITION

Der Zustand macht uns nicht wenig stolz:
unsre Kunst war aus Marmor, jetzt ist sie von Holz.
Ich hatte stets das beste Kleid:
spricht ein Parvenü der Vergangenheit.
Wenn wir so mit dem Gehabten protzen,
hat der Gast nichts zu essen, aber reichlich zu kotzen. (F.472/3:11)

Its [the Burgtheater's] condition makes us not a little proud: our art was of marble, now it's of wood. 'I always had the best dress,' says a parvenu from the past. When we boast so much about what we used to have, our guests have nothing to eat, but ample cause for vomiting.

On resigning, Thimig suggested Holz as his successor, but was blocked by the four actor-directors, Reimers, Devrient, Heine, and Tressler. In commenting on this, Kraus again reminded his readers about the pitiful, degenerate state of the Burgtheater: 'It borrows its style from below and speaks of tradition' (F.457/61:78).

Thimig's successor, Millenkovich, is probably best remembered for an unfortunate press conference at which he called himself 'a German-Austrian who carries in his heart the Christian-Germanic ideal of beauty' (F.457/61:80). Such a statement reminded Kraus too much of the lie behind the First World War. There are two ironic references to it in *Die Fackel*, one when the conference had just taken place and another in connection with the production of *King Lear*:

Wie aber sollte diesem Ideal ein Theater aufhelfen, da es doch seine schönste Erfüllung bereits im Weltkrieg gefunden hat? (F.457/61:81)

Die Unsäglichkeit der heutigen Burgtheateraufführung, die noch tief unter dem Niveau der einer niedrigen Zeit erreichbaren schauspielerischen Möglichkeiten bleibt, also beinahe an das christlichgermanische Schönheitsideal der Direktion hinanreicht, gehört ... der Theatergeschichte an. (F.484/98:89)

However, how was a theatre supposed to further this ideal when it had already found its most beautiful fulfilment in the world war?

The unspeakableness of today's Burgtheater production, which remains well below even that standard that one could expect actors to reach in such degenerate times, and which therefore nearly approaches the Christian-

Germanic ideal of beauty of the management, is worth recording in the history of the theatre.

A revealing statement with regard to Kraus's ideas about both himself and the post of general manager (*Generalintendant*) was made by him when he remarked on the appointment of the diplomat Andrian to that position: he not only commented that this man was impossible for the job, but asked, one suspects only half jokingly, why the authorities had not offered *him* the position:

> Es könnte ... die Frage laut werden, warum man für ein solches Amt nicht den Fähigsten aussucht, nämlich mich, dessen kleiner Finger nicht nur ein besserer Hoftheaterintendant ist als der Herr v. Andrian, sondern auch ein besserer Burgtheaterdirektor, als der Herr Bahr sein wird, und zudem ein besserer Schauspieler, als das ganze Burgtheaterensemble seit zwanzig Jahren gewesen ist.
> ... Die Frage würde ... mit demselben Hohngelächter beantwortet werden, das ich für die Zumutung bereit hätte, eine Lebensaufgabe in der Betätigung meiner weitaus geringsten Qualität einzugehen ... Die Unmöglichkeit, daß sich eine lebendige Kraft in der Niederung heutiger Bühnenreformen versuche, ist identisch mit der Unmöglichkeit, dem Burgtheater aufzuhelfen. Von allen verlorenen Posten, die diese Zeit zu vergeben hat, ist der eines Burgtheaterleiters der hoffnungsloseste, weil die Erkenntnis, daß die Zeit ihre Kunst hat, ausschließlich für das Gewerbe zutrifft, das man heute Theaterkunst nennt. (F.484/98:81–2)

The question could be asked why they did not seek out the most competent person for this position, namely myself. My little finger is not only a better court theatre manager than Mr von Andrian, but also a better Burgtheater director than Mr Bahr will be, and moreover a better actor than the whole Burgtheater ensemble has been for twenty years.
... The question would be answered with the same derisive laughter that I would have ready for the request that I should devote my life to the exercise of what is by far my most modest quality ... The impossibility of a person of real vitality trying his hand in the lowland of today's theatre reforms is identical with the impossibility of helping the Burgtheater up on its feet again. Of all the impossible jobs this age has available, that of a director of the Burgtheater is the most hopeless because the realization that the age has its art holds true exclusively for the business that today is called theatre art.

As Kraus stated that the general manager's job was such a useless one and not worth anybody's while, one wonders why he took so much interest in who received it.

THE BUDAPESTER ORPHEUMGESELLSCHAFT

The only theatre group that won Kraus's unmitigated praise in 1912 was the Budapester Orpheumgesellschaft – 'das einzige künstlerische Ensemble Wiens' (F.343/4:17). This ensemble, which was active from the 1890s until the First World War at least, performed for years in makeshift quarters in the conference halls of hotels in the second – and predominantly Jewish – district in Vienna. Its programme, which was not advertised in the Viennese press, consisted of vaudeville acts and short farces. The group not only had great actors (the genius of the actor Eisenbach was, in Kraus's opinion, comparable to that of Girardi) but their talent was concentrated in a relatively narrow field, that of 'cultural vignettes of petty bourgeois Jewry' (F.341/2:7), where it could best find expression. Their art did not just try to copy reality – rather, it artistically transformed it.

> *Jene [d.h. die Schauspieler Eisenbach und Rott] ... vermögen, den Geschäftsreisenden so hinzustellen, daß man ihn umarmen möchte ... (F.341/2:8)*

> *die Zweideutigkeit der Welt, die sie zur Kunst erheben ... (F.343/4:18)*

> *Ein solcher Selbstspieler in der Verwandlung der Häßlichkeit zum Humor ist auch Herr Eisenbach. (Ibid, p. 19)*

They [the actors Eisenbach and Rott] ... can present the travelling salesman in such a way that one would like to hug him ...

The ambiguity of the world, which they raise to the level of art ...

Mr Eisenbach, too, is such a natural actor who changes ugliness into humour.

It was the actor's gestures and his 'psychic tyranny over everything organic' (ibid, p. 20) that impressed Kraus so much that he could say: 'Es gehört zu den ergreifendsten Eindrücken, die ich in fünfundzwanzig Jahren ... vom Theater bezogen habe' (ibid). [This is among the most moving impressions that I have had from the theatre in twenty-five years.]

The Orpheumgesellschaft was an actors' theatre, and its artistic management had not tried to foist literary pretensions on it. Kraus spoke of the group's 'originality, consistency, and strength of purpose' (ibid, p. 18), all of which were qualities that the Burgtheater management did not seem to be able to cultivate. Kraus had suggested that the Burgtheater management and ensemble should move out and give the Budapester Orpheumgesellschaft a proper place in which to perform (F.341/2:7–8). Berger had, of course, not followed this ironic suggestion, but tried to capitalize on the group's success by adding to the Burgtheater repertoire one of the plays which the troupe had performed so well. The play was *Die fünf Frankfurter* by Karl Rößler; it took place in a Jewish milieu and made use of Yiddish expressions. It was a work for which the Burgtheater actors were not suited and from which they could only draw the basest effects of material humour. Here, then, was a typical example of misguided, misdirected management. As Kraus commented: 'Wenn im Burgtheater gemauschelt wird, so ist damit noch garnichts bewiesen. Es kommt in der Kunst darauf an, *wer* mauschelt' (*F*.343/4:21). [Speaking Yiddish in the Burgtheater proves nothing. In art, it all depends on *who* speaks Yiddish.]

Kraus's enthusiasm for the Orpheumgesellschaft, which performed plays that are long forgotten, is a splendid illustration of the fact that he took his own distinction between literary dramas and stage plays seriously: the latter were theatrical, not literary events, and it was not the quality of the texts, but that of the actors' performance and the spectators' experience that mattered.

KRAUS'S THEATER DER DICHTUNG

In 1910, Kraus began to give public readings of texts he had written for publication in *Die Fackel*. These events attracted a fair amount of attention, but they do not need discussion in the present context. From 1916, however, he began to alternate presentations of his own works with complete readings of plays by Shakespeare and Nestroy – one-man performances which, in the mid-1920s, he called Theater der Dichtung. His reasons for these readings seem to be threefold: he wished to 'rescue' the beauty of the language of literary drama (*Buchdrama*) from what he considered to be the disastrous effects of contemporary theatre productions; he wanted to give these dramas their proper interpretation; and he hoped to rid 'true' literary drama of its associations with what he termed 'false' literary drama.

Kraus began by giving readings only of plays he considered to be genuine literary drama, such as plays in which the main effects, in his view, depended on language rather than on externals such as slapstick or farcical situations. His was a 'theatre' which gave up all visual appeal, such as costumes, props, make-up, and scenery, as well as auxiliary acoustic effects (except music) and relied on the speaker's voice and the listener's ear.[17] As he put it with characteristic immodesty:

Sie [d.h. die Stimme des Vorlesers] würde es sich zutrauen, Vorstellungen von Werken wie Lear, Macbeth, Wintermärchen, Die Widerspenstige mit einer bis in die kleinsten Rollen bewahrten Treue so nachzugestalten, daß ein geschlossenes Auge und ein offenes Ohr der Zeugen jener leben-

digen Herrlichkeit nicht mehr den Apparat vermißte, der heute für das
offene Auge und das geschlossene Ohr seine toten Wunder verrichtet.
(F.426/30:48)

[The voice of the reader] would take it upon itself to reproduce performances of works such as *Lear, Macbeth, A Winter's Tale, The Taming of the*
Shrew with such accuracy down to the smallest roles that a closed eye and
an open ear of those who had witnessed the living splendour [of the old
Burgtheater] would no longer miss the apparatus that today performs its
dead wonders for the open eye and the closed ear.

The theatrical tradition he felt most akin to was that of the 'old' Burgtheater of
the 1870s and 1880s; in fact, he referred to his Theater der Dichtung as 'an
older Burgtheater reconstructed in this way.' He rejected the efforts both of the
contemporary Burgtheater and of Reinhardt's troupe in Berlin. He wrote, for
example, of '[the] honest inadequacy of the present Burgtheater and [the] dishonest one of that Berlin manager' (ibid).

We have discussed at length Kraus's reasons for considering the contemporary Burgtheater inadequate. As for the 'dishonest inadequacy of that
Berlin manager,' the best example of what Kraus and his 'poetic theatre' were
reacting against was Reinhardt's production of *Macbeth* in the Deutsches
Theater (Berlin). There, the main theme, on which variations were played,
was blood. 'Farben und Beleuchtung waren auf Blut gestimmt, und als das
Ehepaar Macbeth den Mordplan aushecke, *umringelten den Hals der beiden*
blutrote Streifen, die von einem Beleuchtungsapparat projiziert wurden.
Ein blutbefleckter Vorhang ging herunter, als der Mord ausgeführt war ...'
(F.418/22:95). [Colours and lighting were tuned to the theme of blood,
and when the Macbeth couple were hatching their plans for murder, blood-red
stripes of light thrown by a projector ringed their necks. A blood-spattered
curtain came down when the murder had been carried out ...] In Kraus's
opinion, such effects were purely decorative and detracted from the poet's
words, which, in the 'good old days,' used to produce horror at Macbeth's
crime.

> *Dekorativ soll se [sic] wirken. Das ist nicht so wie bei armen Leuten.*
> *Ehedem sind bloß Helden aufgetreten, denen das Wort des Dichters aus*
> *dem Hals kam, ohne daß dieser selbst Spuren der dramatischen*
> *Absicht verraten hätte. Traten sie von der Szene, so fiel ein Vorhang,*
> *auf dem nichts zu sehen war als eine Landschaft mit einer Göttin,*
> *die eine Lyra in der Hand hielt, und dennoch war der Zwischenakt voll*
> *des Grauens über Macbeths Tat.* (Ibid, pp. 96–7)

Effects must be decorative. That is not the way it is with poor people.
Before, only heroes came on stage, and it was the dramatist's word

which came out of their throats, without the throats themselves showing traces of the dramatist's intention. When they left the stage, a
curtain fell on which nothing was to be seen but a landscape with a
goddess holding a lyre in her hand, and yet the intermission was
full of horror at Macbeth's deed.

Kraus drew a very strong parallel between the super-productions of Reinhardt and those of the war, where real blood was flowing.[18] Both were based
on technology and depended for their 'effect' on a great quantity of extras.

> *Wie war doch stets und in jedem Belang die Bühne ein Wertmesser der*
> *Lebenskräfte! Die umheimliche Identität der Aufmachung eines Rein-*
> *hardt mit der Regie des jetzt wirklich vergossenen Blutes ist keinewegs zu*
> *übersehen. Schöpfen nicht beide aus Quantität und Technik, aus Kom-*
> *parserie und Mache den Gedanken?* (F.418/22:97)

On every issue the stage has always set a standard of vitality! The sinister
identity of a Reinhardt production with the production of the bloodshed that
is now really taking place cannot be overlooked. Don't they both owe their
guiding thought to quantity and technology, to extras and window-dressing?

For Kraus, poetry had no place in such productions. The preservation of the
beauty of language in the timelessness of his 'poetic theatre' was his
answer to this fraudulence.

Furthermore, in his readings, Kraus sought to give literary dramas their
proper interpretation as revealed through language, and thus to correct in a
small way the misinterpretations of these plays by literary critics and
historians. This applied most often to those dramas by Nestroy which had
been given a political, and especially a liberal, pro-revolutionary interpretation. According to Kraus, the historian Friedjung had been guilty of such
misinterpretation in the chapter on Nestroy in his book *Österreich von
1848 bis 1860.* Kraus sought to show that Nestroy was primarily a satirist and
essentially apolitical – that is, he could see (and consequently show) the
good and bad sides of *both* extreme liberalism and extreme conservatism
(F.343/4:32). 'Aus dieser Absage an jede politische Gebärde, aus dieser
Reduzierung aller Parteimaskerade auf ein streberisches Nichts, aus diesem
unermüdlich abgewandelten Hohn auf die Revoluzzerei entnimmt Herr
Friedjung die gesinnungstüchtige Absage an die Reaktion' (F.345/6:42).
[From this refusal of any political gesture, from this reduction of all attempts
at party masquerade to a pushy nullity, from this tirelessly varied mockery of revolutioneering Mr Friedjung deduces (Nestroy's) staunch rejection
of (political) reaction.]

Finally, through his Theater der Dichtung, Kraus wished to save 'true' literary drama (*Buchdrama*) from the association with 'false' literary drama

that literary critics and theatre directors had forced on it. Kraus provided an example of what he meant by false literary drama in the essay 'Die Literaturlüge auf dem Theater' (F.457/61:53–7), in which he discussed Hebbel's tragedy *Judith* and Nestroy's parody of it, *Judith und Holofernes*. It was Kraus's contention that, if one did not know which play had been written first, one would think the Hebbel play was the travesty.

> *Sie [Hebbel's characters] treten schon mit dem Kopf in der Hand auf und siehe da, es ist der allen gemeinsame, der Hebbel'sche … Die endlose Schnur von aneinandergereihten Überlegungen, die jede Hebbel'sche Figur mitschleppt, weist weniger auf Geburt als auf Selbstmord … Sie alle sind von dem gleichen Wortgeschlecht, von der gleichen intellektuellen Herkunft, alle von Hebbel persönlich ohne die Sprache gezeugt. (F.457/61:55)*

Hebbel's characters come on stage with their head already in their hand and behold! it is the one that is common to all, the Hebbelian head … The endless row of strung-up considerations that each of Hebbel's characters drags along is less indicative of birth than of suicide … They are all of the same linguistic gender and the same intellectual origin, all begotten by Hebbel personally, without language.

Kraus believed that drama ought to be a matter of language rather than psychology. It should synthesize rather than analyse, as Hebbel was wont to do (ibid, p. 54). Referring to his own remark, 'Wissenschaft ist Spektralanalyse: Kunst ist Lichtsynthese' [Science is spectrum analysis: art is light synthesis], Kraus relegated Hebbel's dramas to the category of science, since in them language did not have a synthesizing force.

> *Seine [Hebbel's] dramatische Welt ist wahrlich eine von Punkten, zu denen in nie begriff'nem Selbstzersplitt'rungsdrange das unerforschte Eins und Alles gleich zerstoben war, ohne daß die Sprache ihm die Bindung vollzogen hat. Was er treibt, ist Spektralanalyse, und der deutsche Lesre nennt es 'Gedankendichtung'. (Ibid, p. 56)*

Hebbel's dramatic world is truly one of points, to which the unexplored One and All had immediately been scattered in an unfathomable desire for self-fragmentation without language providing the synthesizing force. What he practises is spectrum analysis, and the German reader calls it 'intellectual poetry.'

But while Hebbel was to be criticized for his inability to characterize and for his over-intellectualization of a problem, Ibsen – in the plays in which he had given up poetry and decided to set up moral precepts – was even worse. Hebbel's plays and Ibsen's social problem plays not only were not 'true' literary dramas, they were failures as stage plays as well, since they were boring. In Kraus's opinion, Nestroy's and Shakespeare's works belonged in his Theater der Dichtung, and the real theatre, which ought to be purged of Hebbel and the later Ibsen, should be devoted to the farces of Scribe and Sardou, which were genuinely suited to it.

Kraus's 'rescue' of the stage for the French comedies was just as vehement and just as quixotic as his campaign to preserve literary drama in his Theater der Dichtung, although he recognized that he was bound to fail in the first case, since he had no control over the stage. The following remarks by him make a point that is worth remembering – that, in the midst of his championing Shakespeare, Nestroy, and other 'literary' dramatists and his condemnation of 'false' literary drama, he did not lose his admiration for the theatrical talent of the genuinely creative actor:

> sei es gesagt: daß ich, wissend daß es Shakespeare und Nestroy gibt, aus der Atmosphäre der Hebbel und Ibsen skrupellos in die der Scribe und Sardou flüchten würde und das lebendige Andenken einer Burgtheatervor-stellung von 'Feenhände' oder 'Die guten Freunde' für alle Verzückungen gebe, zu denen uns die norddeutsche Ersatzweihe seit 1890 herum-kriegen wollten. Was sich die Leute im französischen Lustspiel zu sagen hatten, weiß ich nicht mehr, aber bewahre es in angenehmster Erinnerung, als Rhythmus und Form von irgendetwas, das mit dem Leben zusammen-hing, als Spielraum echter schauspielerischer Kultur, die eine größere Tatsache menschlicher Entwicklung bleibt als die Hervorbringung eines Werkes, in welchem auseinandergesetzt wird, daß das Problem der Geschlechter ein Problem ist. (Ibid, p. 57)

Let it be said that knowing that there are dramatists like Shakespeare and Nestroy, I would unscrupulously flee from the atmosphere of Hebbel and Ibsen into that of Scribe and Sardou and give up for the living memory of a Burgtheater performance of *Fairy Hands* or *The Good Friends* all the ecstasies to which the north German pseudo-sublimity has wanted to win us over since 1890. What the people had to say to each other in French comedy I no longer know, but I have the most pleasant memory of it as the rhythm and form of something or other that had to do with life and provided scope for genuine theatrical culture, which remains a greater factor of human development than the creation of a work in which it is argued that the problem of the sexes is a problem.

KRAUS'S THEATRICALITY

Kraus reminds us over and over again that he saw himself as a kind of actor or player, both in his writings and in his public readings. In 1912 he referred to his thirteen years of night work on *Die Fackel* as his 'comedian's mask': 'Ich würde sonst … meine Komödiantenmaske abnehmen! Ich hatte sie für alle Nächte dieser dreizehn Jahre vorgebunden …' (*F*.345/6:39). When writing, he always imagined a voice from the 'opposition' trying to interrupt him: 'Dieser Widerpart spricht wie irgendeiner, den ich einmal sah; er beugt sich über mich und warnt mich davor, mir Feinde zu machen …' (*F*.309/10:29–30). The voice multiplied to the size of a menagerie, which he had trouble silencing when he tried to sleep: 'Wenn ich einschlafen will, muß ich immer erst eine ganze Menagerie von Stimmen zum Kuschen bringen. Man glaubt gar nicht, was für einen Lärm die in meinem Zimmer machen' (*F*.381/3:70). Even phrases assumed this role of antagonist: 'Im Halbschlaf erledige ich viel Arbeit. Eine Phrase erscheint, setzt sich auf die Bettkante und spricht mir zu' (*F*.389/90:43).

Kraus thought of himself as probably the first writer to have experienced his writings theatrically, in the manner in which an actor would experience them: 'Ich bin vielleicht der erste Fall eines Schreibers, der sein Schreiben zugleich schauspielerisch erlebt' (*F*.389/90:42). However, to the question whether he would therefore 'entrust his text to another actor' (ibid), his answer would have to be no: the gulf between the art of the poet (*Sprachkunst, Wortkunst*) and the art of the actor (*Sprechkunst*) – that is, the difference between *Buchdrama* and *Bühnendrama* – was insurmountable.

Der Dichter schreibt Sätze, die kein schöpferische Schauspieler sprechen kann, und ein schöpferischer Schaupieler spricht Sätze, die kein Dichter schreiben konnte. Die Wortkunst wendet sich an Einen, an den Mann, an den idealen Leser. Die Sprechkunst an viele, an das Weib, an die realen Hörer. Zwei Wirkungsströme, die einander ausschalten … (*F*.389/90:40–1)

The poet writes sentences that no creative actor can speak, and a creative actor speaks sentences that no poet could write. The art of the poet is directed to *one* person, to the man, to the ideal reader; the art of the actor to many, to the woman, to the real listeners. The two streams of action that neutralize each other …

None the less, Kraus did try to resolve these opposites, and thus was himself the embodied contradiction of his own theory. The theatrical experience for him came when he was writing; therefore, paradoxically (but, in his opinion, honestly), he could say that when he read his works at his lectures, he was re-creating what was already there in the word, and not playing or improvising as an actor such as Girardi would do. This is probably what he intended to say in the following, somewhat enigmatic aphorism: 'Wenn ich vortrage, so ist es nicht gespielte Literatur. Aber was ich schreibe, ist geschriebene Schauspielkunst' (*F*.336/7:41). [When I give a reading, I am not performing literature. But what I write is written drama.]

Although they may contradict his theory, remarks such as the one just quoted only strengthen the claim that Kraus's mode of thinking and writing was theatrical and that Kraus himself was keenly aware of this theatricality. For example, by taking a paragraph or a statement from a newspaper and quoting it by itself, perhaps with an added title, Kraus was using *Die Fackel* as a dramatist uses the stage, letting his main 'character,' contemporary times, illustrate or reveal itself in its most characteristic manner. One such item from 1916 is entitled 'Grenzen der Menschheit.'[19] Kraus had taken excerpts from a newspaper critique of the performance of an operetta at the Apollotheater that was filled with such jargon as 'a real smash,' 'a real hit,' 'a new sensation' (F.437/42:126). But Kraus's sense of the theatrical led him to sandwich this critique between two reports from the front lines on the number of dead, thus dramatically underscoring the immoral superficiality of the times.

Kraus's technique of playing off one column against another also demonstrates his flair for the theatrical. Instances of this nature can be found in nearly every issue of *Die Fackel*. For example, under the heading 'Und damit auch der Clown, ders auf Desperanto sagt, nicht fehle,' Kraus ridiculed Harden's circumlocutions for Hamlet, Lear, Shylock, and Othello. Harden had written what stands in the left-hand column, and Kraus's 'translation' is on the right:

der im Mohrenfell	*Othello*
alternde Held, den, in	
einer luftlosen Bürgerwelt,	
blind gläubiger Heroswahn	
aus dem Bezirk sittlicher	
Menschheit treibt. (F.378/80:47)	
the aging hero in a Moor's	*Othello*
skin, whom, in an airless	
bourgeois world, a blindly	
trusting heroic madness	
expels from the realm of	
civilized humanity.	

Another example is in the article 'Ein gut erhaltener Fünfziger' (F.381/3:33–6), in which Kraus dramatized Hermann Bahr's vanity and hypocrisy. The piece opens with a photograph of Bahr in a striped beach-robe on the Lido. The two columns following are entitled 'Gabor Steiner kontra Hermann Bahr' on the left, and 'Das Geld. Von Hermann Bahr' ('Money. By Hermann Bahr') on the right. The first, a newspaper report, tells of how the theatre director Gabor Steiner was trying to get back the royalties that he had paid in advance to Bahr for a revue (*Die Reise nach Eipeldau*) that could not be performed because of the political allusions it contained. The second, a story by Bahr about himself, tells how, even as a youth, he disliked money and equated money with the Antichrist. This technique of visual juxtaposition is far more effective than if Kraus had recounted the two incidents in his own words.

The visual impact of *Die Fackel* was also heightened by the illustrations that Kraus printed from 1912 onwards. Taken from newspapers and magazines, they included caricatures (among them one of Kraus hawking *Die Fackel*, *F*.381/3:42), drawings, advertisements, and photographs. All of these items, when taken out of their context and placed in *Die Fackel*, illustrated in a very theatrical manner the immorality of the times. There was a photo of the novelist Hanns Heinz Ewers in an advertisement for a brand of hair oil; the text was in the form of a poem (*F*.400/3:19). There were drawings of war toys and a sketch of three children playing war, taken from *Ein zeitgemä-ßes Bilderbuch für unsere Kleinen* (A Modern Picture-Book for Our Little Ones) published by the War-Assistance-Bureau of the Imperial-Royal Ministry of the Interior for the benefit of the Red Cross (*F*.454/6:24–5). But it is the war photos which, because of their grotesqueness, make perhaps the deepest impression – a mother and child wearing gas masks and seated by a hearth (*F*.474/83:129), a postcard showing an altar made of pieces of shrapnel and grenades (*F*.431/6, frontispiece). And finally, after the war was over, Kraus printed as a frontispiece to *Die Fackel* no. 499/500 a postcard drawing of Kaiser Wilhelm in medieval armour, with his signature and a quotation by him: 'Wir Deutsche fürchten Gott und sonst absolut nichts und niemanden auf dieser Welt!' [We Germans fear God, and otherwise absolutely nothing and no one in this world!]

There are countless examples of Kraus's sense of the theatrical and the dramatic in his style of writing. A few of the more obvious ones will suffice. In criticizing the technical trickery and heavy-handed symbolism of the blood motif in Reinhardt's production of *Macbeth* ('Shakespeare und die Berliner,' *F*.418/22:95–8), Kraus inserted a surrealistic cry of his own: 'Mir wars, als hört' ich rufen: Schlaft nicht mehr. Reinhardt mordet den Shakespeare, den heil'gen Shakespeare, den stärksten Nährer bei des Lebens Fest – Es rief im ganzen Hause: Schlaft nicht mehr ...' [I seemed to hear the cry: sleep no more. Reinhardt is murdering Shakespeare, holy Shakespeare, the strongest giver of nourishment at this life's feast, – the cry filled the whole house: sleep no more.] Further evidence of Kraus's stylistic theatricality is offered by those articles which take the form of mini-dramas – conversations or dialogues between imagined characters. Under the heading 'Die europäische Kultur hält ihren Einzug' (*F*.372/3:49–52) Kraus published a reprint of a report in the *Neue Freie Presse* about Lehar's operetta *Eva* opening the first theatre in Tripoli, followed by an imagined dialogue between an Arab merchant, his wife, and a young Arab at this performance. Into this little dramatic satire he brought Viennese characters, which were 'arabized' in the conversation (for example, 'Korngold Pascha,' 'Karpath Effendi,' 'Batka Bay'). Even Kraus himself was referred to, by the name popular among many of his opponents: 'Haben Sie gelesen, was der Fackelkraus geschrieben hat? ... Sehn Sie, in allem stehn wir heut doch schon so da, daß wir uns mit Wien vergleichen können. Aber Allah behüt, um diesen Vogel beneiden wir sie nicht ...' (F.372/3:51). [Have you read what Fackel-Kraus has written? You see, in everything, we have reached the point where we can compare ourselves with Vienna. But Allah forbid, we don't envy them this bird ...]

If Kraus often employed the theatrical mode in writing Die Fackel, he was even more keenly aware of its potential in his readings from the lecture stage, where the 'opposition' was right in front of him. Evidence of this was carried over into Die Fackel when, for example, he reprinted at great length the critiques (both negative and positive) of his evenings of readings. (Many Viennese newspapers were still 'silencing him to death,' but the German and Bohemian papers and the Austrian provincial press observed no such ban.) He claimed that he did so in self-defence and that he had at least succeeded in informing his readers of what he was doing. However, to the present-day reader, this seems more like a 'dramatization of Kraus' that, in today's terms, would be called an 'ego trip.' In one instance, he not only published his list of readings (in Berlin) but also recounted incidents that had happened in the lecture hall. For example, he had quoted a 'Desperanto' passage (that is, a passage written by Harden), ending with the words: 'um mit dem Opfer des Hortes ... feindliche Gewalten zu schwichtigen' [in order to appease enemy forces by sacrificing the treasure]. Then:

> (da) hielten zwei Verehrer des Herrn Harden nicht länger und sie ver-
> ließen stampfend – quadrupedante putrem sonitu quatit ungula campum –
> den Saal. Was – um es auf Desperanto auszudrücken – den Erfolg ins
> Riesenmaß recken half; umsomehr, als es dem Vorleser Gelegenheit gab,
> den Desperados schmerzlich nachzublicken und die Worte noch einmal
> nachzurufen: ' – feindliche Gewalten zu schwichtigen!' (F.366/7:33)

[then] two of Mr Harden's admirers couldn't endure it any longer and they stomped out of the room – quadrupedante putrem sonitu quatit ungula campum. Which – to express it in Desperanto – stretched my success to gigantic proportions; even more so as it gave the reciter the opportunity to follow the desperados with his eyes with a pained expression and to shout after them once again: 'to appease enemy forces!'

The reader can sense how Kraus relished that theatrical gesture (schmerz-

lich nachzublicken) and how important it was for him. So much so that his 'threat' to build a theatre when he became tired of the effects he produced as a reciter was probably meant only half-jokingly: 'Damit mich nicht einmal, wenn mir die Wirkungen des Vorlesers nicht genügen sollten, die Lust anwandle, ihnen auf dem von mir ausgebaggerten Sumpf ein Theater hinzubauen!' (F.351/3:39). [So that, if the effects of the lecturer-reciter were not enough for me, the fancy might not sometime take me to build a theatre on the swamp that I have dredged!]

Kraus was doubtless pleased by the image of himself presented in the critiques he reprinted. For example, he cited a critique by a Dr Erich Bien in the *Triester Zeitung* (8 November 1913), adding that this was an exemplary description of his own way of reading. Bien wrote:

> *In ihrer ganzen realen Kraft, in ihrer feisten Gemeinheit hören wir die Stimmen des Alltages, sehen wir den Gestus der Straße, des Zeitungs-pathos, und dann überfällt er diese Halluzinationen in Ekel und Verach-tung ... Er liest 'Die chinesische Mauer' ... Kraus liest ... mit einer Kraft, die geradezu in die Naturmacht selbst hinuntersteigt. 'Die Schale des Zornes gießt er aus ins Meer und es ward Blut als eines Toten und alle lebendige Selle starb in dem Meere', und das Wehe der Apokalypse ruft er mit heulender Gewalt ... (F.387/9:30)*

> In their complete, real strength, in their solid vulgarity we hear the voices of everyday life, we see the gestures of the street, of the pathos of the newspapers, and then he pounces on these hallucinations in loathing and contempt ... He reads *The Chinese Wall* ... Kraus reads ... with a strength that almost descends into the elemental force of nature itself. 'The cup of wrath he pours out into the sea, and it became blood as of a dead man, and every living soul died in the sea,' and the woe of the apocalypse he shouts with howling force ...

This assessment of Kraus's theatrical abilities as a reciter is reminiscent of one of Kraus's own remarks about Girardi, who, in a phrase or two, could reveal the essence of *Wienerthum*. And the evaluation of the power of Kraus's reading –' (eine) Kraft, die geradezu in die Naturmacht selbst hinunter-steigt' – is very much reminiscent of Kraus's own assessment of the quality which made actors like Matkowsky, Baumeister, and Sonnenthal great – their elemental power, which he called *das Elementarische*.

That Kraus's theatricality was not naïve, but was calculated for effect can be seen in his remarks on audiences. He admitted that as individuals he hated the people who made up his audience. Indeed some of his readers saw an unforgivable irony in the fact that he performed for the same people whose hypocrisy he was condemning. In his own defence, Kraus cited a critique printed in a Brünn newspaper,[20] where it was claimed that the tremendous energy and power of Kraus's attacks stemmed from the terrible suffering that emanated from him and which made his criticism genuinely ethical rather than merely witty. His audiences should sense this.

Und dies mag dann auch seinen Vorlesungen Berechtigung geben: daß den Zuhörern vor dem bitteren und furchtbaren Leiden, welches von dem Vorleser ausströmt, die Ahnung aufdämmert, keinen geistreichen und boshaften Witzbold vor sich zu sehen, sondern eine in katastrophalen Krämpfen erbebende Natur, die an der traurigen Unzulänglichkeit unserer Lebensformen oft bis zum Wahnsinn leidet, an ihr aber produktiv wird und sie in die Gefangenschaft unvergänglicher Sätze zwängt. (F.387/8:31)

And this may also *justify* his readings: that, in the face of the bitter and terrible suffering which emanates from the reciter, *the members of the audience may slowly realize* that it is not a clever and malicious joker they see in front of them, but a man shaking with catastrophic convulsions, a man who is made to suffer to the point of madness by the sad inadequacy of our ways or life but whom this inadequacy makes productive, and who then forces it into the confinement of deathless sentences.

Kraus frequently commented directly on the phenomenon of audiences. He could not read to them as individuals, but as soon as they formed the mass unit *Publikum*, they were able to listen to him, and he could dominate them. When the lecture was over and they congregated in the cloakroom, they turned into individuals again, with all their old opinions intact.

Ich könnte mir zu meinen Leseabenden die schlechtesten Leute zusammen-klauben, deren man am Samstag im Volkstheater habhaft werden kann: ich bin absolut davon überzeugt, daß sie mir im Zuhören parieren würden ... und daß erst in der Garderobe die Gesinnung wieder angetan würde. (F.370/1:25)

Man bedenke aber, was es heißt, aus Leuten, die jeden [sic] Früh aufkommen und dann den ganzen Tag wach und intelligent bleiben, am Abend eine willige Einheit zu machen, als Vorleser, ohne Maske, ohne Orchester. (F.384/5:29)

DER VORLESER

Ich muß sie alle vereinen,
die ich einzeln nicht gelten lasse.
Aus tausend, die jeder was meinen,
mach' ich eine fühlende Masse.
Ob der oder jener mich lobe,

ist für die Wirkung egal.
Schimpft alle in der Garderobe,
ihr war't mir doch wehrlos im Saal! (F.472/3:23)

Diese [die Masse] mag, wenn es vorüber ist, in Einzelne zerfallen, deren
Urteil und Tonfall von neuem die Erregung rechtfertigt, aber im Saal
schließen sie sich zu jener Hörfähigkeit ... (F.374/5:29)

I could gather together at my lectures the worst people you could get hold of
on a Saturday in the Volkstheater: I am absolutely convinced that they
would obey me in listening ... and that not until they were in the cloakroom
would they put on their old opinions again.

Just think, however, what it means to take people who get up every morning and then stay awake and intelligent all day and unite them into a
willing, homogeneous unit in the evening, as a reciter, without a mask,
without an orchestra.

THE RECITER

I must unite them all whom I don't accept as individuals. Out of a
thousand, each of whom has his own opinion, I make one feeling mass of
people. Whether the one or the other praises me is unimportant for the
effect. By all means grumble in the cloakroom, you were still in my power
in the auditorium!

This [the mass of people] may, when the performance is over, disintegrate
into individuals whose judgment and intonation justify my rage again,
but in the auditorium they close ranks and become capable of hearing ...

At one point, in a punning sentence that cannot be adequately translated,
Kraus even claimed that he was performing only for his own ears and that it
was a mere concomitant that, in doing so, he also *insulted* (not read to) an
audience: 'Ihnen, den Einzelnen, könnte ichs nicht vorlesen, aber mir selbst
bringe ichs zu Gehör und der Masse sage ichs ins Gesicht' (F.374/5:29).
   As for the effect of his lectures, Kraus seems almost self-consciously
negative and pessimistic. For the most part – as we have seen– he insisted that
the spell was broken as soon as the mass disintegrated into individuals,
who, perhaps in self-defence, had to take up their old attitudes and clichés
again. His lectures might have some unsettling after-effects – 'Was ... mit
nach Hause genommen wird, wirkt nach und stört späterhin Schlaf und Verdauung' (F.374/5:29) – but even if the audience experienced a catharsis
('Reinigung der Leidenschaften,' F.384/5:29), it had no lasting effect.
   The most positive result of his lectures, in Kraus's view, was the magical,

theatrical creation of an 'audience' through the rhythmical effect of the words
he spoke. It should be especially noted that Kraus did not seek to make the
audience *understand*; in his words, the masses could not and should not understand. 'Die Masse kann nicht und soll nicht verstehen. Sie leistet genug,
wenn sie sich aus trüben Einzelnen zu jenem Theaterpublikum zusammenschließt, das der unentbehrliche Koeffizient schauspielerischen Wertes ist'
(*F*.384/5:28). [The masses cannot and should not understand. They accomplish
enough when they cease to be dreary individuals and amalgamate into that
theatre audience which is the indispensable coefficient of good acting.] The
effect he describes is a musical one, based on rhythm – a dynamic appeal to
the whole psyche rather than to reason.

Dieses Publikum ... bewährt sich am besten dort, wo es von der
rhythmischen Wirkung der Pflicht jedes Verständnisses überhoben wird:
an den gedanklich schwersten, aber von der dynamischen Welle zu jeder
Psyche getragenen Stücken, gegen deren Stofflichkeit, deren 'Tendenz'
die fünfhundert Einzelnen rebellieren müßen. (Ibid)

This audience stands the test best there where the rhythmical effect
relieves it of the duty of any understanding: in those plays which are
intellectually most difficult but which are carried by a dynamic wave to
each psyche, and against whose subject-matter and 'message' the five hundred individuals would have to rebel.

In an aphorism from the same period, Kraus made music rather than words
the unifying factor in creating an audience out of individuals: 'Die
Viechsarbeit, neunhundert Menschen, die aus dem Bureau kommen, zur
Empfänglichkeit für das Wort zusammenzuschließen, hat nicht das Wort,
sondern die Musik zu besorgen' (*F*.389/90:41). [The beastly job of uniting
nine hundred people who come from the office and making them receptive to
the word is something not for the word but for music to achieve.]

Some doubts as to the viability of Kraus's position as a critic arise when one
looks a little more closely at this 'musical effect' for which he seemed to be
striving. Although he was probably right that music was a factor in suspend-
ing disbelief, differences, and reason in a crowd, and that music could,
therefore, have a unifying effect on a group of individuals, he was on dangerous ground in desiring the same result from words. What he wanted was,
on the one hand, a completely 'subjective' reaction from his audience – that is,
from a crowd into which all individuality had been submerged – and, on the
other hand, an opportunity to be the 'objective' instigator and the leader of
this subjectivity. What emerges is the prototype of a demagogic situation.
One can of course argue that Kraus had a very strong ethical sense and would
never abuse his powers. But the lecturer who relies on the magical, theat-

rical power of the word rather than on the cogency of his arguments is too closely akin to the political agitator, and the perfect audiences that Kraus tried to create seem uncomfortably like those that were enthralled by Hitler in the 1930s. Here lie some of the pitfalls of Kraus's theatricality.

CONTEMPORARY PLAYS AND PLAYWRIGHTS

The period from 1910 to 1918 was not distinguished by any new development in Kraus's attitude towards contemporary plays and playwrights. Since Kraus rarely visited the theatre or, as far as we know, read modern plays, his remarks about dramas or dramatists had to be less than specific. As usual, he depended on newspaper reports, picking up statements about productions, works, or authors that he could then lampoon or with which he could violently disagree. Predictably, there were ethical implications behind the criticism of artistic inadequacies.

Although Kraus made no reference to any particular play by Strindberg, his admiration for him continued. He published *Eselsdorf*, a one-acter by Strindberg, which appeared the day before that dramatist's death (*F*.349/50: 24–40). At the memorial service on 4 June 1912, he read from some of Strindberg's works. He prefaced these readings with a foreword of his own, which he then published in *Die Fackel* no. 351/3 (pp. 1–3), and which consisted mostly of a clever analysis of the dichotomy of the sexes: the incompleteness of man bothered Strindberg so much that he strove to find the solution in woman, and the chaotic result became the poet's world. 'Er [Adam/ Strindberg] mußte der Nacht verfallen und dem Weib, um auch dort Gott zu erleben ... Er war am Weibe zum Chaos geworden, das Welt wurde im Dichter.' [He (Adam/Strindberg) had to become the slave of night and of woman, in order to be able to experience God there, too ... With woman he became chaos, which became a cosmos in the poet.] This is a very impressionistic piece of prose, and after reading it, we are left none the wiser as to why Kraus admired the dramatist.

Kraus's positive opinion of Wedekind, too, remained unchanged. In *Die Fackel* no. 370/1 (pp. 23–7), Kraus commented on Hugo Heller's production of Wedekind's *Büchse der Pandora*, a production which was supposed to be a 'cultural milestone,' since Heller had had to fight the censors to get permission to stage the play. Kraus pronounced himself in favour of the censors, who protected the play and the playwright from the indiscriminate audiences of Heller's performance. He contrasted what he suspected were Heller's sensationalist motives with his own when he produced the play in 1905.

Ich wollte weder einen Dichter vor der Zensur retten, noch auch durch diese Absicht meinen Kundenkreis vergrößern ... Ich hatte nie einen Markstein

etablieren wollen. Und dennoch gelang mir Ähnliches. Denn die Zensur-
verhältnisse blieben zwar nach meinen zwei Aufführungen der 'Büchse der
Pandora' dieselben, aber ein Dichter war aus dem Dasein eines in Kaba-
rettkreisen geschätzten Gitarrenspielers in das sichtbare Hiersein des
bedeutendsten deutschen Dramatikers eingetreten.

I wanted neither to save a poet from censorship nor even to increase the
number of my customers in this way ... I had never wanted to establish a
landmark. And yet I succeeded in doing something similar. For although
conditions of censorship stayed the same after my two performances of
Pandora's Box, a writer who had been admired in cabaret circles as a guitar
player was revealed as the most important German dramatist.

Kraus then reprinted reviews of the Heller production, most of which agreed
that Kraus's production had been better.

However, Kraus had nothing new to say about Wedekind. This was perhaps
because Wedekind himself had nothing new to say, but this surely would
have been reason for criticism. Also, the occasion of the Heller production
seemed to interest Kraus primarily because it offered him the opportunity
for self-praise. Indeed, he took great delight in reminding his readers of everything that he had done for his own production of *Büchse der Pandora,* when
he had been producer, assistant director, dramaturge, actor, and lecturer, and
had transformed a lecture hall into a theatre.

As for Gerhart Hauptmann, Kraus was always ready to defend him against
the criticism of someone like Goldmann (*F*.354/6:45–6) or the praise of
Bahr (*F*.363/5:56–9). He still admired, and read in his Theater der Dichtung,
Hannele, Die Weber, and *Pippa,* and he still rejected the later Hauptmann
plays. For example, under the title *Drei Engel – drei Räuber oder Gerhart*
Hauptmanns Höllenfahrt, Kraus juxtaposed two passages from Hauptmann,
one from 1894, in which three angels sang of the beauty of earth and
heaven, and one from 1914 about three robbers, 'a Frenchman,' 'a black Rus-
sian,' 'an Englishman,' who were out to rob Germany of her honour.
However, Hauptmann's nationalism during the war years and his weakness
for recognition from the Concordia (*F*.363/5:56–9) evoked sadness rather
than anger from Kraus.

Kraus continued to attack Hermann Bahr whenever the occasion presented
itself and frequently extended his polemics against Bahr to include writers
his bête noire had praised. One victim of these tactics was Hofmannsthal,
and the issue was again ethical rather than aesthetic.

On 16 July 1914 one week before the Austrian ultimatum to Serbia,[21]
Bahr had written an open letter, 'Gruß an Hofmannsthal,' to his friend which
was published in a number of newspapers. Beginning with the sentence, 'I
know only that you are in arms, dear Hugo' ('Ich weiß nur, daß Sie in Waffen

sind, lieber Hugo'), the letter attests to Bahr's patriotic fervour and celebrates the sense of comradeship generated by the impending war. Bahr addressed Hofmannsthal as if he were on his way to Poland and gave him greetings to a mutual friend, Leopold Andrian, the Austrian consul-general in Warsaw, and the same Andrian von Werburg who in 1918 became general manager of the Viennese theatres. This letter, which strikes us now, nearly seventy years later, as rather silly, pretentious, and totally unimportant, was reprinted in spring 1916, and infuriated Kraus to such an extent that he devoted twelve pages of the May issue of *Die Fackel* to a severe attack on both writers involved, under the title 'Gruß an Bahr und Hofmannsthal' (*F.423/ 5:41–52*). Kraus accused Bahr of hypocrisy, claiming that he had known that Hofmansthal was neither in active service nor anywhere near Warsaw and that he had suggested that the poet was on his way east for the sole purpose of casting him in the image of a war hero. Not content, however, with condemning Bahr, Kraus went on to satirize Hofmannsthal, accusing him, among other things, of being a coward while trying to look like a brave 'warrior' in the service of his country. He should, Kraus argued, have responded immediately by a public letter correcting the facts, that is, stating that he was neither in active service nor at the front.

Kraus then extended his attack to include Hofmannsthal's literary activities: the libretti he had written for Richard Strauß, his use of Greek subjects for some of his plays, his eulogies of great Austrians,[22] his plans for an Austrian almanach and for a series of books ('Österreichische Bibliothek') designed to keep alive the roots of Austria's past. The diatribe ends with the complete rejection of Hofmannsthal both as a person and as a spokesman of his country.

> [Hofmannsthal] ist eines der hervorragendsten Beispiele aus der Armee von Literaten, die zur Verherrlichung von Ereignissen ausgesendet wurden, welche sie um keinen Preis erleben möchten ... (*F.423/5:51*)

> Er, der nie mehr war als ein tauglicher Übersetzer fremder Werte oder ihr kunstgebildeter Vertreter, nie mehr als der gefällige Platzhalter eines vor ihm gegebenen Niveaus ... (Ibid, pp. 51 f)

> Österreich irrt wie immer, wenn es in einem, der heute eben noch die Geschicklichkeit hat, sich mit Landesfarben zu schminken, seinen geistigen Vertreter sieht. (Ibid, p. 52)

[Hofmannsthal] is one of the most prominent examples from the army of men of letters who were sent out to glorify events which they would not want to experience at any price ...

[Hofmannsthal], who was never more than the competent translator of foreign values or their tasteful travelling salesman, never more than the obliging representative of a standard that had been established before his time and with which nature had never felt comfortable ...

Austria is mistaken as always when it sees its spiritual representative in someone who nowadays only just still has the skill to paint himself in the colours of his country.

The facts behind this incident are not easy to evaluate. It was of course well known in 1916 that Hofmannsthal had a desk job with the Austrian Ministry of War; but Bahr may have been less dishonest than Kraus made him out to be: on 26 July 1914, Hofmannsthal had reported at Pisino (Pazin) on the Istrian peninsula for service as an officer in the militia and was only subsequently transferred to the Kriegsfürsorgeamt. Thus, when Bahr wrote his letter, he may well have had reason to believe that Hofmannsthal was 'in Waffen,' and he was unlikely to know where his friend was; moreover, a reference to a possible visit to the Austrian consul in Warsaw did not suggest armed combat either in July 1914 or in May 1916. In any case, while Kraus reprinted the whole of Bahr's letter in *Die Fackel*, he did not reveal his source, and we do not know whether Hofmannsthal had seen it. Of course one can well understand Kraus's indignation with all those writers who glorified the war effort from the safety of an office desk in Vienna, and it was only when Hofmannsthal became associated with the Austrian war machine that Kraus's rejection of him turned to hatred; but Kraus had been critical of Hofmannsthal long before the war, and as there is no evidence that he either saw Hofmannsthal's plays and the operas based on his libretti or that he read the texts, it is difficult not to feel that his aversion was based on a prejudice nurtured by second-hand reports in the press. Kraus's intermittent campaigns against Hofmannsthal support such an interpretation, as they proceeded largely by hints and innuendos. Thus, when Hofmannsthal became interested in writing scripts for films, Kraus denied any artistic intent on the poet's part, and, on what seem to be purely malicious grounds, reduced his interest to a financial one: 'Denn daß Herr von Hofmannsthal seine Kunst in einen Dienst gestellt hat und zwar in den des Films, beweist nicht, daß das Kino literarischen, sondern daß Herr von Hofmannsthal kaufmännischen Ehrgeiz hat' (*F*.391/2:18–19). [For that Mr von Hofmannsthal has put his art into a service, namely that of the film, does not show that the cinema has literary ambitions, but rather that Mr von Hofmannsthal has commercial ones.] Or, in the following aphorism, he criticized Hofmannsthal's borrowing from others: 'Die eigenen Lorbeern ließen Herrn v. H. nicht schlafen, aber

auf fremden ruhte er gern aus' (F.360/2:18). [His own laurels did not let
Mr v. H. sleep, but he would like to rest on those of others.]

At best, Kraus criticized Hofmannsthal on the grounds that his 'classical
style' was dated. The journalists and businessmen who inhabited every coffee-
house in Berlin and Vienna spoke like him and even better than he.

> *Das Dionysische ist schäbig geworden und das Apollinische ist auch nicht
> mehr das, was es einmal war. Die gesammelten Werke des Herrn von
> Hofmannsthal ... erscheinen zu spät. Dieser Dichter ist wahrlich nicht zu
> beneiden. Als er siebzehn Jahre zählte, stand er unbeweglich auf der Son-
> nenhöhe des Goetheschen Lebens. Später wurde das Monument gelen-
> ker. Jetzt, wo es Feuilletons und Libretti schreiben möchte, ... muß es sehen,
> daß die geborenen Geschäftsleute es noch besser können. Es ist das
> Schicksal jener, die als Niveau zur Welt kommen, übertroffen zu werden
> ... Wenn Herr von Hofmannsthal seine gesammelten Werke lesen wird,
> wird er erschrecken. Er wird spüren, wie binnen einer Stunde heute
> gerade der veralten kann, dem der Mund von neuen Rhythmen übergeht.
> Die Herren, die in Berliner und in Wiener Kaffeehäusern über Ewigkeits-
> werte und Placierungsmöglichkeiten sprechen, wissen Bescheid und ihre
> Fingernägel haben den Blütenstaub der Bienen des Hymettos. (F.351/
> 3:27–8)*

The Dionysian has become shabby and the Apollonian is no more what it
used to be. The collected works of Mr von Hofmannsthal ... are appearing too late. This poet is surely not to be envied. When he was seventeen
years old he stood firmly planted on the apogee of a Goethean life. Later
the monument became more flexible. Now, when it would like to write
feuilletons and libretti ... it has to see that born business people can do
that even better. Being surpassed is the fate of those who came into the
world as a standard ... When Mr von Hofmannsthal reads his collected
works, he will be shocked. He will sense how within an hour today that very
person whose mouth overflows with new rhythms can become old-
fashioned. The gentlemen who talk about eternal values and marketing
possibilities in Berlin and Vienna coffee-houses know the score, and the
pollen of the bees of Hymettus is under their fingernails.

At worst, Kraus was blindly prejudiced and even cruel. For example, given his
dislike of Reinhardt and his spectacular showmanship, it is easy to see that
Kraus was bound to reject Hofmannsthal's *Jedermann*, staged in 1911[23] by
Reinhardt's 'miracle business' ('Mirakel-Geschäft').[24] Or, in *Die Fackel* no.
311/12 (pp. 52–3), he called Hofmannsthal's work an 'aesthete's bluff' and
stated that his poem 'Zum Gedächtnis eines Schauspielers' read like a
banality from a feuilleton. He then proceeded to make fun of Hofmannsthal's

sensitivity, coupling it with business. 'So viel Impressionabilität und so viel Fragilität wird sicherlich zum Libretto des "Rosenkavalier" getaugt haben. Man kann auf ein höchst exklusives und empfindsames Geschäft gefaßt sein.' [So much impressionability and so much fragility were undoubtedly the right stuff for the libretto of *Rosenkavalier*. We can be prepared for a highly exclusive and sentimental business.] Kraus criticized other critics for their lack of ethics, but this type of criticism is just as unethical.

Although Kraus rejected Schnitzler less savagely than he did Hofmannsthal, he again proceeded by means of evidence gleaned from hearsay and tactics based on innuendo and suggestion. Kraus boasted of having neither seen nor read Schnitzler's *Professor Bernhardi*; since the critics had applauded the play, he concluded that it must be bad. In a short article entitled 'Fern sei es von mir, den "Professor Bernhardi" zu lesen,' he claimed that if he were to read the play, he would feel obliged to quote from it and thus to expose its weaknesses. He called his ability to reveal through quotation 'this secret power that enables me to make German-Austrian authors unpopular before God and man' (F.368/9:1).

There was only one occasion in this period when Kraus wrote about Schnitzler at length, in an article entitled 'Schnitzler-Feier' (F.351/3:77–88); as the title suggests, however, this article did not really deal with Schnitzler's writings themselves, but rather with other critics' evaluations of Schnitzler. From Kraus's reactions to the critics' praise of Schnitzler, we can deduce his reasons for disliking this author, but his criticism tends to be general and impressionistic, proceeding from the particular only in that it takes as its starting point the statement of an individual critic; it never gets as far as a reasoned evaluation of any of Schnitzler's works.

Kraus admitted that Schnitzler was basically a decent person and that he did not take part in the general rush towards financial gain, journalism, and back-patting. Therefore, he did not have any *direct* ethical reason for rejecting Schnitzler. Indirectly, however, he censured him on ethical grounds, contending, for example, that Schnitzler must have something in common with the deficient personalities he attracted:

> er (hat) sich nie um jene zweifelhaften Subsidien mangelnder Persönlichkeit umgesehen ... sondern ... sie (sind) zu ihm gekommen ... Schnitzler ist von ihnen umringt und sitzt in der Fülle aller Leere ... Eine Verwandtschaft mit ihm muß die Welt so hingerissen haben, daß sie ihm entgegenkam. (F.351/3:88)

He never looked around for those dubious subsidies that make up for a lack of personality ... but rather ... they came to him ... Schnitzler is surrounded by them and sits in the fullness of their emptiness ... It must be a kinship with him that so enchanted the world that it came to meet him.

Indeed, throughout Kraus's criticism of Schnitzler there run two seemingly contradictory threads concerning 'blame.' On the one hand, following the example of the statement just quoted, Schnitzler was somehow held responsible for the critics' banality of interpretation, for the 'cliché which demolished him':

> *und wenngleich Schnitzler gewiß besser ist als jene, die ihn so richtig verstehen, so hat sein Werk doch Anteil an der Banalität einer Auffassung, die es mit der zweifelhaften Geistigkeit der Medizin zu verklären sucht.* (Ibid, p. 79)

> *Es ist ein Aberglaube, daß der Künstler für das Klischee nicht verantwortlich ist, das mit ihm fertig wird ...* (Ibid, p. 81)

And although Schnitzler is certainly better than those who understand him so well, his work shares in the banality of an interpretation that seeks to glorify it with the dubious spirituality of medicine.

It is a superstition that the artist is not responsible for the cliché which demolishes him ...

On the other hand, Kraus claimed that Schnitzler's success was due to the fact that the times were out of joint, so that it was the times, not Schnitzler, that were to 'blame' for his success: 'Unsere Explosionen haben keine Ursache mehr. Die Zeit ist ein Knockabout; eine Flaumfeder fällt, und die Erde dröhnt. Wie kann ein Zarter so von Begeisterung umtobt werden?' (ibid, p. 77). [Our explosions no longer have a cause. The times are a knockabout; a down feather falls and the earth rumbles. How can a delicate soul create such an uproar of enthusiasm?]

Most of Kraus's criticism of Schnitzler can be reduced to what Kraus judged to be Schnitzler's lack of greatness. In Kraus's opinion, this stemmed not only from an artistic deficiency but also from an ethical one which Schnitzler had in common with the society which formed the subject of his plays. Kraus expressed this criticism in several ways. He missed in Schnitzler's works the heights and the depths. Schnitzler's 'erotic psychology' was not capable of a metaphysical perspective. His works, with their good taste and well-chiselled external form, had nothing to do with the chaos of life and the power of the spirit of language. His poetic 'strength' was based on and bound by the weakness and pettiness of the world which he described – the Vienna of the turn of the century.

> *Arthur Schnitzler, ein konzentrierter Schwächezustand ...* (Ibid, p. 77)

> *Schnitzlers Seichtigkeit war das Abziehbild eines Jahrzehnts der schlechten Gesellschaft und als solches von Wert für ein weiteres Jahrzehnt;*

Schnitzlers Esprit war die Form der für ein Zeitalter endgiltigen Männer-
schwäche. (Ibid, p. 78)

(Das Leben) läßt sich nicht in allegorische Artigkeiten 'einfangen', und
hat überhaupt etwas gegen diese Beschäftigung, deren Schlagwort die
Marke aller um Schnitzler gruppierten Literatur ist. (Ibid, p. 80)

Was haben die Laubsägearbeiten der Schnitzler und Abschnitzler mit
dem Chaos zu schaffen? Was die Sorgfalt der äußern Form mit der ordnen-
den Gewalt des Sprachgeists? Was geht den guten Geschmack die Kunst
an? (Ibid, p. 80)

Hier ächzt nur als schmerzliche Neugierde intellektueller Nerven, was in
den großen Versuchern als die tragische Sehnsucht wehrhafter Gehirne
brüllt. Es ist nur – wenngleich in der ehrlichsten und saubersten Art –
der Typus, der aus einem fehlenden Ich zwei macht. (Ibid, p. 85)

Arthur Schnitzler, a concentrated condition of weakness ...

Schnitzler's shallowness was the transfer-picture of a decade of bad society
and as such it is of value for a further decade; Schnitzler's *esprit* was the
form for an age of definitive male weakness.

(Life) doesn't let itself be ensnared in allegorical niceties and is quite generally opposed to this activity, whose catch-phrase is the mark of all literature grouped around Schnitzler.

What does the fretwork of these whittlers ['Schnitzler'] and chisellers
have to do with chaos? What does the care bestowed on external form have
to do with the organizing power of the spirit of language? Of what
concern is art to good taste?

What in great tempters roars as the tragic longing of well-armed brains
here merely moans as the pained curiosity of an intellectual's nerves.
Though in the most honest and decent way [Schnitzler] is merely the type
who makes two out of the one individuality that is lacking.

Kraus also pointed out some supposed fallacies in the critics' praise of
Schnitzler. For example, critics had claimed a connection between Schnitzler's
professional insights as a physician and his poetic abilities. Kraus contended
that one did not have to be a specialist in order to be a good writer. This is a
criticism similar to the one he made of naturalism – that an exact depiction
of milieu and dialect did not make great art.

Um Dichter zu sein, muß man nicht eigens Laryngologie studiert haben
... Wenn man selbst in der Medizin gedanklich weiter vorgedrungen wäre,
als der Beruf erfordert und erlaubt, so würde das noch immer nichts

neben der geistigen Eigenmächtigkeit bedeuten, die im künstlerischen Schaffen begründet ist. (Ibid, p. 79)

In order to be a good writer, one need not have gone out of one's way to study laryngology ... Even if a person had a more profound grasp of medicine than the medical profession demands and allows, that would still mean nothing compared with the intellectual autonomy that is bestowed by artistic creativity.

In Kraus's opinion, the critics were also wrong in expecting too much of Schnitzler, since his field was a narrow one: 'die Bedeutung Schnitzlers als eines Befreiers gebundener Unkraft, Dichters eines bestimmten Lebenscottages, soll nicht geleugnet werden. Merkwürdig in die Irre geht diese Intimität nur, wenn sie höhere Anforderungen an ihren Dichter stellt ...' (ibid, p. 82). [The importance of Schnitzler as the liberator of fettered weakness, as the poet of the life that goes on in certain suburban villas, is not to be disputed. This narrow circle goes strangely wrong only when it makes higher demands on its poet ...] Those who hoped that he would one day write 'pure comedy' were mistaken; the true comedian's laugh must (like Nestroy's) be metaphysical – that is, it must come from *above* the situation used by the dramatist. 'Schnitzlers Humor wird keine Verwirrung stiften. Schnitzler blickt jetzt empor. Aber hat etwa der Autor des "Reigen" die Hoffnung auf die große Lache geweckt, zu der nur der Blick von oben auf die Menschlichkeiten fähig wäre?' (ibid, p. 83). [Schnitzler's humour will never create confusion. Schnitzler is now looking up. But did the author of *Der Reigen* ever awaken the hope for truly great laughter, of which only the view from above down on to human nature would be capable?]

Kraus accused Schnitzler of believing that men were marionettes manipulated by the 'great puppeteer' who held all the strings, that fate was to blame for events, instead of showing that man himself was responsible for his problems and failures.

Ich glaube, daß ... die fertige Vorstellung, daß 'der große Puppenspieler uns alle an unsichtbaren Fäden hält', nur eine Ausrede für das schuldbewußte Unvermögen ist, die Stricke zu sehen, mit denen wir uns strangulieren. Wenn die höhere Macht, deren Hand uns zu fassen kriegt, ein Dichter ist, dann braucht er die Verantwortung nicht auf das Schicksal abzuwälzen, und dann erst hat er das Recht, es zu tun. (Ibid, pp. 78–9)

I believe that the ready-made notion that 'the great puppeteer holds us all by invisible threads' is only an excuse for an inability he knew he was guilty of, the inability to see the ropes with which we strangle ourselves. If the higher power whose hand gets hold of us is a poet, then he does not need to slough responsibility off on fate, and it is only then that he has the right to do so.

And, finally, Kraus protested against what the critics – and he himself –
took to be Schnitzler's formula: that each person must find within himself his
own way 'ins Freie.'

*Das Zitat, das in den meisten Festartikeln wiederkehrte, ist wirklich 'die
Formel Schnitzlers': diese Predigt der 'Unbeirrtheit'. Sie könnte das
Erlebnis eines großen Ethikers sein, aber er würde sie schwerlich in solchem
Text halten: 'Jeder muß selber zusehen, wie er herausfindet aus seinem
Ärger, aus seiner Verzweiflung, oder aus seinem Ekel, irgendwohin, wo er
wieder frei aufatmen kann. Solche Wanderungen ins Freie lassen sich
nicht gemeinsam unternehmen, denn die Straßen laufen ja nicht im Lande
draußen, sondern in uns selbst. Es kommt nur für jeden darauf an,
seinen inneren Weg zu finden. Dazu ist es notwendig, möglichst klar in sich
zu sehen, den Mut seiner eigenen Natur zu haben, sich nicht beirren zu
lassen.' (Ibid, p. 84)*

The quotation that recurred in most of the articles in his honour is really
Schnitzler's formula: this sermon of 'doing one's own thing.' It could be the
experience of a great moralist, but he would be unlikely to preach it in
such a text: 'A person must see to it for himself how he finds his way out of
his trouble, out of his despair, or out of his disgust to some place or other
where he can breathe freely again. Such hikes into the open cannot be
undertaken in company, because the roads are not to be found out there
in the country, but in ourselves. For each person it is only a question of
finding his inner way. For this it is necessary to have as clear an insight
into oneself as possible, to have the courage of one's own nature, to not let
oneself be led astray.'

Kraus did not give clear grounds for doubting this view; his reasons, however,
must be linked with his rejection of psychology in general, with his conviction, already noted, that Schnitzler's erotic psychology was not capable of a
truly metaphysical perspective.

*Die erotische Psychologie geht auf eine Nußschale der Erkenntnis, langt
darum nicht zum Aphorismus, nur zur Skizze, deren Technik über dem
Wiener Feuilleton, deren Einfall unter dem französischen Dialog steht.
Dieser Humor geschlechtlicher Dinge lebt von der Terminologie und erst
recht von der durch Gedankenstriche verschwiegenen. Dieser Blick auf
Physiologisches kommt nicht von der Höhe, und darum kommt auch die
Metaphysik Schnitzlers nicht von den Abgründen. Schnitzlers Séparée
und Schnitzlers Kosmos sind von einem Wurzellosen angeschaut.*
(Ibid, pp. 83–4)

Erotic psychology goes for a mere nutshell of knowledge, and so doesn't
suffice for the aphorism. It is only enough for a sketch, the technique of

which is superior to Viennese feuilleton, while its ideas are inferior to
French dialogue. This humour based on sexual matters lives on its terminology, and even more so on that part of its terminology that is replaced by
dashes. This view of the physiological doesn't come from above, and therefore Schnitzler's metaphysics never comes from the depths. Schnitzler's
chambre séparée and Schnitzler's cosmos are viewed by someone without
roots.

A similar view was expressed by Kraus at a later date, in the eassy 'Die Litera-
turlüge auf dem Theater,' when he was criticizing Hebbel's play *Judith*.
'Denn immer noch dürfte das Dramatische, trotz allem, was die deutsche
Bildung so seit Jahrzehnten zugelernt hat, viel eher eine Beschäftigung der
Sprache als der Psychologie sein' (F.457/61:54). [For drama should still be a
pursuit of language rather than psychology, in spite of everything that
German educated minds have been learning for decades.] Kraus was opposed
to taking the science of the psyche or ego as an ontological basis. For him, it
was language that led to the essence of being and provided the metaphysical
dimension necessary for art and life.

Kraus, however, is surely mistaken in ascribing to Schnitzler himself all the
undesirable traits of the Vienna evoked in Schnitzler's plays. He failed to
see that the dramatist himself criticized rather than condoned this society, and
that he was doing so by means of the language that was used all around
him.[25] The decadence and spiritual emptiness of a character such as Anatol and
of the society which he represented is revealed to the audience in, for
example, his conversation with Gabriele in the scene 'Weihnachtseinkäufe.'
Schnitzler accomplished this in a very quiet way; his was not the parodistic,
sledge-hammer technique of Kraus. When Kraus let his characters talk (in *Die
letzten Tage der Menschheit* for instance) the language they spoke was
caricatured and the cliché exaggerated to such an extent that it risked producing the opposite effect to that intended by the dramatist, that is, the brutal-
ization of the reader's (or the spectator's) sensitivity by constant battering.
Here lay the dangers of 'oversell.' Schnitzler, however, risked over-subtlety,
and it took perhaps a finer eye and a more patient ear than Kraus's to ferret
out what he was criticizing in the characters he portrayed. In this case, Kraus
showed himself incapable of subtlety: he was betrayed by his own theatricality. For, although a high regard and even love of language was a major
factor in his life, his love of the theatrical – the bold, the exclamatory,
gesture and mimicry – was just as strong, and sometimes blinded him to the
subtler linguistic accomplishments of others.

George Bernard Shaw came to be an example for Kraus of a bad and even a
false satirist – he was clever but never penetrated beyond surfaces and appearances to the essence. Therefore he, too, lacked a metaphysical dimension
in his work.

In Kraus's opinion, Shaw's irony, his turning morality topsy-turvy, was dubious, if not downright immoral. Although both he and Shaw, as well as Nestroy, attacked some of the same problems (for example, hypocrisy), Kraus persisted in denigrating him. On the last page of the essay 'Nestroy und die Nachwelt,' Kraus accused Shaw of shallowness, superficiality, and arrogance, contrasting him with Nestroy and assigning him a place in the inferior times that had followed the age of the great Austrian satirist.

Herr Bernhard Shaw garantiert für die Überflüssigkeit alles dessen, was sich zwischen Wachen und Schlafen als notwendig herausstellen könnte. Seiner und aller seichten Ironie ist keine Tiefe unergründlich, seiner und aller Flachen Hochmut keine Höhe unerreichbar. Überall läßt sichs irdisch lachen. (F.349/50:23)

Mr Bernard Shaw is a guarantee for the superfluity of all that which could turn out to be necessary between waking and sleeping. For his irony and that of all superficial people no depth is unfathomable, for his arrogance and that of all shallow people no height is unattainable. Everywhere there is worldly laughter.

The final sentence referring to Shaw, 'Überall läßt sichs irdisch lachen' contrasts with the last sentence of the essay, '[Nestroy] lacht metaphysisch.' However, in his own satirical remarks about Shaw, Kraus himself was often quite superficial. For example, Trebitsch, of whose work Kraus had a low opinion, had translated many of Shaw's plays into German and Kraus several times referred to Shaw as 'Trebitsch translated into English.' Such a remark rapidly becomes stale.

Kraus's criticism of Shaw contains some of the same weaknesses as did that of Hofmannsthal and of Schnitzler. It is based on generalization and lacks specific detail. He still relied on the critiques of others for his information about the dramatist and his works; indeed, there is no evidence that he ever saw a performance of a play by Shaw. We cannot be certain that his antagonism towards Shaw did not proceed from his already established dislike for Shaw's translator, Trebitsch. If this was the case, then his criticism is pure prejudice and Kraus, as a critic, was far more dubious than 'der dubiöse Herr Shaw' (F.341/2:34).

While the present reader cannot but deplore the fact that Kraus reacted to the theatre of Hofmannsthal, Schnitzler, and Shaw with moral indignation rather than sympathetic understanding, there were plays then being performed in Vienna and elsewhere to which he had cause to object: propaganda plays such as *Freier Dienst* by Leo Feld (F.418/22: 100–4) and *Könige* by Hans Müller (F.445/53:60; F.454/6:8) that had been written, with inferior artistry and excruciatingly bad taste, in order to support the war effort. That these plays should exploit the blood of fallen soldiers to earn royalties represented for Kraus some of the most obvious evidence of the moral and spiritual leprosy of his contemporaries. 'Von Blut Tantièmen kriegen – daß solches geschehe, hat eine erbarmungslose Untermenschheit geduldet ...' (*F.418/22:102*). That a war playwright such as Hans Müller could claim to be a soldier, to know the reality of the trenches, and could even appear before an audience in the uniform of a soldier at the performance of one of his patriotic dramas, when, in reality, he wrote his war reports and his war plays from the safety of the city and had never been near the frontlines, and that such a playwright could be acclaimed by his contemporaries revealed an abysmal lack of ethics both on his part and on that of his contemporaries. What is interesting, however, in Kraus's handling of war playwrights and of plays that glorified war and propagated patriotism (especially during the First World War) is not that he rejected them – such an observation would be trivial – but rather that they brought him up so abruptly against the problem of illusion and reality with which he had to grapple.

The theme of illusion and reality presented itself to Kraus in many forms: dream/reality, play/reality, theatre/war, war/play, language/reality, as well as sentimentality/brutality, good/evil, and God/Satan. For everyone concerned with theatre and drama, it was a natural theme, since 'play' itself involves the suspension of disbelief and the pretence that the action on stage has a reality of its own. According to Kraus, the confusion of the two opposing factors of illusion and reality came about when producers and audience obscured the dichotomy with the criterion of realism (a realism which in Kraus's opinion was false) and, in so doing, confused realism both with play or illusion on the one hand and with reality on the other. What was thereby – unintentionally – unmasked for Kraus was a vision of a reality so horrible that the viewer must wonder if this could be real, or if it were just a nightmare or an invention of his imagination. This was particularly evident in two contemporary theatre productions. In both, actors were replaced by real soldiers, who then 'played' (that is, pretended to be) real soldiers. In the theatre, they enacted war, a 'pretend' war, which was, however, staged with a false realism to appear genuine and real.

The Munich production of *Der Hias* was reprehensible enough in this regard (*F.426/30:7–10*). Written by a German soldier and performed in 1916 by officers and men of the reserve, the play was about a Bavarian officer, Hias, during the war. Kraus reprinted the report that praised the 'genuineness' of the production: 'was uns bei diesem Theater so mächtig packt, ist der *frische Zug*, der es durchweht, ist die *Ursprünglichkeit und Echtheit*, die ihm anhaften. Es ist Theater und doch keines, vielmehr *in höherem Sinne wahrhaftiges Leben*, das durch die unbeholfene Darstellung nur noch gewinnt.' [What moves us so tremendously in this play is the *fresh breeze* that wafts through it, is the *originality and genuineness* which characterize it. It is theatre and yet it isn't, but rather, *in a higher sense, it is real life,* which only gains from the awkwardness of the production.] Not only did the report claim that the play was really *like* war, since real soldiers were playing, but also that it was genuinely Bavarian. While war was going on in the background, a Bavarian *Schuhplattler* was danced and two soldiers 'played' the role of two young Bavarian girls. '*Und während* ... ein unverfälscht bayrischer *Schuhplattler* getanzt wird – dabei *zwei Soldaten als fesche Dearndln* – arbeitet am Offizierstische das *Feldtelefon* ... arbeitet die Kriegsmaschine ihren eisernen, unerbittlichen Gang!' [*And while* ... a genuine Bavarian *Schuhplattler* is being danced – in which *two soldiers played cute Bavarian girls* – the field telephone keeps ringing at the officer's desk ... the war machine keeps going, inflexibly and inexorably, in full swing!] All proceeds from the performance went to 'military welfare institutions'!

Kraus saw that even the illusion of realism was not genuine and that the play's 'realistic' portrayal of war was false – fake folksiness, fake *Dearndl*, war with its claws removed, without blood and killing. But this very lack of genuineness was the most effective reminder for him of how horrible war was and how superficial and false the society which spawned it. Kraus saw war as a theatre; he employed the Munich production of *Der Hias* to reveal the 'greater play,' to expose, through 'true' re-enactment, the falseness and murder propagated by contemporary German society. In *Die Fackel*, Kraus used *Der Hias* to perform the same function as the play within a play in *Hamlet* – a parallel which he then developed:

> *der Natur gleichsam den Spiegel vorzuhalten: der Tugend ihre eignen Züge, der Schmach ihr eignes Bild, und dem Jahrhundert und Körper der Zeit den Abdruck seiner Gestalt zu zeigen ... O es gibt Schauspieler, die ich habe spielen sehn und von andern preisen hören ... so abscheulich ahmten sie die Menschheit nach ...*

To hold up, as it were, a mirror to nature: to show virtue its own features, shame its own likeness, and the century and body of time the impression of its form ... oh! there are actors whom I have seen play and heard praised by others ... so horribly did they imitate humanity ...

But another theatrical event reported on by Kraus was even more objectionable than the soldiers' performance of *Der Hias*. In June 1916 Kraus tried to publish an article entitled 'Das übervolle Haus jubelte den Helden begeistert zu, die stramm salutierend dankten' (F.426/30: 1–7). [The packed house enthusiastically cheered the heroes, who expressed their thanks with a snappy salute.] It was, however, censored by the authorities and did not appear in *Die Fackel* until October 1917 (F.462/71:1–7). The article included a report (pp. 1–2) from an unnamed newspaper of the performance of 'ein szenisches Vorspiel' written by the poetess Irma von Höfer and performed in the Bürgertheater (Vienna) by the reserve squadron of the 11th Regiment of the Imperial Dragoons. The report was followed by Kraus's commentary (pp. 2–7). This 'theatrical event' provided yet another twist to the illusion/reality dichotomy. For not only did 'real' troops perform on stage, but these soldiers played the 'role' of themselves. This scenic 'curtain-raiser' had as its subject the battle of Uszieczko on the banks of the Dnjestr, a battle in which hundreds of their comrades had fallen. The performance was for the benefit of the widows and orphans of the men who had died. The only person who interpreted a role in it was the Burgtheater actor Skoda, who recited the poetic prologue. 'Während der Kaiserdragoner im Morgengrauen den Überfall des Feindes erwartet, denkt er an sein Heim, an Mutter, Gattin und Kinder, streichelt und küßt die letzte Postkarte von den Lieben und geht darauf vor den Feind' (ibid, p. 2). [While the Imperial Dragoon awaits the attack of the enemy in the dawn light, he thinks of his home, of his mother, wife, and children, he fondles and kisses the last postcard from his loved ones, and then leaves to face the enemy in battle.] All the patriotic stops were pulled as the regimental hymn was sung, a prayer recited, and a pageant of national heroic figures, such as Prince Eugen, Radetzky, and the emperor, was presented. Finally, the national anthem was sung and the audience, which included important civic officials and people from the highest society, joined in. This prologue was followed by the regular, silly Bürgertheater fare: Eysler's Der Frauenfresser.

Kraus's reaction was extreme. He saw real soldiers being used to propagate the myth of war and patriotism for the edification of an upper-class audience. These same soldiers were being used to gloss over the very real suffering that they and their comrades had endured, so that this comfortable audience could continue to live and flourish in the smugness of perfect safety. To Kraus it was beyond imagination that this performance should be staged to aid the victims of a war out of which the audience had profited. Kraus doubted the realism of such a performance. There was a diabolic quality to this spectacle. Were the people on stage actors, the fallen heroes themselves, or soldiers, he asked. Kraus projected the event into the dimensions of 'world theatre' or of the medieval mystery play, with Good struggling against Evil.

> Als die oben niederknieten zum Gebet vor dem Parkett und als die oben stramm salutierten und das Ungeziefer unten ihnen zujubelte und patriotische Lieder sang und in Smokingen dastand Brust neben Brust – da ergriff es ihn [one of the spectators] als der schauerlichste aller Kontraste, wie ein fürchterliches Ringen der Ehre Gottes mit den Argumenten des Satans und wie der Schmerz um eine delirante Menschheit, die sich um des eigenen Opfers willen höhnt. (Ibid, p. 5)

When those up above [on stage] knelt down in prayer before [the audience in] the parquet, and when those up above saluted snappily and the vermin beneath them cheered and sang patriotic songs and stood side by side in dinner-jackets – then it struck him [one of the spectators] as the most horrifying of all contrasts, as the terrible struggle of God's honour with the arguments of Satan, and as the sorrow for a mankind gone mad that derided itself because of its own victimization.

A terrible confusion of illusion and reality was revealed in the intermingling of the areas of theatre and war. Kraus demonstrated this at the level of language. If we can use theatre terms when speaking of war and war phraseology to describe theatrical effects or successes, then there must be a deeper connection between the two areas. This was particularly evident in newspaper reports. On the one hand, we read about the 'war theatre' or the 'theatre of war' when the centre of battle or action is meant. On the other hand, reporters describe actors in terms such as the following: 'Skoda ist ein Schauspieler, hat einen Bombenerfolg, läßt alle Minen springen,' 'Fritz Werner [hat] ... überall durchschlagenden Erfolg erzielt ...,' 'er gab Feuer, hatte mörderische Wirkung.' [Skoda acts in the theatre, his success is explosive, he detonates all the mines; Fritz Werner's success is striking; he set (the audience) ablaze, his effect was murderous.]

Kraus also played on the double meaning of the word *Vorstellung*. War was the most horrible idea imaginable, but it was also a theatrical performance, about which criticism was written; and the people who profited from the war now had the additional advantage of being able to watch it without even having to leave town:

> *Der Reporter sitzt wieder wie einst im Parterre, die Front ist auf die Bühne gekommen, die Helden treten auf. Krieg war ein Theater, worin sie Freiplätze hatten mit dem Privileg, nicht selbst mitspielen zu müssen: sie, Kritiker und Autoren des Werks in einem, wie gewohnt. Nun hat der Krieg noch den Schauplatz gewechselt, der Berg ist zum Propheten gekommen, und der Theaterkritiker selbst schreibt den Schlachtbericht. Das übervolle Haus jubelte den Helden begeistert zu, die stramm salutierend dankten. Von vielen Seiten wurde der Wunsch laut, daß die Dichtung, von tiefem Empfinden erfüllt, auch breiteren Schichten zugänglich gemacht werde und daß die Gefallenen aufstehen, niederknien, stramm salutieren mögen vor den Hyänen, die das so haben wollen und die ja Hunger leiden müßten, wenn der Tod nicht wäre.* (Ibid, p. 6)

The reporter sits in the pit as before, the front has come on stage, the heroes appear on stage. War was a theatre, in which they had free tickets and the privilege that they themselves did not have to perform: they, who were at once both the critics and the authors of the work, as usual. Now, war has again changed its theatre of action, the mountain has come to the prophet, and the theatre critic himself is writing the battle report. The packed house enthusiastically cheered the heroes, who expressed their thanks with a snappy salute. From many sides the wish was expressed that the play which was filled with such deep emotion be made available to broader sections of the population and that the fallen should rise again, kneel down, and snappily salute in front of the hyenas who want to have it this way, and who would have to famish if it weren't for death.

In his article, Kraus employs a very theatrical approach – in his pathos and exclamations, and in his magnifying of the personal implications of the event (the performance took place on 28 April, his birthday).

> *Nein! Nein! Nein! Es kann nicht sein! Gebt den Tag zurück! Es war mein Geburtstag. Ich trat mit diesem Tag ins letzte Aufgebot, bin schon 42 Jahre. Wer weiß, vielleicht liege ich noch als Held auf der Bühne des Krieger-theaters, dem Schlachtfeld des Bürgertheaters ... Man hat mir das Bild des Unvorstellbarsten, was mich die Zeit hat fühlen lassen, zum Präsent gemacht.* (Ibid, pp. 6–7)

> No! No! No! It can't be! Give the day back! It was my birthday. On this day I entered the last reserves, I'm already 42 years old. Who knows, maybe I shall soon be lying as a hero on the stage of the warrior theatre, on the battlefield of the Bürgertheater ... My [birthday] present was the most unimaginable event that the times have inflicted on me.

However, here theatricality on the part of the critic is not out of place, since it emphasizes and echoes on an artistic level the unethical theatricality of war. It also helps him underline the perversion of the theatrical mode of artistic expression: theatre was being used by the contemporary establishment as a tool of self-deception to give a false appearance to the reality of war, illusion or 'play' was being perverted by false realism.

Nor did Kraus's theatricality clash with his language criticism. In the critique quoted, Kraus underlined the sentences in which the reviewer praised the performance, and even took one of them as his title: 'Das übervolle Haus jubelte den Helden begeistert zu, die stramm salutierend dankten.' In so doing, he revealed the lie that was being propagated and showed that, even as a lie, when used by him in this way, language told the truth: 'die Sprache [sagt] noch als Lüge die Wahrheit ...' (*F*.418/22:104). Therefore, for him language assumed an ethical as well as an aesthetic role. By keeping his concept of language pure, by not being misled and diverted by the ornamental and the cliché, he himself was able to perceive the truth masked by the lie and to reveal it.[26]

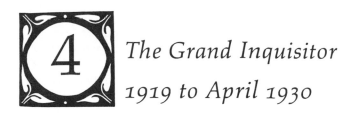

The Grand Inquisitor
1919 to April 1930

The paradox of Karl Kraus became even more striking in the years 1919 to 1930. In 1919 Kraus published relatively few issues of *Die Fackel*, and the articles in them were for the most part rather long and untheatrical. The 1920s, however, formed the period of what was perhaps his most direct and theatrical contact with the world around him. This was evidenced both in *Die Fackel* in his spirited attacks against people such as Bekessy and Schober (attacks which spread to the stage and to placards in the street), in his Theater der Dichtung with his readings to the workers who were members of the Labour party, as well as in his own dramas, most of which were concerned with contemporary issues. However, his theatrical style of criticism did not win him many friends, and by 1929 he had been rejected as an unofficial spokesman for socialism by the officials of the Austrian republic and of the Labour party.

His Theatre der Dichtung, which in the early 1920s had been a tool for criticizing and satirizing society (especially through his readings of Nestroy) and for reaching the people, increasingly became, after 1925, a refuge for a small coterie of followers and for Kraus himself[1] – a refuge where poetry, the 'word,' and the recollection of the magic of the theatre of his youth could be preserved. Paradoxically, too, the Theater der Dichtung, which had originally served poetic or literary drama (*Buchdrama*), now became the stage for his one-man performances of the operettas of Offenbach, which he had previously classified as stage plays (*Bühnendrama*) rather than literary plays.

The breakdown of these classifications of drama and the emergence of stage plays on a literary stage would seem to indicate an increasing preoccupation on Kraus's part with the theatrical, with the profane magic of the theatre rather than the 'pure' study of language. However, during the same period, Kraus began publishing in *Die Fackel* a series of short essays under the general heading 'Zur Sprachlehre,' in which he pinpointed fine distinctions of language. He was also very much involved in the problems of translation – in particular with the revision and adaptation of already existing translations of Shakespeare's plays. And in the following period (1930–6), when Kraus became engrossed in the problems of adapting Offenbach operettas, the division between concerns of language and those of the theatre would break down even further.

If we begin with a study of the antitheses and dichotomies that Kraus set up in his theatre and drama criticism, we can then consider the paradox of Kraus's relation to the theatre and of his own theatricality. The two sides of the basic dichotomy have remained unchanged. It was still the 'old' traditional Burgtheater style versus the 'modern' Burgtheater – or, in another form, his own Theater der Dichtung versus the Berlin theatre experiments. Only the actors and directors varied with the years.

THE BURGTHEATER

Kraus once stated that it was pointless to try to conjure up the past and to bridge the vacuum of twenty-five years to the 'good old days' of the Burgtheater. 'Freilich ... die Vergangenheit heraufzubeschwören, ist purer Übermut. Von den 150 Jahren sind 25, in denen die Größe des Burgtheaters im Foyer beruht hat, glatt zu streichen, und über dieses Vakuum führt keine Brücke zur Vorzeit' (F.726/9:70). [Indeed ... to conjure up the past is wanton insolence. Of the 150 years (of this theatre's past), the 25 in which the greatness of the Burgtheater rested in the foyer count for nothing at all, and there is no bridge that leads over this vacuum to olden times.] Yet he himself could not resist reminding his readers and his audience of the past greatness of the Burgtheater. In the same issue as the one from which the above remark was taken, he printed a photo of Charlotte Wolter in the role of Lady Macbeth and reviewed Helene Richter's biography of Lewinsky.[2] This book, along with the memoirs of Sonnenthal and Zerline Gabillon, formed for Kraus a monument to a culture which he loved. He showed himself once again to be more of a moralist than a theatre critic when he praised Lewinsky for possessing such qualities as 'ethical passion' and 'purity of soul.'

> *Alle ... sollten es lesen, um den Weg zu ermessen, der zum Abgrund des Theaterwesens von einem Kulturmilieu führt, worin das Wunder möglich war, daß sittliche Leidenschaft, Kraft des Willens und Wirksamkeit des Geistes der kargen Natur die Potenz zu genialer Schöpfung abrangen, und woraus das Rätsel resultiert, daß dieser Inbegriff der Seelenreinheit in der Kunst der Scheinbarkeit zum vollen Ausdruck gedieh.* (F.726/9:70)

Everyone ... should read it in order to appreciate the road that leads to the total degradation of the theatre from a cultural milieu in which the miracle was possible, that ethical passion, strength of will, and intellectual effectiveness wrested from his meagre nature the potential for brilliant creation,

and from which the enigma results that this essence of purity of soul
flourished and achieved its fullest expression in the art of illusion.

And again it was ethical as well as aesthetic praise that he bestowed on this
actor whom he called one of the greatest actors of his age:

Das Staunen, daß dieser aus der Einheit sittlichen Wesens und unerbitt-
lichen Kunstverstandes gebildete Denker im Element der Bühne gelebt hat
und, obschon vielleicht der körperlich geringste, als einer der größten
Schauspieler seines gesegneten Zeitalters, wechselt mit der Verwunderung,
daß der Reichtum der hundertmal verwandelten Gestalt noch den Schatz
eines schriftstellerischen Vermögens übriggelassen hat, der in den Aufsät-
zen und Tagebüchern geborgen ist ... (Ibid)

One's amazement that this thinker, who grew out of the unity of moral
character and inexorable artistic sense, lived in the environment of the
stage and, although perhaps physically the slightest, was one of the greatest
actors of his blessed era alternates with one's amazement that the wealth
of this man who could take on a hundred different roles also sufficed for him
to leave behind the treasure of a writer's fortune that is preserved in his
essays and diaries ...

Thus Lewinsky conformed to what must be considered Kraus's ideal of
'morality in artistry.'

A closer reading of Kraus's characterization of Lewinsky shows that there
was a certain amount of self-projection in it. For example, he praised Lewinsky
for seeing as early as 1883 that the Burgtheater was controlled by the press.
He saw Lewinsky's nature as being at odds with the times after about 1890
(that is, during the 'reign' of Bahr as critic and Burckhard as Burgtheater
managing director). The people who turned against Lewinsky, calling his style
old-fashioned, were in reality far inferior to him; he was a great speaker
who could use language creatively, and if his contemporaries called his style
declamatory, this merely showed how superficial they were.

Die unbegreifliche Deckung menschliche und künstlerischer Fülle, vorweg
glaubhaft in dem gigantischen Redner, war am Ende jenem Zweifel ausge-
setzt, mit dem die Zuchtlosigkeit sich selbst beglaubigt, um in der Region
einer niedrigen Natur das ihr Unerreichbare als 'epigonisch' abzutun ...
schon 1883 erkennt er, daß das Burgtheater 'den Pressbuben' ausgeliefert
sei; immer offensiver wendet sich diese Vertretung des Zeitgeistes gegen
den ... (F.726/9:71)

Ist es nicht bezeichnend für ein Mißurteil, dessen eigene Äußerlichkeit
wahrer Wortschöpfung nur die 'Deklamation' abhört, daß es von dem

Erlebnis überrumplte wurde, im zeitwidrigen Lewinsky dem schauspiele-
risch mächtigsten Helfer Ibsens (Bischof Nikolas) und Hauptmanns (Dorf-
schneider) zu begegnen? (Ibid, p. 73)

The incomprehensible congruence of human and artistic wealth, from the
beginning believable in this colossal speaker, was finally subjected to that
doubt with which profligacy attests itself – profligacy that writes off as
'old-fashioned' whatever is out of reach of an inferior nature ... Already
in 1883, he recognized that the Burgtheater was controlled by 'scoundrels of
the press'; these representatives of the spirit of the times turned against
him more and more offensively ...

Is it not characteristic of the misjudgment that in its superficiality hears
nothing but 'declamation' when language is used creatively that it was taken
by surprise when it met in the old-fashioned Lewinsky the most powerful helpmate of Ibsen (in the role of Bishop Nicholas) and of Hauptmann (in
that of Dorfschneider)?

It is interesting that he called Lewinsky a 'helper' of the dramatists (in this
case, Ibsen and Hauptmann). This was essentially the role that Kraus saw
himself playing when he gave play readings in his Theater der Dichtung.
   As well as by implication, Kraus associated himself directly with this actor,
quoting Helene Richter's mention of his defence of Lewinsky, both against
Burckhard and against the critics of the press, and reprinting two of Lewinsky's letters to him (pp. 72–3). In this way, Kraus subtly placed himself in
the same camp as one of the Burgtheater greats, a move which, as we shall see
later, he may have made in order ot link his own Theater der Dichtung with
the tradition of the Burgtheater.
   That Kraus could never forget the former greatness of the Burgtheater
and that this 'reality' assumed almost mythical proportions for him is further
evidenced in *Die Fackel* no. 743/50. Here, he reprinted a short essay by
Zerline Gabillon (a Burgtheater actress of the 1880s whom Kraus greatly
admired) in which she, in turn, remembered the powerful impact that the
performances of the French actress Rachel[3] had made on her. Again, the
impression given is that Rachel was not just an extraordinary actress, but a
great person, and that it was something in her personality that enabled her to
move her audience so deeply. For example: 'Bei aller Macht und Energie
ihres Spiels, bei allem dämonischen Zauber ihres Temperaments hatte sie als
hervorstechenden Zug in ihrem Wesen ein tief rührendes Element, das jede
Gestalt, die sie verkörperte, vibrieren machte ...' (F.743/50:59–60) [With all
the power and energy of her acting, with all the demonic magic of her
temperament, her most impressive trait of character was a deeply moving

element that made every character she portrayed vibrant ...] Directly following this passage is a poem by Kraus, 'Liebeserklärung an Zerline Gabillon' (ibid, pp. 62–3). This is a love poem not just for this actress as an individual, but for all those Burgtheater actors who were her contemporaries, praising their personality, grace, and intelligence, as well as their acting skill. Furthermore, Kraus plainly pictured himself as the heir to and ambassador of this Burgtheater tradition.

...

so unvergänglich standest du dem Sinn
und ließest Rücklauf aller Phantasie.
Denn das Geschaffne lebt in andrem Maß
als dem der Zeit und lebt im Schaffen weiter
...
Was war es nur, daß ...
du das Vermächtnis warst, die treue Botschaft
für mich und durch mich an die leere Zeit? (Ibid, p. 62)
...

You impressed the senses so unforgettably and yet left space for all imagination. For what has been created lives on in a different scale than that of time and keeps on living in creating ... How did it come about that ... you were the legacy, the loyal message, for me and through me, to an empty age?

But the more fervently Kraus praised the past, the more vehemently he deprecated the present.

The end of the Austro-Hungarian Empire and the emergence of the Austrian republic led to changes of both name and substance in the world of the theatre. The Hofburgtheater was now officially known by the name most people had used previously (das Burgtheater) and the Hoftheaterintendanz (Court Theatre Management) became the Staatstheaterverwaltung (State Theater Administration). The 1920s were stormy, quarrelsome years in the Burgtheater. The post of managing director changed hands several times: the actor and director Albert Heine held the position for just over two years (November 1918 to January 1921), the dramatist Anton Wildgans for one and a half years (1921 to July 1922),[4] actor and director Max Paulsen (who had been Wildgans's chief assistant) for one year (August 1922 to July 1923) and Franz Herterich, a director from Munich, for seven years (1923–30). These managing directors had to cope not only with directives from above (the Staatstheaterverwaltung), but also with changing social patterns, financial problems caused by inflation, the need for bigger audiences and the subsequent and very necessary introduction of subscription ticket

sales, as well as with the usual problems with actors. The period was punctu-
ated by crises and disputes – the latest *Burgtheaterkrise* or actors' dispute (such as the Bleibtreu-Medelsky affair in 1924)[5] provided the newspapers
with constant copy. Heine resigned after a conflict with the administration
on policy, Wildgans left the theatre embittered and returned to writing, Paulsen quarrelled with the administration on financial and artistic matters, and
Herterich's resignation was demanded by a group of actors.

Kraus rarely had any direct comment to make about the many Burgtheater
crises; they were just one more sign of a decay that he had been documenting for years and that was now, in his opinion, beyond repair. As he wrote in
Die Fackel no. 726/9 (p. 70): 'Selbst die feierliche Schließung [des Burg-
theaters] käme zu spät.' He did, however, use these crises to satirize critics
who tended to take them seriously, such as Salten, whose talent for saying
the obvious in a 1923 crisis was lampooned by Kraus in two short pieces, both
entitled 'Ruhe!' (F.632/9:68 ff, F.640/8:167 f). When another crisis broke
out in 1926, Salten's motto was 'Das geht nicht,' which Kraus promptly used
as the title of a further satirical article.

> *Schon wieder brach eine Burgtheaterkrise aus, also etwas, was beinahe
> so uninteressant ist wie das Burgtheater, und ich war infolgedessen um
> Salten besorgt. Ich wußte, daß ihn solche Geschehnisse schwer beun-
> ruhigen und daß er dann, die innere Erregung nur mühsam bemeisternd, in
> entschlossenen Maximen und bedächtigen Reflexionen darüber schreibt
> ... (F.717/23:89)*

> *Da sagt er nichts als:* Das geht nicht. *Seit dem Abschiedswort an die
> Iphigenie ist in deutscher Sprache nichts Monumentaleres hingesetzt
> worden.* (Ibid, p. 91)

Once again a Burgtheater crisis broke out, in other words, something
which is almost as uninteresting as the Burgtheater itself, and as a result I
was worried about Salten. I knew that such happenings deeply disturb
him, and that he then, controlling his inner excitement with difficulty,
writes about them in decisive maxims and cautious reflections ...

He then says nothing but 'That won't do.' Ever since the farewell addressed
to Iphigenia [at the end of Goethe's play], nothing more monumental has
been put down in the German language.

The low point of Kraus's relationship with the Burgtheater, both as spectator and critic, came in December 1924, when he attended its production of
Nestroy's *Lumpazivagabundus*.[6] Kraus's reaction to this production was predictable. His immediate response was to hiss during the applause. As a

result of this visit, he also added a verse to Knieriem's song in the play,[7] which he recited when he gave a reading of the play on 28 December 1924, and he published an article, 'Nestroy und das Burgtheater,' in the January 1925 edition of *Die Fackel* (F.676/8:1–40).

With a few exceptions, his evaluation of the performers was completely negative. The two actors most criticized were Thaller as Zwirn the tailor, and Maierhofer as Knieriem the cobbler. His grounds for criticism were a lack of acting genius (Thaller), a lack of humour, the use of Styrian dialect, which obscured the lines and the thought of the play, and a lack of both depth and pathos (Maierhofer). He described Thaller as: 'Aller Nestroyschen Viellebendigkeit bloß mit Routine und den Konturen der Körperlichkeit gewachsen, fern jener Unverantwortlichkeit der Theaterschöpfung, die einer wahren vis major unterworfen ist, der vis comica ...' (F.676/8:14). [Measuring up to all of Nestroy's many-sided liveliness only by dint of routine and the contours of his physical presence, far from that irresponsibility of theatrical creation that is truly subject to a major force, that is, to the comic force ...] The following is typical of what he had to say about Maierhofer:

> *In meinem ganzen an Theatereindrücken so reichen, wenn auch zuletzt versäumnisreichen Leben bin ich einer Humorlosigkeit von derart breiter Spur nicht begegnet wie bei diesem Steirer ...* (Ibid, p. 18)

> *Herr Maierhofer als Knieriem ... (verwandelt) Nestroysche Wortwurf-geschosse – wie den prachtvollen Satz: 'Wann ich mir meinen Verdruß nicht versaufet, ich müßt' mich grad aus Verzweiflung dem Trunk ergeben' – wesentlich und textlich in einen Brei ..., den er mit schwerster Zunge zu schmecken scheint ('so – müßt' – ich mich – rein – dem stillen Suff ergeben') ...* (Ibid, p. 17)

In my whole life, which has been so rich in impressions from the theatre, even though I have mostly neglected going there of late, I have not met a lack of humour of such vast proportions as in this Styrian ...

Nestroy's verbal projectiles – such as the marvellous sentence, 'If I did not drown my anger in booze, my despair would turn me into a drunkard' – are changed by Mr Maierhofer as Knieriem ..., both in their nature and in their actual wording, into a porridge that he seems to savour with the heaviest tongue ('... I'd – really – have to – quietly hit the booze') ...

He blamed both the actors and the director Zeska for the production's lack of depth and greatness, its loss of contact with what in 'Nestroy und die Nachwelt' Kraus had called the 'metaphysical dimension' of Nestroy's plays.

And here Kraus came as close as he ever could to praising Kainz, when he asserted that, by comparison, even Kainz as Knieriem (in the 1901 Burgtheater production of the play) *perhaps* had been believable (although there is no evidence that Kraus saw that performance).

> *Dieses 'Ich halt's nicht aus', das meiner Stimmung an diesem Abend entsprach und besonders beim Abgang dieses Zwirn, war ganz wie der des Knieriem völlig pathosfrei gehalten und ohne jede Fernsicht in den Abgrund, aus dem es nur eine Rettung durch die Geistermacht gibt. Es ist ein Schrei der Herzensangst, den man dem Experiment Kainz in dieser Rolle geglaubt haben mag.* (Ibid, pp. 23–4)

This 'I can't stand it,' which corresponded to my mood of this evening, and especially at the exit of this Zwirn, was spoken like the last lines of Knieriem, absolutely without pathos and without any perspective into the abyss from which one can only be saved through the power of the spirits. It is a cry of despair that may have been believable when, as an experiment, Kainz played this role.

This essay is interesting for several reasons. Since Kraus so rarely visited the theatre, it was seldom that *Die Fackel* contained specific theatre reviews. Kraus's criticism of this production's 'questionable naturalness' (ibid, p. 32) and of the actors' lack of pathos indicates that his criteria for theatre productions had changed little in his twenty-six years of publishing *Die Fackel*.

A look at the number of pages devoted to various topics in this essay reveals that Kraus was just as interested in using the opportunity to attack the critics and other theatrical ventures with which he disagreed as he was in assessing the artistic merit of this particular performance by the Burgtheater, or even in evaluating the Burgtheater-Nestroy relationship over the years, as the title 'Nestroy und das Burgtheater' would seem to indicate. Four of just over thirty-nine pages are devoted to his personal reaction to the production (in particular his hissing) and to his activities as cultural debunker or *Niederreißer*. A further six pages deal with Kraus's negative reaction to the Expressionists' *Raumbühne*, which is surely irrelevant in any essay on Nestroy and the Burgtheater. Nearly one-half of the essay, that is, over seventeen pages, is spent on other critics' remarks about the performance. Kraus moved from rather petty criticism of specific reviewers (such as Auernheimer, Salten, Brečka, and Liebstöckl) to general censure of all critics of the German-speaking stage. It is on them that he laid the blame for (in his opinion) the miserable state of contemporary German theatre, riding, once again, the same hobby-horse that he rode in the first issue of *Die Fackel*:

> *Die Theaterkritik ist in Wahrheit schuld daran, daß das Theater selbst einer Beziehung zum Theater entbehrt, und die Schauspielerschaft von*

heute hat von ihren Altvordern nichts als den Fluch übernommen, dies Geschäft, das innerlich nur mit eigensüchtigem Interesse an dem ihrigen beteiligt ist, zu fürchten ... (Ibid, p. 38)

Es ist eine der perversesten, aber unbestreitbarsten Erscheinungen der Zeit, daß ... das Niveau der Besprechung das Niveau der Leistung gesenkt hat ... (Ibid, p. 39)

It is theatre criticism that is really to blame for the fact that the theatre itself lacks a connection to the theatre, and the acting brotherhood of today has inherited from its ancestors nothing but the curse of being afraid of this business, which, as far as its motives are concerned, is a partner in the actors' business solely for its own selfish interests ...

It is one of the most perverse but undeniable phenomena of the times that ... the level of criticism has lowered the level of performance.

One other point should be noted. Kraus's 'message' is spun out at this stage of his life at much greater length and is often transmitted to the reader less clearly than in earlier years. Though keenly aware of language and style, he himself often practised a style that is virtually incomprehensible. The following may serve as an example:

Und dazu die tödliche Gewißheit, daß es auch nichts hilft, auf den Zeitpunkt zu warten, wo es tunlich wäre, denn es geschähe dann ja doch nicht vor denselben, denen es geschah, und wären es auch dieselben, denn sie sind hier und dort in anderer Wirkungsluft und immer für den Beweis empfänglich, nicht für den Gegenbeweis. (Ibid, p. 3)

Moreover, there is the moral certainty that it won't do any good to wait for the moment where it might be feasible, for then it would not happen in the presence of those to whom it happened, even if they were the same people, for they are in a different atmosphere here and there and always receptive to the proof, but not to the refutation ...

THEATER DER DICHTUNG

In the decade from 1916 to 1925, one-third of Kraus's public readings were of plays by other authors and two-thirds were of his own writings. In the following decade this proportion was reversed: three out of every four readings were devoted to plays and only one-quarter to his own writings.[8] In fact, he himself now stated repeatedly that he did not want to read his own essays and preferred to read dramas written by others. The reasons he gave show his peculiarly paradoxical relationship both to his writings and to those of dramatists whom he admired. When reading from his own writings, he could sense his audience's interest in the content (*Stoff*), an interest which, if we are to believe him, he did not desire and which, in his opinion, detracted from the effect he intended to produce. He also claimed that he was never satisfied with his essays and felt strangely alienated from what he had written. That is why, with the exception of his public readings and his reworking of his essays for collections, he never reread anything he had written once it was printed. When reading the works of others, however, he felt freer and yet for that very reason closer to them[9]: 'Mit keinem andern Werke aber fühlt er sich freier und darum verbundener als mit dem fremden ...' (*F*.781/6:53). In this sentence Kraus could as well be describing the mixture of subjectivity and objectivity that characterizes the creativity of many actors, who can create within a role written for them by a dramatist but who are incapable of writing their own role.

His audiences, however, continued to demand Kraus's highly polemical and satirical writings. Kraus wrote of the little interest that his readings of Nestroy had aroused.

> *Die geringe Teilnahme an den Darbietungen des 'Theaters der Dichtung',*
> *durch die seiner [Nestroys] Geistesgestalt die Ehre wird, die ihr gebührt;*
> *der Umstand, daß es nötig ist, für eines der anmutigsten Humorwerke der*
> *deutschen Sprache [Der konfuse Zauberer] zu werben, um mit seinen*
> *Hörern den kleinsten Saal zu füllen ...* (Ibid, p. 48)

> The lack of interest in the offerings of the Theater der Dichtung bestows upon Nestroy's genius the honour that is its due; the fact that it is necessary to campaign for one of the most charmingly humorous works in the German language [*Der konfuse Zauberer*] so as to fill the smallest hall ...

He even tried to lure the public by promising them his own works and then, when he had a captive audience, giving instead a reading of Offenbach, Shakespeare, or Nestroy.

Kraus's Theater der Dichtung, which had only been open to what he considered to be literary drama, now provided the stage for plays which were actors' vehicles – Offenbach operettas and a play in dialect by Niebergall, *Datterich*.[10] Kraus, therefore, seems to have allied himself more and more with the actor, an alliance which was predictable in view of his penchant for theatricality. In 1920 he admitted, somewhat modestly, that he could not play any of the roles that he spoke. However, he continued: 'ich möchte die Schauspieler auffordern, an diesen Tisch zu treten und auch nur die eine Rolle, die sie spielen, zu sprechen' (*F*.546/50:12). [I would like to invite the actors to come up to the table and to speak just the one role that they act.] In 1926, in a letter to the directors of the Burgtheater, he offered the actors who were appearing in the Burgtheater production of *Macbeth* free tickets for his readings of the play since he thought they could benefit from hearing him.[11] He even reprinted this letter on the programme of his *Macbeth* reading (April 9) and in *Die Fackel* no. 726/9, prefacing it on both occasions with a photo of Charlotte Wolter as Lady Macbeth,[12] thus again allying himself and his performance with the great Burgtheater tradition. In a note following the letter, Kraus remarked that his offer had been neither accepted nor even acknowledged.

Immerhin wäre die Teilnahme von Schauspielern an meinen dramatischen Vorlesungen – die 'aus eigenen Schriften' meide ich selbst tunlichst – aus dem Grunde nutzbringend, weil sie zur Entmutigung, zum Nachsinnen über eine falsche Berufswahl, ja zur Erkenntnis der Absurdität des ganzen heutigen Theaters beitrüge. (F.726/9:69)

At least the attendance of actors at my dramatic readings (whenever possible, I avoid readings 'from my own writings') would be useful because their presence would contribute to discouraging or thinking twice about a false choice of profession, and even to the recognition of the absurdity of everything that is theatre today.

Opinions as to his 'style' of acting and his use of recitative (*Sprechgesang*) to cope with the songs, particularly of Offenbach, vary. Certainly the remarks of critics on his readings from his own works seem to indicate that he had a highly expressive, rhetorical style. The Burgtheater actor and Kraus bibliographer Otto Kerry, who heard Kraus perform an Offenbach operetta, remarked that even there his style was not without pathos ('ziemlich pathetisch').[13] Most of the audience was enthusiastic. Listening to the available recordings of his performances now, one is likely to find that there was more pathos than an Offenbach libretto called for, but, as Kerry points out, this manner of speaking lines was to be expected of a man who so intensely admired the great Burgtheater actors of the past: he would naturally be inclined to imitate them. As for Kraus himself, how well he was aware of the positive aspects of his creativity, of his role as rescuer and preserver of a theatre tradition, becomes obvious to any reader of *Die Fackel*, since Kraus tells him so over and over again. One of many remarks from the essay 'Zweihundert Vorlesungen und das geistige Wien' will serve to demonstrate this point.

Werden wir uns nun, einmal für ein Dezennium, der hier [d.h., in dem 'Theater der Dichtung'] zuwegegebrachten Leistung in den höchsten Regionen des geistigen Schaffens reiner und positiver als alles was sämtliche Bühnen und Podien dieser Landschaft heute geben können, bewußt! (F.676/8:58)

Let us now realize, once and for all in a decade, that what has been accomplished here [i.e., in the Theater der Dichtung] in the highest regions of intellectual creativity is purer and more positive than everything that all the stages and podiums of this country can produce today!

The essay also shows that Kraus was equally aware of the opportunity the Theater der Dichtung gave him to practise his 'negative' creativity: that of the 'demolisher' of cultural institutions and values, in other words, that of the critic-satirist. He did this both in the readings of his own dramas, all of which touched some contemporary problem, and in the verses that he added to the songs of Nestroy and Offenbach. He particularly wanted to destroy the credibility of the press, since he still saw the power of the newspapers as the root of most social evils. The myth of the power of advertising in his opinion could be destroyed by the very existence of the Theater der Dichtung, for he claimed that he always performed before a full house without advertising in any newspaper other than the *Arbeiterzeitung*. Even here, he was quick to point out, what he was doing was not really advertising, but rather 'informing deserving people who were interested of a date they would not want to miss' (ibid, p. 67). His remarks about his sold-out performances were contradicted, however, by his complaints in *Die Fackel* no. 781/6 (p. 48) about the low attendance at his performances of Nestroy. Also, Kraus could not help gloating over the failure of his rivals to attract audiences. The example he gave was of Salten, who had used all the advertising power of the press to get an audience for a lecture he was giving and had managed to sell only two standing-room tickets. Kraus claimed that this case showed the press to be a paper tiger. At the same time, Kraus's comments once again demonstrated his habit of self-glorification.

> *Aber daß sie [die Presse] ihren Lieblingen, ihren eigenen Autoren, deren Namen sie täglich auch gratis unter die Leute bringt, nicht zu helfen vermag, ist die weit blamablere Entblößung ihrer Scheinmacht, als daß meine Gegenwelt des ganzen Plunders ihrer Reklame entraten kann, um zu bestehen, um nach Belieben den größten Saal der Stadt ... zu füllen, ohne ihren Lockruf, ohne die Unsummen, die er kosten würde, auf die schlichte Programmnotiz hin ... ja auf Gerücht und mündliche Überlieferung hin, die einfach jene, die hören wollen, zu der Frage nach der Gelegenheit aufruft.* (F.676/8:66)

But that it [the press] is incapable of helping its favourites, its own authors, whose names it also publicizes daily free of charge, is a far more disgraceful exposure of its sham power than the fact that my counter-world can thrive while dispensing with the whole lot of its advertising, and can fill at will the largest hall in the city, without the press's siren call or the huge amounts that this would cost, just by a simple programme notice

... and even just by rumour and word of mouth, which makes those who want to hear [me] enquire after the opportunity to do so.

Two more points in the essay 'Zweihundert Vorlesungen und das geistige Wien' must be mentioned. First, Kraus's self-assurance was fundamentally of an ethical nature. Here again, we see that peculiar mixture of the ethical and the aesthetic that has been so typical of his criticism. He stated that he wanted to be measured by his work and thereby offer an example that man (the ethical being) and work (the aesthetic product) bear witness to each other (ibid, p. 47). Second, he transmitted and transferred some of this ethical assurance, or self-righteousness, to his audiences. Here, his remarks are somewhat surprising, for his comments about his readers and listeners had been, until this point, for the most part negative or even derogatory.[14] Now, he and his audience are proclaimed to be ethical and intellectual partners, proud that they are in the right and that together they can spite the power of the press.

Wir wollen stolz diesen Verdacht [der Eitelkeit] teilen, stolz auf den Beweis, daß wenn es überhaupt ein geistiges Wien gibt, es in diesem Saal, zwischen dem Tisch auf dem Prodium und dem letzten Stehplatz, versammelt ist, stolz auf die Berechtigung, diesen Namen einer geistigen Fälscherbande entreißen zu können, am stolzesten aber darauf, daß wir, um uns zu begegnen, nicht ihrer Förderung brauchen, und um uns in glücklichster Wechselwirkung zu erleben, frei sind von der Anwesenheit jener, die nicht hören wollen, weil sie zu fühlen fürchten. (Ibid, p. 68)

We will proudly share this suspicion [of vanity], proud of the evidence that, if there is an intellectual Vienna at all, it is gathered in this hall, between the table on the podium and the last standing room behind the last seats, proud of the right to be able to snatch this expression [Viennese culture] away from a band of intellectual forgers, proudest of all, however, that we do not need their assistance in order to meet, and that when we experience the most enjoyable symbiosis, we are relieved of the presence of those who do not want to listen because they are afraid of being chastised.

For Kraus, the audience, simply by being there, became the embodiment of virtue, while those who had the temerity to stay away were condemned as ignorant philistines. This playing on the assumed moral superiority of his audiences may account for his continuing cultlike popularity. It is possible that Kraus attracted people who had a grudge against society or who, when they heard Kraus tell them that they were right, were absolved by association and did not feel compelled to do anything further. It would be interesting to know whether Kraus's criticism did have a catalytic effect among members of his audience.[15]

As we have seen, Kraus was fond of contrasting his own readings with the interpretation of plays on the Viennese stage, but he saw an equally great contrast between himself and what was happening at the same time in the Berlin theatres. First, however, it would be useful to take a look at some of the works he 'performed' most frequently – plays by Nestroy and Shakespeare[16] and operettas by Offenbach.

Nestroy provided Kraus with a creative outlet as satirist and critic, actor-lecturer, and poet.[17] Apart from his readings of Nestroy in the Theater der Dichtung, his 'defence' of that dramatist against the literary critics and historians[18] and against the Burgtheater's productions of his plays, Kraus published in book form his adaptations of Nestroy's *Das Notwendige und das Überflüssige* (from *Die beiden Nachtwandler*) and *Der konfuse Zauberer* (of which the latter at any rate had only a limited success),[19] and almost became involved as director in a production of *Eine Wohnung zu vermieten*.

Kraus's reasons for choosing the Nestroy plays he performed are best revealed in his programme notes and in his essays on Nestroy in *Die Fackel*. His personal bias is immediately obvious: he tended to praise those qualities in the plays which mirrored what he himself was trying to do as a dramatist and satirist. He continued to admire Nestroy's use of language. He praised Nestroy's 'word power' in *Der konfuse Zauberer*, a play which had not been a success in Nestroy's day (F.679/85:38). Regarding another of the dramatist's less successful plays, *Eine Wohnung zu vermieten*, Kraus mentioned that Nestroy's most brilliant and profound use of language often occurred in just such plays (F.613/21:47). He called *Der Talisman* 'one of the most profound and, as far as the dialogue is concerned, most important ... of Nestroy's plays' (F.595/600:76) and found genius even in the dialogue of one of Nestroy's less well known works, *Weder Lorbeerbaum noch Bettelstab* (F.608/12:53). One of the songs of Cajetan in *Eine Wohnung zu vermieten* received praise from him for being '(an) erotic song whose bite is reminiscent of Wedekind' (F.613/21:48).

While such brilliant dialogue and wit could be ends in themselves, Kraus suggested two purposes for them. First, dialogue served the dramatic purpose of revealing character and/or milieu. Thus in the programme notes to *Der konfuse Zauberer*, he remarked:

Seitdem ich Nestroy kenne, ist mir dieses Zauberstück als eines der in ihrer Leichtigkeit und Luftigkeit gewichtigsten erschienen, um der Fülle der Beweise willen, wie da die Charakterzeichnung alles vom Wort empfängt, um ihm nichts schuldig zu bleiben, und jeder Satz förmlich die Kugel ist, die durch die Figur in die Welt schlägt ... (F.679/85:38–9)

Ever since I've known Nestroy, this fairy play, with all its lightness and airiness, impressed me as one of his most important, because it offers so many proofs of the way in which characterization can depend wholly on language and in turn amply gives back to language what it received from it. Every sentence is, as it were, the bullet that passes through the character and strikes the world ...

However, while Kraus tended to belabour the rather obvious role of dialogue as a revelation of character, this could hardly be its main function for him: he had never held with those who saw the creation of characters as an important criterion of dramatic art. What really mattered to Kraus was what he had called the 'intrinsic value of the dialogue': through its humour and wit, dialogue exposed the absurdity and the unfathomable depth of reality. Thus, for example, Kraus spoke of Nestroy's 'fantastic wit' and his 'metaphysical humour ("übersinnlicher Humor"), whose truth portrays the distorted face of reality and whose depth reveals the groundlessness[20] of life' (F.679/85:39). This is the same note on which Kraus ended the essay 'Nestroy und die Nachwelt,' discussed in chapter 3.[21] As in that work, Kraus's description of Nestroy's use of 'fantastic wit' and 'metaphysical humour' sounds very much like a description of what he saw himself doing in his aphorisms and satirical sketches.

Kraus rarely mentioned Nestroy's theatricality. Yet many of Nestroy's plays which he praised so highly depend as much on situation, and therefore on theatrical effects, as on wit to reveal the cleft between appearance and reality. The revelation could be accomplished in various ways – by means of magic (as in Der konfuse Zauberer) or by ghosts and spirits (in Der böse Geist Lumpazivagabundus), by a great climactic scene or exposé (the 'Tafelszene' in Die beiden Nachtwandler) or by some theatrical disguise (the wigs used by Titus to cover his fiery red hair in Der Talisman). In choosing these plays for their 'revelation of reality,' Kraus replaced theatricality with 'Witz' and made them dependent on language for their effect – an effect which he could then claim to reproduce in his Theater der Dichtung.

Kraus was also interested in giving readings of these Nestroy plays for the opportunity it gave him to make specific social criticism in the verses he composed and added to Nestroy's comic songs. Thus, with clever word-play and allusive satire, he not only could satisfy his predilection for language, but give vent to his theatrical flair. His basically personal and subjective criticism, therefore, was given the illusion of objectivity within the borrowed framework of Nestroy's satirical criticism. However, although some of these additional verses can stand on their own as pieces of satire, most demand some specific knowledge of the times that Kraus was criticizing.[22]

Kraus felt free to change Nestroy's verses and even to rework some of the plays. Although he generally thought that Nestroy's plays were not dated, on occasion he updated verses of the songs when he felt the material was too specifically rooted in the Vormärz period.[23] On one occasion, he felt that

Nestroy's message could be misinterpreted by an audience in the 1920s. In the parody *Judith und Holofernes*, the verses accompanying the entrance of Joab tell of the Hebrew army, which had never fought a battle and which had no use for bravery – 'Unsere Leut' sind gar g'scheit,/Hab'n zum Kriegführn ka Freud'' (F.613/21:44). Kraus felt that Nestroy's intended mockery of 'unsere Leut' would miss its objective after all the war disasters of contemporary times and would let the Hebrews (and by extension the Austrians) appear as models of wisdom rather than of cowardice as intended. He was convinced that the song had earned a place in the history of the theatre and provided an actor with a perfect occasion to display his skill (ibid, p. 42), but in order to make it suit the purposes of his own ethical criticism, he felt compelled to add to the existing two verses a third verse of his own, which was to correct the perspective, but which was to remain in the same satirical vein. Here is the complete song:

ENTREE DES JOAB

Krieg von allen Seiten, drum geht auch per se
Auf Urlaub die ganze hebräische Armee;
Der eine hat a Weib und fünf Kinder in der Wiegen,
Der andre wohl nicht, aber er kann s' ja noch kriegen.
Kurz, jeder geht ham. Die Völker, die's nicht verstehn,
Spotten freilich, wenn s' uns sehn mit Waffen herumgehn,
Wir tragen die Waffen nicht als Luxus bloß, wie mancher meint,
Wir müssen doch was haben, was wir strecken vorm Feind.
Unsere Leut' sind gar g'scheit,
Hab'n zum Kriegführn ka Freud'.

Wie Gott freie Wahl unter allen Völkern hat g'habt,
Hat er ohne viel Besinnen auf die Hebräer gleich 'tappt.
Wir sind seine Passion, drum werd'n wir auch reussieren,
Ohne daß wir mit Schlachten uns abstrapazieren.
Tut der Himmel aber auf unsern Fall spekulieren,
Nutzt's uns nix, wenn wir den Feind und uns selbst malträtieren;
Wir Hebräer haben Wunder genug in unsrer G'schicht',
Auf die Wunder der Tapferkeit leisten wir Verzicht.
Unsere Leut' sind gar g'scheit,
Hab'n zum Kriegführn ka Freud'.

Krieg von allen Seiten, das ist ein Vergnügen, ich weiß.
Erst lernte die Welt preußisch, jetzt is der Franzose ein Preuß.
Sie haben halt Waffen und die gehen halt los,
Und kommt der Preuß nicht nach Paris, möcht' nach Berlin der Franzos.

Nur ihr Gott is gemeinsam und eh sie im Feld sich begegnen,
Muß er, ob er will oder nicht, ihre Waffen gschwind segnen.
Denn sie sind nicht bloß Mörder, Gott verhüte den Spott,
Sie sind doch auch Christen und glauben an Gott!
Unsere Leut sind gar g'scheit,
Hab'n zum Kriegführn ka Freud. (F.613/21:44–5)

ENTRY OF JOAB

War on all sides, therefore the whole Hebrew army goes on leave per se; the one has a wife and five children in the cradle, the other doesn't but he can still get them. In short, everyone goes home. The nations who don't understand this make fun of us, to be sure, when they see us walking around with weapons, but we don't carry arms only as a luxury, as many believe, we just have to have something that we can lay down before the enemy. Our people are very smart, they don't enjoy waging war.

As God had free choice among all people, without much hesitation he stumbled right away on the Hebrews. We are his hobby, so we'll succeed without knocking ourselves out in battles. However, if Heaven were to speculate on our defeat, it won't do any of us any good if we maltreated the enemy and ourselves; we Hebrews have miracles enough in our history, we can do without the miracles of bravery. Our people are very smart, they don't enjoy waging war.

War on all sides, that's fun, I know. First the world learned Prussian, now the Frenchman is a Prussian. They have weapons, you know, and these go off, I'm afraid, and if the Prussian doesn't come to Paris, then the Frenchman would like to go to Berlin. They have only their God in common, and before they meet on the battlefield, whether He wants to or not, He must quickly bless their weapons. For they are not just murderers, God forbid such sarcasm, they are also Christians and believe in God! Our people are very smart, they don't really enjoy waging war.

But, although Kraus's verse brings the satire up to date and is ethically sound, it does not fit in artistically. Nestroy's two verses keep up the fiction of the Hebrews, of God's 'chosen people.' Kraus's verse loses contact with the Hebrews as the fictional 'unsere Leut' and brings us crassly into modern times. Therefore, an ethical gain is offset by an artistic loss.

Apart from 'Nestroy und das Burgtheater' and the programme notes to his play readings, only one major statement on Nestroy appeared in *Die Fackel* during these years. This was not by Kraus, but by a critic named Bernhard Gutt, who was a contemporary of Nestroy's. Kraus had been sent a number of Gutt's critiques, which had originally appeared in the newspaper *Bohemia*, and he reprinted them in *Die Fackel* no. 657/67 (pp. 100–20). They dealt with a series of guest performances that Nestroy had given in 1844 in Prague, where he performed for the most part in his own plays. These critiques were recommended by Kraus not only as a monument to Nestroy, but also as exemplary pieces of criticism. Ironically, they in turn expose some of the weaknesses in Kraus's own criticism. For, in the first place, Gutt neither ignored Nestroy's plays as stage vehicles nor did he simply define the plays in terms of language. Instead, he took into account the characters and plot, as well as the manner in which Nestroy, the actor, developed character and idea out of the plot situation without resorting to gratuitous effects. The tone of the performance was, therefore, one of truth and natural necessity.

> *Seine Komik besteht nicht in einem abenteuerlichen, gewaltsam auf das Zwerchfell hinarbeitenden Gebärdenspiele, sondern sie geht aus dem Bewußtseyn der Situation und ihrer Erfordernisse hervor. Daher dieser Ton der Wahrheit, ich möchte sagen der Naturnothwendigkeit ... (F.657/ 67:108–9)*

> *Herr Nestroy zieht seinem Charakter gleich beim ersten Anlegen die weitesten Gränzen. Maske, Haltung und Bewegung, Sprechweise, das ganze Äußerliche der Gestalt wird so entschieden und kräftig als möglich hingestellt. Hiedurch gewinnt er den weitesten Raum zu freier Bewegung und er hat es nicht nöthig, um den Effekt zu steigern, über die ursprünglichen Umrisse hinauszugehen und die Einheit der Leistung zu zerstören.* (Ibid, p. 117)

His technique as a comic does not depend on outlandish gesticulations that aim at forcing us to split our sides with laughter, but is based on an awareness of the situation and its demands. Hence the impression of truth to life – I should like to say, of natural inevitability.

Right from the start, Mr. Nestroy draws the widest boundaries for his characters. His make-up, stance, and movement, his way of speaking, the whole external appearance of the character are presented as distinctly and forcefully as possible. In this way he gains the broadest scope for free movement, and he does not need to go beyond the original contours of the character and destroy the unity of his performance in order to heighten the comic effect.

Of the four qualities mentioned by Gutt that make up the external form of the character – *Maske, Haltung, Bewegung,* and *Sprechweise* – only the last is preserved by Kraus.

Second, Gutt approached Nestroy's plays critically. His evaluation was not always favourable. Although he praised Nestroy's performance as Sebastian Tratschmiedl in the farce *Der Tritschtratsch*, he found the play repulsive and boring.

Die Hauptperson des Tritschtratsch macht einen eben so unangenehmen Eindruck, als das Stück selbst. Bei jenem wird das Mißfallen an der dramatischen Person gemildert durch die virtuose Darstellung, das Stück aber ist so unangenehm als unbedeutend. Dies hämische Ab- und Zutragen von Klatschereien in seiner endlosen Ausdehnung macht einen entschieden widrigen Eindruck. (Ibid, p. 113)

The main character in *Tritschtratsch* makes just as unpleasant an impression as the play itself. With the former, one's dislike of the dramatic character is lessened by the virtuosity of the acting; the play, however, is as unpleasant as it is insignificant. This malicious carrying back and forth of gossip, which is spun out endlessly, makes a decidedly repulsive impression.

He discerned a three-phase development in Nestroy's playwriting. In the first, the plays were characterized by dynamic exaggeration, negation, sarcasm, and the lack of moral and aesthetic convictions: 'der moralische und ästhetische Boden fehlt mehrentheils' (ibid, p. 115). The shoemaker Knieriem in *Lumpazivagabundus* would be a typical character from this period. In the second phase, sarcasm had mellowed to satire, and Nestroy's characters, who previously had been propelled by the plot, began to pulsate and develop. Here, Gutt considered Titus Feuerfuchs in *Der Talisman* to be exemplary. By the third phase, Nestroy had found positive ethical and aesthetic grounds for his satire. The main principle was now humour. Works characteristic of this period were, in Gutt's opinion, *Einen Jux will er sich machen* and *Der Zerrissene*.

In comparison with Gutt's criticism, which is based on a clear sense of aesthetic (as well as ethical) values, Kraus's remarks on Nestroy seem much less impressive. Kraus did not evaluate the relative merit of the works or Nestroy's development as a dramatist. In 1924 he made a very hyperbolic statement about *Der Talisman*, saying that it was Nestroy's poetically most significant work and that some of Titus's speeches far outweighed the whole of Austrian literature: '[Es ist] Nestroys hinreißendstes, dichterisch bedeutendstes Werk, in dem schon die Beschreibung von Titus' Nächtigung im Freien oder das Gespräch mit der Frau v. Zypressenburg die gesamte österreichische Dichtung aufwiegt ...' (F.640/8:81). The only Nestroy play about which Kraus made a comment that could in any way be considered negative was *Einen Jux will er sich machen*, which he admitted appealed to him less (F.622/31:111). Otherwise, the impression that he gave was that all of the plays were equally good. Kraus's approach was not that of either the scholar or the critic, but rather that of the impresario. He made one important discovery: that Nestroy, like himself, was a satirist who used language very cleverly to this end. Kraus then set out to promote this side of the dramatist, and thereby create a Nestroy revival on his own terms. But in so doing, he virtually ignored the theatrical effectiveness and the entertainment aspect of Nestroy's plays, as well as their relative literary merits. Kraus's theatrical, impresario-like approach, with all the bias that this entailed, weakened his criticism and often made it suspect. However, this weakness of Kraus as a critic does not diminish his merits as a promoter of Nestroy.[24]

Kraus's crusade on Nestroy's behalf was matched, if not surpassed, in its tenacity by a very much stranger enterprise – his efforts on behalf of Jacques Offenbach; for whereas Nestroy was a playwright and thus provided Kraus with texts he could read and whose linguistic structure he could extol, Offenbach was a composer who set to music libretti that he had not written himself and that can hardly claim to be linguistic masterpieces. While Kraus made little mention of Offenbach's operettas until the 1920s, his love of them dated back to his childhood.[25] In 1923 he wrote a poem dedicated to Offenbach, praising the magic and sensual wonder of the operetta world (F.622/31:150). In February 1926 he gave a reading of his own reworking of Blaubart. The translation of the Meilhac and Halévy text had originally been made by Julius Hopp. Kraus had taken the published text as well as the prompter's and director's copies from the first Viennese production in 1866 at the Theater an der Wien, and had reworked the dialogue to best fit the music. Kraus called the work 'this crowning work of the comic stage' (F.717/23:99). He 'rescued' it in his Theater der Dichtung after the 'unworthy'[26] production it had received at the Carl-Theater in 1924: 'The Carl-Theater revival of the year 1924 destroyed the magic of the music and the profound but charming nonsense of the farce' (ibid). In Blaubart, the music and the satire of the follies of the state and of mankind could not be separated. 'Hier wie auch sonst hat die freilich von der genialen Musik nicht lösbare Satire staatlicher und menschlicher Narrheit, ganz jenseits der Karikatur des Hofes Napoleons III., ihre Fortsetzbarkeit und also Gültigkeit bewiesen' (ibid). [Here as elsewhere the satire of the follies of state and of mankind, which of course cannot be separated from the brilliant music, proved to continue to be significant and applicable well beyond the caricature of the court of Napoleon III.]

The Offenbach Renaissance had begun. From 1926 until his death, Kraus devoted a great deal of time to the reworking of existing translations of eleven Offenbach texts, as well as to completely new adaptations of Vert-Vert, Madame l'Archiduc, and Perichole, which he published and came to consider as part of his own writings. Kraus placed the works of Offenbach on the repertoire of the Theater der Dichtung. He recited them in Sprechgesang, that is, indicating the melody rather than using a full singing voice, with piano accompaniment in the background. After 1925, more than a third of his readings and recitations (123 out of 346)[27] were devoted to Offenbach. Furthermore, between 1930 and 1932, Kraus prepared and directed for Berlin radio an 'Offenbach cycle' based on his version of the texts.

These activities led to a revival of interest in Offenbach, but this had consequences that Kraus found annoying. Productions of the operettas, often based on Kraus's texts, were made which he considered to be second-rate. He therefore threw much of his energy into the defence of the 'real' Offenbach. This was particularly true in the case of *Pariser Luft*, a version by Peter Scher of Offenbach's *Pariser Leben* produced in Munich in 1929. In the article 'Die Schändung von "Pariser Leben"' (F.827/33:53 ff), Kraus attacked Scher for his lack of taste, the publishing house for its carelessness in looking after the adaptation and translation rights of the operetta, and the music critics for their superficiality and lack of knowledge – not being acquainted with the original work, they had blamed Offenbach instead of the director and Scher for boring them with this production.

If we remember Kraus's distinctions between literary drama and stage drama, it may seem strange that he included operettas in his Theater der Dichtung, which had been dedicated to literary works, in which language was the prime concern. Anticipating this question, in the programme notes to *Blaubart* Kraus referred the reader to his essay on operettas, 'Grimassen über Kultur und Bühne,' originally published in 1909 (F.270/1:1–18). In 'Offenbach-Renaissance' (F.757/8:38–48), Kraus quoted extensively from that essay. This was another attempt to rescue Offenbach from the clutches both of critics who considered his texts 'silly' and of modern producers and directors like Reinhardt who thought it necessary to tamper with the music and the text in order to 'modernize' the works.

> *Denn seit den 'Helena'- und 'Orpheus'- Schändungen des Herrn Reinhardt, der ... schon manche meiner geistigen Direktiven mißbraucht hat, glaubt dieses Aufmachertum ihn [Offenbach] durch musikalische Verödung, textliche Verkitschung und hundert süße Beinchen dem Geschmack einer Jazzbanditengesellschaft annähern zu müssen. (F.757/8:38)*

> For, since the rape of *Helena* and *Orpheus* by Mr Reinhardt, who has already misused many of my intellectual directives, this association of window-dressers believes it has to make him [Offenbach] approximate the taste of a jazz bandits' society by laying waste the music, trivializing the text, and by a hundred pretty legs.

Furthermore, using Offenbach as an example, Kraus again tried to characterize the essence of the true operetta form, and to show where the practitioners of the 'modern' operetta, such as Franz Lehar, had gone wrong.

Having dealt with 'Grimassen über Kultur und Bühne' in chapter 2, only a brief résumé of the points reiterated by Kraus in 1927 will be necessary here: (1) nonsense (*Unsinn*) was the essence of the operetta; (2) in the operetta, music and theatricality fused to form the only perfect composite work of art (*Gesamtkunstwerk*); (3) Offenbach's operettas were a parody of opera; (4) the listener could recuperate from the 'desperate possibilities of life' in the 'bright impossibilities of the operetta world' and could learn from the gracefulness of the operetta foolishness; and (5) the 'modern' operetta's attempts at realism and at rationalizing folly had killed fantasy.

Turning to the situation in 1927, Kraus lamented that the same society that had produced the (in his opinion) monstrous 'modern' operetta (or *Salonoperette*) was now trying its hand at Offenbach. Predictably he rejected all the technical aids of the contemporary operetta stage.

Wie trostlos zu denken, daß ... sich die Wiedergeburt Offenbachs vollziehen soll mit Hilfe ... der Techniken und Praktiken, die die neue Operettenszene zum Schauplatz von allem gemacht haben, was mit dem Theater nichts zu tun hat, von gymnastischen, kosmetischen und sonstigen Geschäften zur Beschönigung des Zusammenbruchs. (F.757/8:42)

How dreary to think that ... Offenbach's rebirth is to happen with the help of the technical aids and devices which have made the modern operetta stage the scene of everything that has nothing to do with the theatre, of gymnastic, cosmetic, and all sorts of other tricks for glossing over the collapse.

However, the essay is most interesting for some of the insights that it provides into the paradoxes of Kraus's criticism. Kraus rejected the many ad libs that had been added to Offenbach's *Pariser Leben* and sought to create the text closest to the original and to the spirit of the music. Yet, he considered the operetta form to be the 'fulfilment of the true sense of the theatre' (ibid, p. 43), which required extemporization. In his original distinction between literary drama and stage drama, the theatre stage was left to the actors, who were allowed to extemporize. No mention is made of this apparent contradiction in the essay 'Grimassen über Kultur und Bühne.' However, in an earlier essay, 'Libretti' (F.172:6–10), he had made a distinction between the libretti of two types of 'older' operetta: those of Strauß operettas, which gave the singer-actor room to extemporize, and those of Offenbach operettas by Meilhac, Cremieux, and Nuitter, which were wittier (*geistvol-*

ler). Therefore, Kraus saw basically the same dichotomy in operetta libretti as he had seen in dramas. Yet, in his operetta criticism, he never made use of this distinction again.

In the essay 'Offenbach-Renaissance,' Kraus insisted that the operetta text should not be judged by literary standards: 'Es beweist aber völlige Kunstfremdheit, den Operettentext als solchen mit literarischem Maß messen zu wollen' (*F.*757/8:43). The text and the music formed a unity, which only an age alienated from the theatre would try to break up into its separate components. The magic of the operetta existed not in spite of but because of the mediocrity of the text. The lyrics had to be suitable to the musical theatre and must not overwhelm the music. Therefore, with the exception of the comic songs, which could stand on their own, Kraus's work at restoring the operetta *Pariser Leben* was, in his opinion, not to be judged on its linguistic merit, separate from the music. In fact, he even stated somewhat modestly, if obscurely, that the work he had done was more valuable than the end-product:

> *die Arbeit (ist) wertvoller … als das Produkt* (Ibid, pp. 44–5)

> *(die alten Operettentexte) waren … gerade so schlecht und so gut, daß sie sich der organischen Verbindung mit der Musik nicht entziehen konnten.* (Ibid, p. 43)

> *Und all dieser Zauber nicht trotz, sondern vermöge der Durchschnittlichkeit eines Wortwerks, das eben die Gabe hatte, solchen Tönen entgegenzukommen. Das Doppelkunstwerk, welches die große Musik und das große Gedicht vereinigt, besteht nicht, denn das Aneinander ist weniger Kunstwerk als das eine und als das andere. Dagegen vermag die scheinbare Albernheit eines Verstextes, zu dem gewiß keine lyrische, aber eine musiktheatralische Begabung erforderlich ist, das Element eines Gesamtkunstwerks vorzustellen …* (Ibid, p. 44)

> *Die Arbeit an diesen unerläßlichen Reparaturen birgt insofern das ganze Problem des Operettenverses in sich, als das Ergebnis keineswegs etwa so beschaffen sein durfte, einen sprachlichen Wert, losgelöst von der Musik, erkennbar zu machen, sondern nur eine analoge Operettenmöglichkeit herzustellen. Darum eignen sich – mit Ausnahme der Coupletstrophen … – die Erneuerungen so wenig zur Publikation wie der beste Operettentext.* (Ibid, p. 44)

The work [I put into it] is more valuable than the end-product …

(The old operetta texts) were … just bad enough and good enough not to be separable from their organic connection with the music.

And all this magic not in spite of but because of the mediocrity of the text, which, however, had the knack of encouraging such music. The composite work of art that combines great poetry and great music does not exist, for the combination is less of a work of art than either of the constituents on its own. Writing such a text requires a talent for operetta rather than a lyrical talent, but its apparent silliness can be the constituent of a composite work of art ...

Doing these essential repairs raised the whole problem of operetta verse, as the result of my labours was by no means to display poetic values in isolation from the music, but merely to create the possibility of operettas that had a value analogous to that of poetry. This is why my revisions, with the exception of the comic songs, are just as little suited for publication as the best operetta text.

In the last sentence of the final quotation above, Kraus claimed that operetta texts were not suitable for publication. Yet he himself, not many years later, published three Offenbach texts that he had translated. He even took songs from these texts, allowed them to stand as individual poems, and included them in volume 9 of his *Worte in Versen.*[28]

In 'Grimassen über Kultur und Bühne' Kraus had insisted on the necessity of fantastic or exotic costume in order to make the operetta singing plausible (ibid, p. 42). Kraus's readings of Offenbach in his Theater der Dichtung, however, removed any such external effects from the operettas and left only voice and gesture. No longer was operetta the sensual experience that it had been for Kraus as a child. Rather, this was operetta that had been spiritualized and reduced to what he considered to be the essence of its poetry, which, in turn, justified his including it in his poetic theatre.

Kraus doubtless considered his 'theatre' to be more genuinely theatrical precisely because of its lack of trappings, since it presented a challenge to the creative powers of the imagination. In fact, his theatre, or at least the world of the texts he was reading, seems often to have been more real to him than the real world around him. The more he cut away appearance or illusion (whether this was costume or make-up, or whether it was the world of newspaper reports), the closer he came to what he now claimed to be reality – the reality of poetry, the reality of theatre. A comment he made about his theatre readings in 1931 illustrates this. In his readings he claimed that it was a question of a making the visible book (from which he read) invisible, so that only the characters would become visible. He did not need spotlights, since they could distract from the 'essence': 'Denn es kommt darauf an, das sichtbare Buch so unsichtbar zu machen, daß nur die Gestalten sichtbar werden, die daraus hervortreten. Scheinwerfer brauchen wir nicht, die könnten vom Sein ablenken' (F.857/63:92).

But in the 1920s Kraus was still very much involved with the times and used the Offenbach operettas to satirize his contemporaries.[29] For example, he gave readings of *Die Briganten* during the period when he was satirizing Bekessy and Schober in his own play *Die Unüberwindlichen*, thereby pointing the Offenbach satire at the modern Viennese brigands. He wrote innumerable topical verses for Offenbach comic songs. A quotation from one of them (from *Pariser Leben*) will suffice.

Ich hör', es wirkt jetzt in Paris
Der Bekessy aus Budapest.
Wenn ich der Tugend Pfad verließ,
Fürcht' ich, daß er mir Geld erpreßt.

Daß die größern Dieb' entrinnen,
da muß man sich trösten.
Dafür bleiben herinnen
hernach doch die größten.

Paris hat Respekt schon
vor'm Monsieur Bekessy.
Er spricht französisch perfekt schon:
La bourse ou la vie!

...
Mancher Name hierzuland ist
durch die Zeitung bekannt.
Ich kenn' einen, der bekannt ist,
weil er nie wird genannt. (F.759/65:31–3)

I hear that in Paris Bekessy from Budapest is now operating. If I were to leave the path of virtue, I'd fear he'd extort money from me.

One has to put up with the fact that the bigger thieves get away. However, the biggest ones still stick around.

Paris already has respect for Mr Bekessy. He already speaks French perfectly: La bourse ou la vie!

Many a name here in this country is known through the newspaper. I know someone who's well known because his name is never mentioned.

Kraus's conviction that it was legitimate for him to add contemporary allusions to Offenbach's operettas doubtless indicates that he found in Offenbach the same kind of timelessness he had pointed out in Nestroy, whose satire, he had claimed, applied to the 20th century even better than to the *Vormärz*. But by 1930 he had come to prefer Offenbach even to Nestroy and did not hesitate to call him the greatest satirist of all times, or, to put it in Kraus's own even more ludicrously excessive terms, 'the altogether greatest creator of satire of all times and cultures' (F.827/33:77).

As in his evaluation of Nestroy, Kraus described Offenbach in such terms as to suggest parallels between himself and the composer. This is particularly evident in his discussion of *Pariser Leben* in the essay 'Offenbach-Renaissance' (F.757/8:38–48). This operetta, unlike Offenbach's others, was set in contemporary Paris. Although Kraus had previously stated that operettas should be made of the fantastic, such was the genius of Offenbach that he could make magic of material based on contemporary reality. For Offenbach, unlike his successors in the operetta field, had 'the power to dematerialize' ('die Kraft der Entstofflichung'), a quality that Kraus had claimed for himself, when, in earlier years, he had asserted that future readers of his works would not need any knowledge of their factual background, since his artistry lay in his language. Furthermore, he stated that 'the life [shown in *Pariser Leben*] is almost as improbable as life really is' (ibid, p. 46). Again, this was what he claimed on behalf of his own works, particularly of the play *Die letzten Tage der Menschheit* and some of the essays in *Die Fackel* which were later gathered into collections such as *Die chinesische Mauer* and *Sittlichkeit und Kriminalität*.

It would not be fitting to leave the topic of Kraus's Offenbach readings without at least one comment from a music expert who had heard Kraus. The composer Ernst Křenek wrote in March 1929:[30]

Während man selbst bei Aufführungen guter alter Operetten meist die Wahl zwischen Davonlaufen oder Einschlafen hat, hört man hier geschlagene dreieinhalb Stunden voll Spannung zu und bedauert schließlich, daß es schon zu Ende sein soll. Das liegt natürlich nicht nur an dem über das Original weit hinaus bereicherten und mit Aktualitäten organisch ergänzten Dialog, in dem jeder Satz ein satirischer Volltreffer ist, und an den genialen Zusatzstrophen zu den Couplets, sondern vor allem an der theatralischen Lebendigmachung des ganzen Werkes durch den Vortrag. Hier macht sich ein ungewöhnlicher Bühnensinn geltend, und die schöpferische szenische Phantasie des Vorlesers zaubert, nur mit der Stimme und ein paar Handbewegungen, ein vollkommen lebendiges theatralisches Bild hervor, so die rezeptive Phantasie des Zuhörers weckend, ohne sie durch die Zufälligkeiten der Kulisse zu beirren. Der besondere Dank des Musikers gebührt Kraus für die Unversehrtheit des musikalischen Textes ... (F.806/9:62–3)

While even at performances of good old operettas one usually has the choice between running away or falling asleep, here one listens with close attention for a good three and a half hours and is sorry that it finally has to be over. Naturally this is not just because of the dialogue, which has been organically enlarged well beyond the original text with references to current topics and where every sentence is a satirical bull's-eye, nor is it just because of the brilliant additional verses to the comic songs, but above all because the recitation makes the whole work come *theatrically* alive. Here an unusual stage sense asserts itself, and the creative theatrical imagination of the reciter conjures up, solely with the voice and a few movements of the hands, a completely lively theatrical picture, which awakens the receptive imagination of the listener without misleading it by the irrelevancies of stage sets. Kraus deserves a special thanks from the musician for leaving the musical text undisturbed ...

Křenek continued:

> [Es] *soll hier darauf hingewiesen sein, daß alle, denen es mit dem Theater Ernst ist, von Karl Kraus mehr für das Theater lernen können als von dessen Mechanikern, und in der Weite seines Vortragssaales bessere Einsicht in das Wesen des Dramatischen gewinnen werden als durch noch so viele Scheinwerfer, die nur den Hohlraum eines beschränkten Rundhorizontes ausleuchten.* (Ibid, p. 63)

One should point out here that all those who take theatre seriously can learn more about the theatre from Karl Kraus than from theatre mechanics, and they will gain a better insight into the nature of drama in the breadth of his lecture hall than by means of no matter how many spotlights, which only light up the hollow spaces of a limited horizon.

Expressions such as 'ein ungewöhnlicher Bühnensinn,' 'die schöpferische szenische Phantasie des Vorlesers,' 'ein vollkommen lebendiges theatralisches Bild,' 'die rezeptive Phantasie des Zuhörers weckend,' 'Einsicht in das Wesen des Dramatischen' reveal that the effect of Kraus's Offenbach readings, at least on this critic, was indeed exactly what Kraus himself had intended.

While Kraus could see himself as the rediscoverer of Nestroy and Offenbach, his concern with Shakespeare, who figures just as prominently in his Theater der Dichtung, was of a different kind. Shakespeare did not need to be rescued from oblivion but, according to Kraus, from the wrong kind of attention – from stage performances that violated the text of his plays and destroyed their spirit.

When in 1912 Kraus began to read texts he had not written himself, he included two major selections from Shakespeare: scenes from *Love's Labour's Lost* and the first three acts of *Timon of Athens*. By 1929 he claimed that he had reworked and adapted ten Shakespeare dramas (mostly from the Schlegel-Tieck translation) – *King Lear, Hamlet, Macbeth, Timon of Athens, Coriolanus, Troilus and Cressida, The Winter's Tale, Measure for Measure,*

Love's Labour's Lost, The Merry Wives of Windsor – as well as parts of
King John and the *Henry VI* trilogy (F.806/9:30). All these plays were
performed in his Theater der Dichtung.

Kraus seldom gave explicit reasons for his choice of these particular
plays. He was extremely positive in his evaluation of *The Merry Wives of
Windsor,* calling it 'Shakespeare's best comedy, which for this very reason
is considered to be his weakest by the asses of Shakespeare criticism'
(F.595/600:72) and 'this most charming of all comedies' (F.806/9:29). One
reason for singling it out for such high praise may have been to spite the
critics. The other reason was that he admired Shakespeare's portrayal of Falstaff: '(here) the sketch of Falstaff in *Henry IV* has grown to complete
and, at the end, almost tragic fullness.' (F.595/600:72). Perhaps, too, he felt
some personal affinity with the tragic character of Falstaff. Such was
certainly the case in his love for *King Lear* and *Timon of Athens.* The title
characters in both these dramas were deceived and wronged by the world
around them. Kraus shared their misanthropy. However, the qualitative difference in the two plays is rarely brought out by Kraus – the reader must infer
this difference when, for example, Kraus states that Lear was 'the greatest
verse tragedy' (F.827/33:73). Indeed, one might wonder at his choice of
Timon even on linguistic grounds. Yet aside from his personal bias, two further reasons may be that here he had an opportunity to 'discover' a
relatively unknown work of Shakespeare's and that, by its somewhat
fragmentary nature, the play afforded him a very fine chance at 'linguistic
re-creation.' Indeed, his own reworking of the play was published in book
form in October 1930, whereas his adaptation of better-known plays such as
Lear and *Macbeth* did not appear until 1934 and 1935 (see chapter 5).

A clue to Kraus's admiration for Shakespeare may be found in *Sittlichkeit
und Kriminalität,* a collection of essays first published in 1908, in which
Kraus damned the moral hypocrisy of his Viennese contemporaries. He prefaced the work with excerpts from *Measure for Measure* and *Lear,* which
he used to underline the main ethical questions in his book. For example, from
Measure for Measure (v, 1) the following quotation appeared:

> *Meiner Sendung Amt*
> *Ließ manches mich erleben hier in Wien:*
> *Ich sah, wie hier Verderbnis dampft und siedet*
> *Und überschäumt. Gesetz für jede Sünde;*
> *Doch Sünden so beschützt, daß eure Satzung*
> *Wie Warnungstafeln in des Baders Stube*
> *Da steht, und was verpönt, nur wird verhöhnt.*

> My business in this state
> Made me a looker-on here in Vienna,
> Where I have seen corruption boil and bubble

Till it o'erun the stew. Law for all faults,
But faults so countenanc'd, that the strong statutes
Stand like the forfeits in a barber's shop,
As much in mock as mark.

In Kraus's opinion, Shakespeare's sensitivity to moral issues was so great that
it seemed he knew everything ahead of time. Referring to a particularly
notorious contemporary court case, Kraus stated:

*Shakespeare hat alles vorausgewußt. Die Dialogstellen aus 'Maß für
Maß' und 'Lear', die ich zum Motto dieser Betrachtung wählte, enthal-
ten das letzte Wort, das über die Moral, die jenen Prozeß ermöglichte
und blähte, zu sagen ist, und selbst der Zufall, der den Dichter für
die Eigenart einer moralverpesteten Stadt den Namen Wien finden
ließ, mag den Glauben an die in alle Fernen reichende divinatorische
Kraft des Genies bestärken ... Von ihm müßten die Moralbauher-
ren aller Völker Werkzeug und Mörtel entlehnen, von seiner Höhe
bietet jede Weltansicht, die konservative wie die fortschrittliche,
ein dem Schöpfer wohlgefälliges Bild; dort ist Kultur, wo die Gesetze
des Staates paragraphierte Shakespearegedanken sind ...*[32]

Shakespeare knew everything ahead of time. The parts of the dialogue
from *Measure for Measure* and *Lear* that I chose as motto for this
essay contain the last word to be said on the morality which enabled
that lawsuit to exist and proliferate, and even the coincidence that
allowed the poet to find the name of Vienna to characterize a morally
infested city may strengthen the belief in the divinatory power of
genius, which reaches out to the remotest regions ... It is from him that
the moral architects of all nations should borrow tools and mortar,
from his height that every world view, the conservative or the progres-
sive, offers a picture that pleases the creator; that place is civilized
where the laws of the state are paragraphed Shakespeare thoughts ...

Thus, in 1908, Kraus's main reasons for praising Shakespeare were ethical
ones.

Kraus's reasons for including Shakespeare in the Theater der Dichtung
were similar to those already observed in the sections on Nestroy and Offenbach. Current stage productions of the dramas were, in his opinion, un-
suited to the heroic spirit of the plays and to Shakespeare's intention. The
Burgtheater lacked actors who could measure up, either in their speech or
in any other way, to the standards of greatness that Kraus remembered from
the Burgtheater productions he had seen in his youth. The Berlin producers
tended to try to revise Shakespeare so as to make his plays more attractive
to contemporary audiences (*F.*751/6:26).

The example Kraus gave of such revision was the production of *Hamlet* in

the Berliner Schauspielhaus by the Expressionist director Leopold Jeßner
– a production Kraus had not seen, so that all his objections to it were based on
hearsay. Apparently Jeßner had staged the play in such a way that parts of
it became a parody of the German Imperial Court; King Claudius, for instance,
was portrayed with a shrivelled arm – an obvious allusion to Wilhelm II.
Kraus was so incensed by this abuse of *Hamlet* that he called Jeßner and his
friends a 'Mafia of literary cheats' (ibid, p. 27) and felt called upon to
defend not only Shakespeare but also Wilhelm II against such 'insolence':

> *Der ehemalige Hausherr des preußischen Staatstheaters, den man ge-*
> *zwungen ist in gemeinsamen Schutz it Shakespeare zu nehmen, hat die*
> *deutsche Welt nicht so zugrunderegiert, wie Herr Jeßner und seinesgleichen*
> *die deutsche Bühne.* (Ibid, p. 28)

The former patron of the Prussian State Theatre, whom one is forced to
protect along with Shakespeare, never reigned so badly that he destroyed
the German world in the way that Mr Jeßner and his kind have destroyed
the German stage.

Kraus believed that the 'heroic feelings' in Shakespeare's dramas (F.827/33:73)
were communicated in his readings, since he alone did justice to the language, to the poetic grandeur of the texts. However, his position regarding the
'sanctity' of every word in Shakespeare's text had changed radically since
1902. At that time, after criticizing Kainz's performance in *Measure for
Measure*, Kraus stated that it was a sacrilege to leave out a single word of
Shakespeare (F.98:15). Now he himself, in his adaptations of the plays for
the Theater der Dichtung, cut at least one-third of the text. Indeed, in his
introduction to Volume I (1934) of his edition of the plays, he claimed that
such drastic editing improved Shakespeare not only for the listener, but also
for the reader.

> *Die innere, nicht bloß die äußere Notwendigkeit des Theaters erzwingt die*
> *Reduzierung jedes Shakespeare-Dramas ... auf zwei Drittel des Um-*
> *fangs, die sich völlig organisch, mysteriös folgerichtig und wie von selbst*
> *ergeben ... Der geistige Organismus wird durch die Beseitigung des*
> *Hypertrophischen nicht nur nicht angetastet, sondern bewahrt ... Shake-*
> *speares Drittel (widerstrebt) menschlichem Fassungsvermögen ... Das*
> *gilt nicht bloß für die Empfangsmöglichkeit des Hörers, sondern auch des*
> *Lesers, und es ist eine der vielen Bildungslügen, daß dieser ... in dem*
> *Gestrüpp der Nebenhandlungen und Nebengespräche nicht ermatte.*[33]

Internal necessity, and not merely the external demands of the theatre,
force the reduction of every Shakespearean drama to two-thirds of its original length – two-thirds that emerge as if of their own accord completely

organically and with mysterious logical consistency ... With the cutting away of the hypertrophic, the spiritual organism (of the play) is not only not hurt, but rather preserved ... Shakespeare's third resists man's ability to comprehend ... This applies not only to the receptivity of the listener, but also to that of the reader, and it is one of the many lies of literary life that the reader does not grow weary in the jungle of sub-plots and speeches by secondary characters.

As Kraus had very little knowledge of English, he was wholly dependent on translations when he prepared Shakespeare's texts for his own readings, although he also drew on his memories of the impression the Burgtheater performances had made on him in his youth. As for his inability to read the originals, he pointed to Schiller as a precedent: 'jede Übersetzung Shakespeares durch einen Nichtdichter (ist) Unfug ... während der Dichter getrost mit Schiller die Nichtkenntnis des Originals und der englischen Sprache gemeinsam haben könnte, um aus einer Übersetzung eine Dichtung zu machen' (F.724/5:38). [Any translation of Shakespeare by a non-poet (is) mischief ... while a poet could easily share with Schiller a lack of knowledge of the original and of the English language and yet turn a (mere) translation into (genuine) poetry.] Besides, he held that it was impossible to translate genuine literature 'accurately'; at most, one could hope to re-create the vision, the thought, and the atmosphere of the original in the second language, and in doing so, one had the right to deviate from the literal meaning of the primary text: 'die wahre Restaurierung (hätte) in der Nachbildung der Vision, des Gedankens, der Stimmungsfarbe mit den Mitteln der andern Sprache zu bestehen ... auf die Gefahr hin, selbst das Vorstellungsmaterial einer Wendung durch ein ganz anderes ersetzen zu müssen' (ibid, p. 43).

He greatly disapproved of Gundolf's translations and for the most part relied on the Schlegel-Tieck version, which he compared with other translations, from which he borrowed a few lines every now and again. The results were by no means uninteresting, but not really satisfactory.

On one occasion Kraus wrote in *Die Fackel* of the problems of adapting Shakespeare from previous translations.[34] The article, entitled 'Hexenszenen und anderes Grauen,' takes up the complete issue of *Die Fackel* no. 724/5 (pp. 1–44) . For the most part, it is about the first two witches' scenes in *Macbeth*, but Kraus also compared translations of speeches in *Hamlet* and *King Lear*. To a large extent, it is also an attack against Gundolf's linguistically accurate but, in Kraus's opinion, unpoetic Shakespeare translations. Kraus took certain lines from various translations of *Macbeth* and either praised their good points or indicated their insufficiencies, sometimes by merely underlining expressions he felt did not fit in. In doing so, he showed that he had a keen ear for rhythm and sound. For example, he compared

Schlegel's and Gundolf's renderings of an excerpt from *Hamlet* (Act II, scene 2). The English version, which Kraus did not offer, is:

> What would he do
> Had he the motive and the cue for passion
> That I have? He would drown the stage with tears,
>
> ...

Kraus claimed that, in Gundolf's version, the lines lost their impetus:

> *Wie Herr Gundolf aber eine Wortreihe umgruppiert, den Sprachschwung-lähmt und die Tirade geradezu in eine Retirade verwandelt, zeigt das folgende Beispiel. Wie mächtig schließt sich bei Schlegel der Kontrast zu-sammen:*
>
> > Hätte er
> > *Das Merkwort und den Ruf zur Leidenschaft*
> > *Wie ich: was würd' er tun. Die Bühn' in Tränen*
> > *Ertränken ...*
>
> *Bei Gundolf setzt sich die Frage, was ihm Hekuba und er ihr ist, gleich-mäßig in die Frage fort:*
>
> > Was würd' er tun,
> > *Hätt er das Stichwort und den Ruf zur Wut*
> > *Wie ich? Die Bühn in Tränenflut ertränken ...* (F.724/5:9–10)

The following example shows how Mr Gundolf regroups a line of words, lames the impetus of the language, and almost turns the verbal attack into a retreat. How powerfully the contrast is integrated in Schlegel's version:

> Had he
> The motive and the cue for passion
> As I: what would he do. Drown the stage
> In tears ...

With Gundolf, the questions of what Hecuba is to him and he to Hecuba smoothly runs on into the question:

> What would he do,
> Had he the motive and the cue for anger
> That I have? Drown the stage in a flood of tears ...

Gundolf's version is closer to the English, but misses the pathos of the Schlegel translation, and pathos was one of the qualities Kraus had associated with the performances of the great Shakespearean actors at the Burgtheater.

One final consideration in this topic must be to what extent Kraus succeeded in his adaptations of Shakespeare. A detailed and systematic comparison of his version and the original would be out of place here, but his adaptation of the first witches' scene in Act I of *Macbeth*, which he printed in *Die Fackel* no. 724/5, offers an example for study:

Erste Hexe
Sagt, wann treffen wir drei zusammen:
Wenn Donner krachen oder wenn Blitze flammen?

Zweite
Wenn verzischt des Schlachtbrands Funken,
Wenn die Erde Blut getrunken.

Dritte
Eh die Sonne noch versunken.

Erste
Wo der Ort?

Zweite
  Die Heide dort.

Dritte
Dort hört Macbeth unser Wort.

Alle drei
Schön ist häßlich, häßlich schön.
Wir weichen wie Wolken und Windeswehn. (F.724/5:1)

Kraus rendered well the 'wenn … wenn' incantation of the first two speeches which the Schlegel-Tieck version misses,[35] and which he criticized Gundolf for omitting (ibid, pp. 39–40). However, he lost the enigmatic note of the second witch's 'When the battle's lost and won' and, by leaving out the lines 'I come, Graymalkin' and 'Paddock calls,' he missed the reference to the supernatural. Here the Schlegel-Tieck text ('Grau Lieschen, ja! ich komme!' and 'Unke ruft: – Geschwind – ') is close to the original and superior to Kraus's version.

In the English text, the first mention of Macbeth's name by the witches is built up to:

1. Where the place?
2. Upon the heath.
3. There to meet with Macbeth.

In the last line, the actress is almost forced to pause before 'Macbeth.' In Kraus's text, 'Macbeth' could too easily become lost in the welter of words that rhyme on 'dort.' The effect of these rhymes is incantatory, but it is awkward. In fact, it is difficult to imagine how Kraus, in his readings, could keep these two lines from becoming tongue-twisters. 'Schön ist häßlich, häßlich schön' is from the Schlegel-Tieck text. It captures the meaning, but misses the quality of a magic, alliterative chant.

In his last line, Kraus employed alliteration with a vengeance. However, although his German version is poetically very good, the English text is subtly superior. 'Hover through the fog and filthy air' forms a unit with the preceding line, both with regard to sound (the repetition of the 'f' in 'fog' and 'filthy') and thought (the 'foul' and the 'filthy' create a link). Kraus's 'Wir weichen wie Wolken und Windeswehn' seems added almost as an afterthought. Moreover Kraus's poetic last line fails to suggest the undercurrent of the horrible and the obscene that runs throughout the witches' scenes and, quite incongruously, has the softness and 'prettiness' of a certain type of romantic poetry. His version of the scene lacks that quality of 'elemental force' ('das Elementarische') that is present in the original. This was, after all, the quality in acting that he so admired in some of his favourite interpreters of Shakespeare – Baumeister and Matkowsky, for example. In this play, the elemental passions of characters such as Macbeth and Lady Macbeth are prefigured in the horror and mystery of the witches' scenes. The language in Kraus's translation often misses those qualities. His are the witches of ballads and not the 'weyard sisters' of Shakespeare's play.

In conclusion, we can return to Kraus's statement of what the 'true restoration' of a text in a second language could hope to achieve: 'die wahre Restaurierung (hätte) in der Nachbildung der Vision, des Gedankens, der Stimmungsfarbe mit den Mitteln der andern Sprache zu bestehen ...' (ibid, p. 43). [The true restoration should consist of a reconstruction of the vision, the thought, the atmosphere (of the original) with the resources of the other language ...] In his version of the witches' scene, Kraus failed in the latter of the three areas, that of atmosphere or *Stimmungsfarbe*. This can hardly be the exclusive fault of the second language, as the Schlegel-Tieck version does manage to conjure up the mood. More likely reasons are that he edited drastically and that he did not know English. His contention that the person reworking a translation did not have to know the original text but only needed to compare translations is dubious.[36] Although his adaptations of the texts and his subsequent public readings of them undoubtedly satisfied the theatricality of his nature, the result was very much Shakespeare 'à la Kraus.' One wonders if Elizabethan theatre-goers would have recognized their dramatist.[37]

THEATRE EXPERIMENTS IN BERLIN

Kraus's many lecture tours often took him to Berlin, where, in marked contrast to his virtual boycott of the Viennese theatre, he visited the theatre several times. At the turn of the century he had rejected Brahm's Berlin troupe of naturalist actors. Now he strongly criticized the political theatre of Erwin Piscator, the experiments in Expressionist theatre by such directors as Leopold Jeßner, Jürgen Fehling and Karlheinz Martin, as well as all efforts by Max Reinhardt and by anyone associated with him. This included the actor Alexander Moissi, a star member of Reinhardt's troupe, who became for Kraus the model of the bad actor, the same 'role' that Kainz had played in his criticism up to 1910. In fact, there was only one Berlin director who received Kraus's praise. This was Berthold Viertel, whose ensemble, 'Die Truppe,' staged Kraus's *Traumstück* and *Traumtheater*.[38]

Kraus saw a performance of Schiller's *Die Räuber* by Piscator's group at the Staatstheater. His reaction was one of disgust, which first found expression in the poem 'Berliner Theater' (*F.*743/50:88–9); the following year, he deemed it necessary to blow up these two pages into a thirty-page essay, 'Mein Vorurteil gegen Piscator' (*F.*759/65:45–75).

The message of the poem is that Berlin theatre had revealed the times in all its horror.

Dies Gesicht, das ich erfasse,
wenn es in den Traum mir dringt:
Zeit, du Scheusal, das ich hasse,
hier erscheinst du ungeschminkt.

This face that catches hold of me when it forces its way into my dreams:
Time, you monster that I hate, you appear here without make-up.

Ethical values had been turned topsy-turvy (stanza 3) and a frenetic message of progress had been imposed on the theatre (stanzas 4 & 5). As for the aesthetic aspect of the productions, the set no longer had scenery but was built of blocks and stairs. The actors lacked temperament and tried to make up for this by rushing through their lines. Consequently, the words of the text were lost.

Alles schiebt und stampft besessen
und die Wirkung ist enorm,
nichts bleibt als das Wort vergessen
in des Rhythmus Uniform.

Alles rennt in wilder Hetze,

was ist los, nanu, wo brennts,
sie zertrampeln schon die Sätze –
Tempo statt des Temperaments.

Everything shoves and stamps madly and the effect is enormous; nothing but the word is forgotten in the uniform rhythm.

Everybody runs around in a wild hurry; what's up, hey! where's the fire? They're already trampling down the sentences – tempo instead of temperament.

Kraus ended the poem by claiming that he wanted to get out of Berlin, since Vienna, although it had much to be criticized, was better.

Ich, der Heimat treuer Hasser,
will aus dieser Gegend weg.
Blau war nie das Donauwasser,
doch die Spree hat noch mehr Dreck.

I, the faithful hater of my homeland, want to get out of this country. The Danube water was never blue, but the Spree has even more muck.

Kraus's reasons for censure in 'Mein Vorurteil gegen Piscator' were essentially the same. Here he offered objections that were similar to those he had raised against Jeßner's production of *Hamlet*. It was in the theatre that Kraus claimed he saw the true face of the times – or, as he put it, he saw the true *Zeitgesicht* of the theatre in this production by Piscator. In his production of *Die Räuber*, Kraus complained, Piscator had tampered with the text by changing and cutting lines (for example, the role of Kosinsky was missing). This was, of course, an activity that Kraus himself indulged in, but he would insist that when *he* cut a line, the text was strengthened and the intention of the poet-dramatist reinforced. Piscator, in contrast, had superimposed his own Bolshevist intention on the text. He had allowed actors to 'massacre' their lines – words were mispronounced and rattled off at high speed. Furthermore, such a production demonstrated for Kraus the perverted 'purposefulness without purpose' that was characteristic of the times.

> *Diese Prozedur wird durch das Zauberwort 'Tempo!' bewirkt, und wie Piscator seine Leute durch die von ihm hergestellte Textwüste einherjagte, das bot in seiner Art wirklich das imposante Bild jener zeitgemäßen Zweckhaftigkeit ohne Zweck, die aus dem Hohlraum alles herauspumpt, was nicht vorhanden ist, zwischen keinem Ursprung und keinem Ziel sich Bewegung macht und nichts Fixes kennt außer der Idee, daß eben dies der Fortschritt sei. (F.759/65:49)*

This procedure was dominated by the magic word 'Tempo!' and Piscator's chasing his people through the textual wasteland that he has produced truly offered in its own way an imposing picture of that modern 'purposefulness without purpose' which pumps out of the vacant space everything that doesn't exist, which goes through its motions between no origin and no goal, and which has nothing to depend on except the idea that this, of all things, is progress.

In Kraus's eyes, the Berlin actors had not progressed artistically at all. They were no longer great individuals with humour and imagination as actors of the 'grand style' had been. In his opinion, the critics had been forced to reject the older style of acting, since the actors whom they supported were incapable of it.

Daß es einst für Karl und Franz einen Matkowsky und einen Lewinsky, ja daß es überhaupt je eine Schauspielkunst gegeben hat ... läßt, was sich da oben abspielt, zunächst nicht einmal ahnen.
   ... die Tonfallsschnoddrigkeit, mit der sich das Elend tröstet, wirkt als der eigentliche Stil dieser Schauspielerei, bekräftigt von einem kritischen Neulingtum, das auch alles Elementare der Vorzeit als 'epigonisch' abtut. Was in der frechen Willkür dieses Reformertums einzig als Zeitnotwendigkeit begründet erscheint, ist: nichts anders zu können, als das, was es nicht kann, zu verunehren. (Ibid, p. 50)

That there was once for Karl and Franz [Moor] a Matkowsky and a Lewinsky, and indeed that there ever was such a thing as the art of acting ... cannot even be suspected from what is being played on that stage.
   ... what strikes one as the essence of this style of acting is the sassy, self-assured manner of speaking with which impotence consoles itself – a manner supported by critical Johnny-come-latelies who shrug off the elementary power of earlier times as 'old-fashioned.' What seems to these self-styled reformers, in their wilful insolence, to be grounded in the necessity of the times is, in fact, nothing but their inability to do anything other than heap dishonour on what they can no longer do.

Piscator's solution to the dearth of good actors had been to make the mass or crowd the only 'individual' on stage; the noise and movement that resulted, and the use of mechanical contraptions to produce theatrical effects, merely served to distract the audience, whose attention should have been on the dialogue.
   Such a theatre was a director's theatre, since every possible effect depended on him alone. 'Seitdem es [das Theater] aufgehört hat, auf den Beinen der schauspielerischen Persönlichkeiten zu stehen, bedarf es der Prothesen, die ihm die "Regie" beistellt' (ibid). [Since the theatre no longer has real legs

to stand on – the legs of actors with masked individualities – it requires the artificial limbs supplied by the stage director.] One of the 'artificial limbs' provided by the director was the doctrine of the 'timeliness' of a play – that is, a drama was only valuable and worthy of being performed if it contained some kind of contemporary message (usually foisted on it by the director).

> *Denn dieser auftrumpfende Flachsinn macht ja nicht nur ein Geschäft damit, sondern auch eine Doktrin daraus, den Zeitwert des Kunstwerks in seiner Eignung zu erkennen, sich von der Kommishand, die danach greift, 'aktualisieren' zu lassen. And den 'Räubern' ... ist eine Arbeit verrichtet worden, die dem Erneuerer weniger den Vorwurf einträgt, daß er Schiller verkürzt als daß er dessen Namen stehen gelassen hat: keinem Hörer wäre es eingefallen, ein Plagiat zu vermuten.* (Ibid, p. 51)

For this arrogant shallowness of mind not only makes money but also a doctrine out of the practice of discovering the current value of a work of art in the extent to which it can be made 'topical' by the sales clerk that handles it. *Die Räuber* has been worked over in such a way that its adaptor is to be chided less for having short-changed Schiller than for having let Schiller's name stand at all: [otherwise] no person in the audience would have even hit on the idea that a plagiarism had been committed.

Furthermore, Kraus was appalled that the theatrical ventures of Piscator, and others like him, were supported by the state; this was but one more sign of the decline and fall of the theatre.

> *Alles in allem kann ich sagen – aber vielleicht nur, weil ich Jeßners 'Hamlet' und den 'Faust' der Volksbühne nicht mitgemacht habe:– ein schmählicheres Bild vom Untergang des Theaters, ein aufreizenderes vom Übermut einer Libertinerbande, die das Vermögen der Gemeinschaft zur Aushöhnung ihrer kulturellen und nationalen Besitztümer verwendet, wäre nicht vorstellbar.* (Ibid, p. 53)

All in all I can say – but perhaps only because I did not attend the performances of Jeßner's *Hamlet* and *Faust* of the Volksbühne – that I cannot imagine a more disgraceful picture of the ruin of the theatre, a more outrageous example of the insolence of a gang of libertines that uses the assets of the community to make mockery of its cultural and national possessions.

This decline, supported as it was in the name of progress by many literary critics, was part of the general literary swindle propagated by both critics and literary historians (ibid, pp. 54–5).

Only the first third of Kraus's essay on Piscator contains theatre criti-

cism, that is, mostly the attack on his production of *Die Räuber* from which
we have quoted. In the remainder of the essay (ibid, pp.56–75), Kraus
broadened the scope of his attacks to include contemporary society, using
Piscator and his production as evidence of its rottenness. Kraus now turned
to the title of his essay 'Mein Vorurteil gegen Piscator,' and sought to
explain what he meant by his 'prejudice.' Piscator had asked Kraus to lecture
at a charity event sponsored by the Künstlerhilfe to benefit the starving
people in Russia. Kraus had refused. In the essay, he went on at great length
to explain why he had done so (he had not wanted to lecture on Dostoiev-
sky) and to show Piscator up as a sly, unscrupulous manager (Piscator, for
example, had not accepted Kraus's refusal and had advertised him as a
speaker). Nine pages of the essay contain the letters and telegrams documenting this affair.

In assembling his evidence against Piscator, Kraus again linked ethical and
aesthetic criteria. Thus he comments on one of Piscator's letters: 'I gathered that he was a writer from the stylistically and morally idiosyncratic
construction of his wishes and hopes ...' (ibid, p. 61). Piscator had sought
to demonstrate man's progress with an example that Kraus considered ethically abhorrent: that is, that man was much more advanced in the way he
conducted war in 1914 than he had been in 1814. Piscator had stated: 'Welch
ein Fortschritt von der Postkutsche zum Flugzeug, dem wochenlang lau-
fenden Brief zum Radio ... *welch ein Fortschritt in der Kriegsführung von
1814 zu 1914*' (ibid, p. 66). [What progress from the post-chaise to the
airplane, from the letter that took a week to deliver to the radio, *what progress
from 1814 to 1914 in the conduct of war* ...] Claiming that such 'progress'
was only possible because man's imagination had atrophied, Kraus damned all
theatre experiments, and not just Piscator's, based on and claiming to be
products of such questionable progress.

> *Aber anstatt die stahlharte Erkenntnis zu formulieren ... daß der mili-
> taristische Aufschwung von 1814 zu 1914 eben durch die Verkümmerung
> der Phantasie erst ermöglicht wurde, anstatt dessen reformieren die
> Literaten das Theater nach den Bedingungen des luftleeren Raums und
> opfern der Ideologie des Schwachsinns die überkommenen Kulturwerte.*
> (Ibid, p. 67)

But instead of stating the irrevocable fact that the militaristic advance from
1814 to 1914 was made possible precisely because man's imagination
had atrophied, these scribblers reformed the theatre according to the conditions of empty space and sacrificed traditional cultural values to the
ideology of feeble-mindedness.

Kraus contrasted his own concept of what was timely with that of the Berlin innovators. For him, timeliness meant the return to what was essential in life. For the others, timeliness was rooted in the noise and trappings of modern times.[39]

> 'Aktuell' ist die Überwindung des Zeitwiderstands, die Wegräumung des Überzugs, den das Geräusch des Lebens dem Gehör und der Sprache angetan hat. Für aktuell aber halten die Zutreiber der Zeit den Triumph des Geräusches über das Gedicht, die Entstellung seiner Geistigkeit durch ein psychologisches Motiv, das der Journalbildung erschlossen ist ... Der unergründliche Flachsinn gibt vor, der Erkenntnis, daß Shakespeares Gehalt 'in jeder Gestalt zur Wirkung gelangt', am besten durch einen Hamlet im Smoking zu dienen und einen Fortinbras, der mit Tanks ankommt, um eine Thronrede abzuschnarren. (Ibid, p. 71)

What is 'timely' is to overcome the resistance of the times, to remove the cover which the noise of life has placed over man's capacity to listen and to speak. However, what the whoremongers of the age consider to be timely is the triumph of noise over the poem, the perversion of its spirituality by means of a psychological motive that is accessible to anyone whose mind is furnished by the newspapers ... This unfathomable shallowness pretends that the discovery that what Shakespeare has to say can be 'put across in any form' is best served by a Hamlet in a dinner-jacket and a Fortinbras who arrives with tanks to rattle off a throne speech.

In particular, Kraus felt called upon to protect the classics against such a concept of timeliness.

> Nein, mein Zeitbewußtsein, hellhörig jedem heutigen Mißton erschlossen und die Gerechtsame des Gedenkens einer hohen Vergangenheit wahrend, dringt aus dem rechten Verständnis für die aktuellen Nöte auf Bescheidenheit. Wohl wäre es unnütz, Verluste zu beklagen, und unbillig, dem Mangel aus ihnen einen Vorwurf zu machen. Aber seinem impertinenten Versuch, sich nicht allein durch Künste des Ersatzes, sondern auch durch die Verunehrung des Wertes schadlos zu halten, werde ich entgegenstehen, solange mein Dasein mit meiner Erinnerung reicht! (Ibid, p. 74)

No – my consciousness of the age, quick of hearing and sensitive to every false note, safeguards the privilege of remembering an illustrious past; rightly conscious of the present misery, it insists on modesty. It would be useless to mourn the riches we have lost and to reproach the present poverty with these losses. But the impertinent attempt of the impoverished to make up for the losses not only through the art of creating substitutes but by dishonouring the [the old] values – this attempt I shall resist as long as I have breath and memory.

Returning at the end of the essay to his 'prejudice' against Piscator, Kraus asked somewhat obscurely: 'But could you believe that my judgment would not have been strong enough to do without prejudice?' (ibid). The reader might indeed wonder why Kraus included this 'prejudice,' for it does not strengthen the article. Rather, it seems like a weak attempt to bolster his ethical interpretation of an artistic experiment which he judged to be a failure. Such a manoeuvre was in keeping with Kraus's technique of using both ethical and aesthetic criteria. However, in including the Künstlerhilfe episode and in documenting in detail his reaction to Piscator's telegrams and letters of invitation and excuses, Kraus showed that he was not able to resist bringing himself into the picture in one of his favourite roles: that of rescuer and defender of both theatrical and ethical values.

Kraus's affirmation of the role of illusion in the theatre is nowhere more clearly evident than in his rejection of all attempts by the Expressionists to break away from the picture-frame stage (*Guckkastenbühne*). *Raumbühne* was the term given to many efforts in this field, whether it was the 'theater-in-the-round', which Kraus likened to a boxing ring, or the apron stage. The scenery on such a stage had been replaced by stairs and cubes. The spectator could view the actor from all sides and get a glimpse behind the scenes.

RAUMBÜHNE

Das Instrument, geschaffen, daß wir wissen,
wie's zugeht hinter den Kulissen,
Raumbühne der Geist der Neuerung nennt's.
Der Komödiant stellt leicht sich darauf ein:
er muß von allen Seiten sichtbar sein,
nur nicht von der des Talents. (F.691/6:60)

THEATRE-IN-THE-ROUND

The instrument that was created so that we may know what goes on behind the scene – 'theatre-in-the-round' the spirit of innovation calls it. The actor adjusts himself easily to it: he must be visible from all sides, only not from that of talent.

In trying to bridge the gap between stage and audience, the Expressionists, in Kraus's opinion, had destroyed the genuine artistic unity that existed (*because* of the separation of stage and auditorium) between the spectator and the 'illusion of a higher reality' that set, costumes, the actor's talent, and music, particularly the incidental music between acts, helped 'the word' in the theatre to produce.

Zu diesem [d.h. dem Wesen des Theaters] gehört eben die altherge-
brachte, durch keinen Literaturwillen abänderliche Illusion der Szene,
deren Überladung das Wort bedrücken mag, deren Entleerung es todsicher
erstickt. Die Illusion einer höheren Wirklichkeit, zu der das Wort nun selbst
des Übergangs entbehren muß, den diese verdammten Reformpfuscher
und Kulissenvegetarier ihm mit der Zwischenaktsmusik geraubt haben ...
Sie wollen die Vereinigung, indem sie das Orchester überbrücken; sie
verbinden die Räume und trennen die Sphären. (F.668/75:90–1)

The illusion created by the traditional stage setting, which cannot be
tampered with by any literary whim, is a part of the essence of the theatre.
If the *mise-en-scène* is excessive, it can oppress the word, but if it is
missing, the word will most certainly be choked to death. [This is] the illusion
of higher reality, to which the word must now do without the bridge provided by the music between the acts which these damned reformist bunglers
and stage-prop vegetarians have robbed it ... They want to connect [the
stage and the audience] by covering up the orchestra; they connect the
spaces and divide the spheres.

In his opinion, only 'literary' people or literary theatre people (*Literaturthea-*
terleute) could be so alienated from the essence of theatre as to attempt such
a move – for the essence of art was illusion.[40]
Kraus was quick to distinguish between his podium stage and the theatre
stage. He thought the effect he achieved from the podium was unique
(F.668/75:90). In his performances, the world of poetry blossomed from the
word alone. But, although Kraus did not put it this way, he did preserve the
distance between podium and auditorium. He claimed that he achieved the
'illusion of a higher reality' through the word and through music, but he
needed distance as well. As long as both factors functioned – that is, (a) the
man, without costume or make-up, sitting at a table, making no attempt at
imitating the actions of the play, portraying *all* characters and (b) the magic,
conjuring power of the words that he read, supported by the harmonizing
force of music – the dialectical process that is 'theatre' could operate. However, if Kraus had started to move about the podium and had tried to imitate
the characters he portrayed, the dialectical process would have been destroyed,
as would the illusion that it created. It was this process that, in his opinion,
Expressionist directors such as Karlheinz Martin failed to understand when
they claimed that the power of the poet's word would be that much greater
if the stage were cleared of sets and props and the actors appeared in street
clothes. Martin also failed to see that in order to let the word come into its
own, he would need actors who could speak properly. Kraus commented:

So versichere ich dem Herrn Martin, daß, wenn ich die 'Weber' vorlese,
'aus dem Wort und nur aus dem Wort allein die Welt der Dichtung erblüht'

*[a quotation from Martin] und daß da trotz allen Widerständen einer
verdorbenen Zeitakustik und auf einem Podium, auf dem nichts für ein
Tisch ohne ein Wasserglas steht, eine zehntausendmal belebtere und
wortlebendigere Bühne vor das geistige Auge des Hörers gerückt ist als
durch seine Regie mit achzig Schauspielern, die ich als ein Schulbeispiel
der Armseligkeit und Wortverkümmerung halte. (Ibid, p. 90)*

So I assure Mr Martin that, when I give a reading of *Die Weber*, 'the
world of poetry blooms out of the word and only out of the word alone'
[a quotation from Martin], and that there, in spite of all the resistance of
the spoiled acoustics of our times, and on a podium on which there is
nothing but a table without a water glass, a ten thousand times more
animated and linguistically livelier stage is placed before the inner eye of the
audience than by eighty actors under his direction, which I consider to be
a perfect example of impoverishment and linguistic atrophy.

Furthermore, Kraus saw these stage experiments as triumphs of technology
over the human spirit. They were, therefore, both product and evidence of the
sickness of the times.

*Und so völlig verödet und verblödet, so jedem Trugschluß preisgegeben, so
gegen alle Notausgänge orientiert ist dieses Denken, daß es dem Mangel
an Natur und also an theatralischer Potenz homöopathisch mit den Giften
beizukommen wähnt, die das Siechtum bewirkt haben, und daß sie wirklich glauben, oder so tun als glaubten sie, die absterbende Kunst galvani-
sieren zu können, wenn sie ihr unmittelbar etwas von dem Dynamo-
motorischen, durch das alles Organische verheert ward, hinzufügen.*
(Ibid, p. 61)

And this way of thinking is so completely desolate and stupid, so much at
the mercy of every fallacy, so dependent on all the emergency exits, that it
hopes to remedy its lack of naturalness, and therefore of theatrical power,
homeopathically, with those poisons that have caused the sickness, and that
they really believe, or pretend to believe, that they can galvanize a dying
art by directly adding to it something of the dynamo-motor that has devas-
tated everything organic.

Again, we see Kraus's mixture of ethical and aesthetic criticism when he
charged that these attempts at innovation were a swindle that sought to
gloss over the basic evil – man's alienation from language. He, of course, had
seen through these attempts long ago.

*Ich jedoch ... stehe nun seit zwei Jahrzehnten diesem Treiben mit einem
geradezu heroischen Ekel gegenüber, indem ich alle Versuche mit Licht-
kegeln, Orchesterbrücken, Treppen, Würfeln, alle Strapazen einer kubisch erhöhten Impotenz, alles Getue einer usurpierten Regieallmacht,*

allen Wahn, die szenische Wirklichkeit, die noch kein Genie beengt hat,
durch groben Unfug 'anzudeuten' und die Untalente mit Metaphern zu
umgeben, die auf der Bühne als Körper, als Fremdkörper in Erscheinung
treten wie jene selbst – indem ich all diese Hochstapelei der Neben-
sachen und diese ganze Problematik der Kulisse, die über das Grundübel
der Wortfremdheit hinüberschwindeln will, nicht als Hilfe, sondern als
Hemmnis der Wortbühne betrachte. (Ibid, p. 62)

I, however, have been opposing these manoeuvres for two decades by
now, with a disgust that borders on heroism. All these experiments with
searchlight beams, decks over the orchestra, stairs and cubes, all these
efforts of a cubically intensified impotence, this display of omnipotence
usurped by the stage director, all this craze for 'indicating' the reality of
the scene, which has never hampered an actor of genius, by sheer idiocies,
and for surrounding actors without talent by metaphors that appear on
the stage as bodies and indeed foreign bodies, like the actors themselves – all
this fraudulent promotion of trivialities and this whole problematic of
stage props that seeks to gloss over the basic evil of man's alienation from
language – all this I regard not as an aid, but as a hindrance to the
presentation of language on the stage.

Having established his own Theater der Dichtung as the only 'theatre'
which solved the problem of *Wortfremdheit*, Kraus found it ironic that others
thought that the *Raumbühne* was particularly suitable for his own play *Die
letzten Tage der Menschheit*: 'In fact, it so turns out that it was from the
Pandora's box of my work that the idea of *Raumbühne* emerged ...'
(F.676/8:37). Altogether, his attitude towards the stage and the theatre was
extremely conservative,[41] and he admitted this: 'Denn ich bin, mit allem Verständnis für die bunten Möglichkeiten des Lebens, in Dingen der Kunst
unbelehrbar, rückständig, voll Vorurteil und keines Vorteils gewärtig'
(F.668/75:63). He would probably have rejected out of hand the theatres of
Shakespeare's day. And yet in such a theatre the sense of illusion and wonder
is not destroyed by the stage. True, this sense of illusion was aided by costumes, props, and stage effects, as was apparently not the case in the Berlin
productions Kraus spoke of. And productions in Shakespeare's day would
probably have been failures without one theatrical ingredient that Kraus considered essential – good actors who spoke well. But given these factors, even
though a production of Shakespeare on such a stage may not have given full
predominance to language, it must have created that other quality that
Kraus considered indispensable to the theatre – theatrical illusion ('die Illusion
der Szene').[42]

Kraus's opposition to Reinhardt increased in vituperative quality in this
period. Reinhardt no longer limited his theatrical activities to Berlin. In 1920,

with the rise of Jeßner and other Expressionist directors, he left Berlin, and from then till 1924, he was active in Vienna and Salzburg. In Vienna, the Theater in der Josefstadt was renovated and opened under his direction, while in Salzburg he, Richard Strauß, Hofmannsthal, and others founded the Salzburg Festival. Reinhardt's concept of theatre as a spectacle or festival,[43] with language assuming secondary importance and sometimes even being lost in the theatricality of effect, was diametrically opposed to Kraus's reverence for the word. Kraus could not help but see the tremendous influence that Reinhardt, with his avowed return to the baroque tradition of Austrian theatre, exerted on the contemporary and local theatre scene. Undoubtedly there was envy on Kraus's part; for good or ill, Reinhardt's influence on the theatre had been much more substantial than his own. But although Kraus rejected spectacle and show in his own Theater der Dichtung, his encounters with the Reinhardt phenomenon, in both *Die Fackel* and his public lectures, did not lack theatrical and dramatic dimensions.

The best illustration of the mode of Kraus's criticism of Reinhardt is the article 'Vom großen Welttheaterschwindel' (F.601/7:1–7). In 1911 Kraus had converted to Roman Catholicism. Now he announced that he was leaving the church, for no other reason than that Reinhardt's production of Hofmannsthal's play *Das Salzburger Große Welttheater* had been staged in a church – the Kollegienkirche in Salzburg. Although the decision to leave had been reached earlier,[44] Kraus waited for an occasion to dramatize his criticism of both the church and Reinhardt. In Kraus's opinion, the play was being performed for business reasons and not out of any convictions of faith. Any attempt to present the play as a religious drama would consequently be fraudulent. Here, not only was Reinhardt faulted, but the church was also criticized for lending its sacred building to such an 'obvious' swindle.

Kraus had originally read his article in his Theater der Dichtung in September 1922, nearly two months before printing it in *Die Fackel*. This reading had formed the preface to his performance of Nestroy's *Der Talisman*, a play from the 'old' theatre world, which Kraus used as a means of protest against the Reinhardt production of Hofmannsthal's drama. In the Nestroy play, people had only been duped by wigs. Now, they were being cheated by a combination of aesthetics, religion, and business that he summarized in the word *Messe*, with its double connotation of religious mass and market: '(eine) Gegenwart ... wo Hochamt und Großmarkt in dem Einheitsbegriff jener "Messe" verschmelzen, die die Gelegenheit für Händler und Mysterienschwindler bedeutet ...' (F.601/7:3).

Kraus claimed that he had originally entered the church in order to flee from those *Literaturhändler* whom he associated with his original Jewishness, only to find similar characters involved in the Catholic church. He was thinking in particular of Reinhardt, Hofmannsthal, and Moissi, since they had collaborated in the *Salzburger Großes Welttheater* production. For Kraus, the use of the word *Welttheater* was appropriate because, for him, the state of the theatre paralleled and mirrored the state of the world, and he felt the Roman Catholic church should be damned for condoning both. He contrasted the 'good old days' of the theatre, when both theatre and world were in a better state, with the fraudulence and the artificial but lucrative baroque quality of a Reinhardt production (ibid, p. 6). And, as usual, he blamed the press for its complicity in propagating this deceit. The first five verses of a long poem, *Bunte Begebenheiten*, published the following year, perhaps sum up best Kraus's picture of Reinhardt in Salzburg:

> *Seit jener göttliche Regisseur*
> *dort erschaffen sein Welttheater,*
> *geht in die eigene Kirche nicht mehr*
> *der gute Himmelvater.*
>
> *Wo er hinblickt steht ein Dramaturg*
> *und gibt den sakralen Stempel.*
> *Doch was tut Gott? Nicht um die Burg*
> *betritt er mehr diesen Tempel.*
>
> *Die Plätze gleich vorn beim Hochaltar*
> *sind reserviert für die Fremden,*
> *dort kann man am besten auch sehn, wie der Bahr*
> *wechselt die Büßerhemden.*
>
> *Und täglich betet ihm nach jeder Schmock,*
> *wenn von Kultur sie schmocken:*
> *Herr, gib uns unser täglich Barock!*
> *Und da läuten die Kirchenglocken.*
>
> *Mit dem Zirkus ist das Geschäft vorbei,*
> *jedoch mit der Kirche gelungen,*
> *drum gloria in excelsis sei*
> *von der Presse dem Reinhardt gesungen.* (F.622/31:65)

COLOURFUL EVENTS

Since that divine director created his theatre here, the good Heavenly Father doesn't go to church anymore.

Wherever he looks a dramaturge stands and gives the sacred stamp. But what does God do? Not for the life of the Burgtheater would he enter this temple any more.

The seats right at the front by the high altar are reserved for the tourists; there one can also have the best view of how Bahr changes his hair-shirts.

And daily all the fops parrot him whenever they brag culture: Lord, give us our daily Baroque! And then the church bells ring.

You can't make money with the circus anymore, but you certainly can with the church. Therefore let gloria in excelsis be sung by the press to Reinhardt.

The article immediately following 'Vom großen Welttheaterschwindel' was also concerned with Reinhardt. Its title, 'Preßburgtheater,' not only alluded to the fact that Reinhardt was a guest producer in Preßburg at the time, but punned on the word Burgtheater, suggesting that the Burgtheater was now as provincial as if it were in Preßburg, which was notoriously provincial, and at the same time insinuating that the Burgtheater was a *Burg* (fortress) formed by the press, from which Reinhardt ruled over the theatre. Kraus made fun of the feuilleton writers' (here, Salten's) adulation of Reinhardt, and tried to cut Reinhardt down to size. His direction, based on flashy effects, did not get to the heart of a play, nor had it succeeded in raising the level of either the theatre or the times. His accomplishments were 'nothing but the glorious feats of the director of a group of extras, which haven't raised the standards of a depraved age and the stagecraft appropriate to it by one iota ...' (F.601/7:9).
Apart from Kraus's *bête noire* of the 'business' of press and theatre, the article contains a very revealing and unintentionally ironic statement by Kraus, in which he characterized Reinhardt as 'that director who had the talent to stage himself even better': 'Was meine isolierte Wenigkeit betrifft ... so kann ich nur sagen, daß ich an diesem Regisseur stets das Talent anerkannt habe, sich selbst noch besser zu inszenieren ...' (ibid). The comment could just as easily pertain to Kraus himself, for he, in using his own case as his best example, was constantly 'staging himself.' And there could be no better illustration of this than the preceding article, 'Vom großen Welttheater-schwindel,' in which Kraus dramatized his exit from the Catholic church, very theatrically using himself as the example with which he contrasted a sick theatre and an equally sick world. The role in which he cast himself (at least by allusion) in the concluding paragraph of this article is even more revealing. Here, twisting the episode of Christ driving the money-lenders from the temple, Kraus claimed that he would drive from the altar (the stage provided by the church) those worshippers who intended to perform for the traders and money-changers. 'Der Vorhang ist von Reinhardt. Auf der Bühne ist etwas gestorben. Ich halte den Nachruf und treibe die Beter vom

Altar, die dort den Händlern und Wechslern etwas vorspielen wollten' (ibid, p. 7).

Therefore, both Kraus and Reinhardt were similar at least with respect to their theatricality. If Kraus accused Reinhardt of behaving like 'that divine director' ('jener göttliche Regisseur') (F.622/31:65) in his 'world theatre' in Salzburg or like a king in the aesthetic splendour of his castle at Leopoldskron, then Kraus could just as easily be accused of casting himself in the role of Christ. Their mode of theatricality was different, Reinhardt's being more visual and spectacular, Kraus's appealing to the ear and the intellect. This helps to explain the differences in their aesthetic approaches to theatre. Reinhardt's great success in the theatre world doubtless annoyed Kraus. In criticizing Reinhardt, he could not just use artistic criteria, since his dislike of Reinhardt's productions could be attributed to differences in taste. Therefore, his main criticism (rightly or wrongly) had to be of an ethical nature – Reinhardt's church theatre was a dishonest trick to make money. From that point on, Kraus used Reinhardt as a symbol of fraudulence in art, of the interests of business and the press disguised as *Regisseur*.

As may be expected, Kraus's detestation of Reinhardt extended to some of his entourage, and particularly to some of the actors Reinhardt liked to work with. Among the most famous of these was Alexander Moissi, who also had a second strike against him: he had been discovered by Kainz.[45] Two comments by Kraus best characterize his image of Moissi. In the first, in an article entitled 'Der Zeit ihre Kunst,' Kraus remarked sarcastically: 'Wohl weiß ich, daß wenn es je eine Primadonna gegeben hat, von der das Nestroy'sche Wort gilt: "Aus Neid sein die Nachtigall'n hin wor'n im Nest", dies auf Herrn Alexander Moissi zutrifft' (F.595/600:99). [I well know that, if ever there was a prima donna to whom Nestroy's statement 'The nightingales died of envy in their nest' applies, it is Mr Alexander Moissi.] In the second, Kraus admitted that Kainz had been far more effective on stage than Moissi would ever be.[46]

> Josef Kainz, einer der größten Bühnenredner, war ein zweidimensionaler Schauspieler oder eigentlich nur der der Linie ... Freilich, wem sein Richard II. nach Robert und Matkowsky gestaltlos erschien, dem mag seine Bühnenfülle vorschweben, wenn er an die Möglichkeit denkt, Herrn Moissi in dieser Rolle zu sehen. (F.622/31:121)

> Josef Kainz, one of the greatest stage orators, was a two-dimensional or, actually, only a one-dimensional actor ... However, a person who finds his Richard II insubstantial by comparison with Robert and Matkowsky may consider his stage presence imposing when he considers the possibility of seeing Mr Moissi in this role.

The first remark shows Kraus's reaction to the critics' overwhelming praise of Moissi's musical delivery of lines[47] and his lack of pathos. Therefore, in this respect he did not meet Kraus's ideal of the great Burgtheater actors. The second reveals that Kraus considered Moissi's stage presence and his ability to characterize three-dimensionally to be minimal. This was as much a criticism of Moissi's personality as of his acting skill. Kraus's old Burgtheater heroes had been able to create convincing characters *on* stage because *off* stage they were great personalities.[48]

Kraus's chief comment was that Moissi's great success as an actor mirrored and was a criticism of the times. Only an age which lacked an ethical basis for heroism could, in Kraus's eyes, be so wrong about what constituted the artistically heroic. The times and not the individual actors, therefore, were to blame for the miserable state of acting in the 1920s:

> *(ich) bin ... nicht ... der Ansicht, daß die heutige Schauspielkunst, als deren Repräsentant mit Recht Herr Moissi angesehen werden dürfte, das Publikum gewandelt hat, sondern ich meine, daß eher das heutige Publikum die Schauspielkunst gewandelt hat ... Ferner wäre es auch verfehlt zu glauben, daß der vorhandene Moissi eine andere Wahl hatte, bevor er etwa eines Tages der sich ihm darbietenden Möglichkeit, ein Matkowsky zu sein, heroisch entsagte, um nur aus Gefühl für die Zeitfordernisse ein Moissi zu bleiben.* (F.595/600:100)

> (I) ... do not hold the view that today's art of acting, of which Mr Moissi may rightly be considered representative, has changed the public, but I believe that the public has changed the art of acting ... It would also be wrong to hold that Moissi, such as he is, had any choice in the matter when one day he heroically renounced the possibility of becoming a Matkowsky in order to remain a Moissi, simply because he felt it was right for the times.

Furthermore, the critics were doubly culpable since they also tried to pass Moissi's defects off as assets. And finally, the injustice of such a state of affairs concerned Kraus. For instance, Moissi, who had originally been rejected as 'untalented' by a committee of Burgtheater directors that included Sonnenthal, Lewinsky, Baumeister, and Hartmann, was now richer and more famous than all the others had been together.

> *Nun muß man freilich sagen, daß es vier Gewaltigere in der Kompetenz über schauspielerische Befähigung weder damals gegeben hat noch auf absehbare Zeit geben dürfte ... Aber die Welt läuft eben so, daß Herr Moissi heute mehr Ruhm hat und mehr Gewinn als dazumal sie alle zusammen.* (F.743/50:57)

It must be admitted that four more competent judges of acting skills neither existed then nor are likely to be found in the foreseeable future ... But it is the way of the world that Mr Moissi should enjoy more fame and money today than all four of those others together enjoyed in their own day.

In his censure of Moissi, Kraus proceeded in much the same manner as he had against Kainz, methodically setting him up as the villain in his criticism. And in 1922, as previously, Kraus operated almost solely on the basis of prejudice.

Aber zum Glück kann ich beweisen, daß ich seit jeher ein Vorurteil gegen Herrn Moissi gehabt, daß ich die Übertragung des Kainzzeichens der Schauspielkunst auf seine noch weit schmächtigere Grazie immer für einen Beweis des Fortschritts ihres Rückschritts gehalten ... habe. (F.595/600:103)

But fortunately I can prove that I have always had a prejudice against Mr Moissi (and) that I have always seen a proof of the progress of the retrogression in the art of acting in the fact that its sign of Kainz has been bestowed on his still feebler grace ...

Moissi was blamed by Kraus for his complicity in Reinhardt's production of the *Salzburger Großes Welttheater* (he played the leading role), but since Kraus had never seen the play, he had no objective grounds for criticism. In fact, at no time did he give any indication that he had ever seen a performance by Moissi. Kraus admitted, for example, that he had not seen Moissi's Faust: 'Ich habe Herrn Moissi Fausts Tod weder spielen gesehn noch sprechen gehört, aber ich bin natürlich dagegen' (F.577/82:38). [I have neither seen nor heard Moissi portray the dying Faust, but of course I object to his performance.] Therefore, as theatre criticism, his articles on this actor are worthless.

DRAMA CRITICISM

Kraus's defence of Nestroy led him to a somewhat controversial position vis-à-vis Grillparzer. For example, he claimed that if Austrian literary historians heard him give a reading of Nestroy's *Talisman*, they would immediately recognize that the speech in which Titus boasted about how he had got grey hair far outweighed Grillparzer's or Anzengruber's life's work (F.679/85:82). Until that period, Kraus had been curiously silent about Grillparzer as a dramatist. Now, however, on at least two occasions, he denied that Grillparzer was a great playwright and tried to win the position of 'Austrian classic' for Nestroy.

The first instance was in *Die Fackel* no. 679/85, in the article from which the remark about Titus's grey hair was taken. Kraus's judgment, based on the criterion of language, is of a very general nature. Two plays, *Medea* and *Der Traum ein Leben*, were deemed by him to be theatrically effective, but censured on the grounds that they contained the worst kind of occasional verse, worthy of any high-school dilettante. He considered *Ein treuer Diener seines Herrn* to be linguistically sounder (ibid, p. 81), but as he supported neither his praise nor his blame by any specific examples, his criticism is not very enlightening.

In a longer article, entitled 'Grillparzer-Feier,' Kraus was more specific. He blamed the literary historians for establishing Grillparzer as an Austrian classic and the journalists for keeping this myth alive. In Kraus's opinion, the basic reason for the creation of this myth was the Austrians' need for a classic, as well as their childish delight in having one of their own poets share the limelight, albeit as number three, with Goethe and Schiller (F.588/94:12).

Kraus condemned Grillparzer as lacking in depth and substance, and even ranked Hebbel higher than him as a dramatist.

Und so problematisch etwa die Erscheinung Hebbels sein mag, so bietet sie doch – nebst aller nicht kunstgelösten Problematik – wenigstens ein Problem gegenüber der papiernen Ebenheit der Welt Grillparzers, den die Literarhistoriker in die Nähe jenes rücken ... Keines der Grillparzerdramen, so außerordentlich sie zur Unterlage einer hohen Schauspielkunst taugen mochten ... wäre imstande, einer lesenden Nachwelt die Überzeugung beizubringen, daß der Versuch, den Himmel Griechenlands über dem Wienerwald zu wölben, geglückt sei. (Ibid)

Überall die mittlere Kultur eines vorhandenen, unerschaffenen Ausdrucks und dennoch, vielleicht eben darum, der österreichische Klassiker. (Ibid)

Hebbel may be a problematic figure, but – with all the problems he could not resolve into art – he at least does present a problem, as opposed to the cardboard smoothness of the world of Grillparzer, whom the literary historians place side by side with Hebbel ... Grillparzer's plays may provide great actors with the most extraordinary opportunities to display their art, but ... not one of them is apt to persuade a literate posterity that the experiment to spread Greek skies over the Vienna woods has been successful.

Everywhere [he displays] the average skill of expressing himself in a language that he had inherited, not created, and yet – and perhaps for this very reason – [he is] the Austrian classic.

The above quotation also indicates that Kraus considered Grillparzer's plays to be stage plays rather than literary drama – that is, they could serve as the basis or outline for an actor's art, but they could never satisfy future generations of readers. Here again, in Kraus's opinion, it was the literary historians and the 'psychological windbags like Bahr' ('die psychologischen Schwätzer wie jener Bahr') who were at fault for transforming Grillparzer into the great Austrian classic.

In his second point of criticism, Kraus took issue with Grillparzer's message, a message which in turn deadened the world Grillparzer was trying to create. The main idea, that the hero must bow to the powers of life and of the state, was a lifeless and essentially undramatic one:

> (sein Wirken) setzt sich ... in keiner lebendigen Wirkung fort. Wie sollte dies auch der Gestaltung einer Welt gelingen, in der bei aller Vornehm-heit, Würde und Feinheit der formalen Bildung doch ein vor allen Gewalten des Lebens und des Staates unterduckendes Gemüt seine Bene-diktion findet ... wo selbst der Traum von des Lebens bunten Abenteuern nur als der Umweg zu der bleibenden Erkenntnis sichtbar wird, daß der Österreicher im Ausland nichts zu suchen habe. (Ibid, p. 13)

> [His work] ... has had no lasting effect on life. And indeed, how could such an effect be produced by the creation of a world in which, in spite of all the nobility, dignity, and refinement of its external form, the kind of person approved is the one who gives way before the forces of life and the power of the state [and] where the dream of life's gay adventures is unveiled as nothing but a circuitous route to the lasting conviction that an Austrian has no business to go abroad.

Kraus's third point of criticism was included in the opening of the above quotation. In his opinion, Grillparzer's dramas had no bearing on the twentieth century: 'No one who wrote a commemorative article on the 50th anniversary of Grillparzer's death was able to show that he has anything to say to our era' (ibid, p. 19). Kraus allowed one exception, which, however, had nothing to do with Grillparzer as a dramatist, namely a poem against journalists, which he had already published many years earlier in *Die Fackel*. This poem not only demonstrated Grillparzer's critical abilities with re-gard to a topic that was still of current interest in the 1920s, but also showed Kraus's personal bias, in that Grillparzer's poem could not help but lend weight to his own fight against the press.

Kraus's criticism of Grillparzer is not based on personal motives and is, therefore, less suspect than some of his criticism of contemporary dramatists. There are readers of Grillparzer who would agree that his message, as

Kraus construed it, is deadening and has no appeal to modern times. It could also be argued that some of Grillparzer's plays make far better stage dramas than reading or literary dramas. *Sappho,* for example, may not always hold the reader's interest with either its language, plot, or characters, but it could be an excellent vehicle for a talented actress. *Der Traum ein Leben* begs for a stage production, with costumes and colour and lighting effects. Although he should have supported his arguments with more examples from the texts of the plays, Kraus's criticism of Grillparzer as 'the Austrian classic' is perhaps quite defensible and certainly not as far-fetched as it might have seemed at first.

Kraus's comments on contemporary dramatists can hardly be classified as drama criticism since he rarely seems to have read their plays or seen productions of them. His information came almost entirely from newspapers. He remained loyal to those playwrights whom he had supported in the 1890s and early 1900s, particularly to Wedekind and the early Hauptmann. In addition to reading some of Wedekind's works in the Theater der Dichhtung, in 1925 he reprinted his own essay 'Die Büchse der Pandora' (F.691/6:43–55)[49] and published Wedekind's correspondence with him from 1903 to 1907.

As for Hauptmann, Kraus continually tried to recall the memory of Hauptmann as a young playwright and thus to illustrate the turn for the worse that both Hauptmann's life and works had taken since the beginning of the century. To do this, Kraus gave readings of some of the early Hauptmann plays, including, in 1923, his first complete reading of *Die Weber* since his successful youthful efforts in 1893. He also reprinted two favourable press critiques of the 1893 readings, thus associating himself with the early Hauptmann.

He was adamant, however, in rejecting the Hauptmann of the 1920s. His comment on the play *Gabriel Schillings Flucht* was: 'It is probably the most desolate stop on Hauptmann's dreary route that starts with the play *Einsame Menschen ...*' (F.726/9:66). But again, as in the previous decade, most of Kraus's reasons for criticism were of an ethical nature. He could not forget, for example, that Hauptmann had become a patriotic nationalist during the war, instead of bearing witness to the horrible inhumanity of those years. Kraus was saddened and disappointed at Hauptmann's associations with people such as Reinhardt and the banker Castiglioni.[50] When Hauptmann's play *Dorothea Angermann* was premiered in Reinhardt's Theater in der Josefstadt, Kraus reprinted newspaper reports of the performance, as well as the following: 'Nach dem Premiereabend hatte *Präsident Castiglioni* einen Kreis von Freunden zu Ehren Gerhart *Hauptmanns,* Max *Reinhardts* und Tristan *Bernards* zu sich zum Souper gebeten. Es nahmen ungefähr zwanzig Personen daran teil' (F.743/50:43). [After the première, *President*

Castiglioni had invited a circle of friends to his place for supper in honour of Gerhart *Hauptmann*, Max *Reinhardt*, and Tristan *Bernard*. Approximately twenty people were present.] His own comments were:

> *Drei hat man. Der eine ist ein Theaterhändler, der andere ein Lustig-*
> *macher, der hier gleich bei der Ankunft vor Journalisten Purzelbäume*
> *schlug; geht in Ordnung. Doch der dritte, ach der dritte hat die*
> *Himmelfahrt jenes hungernden Kindes geschrieben, das erst am erträumten*
> *Ziel von goldenen Schüsseln speiste. Und der Mann, dem der Bundespräsi-*
> *dent den Dank des armen Österreich abstattet, läßt sich von dem Präsidenten*
> *fetieren, der Österreich arm gemacht hat. Wie traurig sind doch dieses*
> *Lebens Feste!* (Ibid)

> *Den Mann, der diese Verse* [Hanneles Himmelfahrt] *geschrieben hat,*
> *heute mit Schmöcken gepaart zu sehen, ist eine Tragödie der Zeit, die er*
> *nicht mehr schreiben könnte.* (Ibid, p. 101)

We have three. The one is a theatre-monger, the second a merrymaker who turned somersaults as soon as the journalists arrived; that's fine. But the third, alas! the third wrote [the play about] the ascension of that starving child who only ate from golden plates when she reached the goal that she dreamed of. And the man to whom the president of this country rendered the thanks of poor Austria allows himself to be fêted by the president who made Austria poor. How sad are the fêtes of this life!

To see the man who wrote these lines [*Hanneles Himmelfahrt*] paired with the snobs is a tragedy of the times which he would no longer be able to write.

Thus Hauptmann was rejected by Kraus for becoming a part of the establishment. But most other successful contemporary dramatists, as far as Kraus was concerned, had never been anything other than members and even dependents of the established order. Schnitzler is the one who perhaps came off best, but only, one suspects, because Kraus judged that he had acted decently during the war.

> *Nun sind freilich die Ehrungen, die ihm* [Schnitzler] *in so überreichem,*
> *wenngleich nicht mehr überraschendem Maß zuteil wurden, einem*
> *Manne wohl zu gönnen, der zwar den 'Reigen' geschrieben hat,*
> *aber immerhin einer der wenigen Schriftsteller ist, die sich während*
> *des Krieges anständig benommen haben, was man zum Beispiel von*
> *seinem Mitklassiker einer unteren Klasse, dem Herrn von Hofmannsthal,*
> *nicht sagen kann ...* (F.595/600:90)

Now, to be sure, the honours which were heaped on him [Schnitzler] in such an abundant, although no longer surprising, measure cannot be begrudged a man who, though he has written *Der Reigen*, is nevertheless one of the few writers who behaved decently during the war; this cannot be said, for example, of his fellow classic of a lower class, Mr von Hofmannsthal.

But Kraus did not hold Schnitzler's artistic abilities in very high regard:

Außerdem ist ja gewiß nicht zu leugnen, daß Schnitzler seine Meriten hat, indem er nach amourösen Anfängen eben den Kreisen, deren genußfroher Lebensrichtung er entgegengekommen war, auch vertieftere Einsichten vermittelte, ja sich in seinem Schaffen zu der Erkenntnis durchrang, daß wir alle sterben müssen. (Ibid)

Besides, it certainly cannot be denied that Schnitzler has his merits in that, having begun as a writer about sex, he then provided those very circles to whose life of pleasure he had accommodated himself with more profound insights, so that in his later works he even progressed as far as the discovery that we all have to die.

As for the play *Der Reigen*, Kraus considered it to be both a literary and moral failure – a box-office success, consisting of ten acts that were begun but never completed, and depending for its success on titillating the audience.

Denn darüber wollen wir uns wohl gar keiner Täuschung hingeben, daß, wie immer man über das Moralproblem der Bühne denken und den literarischen Wert des 'Reigen' einschätzen mag, sein Bühnendasein sich doch ausschließlich jenem Augenblick verdankt, wo der Dialog aufhört; daß sein typischer Zuschauer doch kein anderer ist als jener Voyeur, der, da über einer Entkleidungsszene der Vorhang eines Pariser Theaters fiel, ihm mit beiden Armen Halt gebieten wollte ... (Ibid, p. 91)

For let us not try to deceive ourselves and forget that, no matter how one may assess the problem of the morals of the stage and the literary value of *Der Reigen*, in the final analysis it owes its place in the repertoire to that moment when the dialogue stops; that the typical member of the audience is none other than that voyeur who held out both arms to try to keep the curtain of a Paris theatre from falling when the actors began to undress.

Kraus's criticism remained fixed on the subject matter of Schnitzler's plays; he himself made no attempt to analyse how Schnitzler used this material. This kind of criticism seems particularly unfair when one remembers that Kraus, less than twenty years before, had rushed to the aid of Wedekind against just such critics who could not see beyond the subject matter.

Kraus's criticism of Hofmannsthal continued to be equally unfair. We have already discussed his reaction to *Das Salzburger Große Welttheater* and must now point out again that he rejected this play in the strongest terms while admitting that he knew next to nothing about it.

> *Es mag ja gewiß erstaunlich sein, daß ich, statt in die Kirche einzutreten, um mir ein Urteil über ein Stück des Herrn Hofmannsthal zu bilden,[51] aus ihr austrete. Aber zu jenem befähigt mich allein schon mein Geruchs-vermögen für alle Unechtheit, mein Spürsinn für das Talmi einer 'gol-denen Gnadenkette' und ein unzerstörbares Gefühl für den Takt der Zeit, die auf Leichenfeldern nicht Festspiele zu veranstalten hat, jedoch auch die Lektüre einer einzigen Szene, die ich für einen so aberwitzigen Dreck halte, daß ich selbst dieser unverlegensten aller Epochen nicht zugetraut hätte, so etwas mit den höchsten Begriffen der Menschheit in Verbindung zu bringen ... (F.601/7:5)*

It may certainly seem surprising that instead of entering the church in order to form an opinion of a play by Mr Hofmannsthal, I am leaving it. But to form that opinion, all I need is my good nose for everything that is false, my flair for the talmi-gold of a 'golden chain of grace' and an indestruc-tible feeling for the taste of the times, which should not stage festival plays on fields of corpses, but also my reading of one single scene, which I consider to be such absurd rubbish that I would not have believed even this most shameless of all eras capable of combining that sort of thing with the highest concepts of humanity ...

Kraus never forgave Hofmannsthal his activities as a propagandist in the First World War (see p. 135 above), but this hardly gave him the right to damn a play of which he had read no more than one scene. His prejudice was revealed even more unpleasantly in another instance, when he remarked on a printing error in Salten's report on Hofmannsthal's *Der Schwierige*: 'an-mutigen menschlichen Schamlosigkeit ...' ('charming human shamelessness') instead of 'anmutigen männlichen Schamhaftigkeit ...' ('charming manly bashfulness'). His comment was: 'Interessant, ich hatte den sinnstörenden Druckfehler zwar bemerkt, aber er ist mir nicht aufgefallen, so wenig wie wenn etwa statt des "Schwierigen" "Der Schmierige" gedruckt worden wäre' (F.759/65:98–9). [It was interesting; I had indeed noticed the printing error, which spoils the meaning, but which did not at all strike me any more than if, instead of *Der Schwierige* (*The Man Who Is Difficult*), *Der Schmierige* (*The Man Who is Smutty*) had been printed.] Although the remark is ambiguous – it could refer to Salten – the reader's first reaction is to associate the adjective *schmierig* with Hofmannsthal. In such a case, Kraus's 'criti-cal techniques' are nothing more than smear tactics.[52] Therefore, his protestations against the press's lack of taste in its treatment of the 'tragic death' of Hofmannsthal in 1929 can only seem somewhat hollow (F.811/19:138).

Kraus's comments on Pirandello's *Six Characters in Search of an Author* were quite unspecific and entirely assertory, and were perhaps typical of his criticism of contemporary dramatists in this period. The short poem entitled 'Pirandello' makes only one point about the drama – that it was boring – but presents no evidence or argumentation.

Ein schaler Witz zwischen Schein und Sein,
Rosinen schmecken nach Kuchen.
Der Autor aber bildet sich ein,
daß sechs Personen ihn suchen. (F.697/705:90)

A shallow joke between appearance and reality, raisins taste like cakes. The author, however, imagines that six characters are looking for him.

Elsewhere in the same issue he stated that if there was one thing in the world of which he was proud, it was of not having written Pirandello's *Six Characters in Search of an Author*. He characterized the play, again without evidence, in the following very general terms:

jenes Stück des Herrn Pirandello, das den Gipfelpunkt der geistigen Scham-
losigkeit bedeutet (den Schlußpunkt der Entwicklungslinie eines sich
selbst verwerfenden Theaterwesens und die Eröffnung seines inneren Kon-
kurses) ... das Stück, dessen Langweiligkeit selbst den unleugbaren zeit-
pathologischen Reiz gefährdet ... (Ibid, p. 133)

That play of Mr Pirandello's which signifies the peak of intellectual shamelessness (the end point of a line of development of a theatre which rejects itself and the beginning of its inner bankruptcy) ... this play, which is so tedious that it even imperils the undeniable pathological attraction it has for its time ...

But two considerations make these remarks suspect. First, Reinhardt had staged a production of this play in Berlin the year before (1925). Reinhardt's approval of a new dramatist would almost automatically entail Kraus's disapproval. Second, the remarks quoted above were printed in conjunction with a report of Bernard Shaw's evaluation of the play as 'the most original and most powerful work of the ancient and modern theatre of all nations' ('das originellste und stärkste Werk des antiken und modernen Theaters aller Nationen') (ibid). Such approbation from someone whom Kraus so intensely disliked could also be expected to evoke his censure of Pirandello.[53]

Although Shaw was rarely mentioned in *Die Fackel* in this period,

Kraus retained his negative attitude towards him. This was particularly evident in an article entitled 'Aus dem Reich der Vernunft' (F.735/42:50–4), in which he cited and commented on some of the articles published in honour of Shaw's seventieth birthday. Kraus was most effective when he quoted Shaw's admirers, letting them reveal their own silliness. For example, Alfred Kerr, the Berlin critic (referring perhaps to *Back to Methuselah*), had greeted Shaw in the following manner:

X

Manches noch schrieb ich. Aber ich will's jetzo fast in Kinderworte *kleiden:* weil diese Sprache von Rechts wegen zu uns Kleinjährigen paßt. Du Mann mit dem länglichen Körper, *mit dem länglich-weißbärtigen Gesicht, rötliche Farben darin und ein wasserblaues Augenpaar!*

Wenn Du jetzt, im fast erreichten Viertel des Lebens, nur ein Jüngling bist, bin ich erst ein Knabe. Du ein Süngling, is ein Tnabe. [sic] Genug!

XI

Thanks.

X

I wrote a lot more. But now I want to say it almost as a *child* would: *because this language by rights is appropriate for us youngsters.* You, man with a longish body, with the longish white-bearded face, with reddish colours in it and a water-blue pair of eyes!

If you now, having lived almost a quarter of your life, are just a youth, then I am just a boy. *You youth, me boy.* Enough!

XI

Thanks.

Kraus continued, however, to make Shaw responsible for evoking such stupidity. Here, as usual, Kraus mixed ethical and aesthetic criticism: Shaw was typical of the times which had made him so popular; lacking greatness, personality, and respect, he destroyed standards and negated everything of 'eternal value.'

Ich halte ihn [Shaw] bloß für eine Station im dichten Bahnnetz mittel-europäischer Verirrungen, wenngleich für einen Hauptknotenpunkt des Verkehrs. Für die hohle Gasse, durch die alles liberalisierende und journalisierende Gelichter dieser Tage kommen muß. Für die Einkehr aller Zweifelsucht und für die tiefste Stelle im Geistesleben, in die

sich der Flachsinn versenken kann. Daß die Substanz, der diese Negie-
rung alles überzeitlichen Wertes entspringt, Geist sein soll, bejaht den
zeitlichen ganz und gar. Aber vielleicht kommt es nur daher, daß es aus
dem Irischen kommt und ins Deutsche geht, wo die ausgehungerte Phan-
tasie leicht geneigt ist, jeden Bocksfüßer für den Pan zu halten. Doch
im Erfolg dieses Aufrieglers soll das Bedürfnis der Epoche, von der er ge-
macht wurde, nicht verkannt werden. Mit seinem Gemeinverstand demen-
tiert er das Ungemeine und mit seinem weißen Haar bürgt er für eine
Generation, die den Mangel an Persönlichkeit durch den Mangel an
Ehrfurcht wettmacht. (F.735/42:54)

I consider Shaw to be a mere station in the dense network of middle European aberrations, although I admit he is a main junction point for the
traffic. I consider him to be the empty narrow lane through which all liberal-
izing and journalizing scoundrels of these days must pass. I consider him to
be the resting place of all scepticism, the lowest point in intellectual life
to which shallowmindedness can sink. That the substance from which this
negation of all eternal values springs is supposed to be intellect only
completely affirms the temporal values. But perhaps it is only because it
comes from the Irish and goes into the German, where the starved
imagination is easily inclined to consider anyone with cloven hooves to be
Pan. But in the success of this innovator we must not fail to recognize
the impoverishment of the age which made him. With his common sense he
denies all that is uncommon, and with his white hair he vouches for a
generation that makes up for a lack of personality with a lack of respect.

Hans Weigel, in his book on Kraus, praises this article, stating:

[Kraus] erhebt ... sich zu einer grandiosen Charakterisierung dieses Über-
schätzten [Shaw] ... Es war sinnvoll, und es ist tragisch, daß Karl Kraus
... derartige wesentliche, literarisch und zeitkritisch unschätzbare und gleich-
zeitig so brillant pointierte Erkenntnisse formulierte, die Allgemeingut der
geistigen Menschheit zu sein verdienten und in irgend einer Glosse
versteckt bleiben.[54]

[Kraus] rises to a grandiose characterization of this man who has been
so overestimated [that is, Shaw] ... It was meaningful, and it is tragic that
[when] Karl Kraus ... formulates such substantial *aperçus*, which are
invaluable from both a literary and a topical point of view and which at the
same time are so brilliantly pointed, *aperçus* which deserve to become
the common property of the intellectual world, they remain hidden in some
gloss or other.

However, he fails to note that, although some of the *aperçus* may be brilliant, what Kraus produced was not literary criticism. Nowhere in *Die Fackel* is there a well-reasoned evaluation of a Shaw play. Kraus's attack was against a society that he considered third-rate. Since Shaw elicited admiration from such a society, Kraus concluded that the dramatist must share in its mediocrity. However, if indeed Shaw *was* overrated by his contemporaries, Kraus would have been on firmer ground if he had offered arguments based on aesthetic criteria rather than criticizing him for the sins of contemporary society.

KRAUS'S DRAMAS

That Kraus would sooner or later write plays of his own was only to be expected, given the theatricality of his style in *Die Fackel* and his readings of other authors' plays in the Theater der Dichtung. The questions that will be considered here will be to what extent the plays that he wrote were projections of his ideas on drama and the theatre, as well as of his previous mode of writing, and to what degree these plays can be considered successful. No attempt at a detailed study of the plays will be made, since Hans Heinz Hahnl has already done so in his dissertation 'Karl Kraus und das Theater.'

Following is a chronological reference list of Kraus's dramas, with the subtitles given by Kraus and a short indication of the subject of each:

1a. 1918ff *Die letzten Tage der Menschheit*
Tragödie in fünf Akten mit Vorspiel und Epilog
– A dramatic document of the First World War.

1b. 1918 *Die letzte Nacht*
– A separate printing of the epilogue to *Die letzten Tage der Menschheit*; this was given several performances on its own.

2. 1921 *Literatur oder Man wird doch da sehn*
Magische Operette in zwei Teilen
– A satire of Werfel and contemporary Viennese writers (especially the Expressionists) prompted by Werfel's 1920 play *Der Spiegelmensch* (Magische Trilogie), in which Kraus was lampooned.

3. 1923 *Traumstück.*
– Criticism of post-war times in the form of a poet's dream.

4. 1923 *Wolkenkuckucksheim.* Eine Verskomödie
Phantastisches Versspiel in drei Akten auf Grund der 'Vögel' von Aristophanes
– A satirical picture of Vienna (depicted as Cloud-Cuckoo-Land), ending on a note of optimism for the (Austrian) republic.

5. 1924   *Traumtheater*. Spiel in einem Akt
           – Written in memory of the actress Annie Kalmar,[55] this play
           concerned the poet's attempt to fathom the essential attraction of
           the actress.
6. 1928   *Die Unüberwindlichen*. Nachkriegsdrama in vier Akten
           – A very thinly disguised dramatization of Kraus's campaign
           in the mid-1920s against post-war corruption. The three 'invin-
           cible' men attacked most vehemently were the editor of *Die
           Stunde*, Bekessy (who became Barkassy in the plot), the financier
           and banker Camillo Castiglioni (Camillioni), and the Vien-
           nese chief of police, Schober (Wacker).

Most of Kraus's plays are closet dramas, and are not suitable for the three-dimensional reality of the stage. *Die letzten Tage der Menschheit*, with over 600 pages of dialogue, was never intended for the stage.[56] 'The performance of this drama, which, in its entirety, would take ten evenings measured according to our time, is intended for a Marstheater.'[57] According to Weigel, even the shorter 'stage version' (*Bühnenfassung*), which could be produced in two evenings, was not effective on stage and made those in the audience who had heard Kraus read the play realize the superiority of a purely aural approach.[58] The importance of music in so many of his plays is further evidence of the aural approach. *Literatur oder Man wird doch da sehn* was a 'magic operetta' with music according to the specifications of the author. In *Die Unüberwindlichen* Kraus employed songs, as Nestroy had done in his plays. In *Traumstück* he used music from Offenbach's *Tales of Hoffmann*.[59]

In his drama criticism, Kraus always stressed the importance of the thought or idea of a play (as well as the language which revealed the thought) and tended to ignore character and plot as ingredients of a successful drama.[60] If one now considers his own plays, it becomes obvious again that plot and character were not of great importance for him. In all of his dramas, there is virtually no plot. The play in which Kraus copes best with the lack of plot is *Die letzten Tage der Menschheit*. Here, Kraus orchestrated the themes and achieved some of his most dramatic effects through the use of repetition. Each act, for example, opens with a scene on the Sirk-Ecke of the Ringstraßen-korso in Vienna. As the war progresses, this locale becomes increasingly seedy and depressing. Kraus also uses the scenes of the *Nörgler* ('Grumbler') and the *Optimist* as a kind of counterpoint to the main drama. But as the following programme note reveals, Kraus even saw 'plot' in linguistic terms, the dramatic issue being none other than the revelation of the reality beneath the cliché:

> *Die Handlung entwickelt unter Verzicht auf jede äußere Begebenheit,*
> *das ruchlose Weltbild der Personen auf dem rein assoziativen Weg der*
> *Redensarten, die sie einander zuwerfen und abfangen, und das drama-*
> *tische Ergebnis ist nichts weiter, als das fingierte Leben, das sich zwischen*
> *diesen Kreaturen abspielen muß, wenn die Phrase einen*
> *Inhalt bekommt.*[61]

The plot does without any external incident and develops the infa-
mous view of life of the characters in a purely associative way through
the use of the clichés that they bandy about, and the dramatic outcome is
nothing other than the sham life that must be played amongst these
characters when the cliché receives some content.

As for the characters, they tend almost without exception to be two-
dimensional types who talk a lot. In many of his plays, they are not even
individualized by names, but are either labelled according to family
relationship or profession (Der Vater, Ein entfernter Verwandter [The Father,
A Distant Relative] in *Literatur*; Dichter, Regisseur, Schauspielerin [Poet,
Director, Actress] in *Traumtheater*) or are concepts that have been personified
(Valuta und Zinsfuss, Imago, Geräusch, Der Traum [Currency and Bank
Rate, Imago, Noise, The Dream] in *Traumstück*). This lack of characterization
was in part attributable to Kraus's stylistic technique of quoting, a technique
which he had practised very often in *Die Fackel*, and which he now used
particularly in *Die letzten Tage der Menschheit*, *Literatur*, and *Die Unüberwindlichen*. A large part of *Die letzten Tage der Menschheit* is made up of
quotations from newspapers. Such a stylistic technique is excellent for caricatures and flash impressions, as well as for building up an overall picture of a
group or an era, but it inhibits any atttempt by an actor to create a three-
dimensional character from the material.

Another point of comparison with both *Die Fackel* and the plays of Nestroy
that he read in the Theater der Dichtung would be the high incidence of
satire and social criticism in Kraus's dramas. However, unlike Nestroy, Kraus
never managed successfully to make his satire the subject of a fictive plot,
not even when he adopted the external plot framework of Aristophanes' *The
Birds* in his *Wolkenkuckucksheim*. Rather, satire in his plays remained
very much rooted in the material of the times. Herein lies one of the weaknesses of his plays, for most often, instead of transcending the material, they
present the reader or spectator with the task of deciphering the code. This
might have been an interesting task in Kraus's time, but nowadays it is
questionable whether the results would be rewarding. This criticism applies
least to *Die letzten Tage der Menschheit* and most to *Die Unüberwindlichen*. In the first case, the First World War is sufficiently well known and
important to warrant the effort on the part of the reader, whereas the

events of the second play, no matter how symbolically significant they may have been for Kraus or how praiseworthy his struggle may have been, do not evoke in the reader or the audience the instinctive moral reaction they presumably did in Kraus's day. Not only was the ethical argument not supported by the artistic form of the play (both plot and characterization, as well as Kraus's use of language, are weak), but the dramatic aspect was hindered by the specific details of the moral argument. Weigel sums up the weaknesses of *Die Unüberwindlichen* as follows:

> Doch 'Die Unüberwindlichen' sind kein großes Panorama einer Welt, son-
> dern nur ein Schlüsselstück; sie stellen eine (gewiß bedeutende) Affäre
> dar, aber gleichsam als dramatisierte 'Fackel', auf der Basis realer, allzu
> realer Fakten ... da gibt es große (aber zu lange und zu wortreiche)
> Szenen mit einzelnen herrlichen Pointen ... doch die angestrebte Wirkung
> bleibt aus, die dramatische Machart ist, brutal gesprochen, dilettantisch
> und streckenweise nur ein Protokoll tatsächlicher Vorgänge und
> Gespräche ...[62]

However, *Die Unüberwindlichen* is no great panorama of a world, but rather a drama à clef; it depicts an (albeit important) affair, but does so just as if it were a dramatized *Fackel*, on the basis of real, only too real facts ... There are great (but too long and verbose) scenes with a few isolated marvelous punchlines ... but the desired effect is absent, the dramatic construction of the play is, to be brutally honest, amateurish and, in parts, only a transcript of actual happenings and conversations ...

All of Kraus's plays, except *Die Unüberwindlichen*, make use of dream, fantasy, or magic. This is evident in the titles (*Traumstück, Traumtheater*), in the subtitles ('Magische Operette,' 'Phantastisches Versspiel'), and, in *Die letzten Tage der Menschheit*, in the list of characters (some with fantastical names: Hofrat i. P. Dlauhobetzky von Dlauhobetz, Géza von Lakkati de Némesfalva et Kutjafelegfaluszég; others directly out of a nightmare: Larven und Lemuren, Männliche Gasmaske, Weibliche Gasmaske, Der Herr der Hyänen [Masks and Lemurs, Male Gasmask, Female Gasmask, The Lord of the Hyenas]). By these artistic means, Kraus tried to escape the problem of subject matter that is rooted in a particular era. In a sense, he was perhaps using Offenbach as his example here, for that composer managed to give an imaginative framework to his social satire through his use of music and fantasy. However, Offenbach's music carried the day, and his operettas were entertaining in their topicality. Kraus's situation was slightly different. He was not a composer and music had to assume a somewhat subordinate role in his plays. (Since he could not read music, he had to 'suggest' melodies for his plays to friends who would then score them.) Moreover, underlying his criticism of society, there was a concern of a more ontological nature. Kraus continually found himself confronted with the problem of illusion and reality. This was particularly evident during the war, as seen in his criticism of war plays.[63] Kraus had discovered that language (for him, at any rate) always spoke an essential truth – that a person's language revealed any discrepancy between what he said and what he meant. War widened that gap between appearance and reality, as more and more clichés and phrases were used to try to cover up the essential immorality of war and of a society which tolerated it. The drama and the theatre were the perfect artistic devices to expose this gap, since they 'played' with illusion and could go beyond realism through the dramatist's use of dream, fantasy, and musical effects. This is evident in Kraus's *Letzte Nacht*, which is pure surrealistic theatricality and in which, in the apocalyptic aftermath of the war, the lack of plot and of character development are essential.

In the operetta *Literatur oder Man wird doch da sehn*, Kraus 'played' with illusion and attempted to reveal what he considered to be the reality of the contemporary literary scene. He satirized Werfel and the Expressionists by confronting what they pretended to be (that is, great, inspired poets) with what they really were in his opinion (that is, mediocre poets, interested in financial gain through literature). In his criticism in *Die Fackel*, Kraus had accused Werfel of trying to imitate Goethe. In the operetta, he twisted the theme of 'appearance' further by naming the Werfel figure Johann Wolfgang, who in turn was an imitator ('ein Epigone') of the original great poet, named Werfel. Also, within the fantasy of the operetta, Kraus revealed the essential nature of newspapers and their editors; here he combined ethics and aesthetics in a very successful song, sung by Schwarz-Drucker, a character in the play:

Im Anfang war die Presse
und dann erschien die Welt.
Im eigenen Interesse
hat sie sich uns gesellt.
Nach unserer Vorbereitung
sieht Gott, daß es gelingt,
und so die Welt zur Zeitung
er bringt.
...
Wenn auch das Blatt die Läus hat,
die Leser gehn nicht aus;
denn was man schwarz auf weiß hat,
trägt man getrost nachhaus ...
...
Wir bringen, dringen, schlingen

uns in das Leben ein.
Wo wir den Wert bezwingen,
erschaffen wir den Schein.
Schwarz ist's wie in der Hölle,
die auch von Schwefel stinkt ...[64]

In the beginning was the press and then appeared the world. In its own interest it associated itself with us. After our preparation God sees that it is successful, and so he brings the world to the newspaper ...

Even when the paper has lice there is never a lack of readers; for what one has in black and white one can safely take home ...

We report, intrude, creep our way into life. Where we defeat things of value we create appearances. It's as black as in hell, which also stinks of sulphur ...

Traumtheater is the play in which Kraus is least concerned with criticism of society. Here, through theatre and the dream, he tried to capture the paradoxes of the essential appeal of the actress. The play is dedicated to Annie Kalmar, whose death in 1901 had been such a blow to him. However, it undoubtedly also had its roots in Kraus's admiration of the great Burgtheater actresses of the previous century such as Zerline Gabillon and Charlotte Wolter, as well as in his interest in the problem of the attraction of woman, which had been posed in Wedekind's 'Lulu' plays. Indeed, there are traces of Lulu here, as, for example, when the poet in the play states that the actress is, for every man in the audience, exactly the woman *he* desires ('Sie gibt jedem die Seine').[65]

The poet must come to terms with the paradox that the actress, who belonged to him alone on stage, could then belong to everyone else off-stage and still be true to herself and her sensuality, as well as to him. Kraus twisted the dichotomy of illusion and reality, so that the relationship between poet and actress is real when she, the medium of illusion on the stage, acts in the roles that he has created for her. Then she is completely his. Life off-stage has only an illusory reality in their relationship. As the poet says to her at the beginning of his dream:

Sei wie du bist, so sinds genug der Farben,
die in beglückendem Verein
sich um dein Wesen, deinen Schein
zu ihrer eignen Lust bewarben.
Ich nähre dich als schönste von den Flammen,
die mir aus dem Gedanken schlug.
Dies Geisteswerk und dieser Sinnentrug,
so spielen sie vor aller Welt zusammen![66]

Be as you are, then there will be colours enough that in delightful harmony court the real you and the make-believe you for their own pleasure. I nourish you as the most beautiful of the flames that sprang from my thoughts. This creation of the mind and this illusion of the senses play together in front of the whole world!

Or in the words of the actress:

Spielend erfaßt' ich, daß dies Spiel der Welt
dem Ernste meines Freundes wohlgefällt.
Mein Sinnenspiel: dein Spiel der Phantasie,
daß mir's zur Lust und dir zum Geist gedieh.
Sieh es wie damals, da es dir gefiel:
wie ich auch spiele, du bist mit im Spiel.[67]

Playing, I realized that my make-believe world pleases my friend's earnestness. My sensual play: the play of your imagination – I realized that they flourished to give me physical joy and to enrich your thought. Look on as you used to do when my playing pleased you: whatever role I play, you too have a part in it.

However, the play is not very successful, even as a reading drama. As a stage play, it fails because there is too much talk about paradox and very little action. Ironically, the two most realistic scenes come off best. Each shows the actress with one of her admirers – the first with an older man (Der alte Esel), who wants to start an affair with her as long as his wife does not find out; the second with Walter, a young high-school student. Here Kraus has created individuals, albeit caricatures, whereas the poet and the actress are rather colourless and two-dimensional. The play fails as a reading drama since it is not poetically great. The reader has the impression that Kraus was perhaps trying too hard. For example: 'Mein Herz hat es im Traume aufgewühlt/mit der Naturempfindung süßer Schmerzen.'[68] [In my dream, my heart stirred with the natural feeling of sweet pains.] Or:

Das Stichwort fällt, gleich trittst du auf,
es drängen Partner sich zuhauf,
und stets gebeten, nie bedankt
spielst du, was man von dir verlangt,
und wie den vielen es gefiel,
stehst du und alles auf dem Spiel ... [69]

The cue is given, at once you appear on stage, partners swarm around you, and, always asked and never thanked, you play what they demand of you, and, as your playing pleased so many, you and everything are at stake ...

Part of the evidence of Kraus's theatricality in *Die Fackel* had been his use of paradox and his juxtaposition of extreme opposites. Although he employed these stylistic devices in his dramas, this, as in the case of *Traumtheater*, did not necessarily mean that the plays were theatrically effective. Another measure of Kraus's theatricality in his articles in *Die Fackel* had been his practice of transforming himself into his main character, whom he pitted against the world. This was also true in the dramas.[70] Here, Kraus either appeared directly as a protagonist under an easily recognizable pseudonym (as the 'Dichter' in *Traumstück* and *Traumtheater*, the 'Nörgler' in *Die letzten Tage der Menschheit*, 'Spiegelmensch' in *Literatur*, and the editor Arkus in *Die Unüberwindlichen*) or his presence was felt when characters made mention of 'Fackelkraus' (in both *Die letzten Tage* and *Literatur*). In all of these disguises, Kraus played the same role he assumed throughout the publication of *Die Fackel*, that of the Outsider, of the opponent of the times. The 'Nörgler' is probably the strongest, most vehement projection of Kraus. He is the chorus of *Die letzten Tage der Menschheit*; the scenes with him and the Optimist form a kind of choric interlude.[71]

However, Kraus's appearances in his plays are also evidence of his inability to objectify his theatrical instincts and his sense of ethics in a situation *outside* himself and the immediate problems of his times. His plays are projections of what is a very ethical, but at the same time extremely subjective, egocentric reaction to the world, as well as an equally personal and ethical attitude towards language. They do not, however, constitute good drama. The following quotation perhaps provides a clue to the reason for Kraus's failure as a dramatist: 'One reason good new drama is scarcer than hen's teeth in today's theatre is that today's serious dramatists often write out of a fiery indignation over the state of the world; and pure indignation, however well justified, seldom makes good drama. Something else must be added. Sophocles and Shakespeare were indignant, secondarily, over the cruelty of Greek fate and the corruption of the Danish court. But what really excited them was the unholy mess, the human dilemma, of overconfident King Oedipus and underconfident Prince Hamlet.'[72] In order to transcend 'fiery indignation' and to present the 'human dilemma,' Kraus not only would have had to construct a drama with plot and characters, but a plot and characters that did not necessarily have anything to do *directly* with either contemporary times or himself.

One final paradox must be considered. In answer to the question, 'For what medium did Kraus write?' many critics point to the technical impossibilities of *Die letzten Tage der Menschheit*, as well as the intellectual appeal of Kraus's language and the challenge of the plays to the imagination, and remind us that these texts were perfect vehicles for Kraus's own Theater der Dichtung.[73] Others, while differing in opinion on the stage potential of

Kraus's dramas, insist that some of them at least were intended to be performed on a real stage.[74] There are even those who think that Kraus had a decisive influence on German theatre.[75]

As for Kraus himself, the stage production of his plays could not have been a matter of indifference to him or something he wished to avoid completely. He would not give permission to produce his plays to someone whom he disliked (he denied Piscator and Reinhardt the production rights to *Die letzten Tage der Menschheit*), but he was extremely interested in those productions of which he approved. There is ample evidence of this interest. In *Die Fackel* no. 613/21, he devoted eighty-six pages to material about performances of *Die letzte Nacht*, in which he took the role of 'Der Herr der Hyänen,' and which he modestly called 'one of the most incredible experiments in all of theatre history' (ibid, p. 64). Most of the article was, of course, dedicated to the study and criticism of the critics' response. When Berthold Viertel produced *Traumstück* and *Traumtheater* in 1924, Kraus filled seventy pages of *Die Fackel* no. 649/56 with his own and other critics' reports of the production.[76] And the first forty-one pages of *Die Fackel* no. 827/33 dealt with the performance in Berlin by the Volksbühne of *Die Unüberwindlichen*.

Nor are Kraus's plays completely devoid of visual theatrical effects. This is particularly true of *Die letzten Tage der Menschheit*. Near the end of this drama there is a series of 'apparitions,' most of which are based on war photos. For example:

Einäscherung der Meierei Sorel bei Loison und Verbrennung von 250 dort befindlichen Verwundeten.
(Die Erscheinung verschwindet.)

Versenkung eines Spitalschiffes.
(Die Erscheinung verschwindet.)

Longuyon mit Petroleum-Eimern in Brand gesetzt, Häuser und die Kirche geplündert. Verwundete und kleine Kinder verbrennen.
(Die Erscheinung verschwindet.)

Flandern. In einer ausgeplünderten Hütte sitzt vor einem Kessel eine Gasmaske. Auf ihrem Schoß eine kleinere Gasmaske.
(Die Erscheinung verschwindet.)[77]

The incineration of the Sorel diary-farm near Loison and the burning to death of the 250 wounded there.
(The apparition disappears.)

The sinking of a hospital ship.
(The apparition disappears.)

Longuyon set ablaze with buckets of petroleum, houses and church plundered. Wounded and little children burn to death.
(The apparition disappears.)

Flanders. In a looted hut a gas mask sits in front of a kettle. On its lap a smaller gas mask.
(The apparition disappears.)

Such descriptions suggest that Kraus may have been considering a theatre that, at least through the use of slides, went beyond the purely linguistic boundaries of the Theater der Dichtung.[78]

But if Kraus was intrigued by the stage possibilities of his plays, he failed, at least in part, because he did not follow his own advice as a critic. When he distinguished between stage drama and literary drama, his specification for stage drama was that it should provide the basic framework within which the actors could improvise. But in his own plays he would not allow any actor to tamper with the language. Weigel saw this problem, which he outlined as follows:

Und immer liegt der Reiz und das Besondere [in Kraus's plays] in den Gedanken, in der Sprache, nicht im Dramatischen. Alle seine Bühnenwerke widersprechen dem, was Karl Kraus vielfach als das wesentliche Element des Theaters erkannt hat, sie fordern dem Schauspieler das Wort ab, statt ihm nur das Stichwort für seine Persönlichkeit zu geben.[79]

Er hat das Wesen des Theaters erkannt, hat aber gegen diese Erkenntnis für das Theater, also eigentlich gegen das Theater geschrieben, immer für ein Traumtheater, ein Wolkenkuckuckssheim-Theater; so mußte er scheitern und die Andeutung des Vortragssaales gegen die erträumte Wirklichkeit setzen.[80]

And the fascination and the uniqueness [in Kraus's dramas] always lies in the thought, in the language, and not in the dramatic element. All his stage works contradict what Kraus frequently recognized as the essential element of the theatre: they demand the word of the actor, instead of just giving him the cue for his character.

He knew the nature of the theatre, but when he wrote for the theatre he did so against his better knowledge and thus really against the theatre – for a dream theatre, a cloud-cuckoo-land theatre; hence he was bound to fail and to set off the suggestion of the lecture hall against the reality he dreamed of.

The only place left for Kraus's dramas, therefore, was the Theater der Dichtung. 'Das Gastspiel in der Dreidimensionalität war zu Ende. Das Wort hatte das Wort.'[81] [The guest performance in three-dimensionality was over. The word now had the floor.]

THE OTHER STAGE: 'DIE FACKEL'

After this lengthy consideration of Kraus's ventures into two- and three-dimensional theatre, it seems appropriate to return to *Die Fackel*, which Kraus constantly used as a kind of stage. In this period, it was the scene of a number of dramas in which Kraus featured himself, either in the role of defending himself against the wrongs done to him by the times, or in that of challenging the people he considered to be symptomatic of the evils of contemporary society.

There are many examples of the first type of drama, that of Kraus in self-defence. One of the earliest during these years concerned a public reading of scenes from *Die letzten Tage der Menschheit* that he gave in Innsbruck in 1920. Members of the Tiroler Antisemitenbund created a disturbance at the first lecture and caused the cancellation of the second. They charged that one of the scenes, 'Wilhelm und die Generale,' which did not cast the emperor in a very heroic role, was defamatory, whereas Kraus insisted that every scene in the play was true. He devoted the complete issue of *Die Fackel* no. 531/43 to 'Innsbruck und Anderes.' (The *Anderes* referred to a disturbance at a Berlin reading.) It included long essays in his own defence, as well as a detailed reprinting of the opinions of other critics on the case, along with his own rebuttal and his justification of his opinion that Emperor William II was a charlatan. The issue is 206 pages long.

After the war, Kraus's political sympathies were on the side of the republic; he supported the Social Democrats and often gave readings for the workers under the sponsorship of the socialist Kunststelle, especially on May Day and on the Day of the Republic (12 November). However, Kraus's independent stand and his criticism of what he considered to be the increasingly bourgeois, conservative tone of the party won him enemies among the officials of the Social Democratic party, even though he kept his popularity among the workers. The break with the Kunststelle came in 1925, when Kraus was not asked to speak at the celebration of the Day of the Republic. This evoked an article of explanation from Kraus (F.706/11:58–70), as well as an address of his own to the workers on 9 December 1925, published in *Die Fackel* no. 712/16 (pp. 1–18) under the title 'Nachträgliche Republikfeier.' Among other things, Kraus criticized the theatre – instead of being an instrument of revolution and a tool for the betterment of the working class, it remained under the control of the forces of reaction, which sought to divert attention from the real issues of the times with bourgeois plays and silly modern operettas.

Denn von da [d.h. November 1918] an hat man die unverbrauchte Seele
des arbeitenden Menschen ... deren Natur doch alle politischen und
sozialen Früchte reifen soll, dem Unheil ausgeliefert, dort wo es zu vor-
bildhaftem Ausdruck auf die Szene tritt, auf die Szene des bürgerlichen
Theaters, in welches dem Proletarier Eingang zu ermäßigten Preisen
verschafft zu haben man für eine revolutionäre Errungenschaft hält. Aber
selbst wenn der Eintritt gratis erfolgte, würde ich darin einen Plan der
finstersten Reaktion erkennen, ausgeheckt, um die politische Drohung, um
den Ernst der Forderung nach Brot durch Spiele abzulenken, durch Spiele,
deren Sinn selbst nichts anderes ist als die Ablenkung des geistigen
Anspruchs einer aufstrebenden Menschheit durch die schnöden Tändeleien
der herrschenden Gesellschaft ... Sie [the workers he is addressing] genie-
ßen die parfümierten Ausdünstungen des Bürgergeistes, die man Operet-
ten nennt, die Verlockungen in die Gefühlswelt des Schiebertums, die
sinnbetrügend mit dem Klingklang des unsterblichen Geldgedankens Ihnen
von Woche zu Woche geboten werden als die Erfüllung Ihrer kulturellen
Sehnsucht, als der Inhalt eines lichteren Lebens, in das Sie aus dem Arbeits-
tag hinaufwollen. (F.712/16:2–3)

For from then on [November 1918], the unspoiled soul of the working man
... which should have brought all the cultural and political achievements
to their fruition, was perverted in exactly that place where it has the function of serving as an example: on the stage of the bourgeois theatre, the
theatre to which the proletarian can now gain access at reduced prices – an
arrangement considered [by the bourgeoisie] to be a revolutionary advance. But even if admission were free, I would regard this as a plot hatched
by the forces of darkest reaction, a ploy to offer entertainment instead of
the bread they [the proletarians] so seriously demanded and thus to divert
the political threat. The purpose of these entertainments is nothing other
than the diversion of the intellectual demands of an aspiring people by the
shameless triflings of the ruling establishment ... You [the workers Kraus
is addressing] are enjoying the perfumed exhalations of the bourgeois
spirit that are called operettas, these enticements into the emotional world
of the racketeers, which, confusing your senses with the jingling of the
eternal thought of money, are offered to you week after week as the fulfilment of your cultural longing, as the substance of a better life to which
you aspire out of your workaday world.

Such an argument, with its mixture of ethical and artistic factors, was typical
of Kraus's criticism of both the times and the theatre. In his censure of the
reactionary, conservative role of the theatre, Kraus seems to subscribe to the
theory that the theatre should be an instrument of revolution[82] (ibid, p. 4).

However, later in the essay, he takes a somewhat more cautious stand – that is, if the theatre could not become a 'party theatre,' at least it could be cleaned up artistically, and a repertoire with the goal of 'popular culture' could be introduced:

> *wäre es in der Tat heute unmöglich, an die Wiedererrichtung eines Partei-theaters zu schreiten ... trotz allem bliebe dennoch zu fragen, warum denn auf diesem Gebiete Schaden gestiftet werden muß, wenn schon nicht Nut-zen gestiftet werden kann. Warum er [der Versuch] denn nicht ... wenigstens so weit zu stiften wäre, daß man die vorhandene Möglichkeit und die gebotene Gelegenheit benützt, dem wankenden Kulturgeschäft einer feind-lichen Gesellschaft für die pekuniäre Unterstützung doch künstlerische Bedingungen aufzuerlegen und ein Repertoire durchzusetzen, das dem Ziel volkstümlicher Bildung förderlicher wäre als die Taten einer Direktion Beer ...* (Ibid, p. 6)

if it were really impossible today to begin to re-establish a party theatre ... the question would still remain why, even if the theatre cannot do good, it must do harm. We would still have to ask why it [the attempt] ... should not be instituted to use the present possibility and the offered occasion at least to the extent of imposing on the disarrayed cultural racket that is run by a hostile society certain conditions in return for the financial subsidies [paid out of the workers' taxes]; why a repertoire should not be insisted on that would be more suitable for the education of the people than the proud deeds of director Beer ...

(It should be noted in passing that as a result of his pouring out countless pages of invective month after month and year after year, Kraus's style had become increasingly involuted, not to say bombastic. The pronoun *er* in the passage just quoted is separated from its antecedent, *Versuch*, by five lines of print, and one has to reread the passage to realize that this *er* refers to *Versuch* and not to *Nutzen*. Kraus can no longer 'make' an attempt – he must 'institute' it (*stiften*). He can no longer 'use the opportunity,' but must 'use the present possibility and the offered occasion.' His sentences now run to an average of some eight or ten lines at least. That they constitute a translator's nightmare is hardly to be held against him, but one wonders whether the people he was addressing could understand what he was saying.) Kraus's criticism of the Kunststelle at this point tied in with his dramatic battle with Bekessy, the editor of *Die Stunde*, who became one of the targets of attack in the play *Die Unüberwindlichen*. In the 1920s Bekessy assumed all the symbolic proportions of 'the enemy' that the *Neue Freie Presse* had had at the turn of the century – except that Bekessy was even more influential and, therefore, in Kraus's opinion, even more evil and dangerous. In part, of course, Kraus's reactions to Bekessy were very personal and subjective, although Bekessy repaid him in the same coin. He had, for example, reprinted a photo of Kraus as a young boy, with one of his sisters, in which Kraus's facial features had been retouched to make him look like an idiot (F.686/90:12–13). As for the Kunststelle, Kraus insisted that he broke with this organization because it had shown itself too closely allied with the forces of the status quo and especially with Bekessy. Part of his evidence for this statement was that the Kunststelle had not been willing to challenge a statement in *Die Stunde* to the effect that Kraus and his readings had been forced on the workers. According to Kraus, the opposite was true: the workers had forced him on the Kunststelle.

However, the Bekessy case grew from a drama of self-defence to one of challenge. This was apparent in the play *Die Unüberwindlichen*, but it was also dramatically evident in lectures and in numerous articles in *Die Fackel*, in which Kraus gave vent to his theatrical instincts. One lecture article entitled 'Vor neunhundert Zeugen' (F.706/11:101–20) ended with the sentence 'Hinaus aus Wien mit dem Schuft!' [Get that scoundrel out of Vienna!] This became Kraus's anti-Bekessy slogan; he had only to begin the sentence in his lectures and the whole audience joined in with him. Kraus even nailed placards with this slogan all over Vienna. Complete issues of *Die Fackel* were devoted to his fight (F.730/1 – 'Die Stunde des Gerichts'; F.732/4 – 'Die Stunde des Todes'). And indeed, in 1926 Bekessy did finally have to leave Vienna – he went to Paris.

But the 'drama' of 'Die Unüberwindlichen' which Kraus staged in *Die Fackel* did not end here. On 15 July 1927, during a workers' demonstration, the Palace of Justice in Vienna was set on fire. Schober, the Viennese chief of police, ordered the police to charge the crowd with their horses and to open fire. Ninety people, including innocent bystanders, were massacred. Two months later, the following placard was posted throughout Vienna:

An den Polizeipräsidenten von Wien
JOHANN SCHOBER
Ich fordere Sie auf, abzutreten.
KARL KRAUS
Herausgeber der 'Fackel'

To the President of the Police of Vienna
JOHANN SCHOBER
I demand that you resign.
KARL KRAUS
Editor of *Die Fackel*

The moral stand that Kraus took here was reiterated in long issues of *Die*

Fackel, which were completely devoted to a condemnation of Schober and the killings (*F.766/70* – 'Der Hort der Republik'; *F.771/6* – 'Mein Abenteuer mit Schober'; *F.777* – 'Das Ereignis des Schweigens'; *F.778/80* – 'Blut und Schmutz oder Schober entlarvt durch Bekessy'; also *F.781/6:105–21* – 'Schober im Liede,' which consisted of all the topical verses about Schober that Kraus had written).

The problem here is not whether Kraus was right or wrong – obviously his stand was morally justified. However, today the artistic effect of such lengthy articles, which constantly batter the reader with Kraus's pathos, combined with facts and figures from newspapers and court protocols, may not be what he had intended. Kraus rightly capitalized on the drama of the police shootings, but lost much of the continuing dramatic effect when his theatricality became too long-winded.

Wordiness was also the drawback of the next major drama of challenge that he staged in *Die Fackel*. This time his object was Alfred Kerr, whom he had attacked on stylistic and ethical grounds in the 1910s.[83] This attack was 'dramatized' in the 208 pages of *Die Fackel* no. 787/94, and was entitled 'Der größte Schuft im ganzen Land … (Die Akten zum Fall Kerr).' Again, Kraus's ethics were undoubtedly sound. During the war, under the pseudonym Gottlieb, Kerr had published some artistically bad patriotic war poems, in which he had made fools of such wartime enemies as the French and the Rumanians. However, in the 1920s, his past well hidden, he turned up on a lecture tour in Paris, preaching the gospel of pacifism and ready to make money from the people he had treated so shamelessly a few years before. Kraus had already attacked Kerr on this issue in 1926 (*F.735/42:70–95*). Nor was 'Der größte Schuft im ganzen Land …' the end of the matter; *Die Fackel* no. 795/9 contained the follow-up in 'Der größte Schriftsteller im ganzen Land' (pp. 52–104). But in these articles the conflict becomes lost in an endless torrent of words, and the reaction of the present-day reader may be, perhaps unjustly, that here surely a mountain has been made of a molehill.

As for the other literary critics whose names had become slogans for the stylistic and moral ills of the times, they still turned up in *Die Fackel*, but Kraus had much less evidence to pin on them, and therefore they were no longer the symbolic creatures that they used to be. 'Desperanto' only warranted a little over a page, for example (*F.759/65:102–3*), and could merely conjure up faint echoes of the Harden of nearly twenty years before. Bahr received much more frequent mention, and here, at times, Kraus had not lost his old theatrical touch. In reporting the newspapers' reaction to Bahr's sixtieth birthday (*F.632/9:101–7*), through clever arrangement of quotations and a photo of Bahr and his wife (which he titled 'Pietà'), Kraus managed to make Bahr appear very foolish. His tactics, though, were those of a showman and not of a literary critic.

The period 1919 to 1930 formed the high point of Kraus's interest in the theatre. His Theater der Dichtung provided him with what was probably his most rewarding method of satirizing society, indulging in fancies, and revelling in the greatness of language. There his theatricality and his love of language met on equal terms. Ironically though, his own dramas did not provide an answer to the ills of the theatre, since in them Kraus became lost in issues and words, and was unable to provide either plots of sufficient dramatic impact or clearly drawn characters that actors could work with. It was a period in which the wish he expressed in 1923 in the poem 'Wiedergeburt' for a rebirth of the theatre was to remain unfulfilled.

WIEDERGEBURT

Lange Jahre war das Theater verraten
an Kastraten und Literaten.
Wann bringt die Zeit wieder Spieler hervor,
die Bühnenfüllenden, die Lebendigen,
oder wann raffen empor sich die Toten
und heften die Warnung ans Bühnentor:
Den hier Unzuständigen
ist der Eintritt verboten! (F.622/31:73)

REBIRTH

For many a long year the theatre was betrayed by castrati and literati. When will time again give birth to players, or who fill the stage with life, when will the dead ones gather themselves up and pin their warning on the stage door: Entrance forbidden to those who are incompetent!

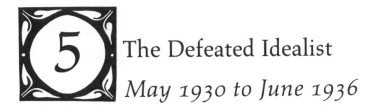

5 The Defeated Idealist
May 1930 to June 1936

Paradoxes abound in the final period of Kraus's life. Kraus, the servant of the word, found himself abandoned by language and thus unable to 'put the word' to the social and political upheavals in Germany and Austria in 1933 and 1934; but it seems in retrospect that he expressed his opposition to the times most eloquently by the silence he kept in both his 'theatres.' With the exception of two evenings in Zagreb in January 1934, he gave no lectures between 4 April 1933 and 19 November 1934. In the publication of *Die Fackel* Kraus observed a twenty-seven month silence, from January 1933 to April 1935, broken only by the appearance of three issues.

Kraus's breaks in his silence represent two completely antithetical attempts to come to grips with the world around him through the medium of language. *Die Fackel* no. 888 consisted of four pages, containing his funeral speech for the architect Adolf Loos and a ten-line poem about his (by then ten-month-old) silence. In contrast, *Die Fackel* no. 890/905, which appeared nine months later, reached a length of 315 pages, in which Kraus tried to explain his reasons for not publishing. However, both his silence and the short poem in which he first commented on it were far more dramatic and effective than the voluminous apologia that followed. Traces of Kraus's theatrical approach to the problems of the times can still be found in this multiple issue of *Die Fackel*, but no matter how hard he tried to enliven his arguments, he became repetitive and enmeshed himself in his own words.

In spite of – or perhaps because of – his difficulties in expressing the ills of the times in words, Kraus devoted a great amount of time and energy to the study of language. In 1932 he announced the publication of a collection of his remarks on language, to be entitled *Die Sprache*, which, however, was only published posthumously in 1937; and in 1934, he planned, but did not actually hold, a seminar on language. His Shakespeare and Offenbach adaptations were, in his opinion, triumphs of language. Kraus regarded language as a treasure to be preserved and its proper usage as a bastion against the immorality of the times, but present-day readers cannot but suspect that his preoccupation with semantics and grammar, far from sharpening his eye for politics, may have served as a kind of narcotic and actually cushioned the shock of confrontation with the mounting horror that surrounded him.

Unable to satirize the main social and political representatives of an era that was so out of joint that it defied satire, Kraus turned all his satirical and critical energies to issues which now seem to be of minor importance. He was still particularly obsessed with Reinhardt. But although Kraus retained his theatrical mode of criticism, he again became repetitive and his grounds for criticism were increasingly personal.

More and more during this period, Kraus found both solace and a refuge for his own theatricality in the theatre of the past. A reader of *Die Fackel* may have the peculiar sensation that Kraus's life had come full circle, since the recollection, albeit idealized, of the performers and plays he had loved in his youth was so strong. Even negative youthful memories (such as his performance in *Die Räuber* in 1893) came to the fore. In his Theater der Dichtung, he continued to shy away from readings of his own works and to read mainly from the works of Shakespeare, Offenbach, and Nestroy to the devoted but small audience assembled to hear him. He also published three volumes of his Shakespeare adaptations[1] (intended for recitation or silent reading rather than the stage), as well as separate editions of Offenbach's *Perichole* and *Vert-Vert*.

Kraus's adaptations seem particularly suited for radio performance. Indeed, it was through the medium of radio that he reached the greatest number of people and effected a renewed interest in Offenbach. For the most part, Kraus directed the speaking parts in order to make sure that the actors kept to his text.[2] He also gave one-man readings in the style of the Theater der Dichtung, and took the title role in a broadcast performance of *Timon of Athens*. These radio broadcasts continued well into 1932. But ironically, after Kraus had begun to popularize Offenbach in this manner, he withdrew his adaptations from circulation because he discovered that others were using them to stage productions which were contrary to his intention.

THE FAILURE OF 'DIE FACKEL' AS A THEATRE OF THE TIMES

If *Die Fackel* can be thought of as a stage on which Kraus fought those he felt to be responsible for the problems of the times, in a fight in which he used all the theatrical means at his disposal, this *Zeittheater* now turned out to be a failure. In the face of the events of the 1930s, words failed him, and, therefore, his theatricality, which was so strongly based on language, was denied its medium of expression.

In 1930, in the essay 'Timons Mahl,' Kraus expressed his doubts that the human imagination would ever be able to give satirical expression to an era whose very material outdid satire.

Nicht darum allein steht die Satire ohnmächtig vor der Wirklichkeit, weil sie sie nicht verändern und nicht materiell bezwingen kann – solches war ihr in den Maßen der Zeitgenossenschaft niemals gegeben; sondern: weil sie sie nicht mehr geistig bezwingen kann. Sie wird von ihr erreicht und übertroffen, sie wird eingeholt und abgewürgt von der Spottgeburt, und Phantasie erstarrt vor dem letzten Wunder, das sich nebst denen der Technik begibt: Lächerlichkeit macht lebendig; der Stoff übertreibt die Satire, die ihn geformt hat ... (F.845/6:30)

Satire is not only powerless in the face of reality because it can neither change it nor control it in its physical substance – this power satire was never accorded by the contemporary masses – but also because it can no longer control reality's informing spirit. Satire is equalled and overtaken by reality, this absurd monstrosity has caught up with it and is choking it to death, and the imagination stands petrified in face of the last miracle that matches the miracles of technology: the content exaggerates the satire that has given it form.

Kraus none the less tried to use *Die Fackel* to satirize the times until December 1932; but when Hitler was appointed chancellor of Germany, when there was a general strike in Austria, and when Dollfuß suspended the Austrian parliamentary constitution, Kraus's reaction was silence. He published one single issue of *Die Fackel* in 1933, no. 888, which came out in October and contained the much-quoted poem in which he explained his apparent inactivity:

Man frage nicht, was all die Zeit ich machte.
Ich bleibe stumm;
und sage nicht, warum.
Und Stille gibt es, da die Erde krachte.
Kein Wort, das traf;
man spricht nur aus dem Schlaf.
Und träumt von einer Sonne, welche lachte.
Es geht vorbei;
nachher war's einerlei.
Das Wort entschlief, als jene Welt erwachte. (F.888:4)

Do not ask what I was doing all the time. I remain silent; and I do not say why. And there is stillness, since the earth was roaring. Not a single word that was to the point; we talk only in our sleep. And we dream of a sun that laughed. It passes; afterwards it made no difference. The word fell asleep when that world awoke.

The poem is the logical conclusion of his remark in 1930 that satire could no longer master contemporary reality. Paradoxically, here the word has illuminated the essence of Kraus's silence. But there is a tragic irony in the fact that the man who had placed so much faith in the word could now only write about his own silence.

Kraus, however, could not leave what he considered to be his own reality unexpressed, nor could he put aside his old roles of challenger and defender. Earlier in 1933, he had already begun to work out the themes for *Die Dritte Walpurgisnacht*, which he originally intended to publish as a regular issue of *Die Fackel* in October of that year. Publishing the poem instead, he nevertheless continued to work on this prose attack on Hitler and Naziism. It was completed and type-set by early 1934, but only appeared posthumously in 1952, although parts of it were worked into the two essays which make up *Die Fackel* no. 890/905.

No. 889 of *Die Fackel*, published nine months after his ten-line poem, consisted of sixteen pages of quotations from critics who had commented on Kraus's long silence, with the title 'Nachrufe auf Karl Kraus.' This served the purpose of setting up his opponents, whom he proceeded to knock down a few days later in the mammoth issue no. 890/905, paradoxically entitled 'Warum die Fackel nicht erscheint' ('Why *Die Fackel* Has Ceased Publication'). Kraus tried to enliven this 315-page rebuttal with some of his old theatrical tricks. For example, the first part of the issue (pp. 1–169) takes the form of a letter, dated 'Anfang Januar bis 12. Februar 1934,' from the 'Verlag der Fackel' ('*Die Fackel* Publishers') to a fictitious reader. Kraus, the author, thus acts out the role of the editorial 'we,' speaking of 'Kraus' in the third person – a device by means of which he tried to give some objectivity to his central assertions, for example, that writers and journalists were responsible for the death of imagination, thought, and language, and were, therefore, to blame for the growth of Naziism. As regards the press, he stated: 'Denn der Nationalsozialismus hat die Presse nicht vernichtet, sondern die Presse hat den Nationalsozialismus erschaffen. Scheinbar nur als Reaktion, in Wahrheit als Erfüllung. Jenseits aller Frage, mit welchem Humbug sie die Masse nähren – sie sind Journalisten.' (F.890/905:141). [For National Socialism has not destroyed the press, but on the contrary, the press has created National Socialism. Apparently only as a reaction, but in reality as the fulfilment. Beyond all question of what kind of humbug they feed the masses – they are journalists.]

In the second part of the issue, Kraus put himself in the foreground, again assigning himself a 'role,' writing this section in the form of another letter, in this case an unsigned one from himself to the 'Verlag der Fackel,' dated 'April bis Anfang Juli 1934' (pp. 170–313). It contained a bitter attack against the tactics of the Social Democrats.[3] The final, short section (pp.

314–5), dated 'Mitte Juli' and entitled 'Ad spectatores,' resembles a programme note. Having presented the spectators with the 'drama,' Kraus quoted from *Macbeth* and drew parallels between that play and the 'drama' of evil being played out in contemporary society.

In the first part of this issue, Kraus quoted sections of his unpublished *Dritte Walpurgisnacht* in which he criticized the Nazis on the basis of their language. As had so often been the case before, language was Kraus's ethical criterion, as he sought to reveal inhumanity through atrocities of style and syntax. He gave examples of words the Nazis had made up (*Reichskulturkammer, Gaukartei, Reichsfachschaftsleiter, Gaukulturwart*, ibid, p. 91) and words that were abbreviations (Gestapo, Fepo, SA, SS, ibid, pp. 92). He was particularly horrified by the Nazis reverting to the literal meanings of phrases which had long been used strictly as metaphors.

> *Und welch Enthüllung für den, der der Sprache nahekam, wäre überraschender, welcher Anblick schlagartiger als der der Worthülse, die sich wieder mit dem Blute füllt, das einst ihr Inhalt war? ... Denn dem wahren philosophischen Sinn des Ereignisses: daß sich hier zum erstenmal, seit es Politik gibt, der Floskel das Wesen entband, und daß nun etwas wie blutiger Tau an der Redeblume haftet – solchem Sinn gehorcht auch die Metapher, die man in ihre Wirklichkeit zurückgenommen sieht ... Die Regierung, die 'mit aller Brutalität jeden niederschlagen will, der sich ihr entgegenstellt' – tut es ... und vollends erfolgt die Absage an das Bildliche in dem Versprechen eines Staatspräsidenten: 'Wir sagen nicht: Auge um Auge, Zahn um Zahn, nein, wer uns ein Auge ausschlägt, dem werden wir den Kopf abschlagen, und wer uns einen Zahn ausschlägt, dem werden wir den Kiefer einschlagen.'* (Ibid, pp. 94–5)

And what revelation could be more surprising for a person concerned with language, what spectacle could be more stunning than that of the skin of the word being filled again with the blood that had once been its content? ... The true philosophical significance of what is now happening – the fact that now, for the first time since there is such a thing as politics, the empty phrase has turned into reality and that something like bloody dew is clinging to the flowering clichés – this significance is observed by the metaphor that has its literal meaning restored to it ... The government that 'will beat down with utter brutality everybody who resists it' really does so ... and the relapse from the metaphorical to the literal meaning is complete when the president of the state promises: 'We do not say an eye for an eye and a tooth for a tooth, but on the contrary: if someone strikes out one of our eyes, we shall knock off his head, and if someone knocks out one of our teeth, we shall smash his whole jaw.'

Kraus's language-based criticism is convincing, but his own style is very bad in this essay. His complicated syntax slows down the reader, and his polemic frequently bogs down in repetition (such as his repeated attempts at self-defence) and so loses its dramatic impetus. Some of the misunderstandings that this essay brought about stemmed from his very idiosyncratic use of language – a combination of ellipses, obscure allusions, and excessively complicated syntax. Probably Kraus's most notorious statement is the opening sentence in *Die Dritte Walpurgisnacht*, which he quoted on page two of 'Warum die Fackel nicht erscheint': 'Mir fällt zu Hitler nichts ein' ('I can find nothing to say about Hitler'). Within the context in which the remark was written – that of *Die Dritte Walpurgisnacht* – the remark makes sense: there, it partly serves the purpose of further provoking the writer who had reproached Kraus for his silence, but mainly that of stating as dramatically as possible that with Hitler and his gang, reality had reached a degree of monstrousness that surpassed the satirist's wildest fictions. As Kraus explained in the essay:

> *Wenn man ihnen sagt, daß einem nichts dazu eingefallen ist, so ist das natürlich eine Hyperbel, man will damit nur sagen, daß man sein Wort für unzulänglich hält, weil einem bloß mehr als ihnen eingefallen ist und weil – so bescheiden ist man wieder – solches noch geringern praktischen Wert hat. Man ist sogar bereit, ihnen Bruchstücke hinzuwerfen, aus denen sie ersehen, daß ... der Verzicht der Unmöglichkeit entstammt, das Grauen zu bewältigen ...* (Ibid, pp. 137–8)

> If you tell them that you can find nothing to say on that subject, that is of course hyperbolical. You only wish to say that you consider your powers of expression to be inadequate because you really have more to say than they have, and because – and here you are so modest again – anything you might say has even less practical value. You are even ready to throw them scraps from which they can see that ... your abandoning speech comes from the impossibility of coping with [your own] horror ...

However, the context of *Die Dritte Walpurgisnacht* was not accessible to Kraus's contemporaries, and he seems to have upstaged himself with his short remark, which became nothing more than a cliché that people began to use against him. If Kraus has not succeeded in explaining his silence in these essays, one reason is that they lacked clarity. Paradoxically, language seems sometimes to have failed him as a means of communication.

Kraus's belief that it was no longer possible to express the reality of the 1930s in words, and his occasional failure to employ language effectively as a means of communication, are two reasons for the demise of *Die Fackel* as a kind of *Zeittheater*, a stage on which Kraus could, with pathos or satire, confront the issues of the times. The third reason for *Die Fackel*'s failure in this area is itself an indictment of the times. In *Die Dritte Walpurgisnacht*, Kraus amassed evidence gleaned from newspapers to dramatize the horror of Naziism. In a sense, this work, although not a play, was a sequel to *Die letzten Tage der Menschheit*. Originally, Kraus had intended to publish this document of evil in *Die Fackel*, if only to bear witness against the atrocities committed by Hitler and his gang. He withheld publication because he feared that the Nazis would take their revenge for this 'provocation' by punishing innocent people. As Frank Field states in his study of that era based on Kraus's works: 'The principal reason why this document did not appear in 1933 was that, in Kraus's own words, "This book includes among other things a description of the 'mentality' of the Minister of Propaganda. It could happen that if his eyes saw my work he would, out of rage, order fifty Jews from Königsberg into the living death of a concentration camp. How could I be responsible for that?" '[4] Similarly, Schick explains:

> *Diese 'Dritte Walpurgisnacht', an der er vom Mai bis September schrieb,*
> *war ursprünglich für die 'Fackel' gedacht. Die 'Fackel' war schon gesetzt, die*
> *Druckfahnen korrigiert, als Kraus sich entschloß, auf die Veröffentlichung*
> *vorerst zu verzichten. Es war nicht die persönliche Gefahr, der er sich*
> *schon beim Schreiben bewußt war ... die ihn von der Veröffentlichung*
> *abhielt, sondern das Verantwortungsgefühl, die Furcht, daß die National-*
> *sozialisten sich für die 'Provokation' an unschuldigen Geiseln rächen*
> *könnten. Er selbst bekannte, daß er 'den schmerzlichsten Verzicht auf den*
> *literarischen Effekt geringer achtet als das tragische Opfer des ärmsten*
> *anonym verschollenen Menschenlebens'.*[5]

This *Third Walpurgisnight*, which he worked on from May to September, was originally intended for *Die Fackel*. *Die Fackel* had already been type-set, the proofs corrected, when Kraus decided to forgo publication for the time being. It was not personal danger, of which he was already aware when he was writing ..., which kept him from publishing, but rather the feeling of responsibility, the fear that the National Socialists could take vengeance on innocent hostages for such 'provocation.' He himself acknowledged that he 'attached less weight to the most painful renunciation of·the literary effect than to the tragic sacrifice of the poorest soul who disappeared anonymously.'

Repelled by the epoch in which he lived, unable or unwilling to freely publish his opinions on most of the topics that it offered him, Kraus began to use *Die Fackel* increasingly as a vehicle for his opinions on theatre and drama, and engaged only one more time in a polemical argument of a political nature, 'Wichtiges von Wichten (In verständlicher Sprache)' (F.917/22: 94–112), an attack on those former supporters of his who had become Communists and who censured him as a *Kleriko-Faschist* from the safety of Prague and Brünn. Otherwise, as a satirical-political stage, *Die Fackel* was dead.

THEATER DER DICHTUNG AND A RETURN TO THE PAST

Kraus ended the first essay of 'Warum die Fackel nicht erscheint' with a pledge to preserve the values threatened by National Socialism by honouring language through his public readings and through his work on language (F.890/905:168). During the 1930s and particularly 1935 to 1936, his public readings were largely devoted to his Theater der Dichtung. As before, he tried to win his audiences over to an appreciation for Offenbach, Shakespeare, and Nestroy. He demanded that his audiences accept his adaptations of the works of others as his own works; those who did not do so, he insisted, should stay away from his readings. In fact, he estimated the 'real' audience of his theatre to be no more than a hundred people. When his readings were disrupted by supporters of the Social Democrats, who disagreed with his individualistic stand for Dollfuß and against their own party, he restricted admission to his performances; from November 1935 until 2 April 1936 (the occasion of his 700th – and last – lecture), tickets had to be obtained in advance. His Theater der Dichtung had thus become a refuge from reality for himself and an exclusive few. This escape from reality was equally evident in the activities subsidiary to his 'theatre' – his adaptations and 'translations' of Shakespeare and Offenbach, his research on Offenbach and Nestroy, his programme notes and introductions to his adaptations, which formed the bulk of the issues of *Die Fackel* published in 1935–6. The 'retreat into intellectual matters' ('Flucht in die geistigen Dinge,' F.845/6:3) which he had announced in 1930 was nearly completed.

The reader of *Die Fackel* of the 1920s cannot help but notice that throughout his criticism, Kraus had increasingly turned to the nineteenth century for his standards of excellence in theatre and drama. This tendency became even more pronounced in the 1930s. The comic and musical roots of his Theater der Dichtung extend back one hundred years into Vienna's theatrical past, the popular theatre of the 1830s with the works of Raimund and the early plays of Nestroy (such as *Lumpazivagabundus*), the 1840s and 1850s, when Nestroy was Vienna's leading dramatist, and the 1860s and 1870s, when Offenbach's operettas were in vogue in both Paris and Vienna and when, in 1860 and 1861, Nestroy acted in these operettas.

It is the intensity of the nostalgia with which Kraus turned to the past during the troubled 1930s and the quality of the traditions which he sought out that are worth noting. It was a very Viennese past. Given what

Kraus considered to be the absence of ethics in the press, theatre, politics, and society, and the lack of genius in the theatre in the twentieth century, he was trying to find something ethically and artistically good in the culture that was so much a part of him. His view of the past was, to be sure, an idealized one, as he appears to have for the most part ignored the political and theatrical intrigues of the previous century. However, what seems to have been important to him was that the plays of Raimund and Nestroy and the operettas of Offenbach were works of artistic merit by essentially decent and imaginative men, works which he now no longer primarily used as a means of indirectly criticizing his own contemporaries, but as a welcome escape from the horror of his own times into the world of poetry and imagination.

Kraus's interest in Raimund is a case in point. Although he had previously given readings of sequences from Raimund's plays,[6] he had never 'performed' a full-length play by this dramatist, and had never had very much to say about him. His earlier remarks were mostly of a very general nature,[7] made with little attempt at accounting for his admiration of the dramatist: 'I consider ... Raimund to be the greatest Austrian poet ...' (F.232/3:27) and, comparing him with Grillparzer, '(Raimund is) the more genuine poet ...' (F.588/94:13).

By 1935, not only had the number of Kraus's readings of separate scenes from Raimund's plays increased, but he had also added Der Verschwender to his repertoire (F.909/11:5).[8] He complained that Viennese newspapers had largely ignored this addition. To counteract this negative attitude of the press, he reprinted a review[9] by Armin Friedmann, 'Karl Kraus liest Ferdinand Raimund (Bericht und Betrachtung, nicht Kritik)' (F.917/22:43–5), which was recommended by Kraus since it reminded the reader that a 'relationship still existed with lost values and especially with the spheres of Raimund and Nestroy' (Ibid, p. 43). The article by Friedmann was very complimentary to Kraus. The reviewer found that Kraus had discovered the Nestroy note in Raimund (ibid, p. 44). He admired the 'acoustic miracle' of Kraus's singing both solo and chorus parts, as well as Kraus's sensitivity to the change in pace necessary in reading Raimund after he had spent so much time on Nestroy.

> War Nestroy impulsiv und aggresiv, so ist Raimund meditativ und kontemplativ. Den dadurch bedingten Tempounterschied fühlt Karl Kraus stärker als wir alle ... Wie er Solo – Chor singt, bleibt ein akustisches Wunder für sich. Das Hobellied blüht ihm wurzelwarm herauf. Der letzten Strophe gibt er eine Dämonie, die vor ihm keiner gab. Sein Tod winkt wirklich schauervoll liebreich, einladend-unerbittlich: 'Brüderl kumm.'
> (Ibid)

If Nestroy was impulsive and aggressive, then Raimund is meditative and contemplative. Karl Kraus feels more strongly than any of us the change in pace that such a difference demands ... The way he on his own sings the choruses is an acoustical miracle. The *Hobellied* [the most famous song from *Der Verschwender*] blossoms forth from his very roots. His interpretation of the last verse has a demonic quality that no one before him gave to the song. Kraus as Death beckons in a manner both awful and sweet, inviting inexorably: 'Little brother, come.'

There is an ironic appropriateness in Friedmann's description of Kraus in the role of Death, appearing as it did in the last issue of *Die Fackel* before Kraus's own death.

Although this report, as well as the fact that Kraus chose to read more of Raimund's works, suggests that he now felt a great affinity for these dramas, he was no more explicit than he had been in previous years as to the *reasons* for his choice.

Although Nestroy did not disappear from the repertoire of the Theater der Dichtung, the ten years before 1935 saw Kraus spend relatively much more time on Shakespeare and Offenbach. But his return to the past in 1935 also included a return to Nestroy, with Kraus adding two more Nestroy plays to his readings – *Liebesgeschichten und Heiratssachen* and *Eisenbahn-heiraten oder Wien, Neustadt, Brünn*.[10]

One of the purposes of Kraus's Nestroy performances was to 'rescue' the plays and the playwright from current productions, such as the Volksoper's *Talisman*, which he considered inferior. Kraus reprinted a positive critique of this production from the *Reichspost*,[11] in which, however, he under-lined the critic's praise of those qualities of the production that in his opinion went against Nestroy's intention:

an sich eine Mixtur von Marionettenbühne und Spieluhr, von Revue, Dreigroschenoper, Kino, Opernparodie, Girls, Jazz und Bauerntheater, Posse, Bühnenexpressionismus, Operette, Philosophie und von – Nestroy, *der hier* voll und ganz zu Worte *kommt, wenn auch* oft nicht wörtlich *nach dem Original; wenn auch oft 'frei nach Nestroy'*. (F.909/11:41)

A mixture of puppet theatre and musical clock, of musical show, Three-Penny-Opera, cinema, parody of opera, dancing girls, jazz and peasant theatre, farce, expressionism, philosophy, and of – Nestroy, who here gets a full and complete hearing, if often not a literal one according to the original text; indeed, often 'freely, according to Nestroy.'

Kraus was against any attempt at updating Nestroy or at making him topical, except of course in the comical songs ('Couplets').

(Jeder dramaturgische Eingriff in ein Werk Nestroys) stellt sich ... als frecher Übergriff dar. Erneuerung oder Aktualisierung – die kürzlich [i.e., at the Volksoper] mit dem entzückenden 'Talisman' bis zur Unkenntlichkeit vorgenommen wurde – ist einzig als Zutat zu den Couplets denkbar, deren Strophen, als Zeitstrophen von damals, oft stofflich wie gedanklich antiquiert und daher unverständlich sind, während ihr geistgeborner, nie veraltender Refrain jeder Gegenwart die Spitze bietet. Der geringste Versuch jedoch, der Zeit auch den Dialog anzupassen, würde ein Gesetz zum Schutze von Sprachdenkmälern erforderlich machen. (F.917/22:41)

(Any interference by a dramaturge in a work of Nestroy's) is an impudent encroachment. Attempts at renewing or updating – such as were recently made on the charming play *Der Talisman*, with the result that the play became almost unrecognizable – are only conceivable as additions to the comical songs, whose verses were topical in their times, but now often appear antiquated both in their subject matter and in their style of thought and are therefore incomprehensible, while their witty, ever youthful refrain defies time. However, the slightest attempt at making the dialogue suit the times would demand the passing of a law for the protection of linguistic monuments.

Kraus also approached the problem of the use of dialect in the performance of Nestroy's plays. This question had been raised by him before, in 1925, in a footnote to the essay 'Nestroy und das Burgtheater' (F.676/8:24–8). At that time, he objected to Leopold Liegler's 'translation' of Nestroy into Viennese on the grounds that this killed Nestroy's rhetorical satire.

Nestroy, der kein österreichischer Dialektdichter, sondern ein deutscher Satiriker ist, ins Wienerische übersetzen heißt ihm eine Anzengrube graben. Was wird aus dem Schillerpathos seiner Domestiken? Wie nimmt sich der klischeezersetzende Witz dieser Geschwollenheiten im Einheitsdialekt aus? (F.676/8:25)

Nestroy is no Austrian dialect writer, but rather a German satirist. Translating him into Viennese would make him as tedious as Anzengruber. What is to become of the Schillerian rhetoric of his servants? The wittiness of this bathos that unmasks clichés – how would it come off in the standardized dialect [of Vienna]?

In the final issue of *Die Fackel* (1936), Kraus again pointed out how ridiculous some of Nestroy's speeches ('diese Gedankensprache') would sound if translated into 'Neuweanerisch' (F.917/22:71). In his opinion, the region of Nestroy's speech was neither the extreme realism of popular speech nor, at the other end of the scale, stilted *Hochdeutsch*. Rather its inimitable quality was what Kraus called 'topsy-turvy Schillerian rhetoric, which only a leap into the trivial distinguished from the speech of a Moor or a Mortimer' (ibid). For Kraus, the proof that Nestroy's roles went beyond the limits of dialect actors was the fact that German actors had excelled in them.

> *Der Hamburger Carl Treumann, der Rostocker Knaack hat es getroffen und gar der Breslauer Beckmann, der den Knieriem größer als dessen Schöpfer gespielt haben soll ... Könnte es einen stärkeren Beweis für die lokale Unbegrenztheit dieser Sprachschöpfungen geben?* (Ibid, p. 72).

Carl Treumann from Hamburg, Knaack from Rostock succeeded (in playing Nestroy's roles), and so, above all, did Beckmann from Breslau, who is said to have played Knieriem better than Nestroy himself ... Could there be more powerful evidence that these linguistic creations know no local boundaries?

With the exception of the crisis years 1933 and 1934, every issue of *Die Fackel* in this period carried some mention of Offenbach. Until 1932 Kraus continued the Offenbach cycle that had been broadcast since the end of the previous period, and published his versions of *Perichole* (1930) and *Vert-Vert* (1931). On the programmes of his operetta readings, which were reprinted in *Die Fackel*, he still customarily gave information about the first Paris and Vienna performances (in the 1850s and 1860s). This was one way in which he tried to associate his Offenbach readings with the tradition of the composer. In answer to critics who claimed that he did not do justice to the music of Offenbach,[12] he reprinted critiques by those who asserted that he did succeed in this respect.[13] His most convincing piece of evidence in his favour was probably a letter to him by Offenbach's grandson, Jacques Brindejont-Offenbach,[14] praising Kraus's ability to re-create the music and spirit of the composer: 'Vous avez su, en effet, donner à cette musique son sens véritable en révélant son inspiration classique, en exprimant son véritable rythme, en dégageant sa bouffonnerie comme sa mélancolie ... Ah, qui ne vous a pas entendu "indiquer" la musique et l'esprit d'Offenbach ne connait pas Offenbach. Si tous ceux qui l'interprètent ou qui croient l'interpréter et le servir avaient pu se rendre compte de ce qu'est Offenbach, à travers vous, quelle révélation pour eux ... Je croyais, moi-même, bien comprendre ce rythme, et plusieurs fois, vous m'avez éclairé, surpris, emporté, entraîné' (F.909/11:26–7).

As already noted in the previous chapter, Kraus's Offenbach readings were often part of his battle to 'rehabilitate' the composer in the face of what he called the 'Offenbach-Schändungen' that had sprung up as a result of the renewed interest in the composer created, paradoxically, by Kraus himself. His criticism of these 'desecrations' was more convincing than most of his theatre and drama criticism of the previous decades, since he did not merely rely on newspaper reports, but actually attended at least five of the performances he discussed.[15]

Kraus claimed that the 'style of the times' had been imposed on Offenbach's works and had dragged them down to the level of the contemporary *Salonoperette*. He characterized this style as a combination of realistic, contemporary detail and trashy and spectacular sentimentalism (*Kitsch* or *Schmalz*). For him, the Prague production of *Madame l'Archiduc* was a particularly galling example of the impossibility of doing justice to an Offenbach operetta while playing it in the 'style of the times.' Kraus had given permission for his own text to be used, after having extracted promises from the producers that his directions (*Wortregie*) would be followed. However, by the opening night, the *buffo*, Erich Dörner, who played the role of Giletti, had added expressions and comic touches of his own that appalled Kraus, especially since the audience was obviously greatly entertained.

> *Die erste Heiterkeitswelle des in musealer Beschaulichkeit dahinziehenden Abends erhebt sich, wenn sein [Dörner's] Wort, seine Bewegung den Anstoß gibt, wenn ein Zeitton, den der Hörer identifizieren kann, wie eben jenes Zerspringen oder eine Wortverrenkung oder auch nur eine Geste, ein komisch aufgestülpter Zylinderhut, von Tönen, die sonst an Mozart erinnern könnten, ablenkt. Er kann nichts dafür, er muß; es ist eine vis comica major. (F.885/7:37–8)*

The contemplative attitude that prevails this evening – an attitude like that in a museum – is interrupted by a burst of laughter when a phrase spoken by Dörner, or one of his gestures, gives rise to it, when the attention is diverted from melodies that could remind you of Mozart by a note of the times that the listener can identify, like that phrase 'And if you blow your top' [a phrase that Dörner added to the text] or a malapropism or a gesture, a top hat that is put on in a funny way. Dörner cannot be blamed for this, he can't help it – he is in the grips of a comic force majeure.

In his essay 'Madame l'Archiduc in Prag,' from which the above quotation was taken, Kraus claimed that the contemporary style of stage productions reflected the degraded character of contemporary life in general and that the commercialism of the stage (ibid, p. 39) was but an extension of the commercial and servile spirit of the whole age. This assertion is typical of Kraus's tendency to give aesthetic criticism an ethical basis. His double grounds for attack are indicated in the words which he felt described the

Prague effort best: *Dilettantismus* ('amateurishness') and *Schweinerei* ('smut') (ibid, p. 34), the first indicating artistic censure, the second ethical censure. He wrote that he was fighting an artistic battle ('die Bitternis des Kampfes um Bewahrung einer Kunstwelt,' ibid); however, he had just characterized his fight for Offenbach as 'die *Leidensgeschichte* des Kampfes um Offenbach' ('the *Passion* of the battle for Offenbach') (ibid., emphasis mine), a term which suggests the trials and sufferings that go with a moral or even a religious cause.

Expressions such as *Kampf* and *Leidensgeschichte* reveal that Kraus still saw himself in the role of champion, rescuer, and defender. He was defending not only Offenbach and his operettas but also the nineteenth-century Parisian and Viennese style of performance. In the introduction to his 'rehabilitation' of *Die Großherzogin von Gerolstein*, Kraus called Mehring's version of the operetta an absurdity:

> *Mehring gehört zu unseren stärksten Nichtskönnern, und ich spreche es vor einem Berliner Auditorium aus, daß selbst wenn er bessere Verse schreiben könnte, eine norddeutsche Fassung Offenbachs ein Unding ist ... Eine Wiederherstellung dieser Welt von Witz und Aberwitz ist ... nur im festgelegten Stil der Pariser und der Altwiener Operette, der natürlich auch in Wien längst in Verlust geriet, denkbar.* (F.868/72:41–2)

Mehring belongs in the ranks of our most powerful incompetents, and I say in front of a Berlin audience that even if Mehring could write better verse, a North German version of Offenbach is an absurdity ... It is only possible to reconstruct this world of wit and folly in the well-defined style of the Parisian and old Viennese operetta, which, of course has long since died out in Vienna as well.

In defending *Madame l'Archiduc*, he wrote:

> *Das 'Historische' (1820) ... und das Milieugemäße (Parma) bilden eben das Niemandsland der Operette, die zwar phantastisch aber niemals gegenwartsgemäß ist, die ihre unabänderlichen Normen und Formen hat, an welchen der Banalverstand nicht rütteln kann, und deren Stil, in französischen und altwiener Elementen beruhend, immer gültig und überall verständlich dem Ohr bleibt, das vom Schmalz des neuen Singspiels noch frei zu machen ist.* (F.885/7:41)

It is precisely the 'historical element' (1820) and the milieu (Parma) that constitute the no-man's-land of the operetta, which is fantastic, but never topical, and which has its own immutable norms and forms which banal common sense cannot change. The style of the operetta has its roots in French and old Viennese elements, and will always remain valid and accessible to the ear that can still be cleansed of the sentimentalism of the new musical comedy.

Kraus's defence of Offenbach's operettas was so passionate that one might think he thought of himself as having exclusive rights to these works. He wrote that by withholding his text of the operettas from public performance, he was forcing others to perform inferior versions, so that he, in turn, could show them up with his performances: 'So zwinge ich sie eigentlich, den Dreck aufzuführen, gegen den ich dann eine Strafexpedition in Form des Vortrags unternehme' (F.868/72:15). Indeed, after his experience with the producers in Prague, he opposed anyone else's attempts to stage his Offenbach texts as he considered these works to be his own linguistic creations. He wrote somewhat hyperbolically of his 'word service to the rhythm' and of the 'triple linguistic bondage' under which he toiled:

> Denn meinen Wortdienst am Offenbachschen Rhythmus verhöhnen sie [the music critics] als 'brave und biedere Mühe' ... Wenn diese Gesellschaft eine Ahnung hätte, welch ein rein poetischer Aufwand – selbst George, Hofmannsthal, Rilke und sogar dem Werfel unerreichbar – dazu gehört, in dreifacher Sprachgebundenheit – an den Vers, an den Text und an die Musik – eben dieser zu neuer und doch alter Paarung zu verhelfen und wie noch das Problem der Interpunktion für den musikalischen Ausdruck eine Bedeutung gewinnt, vor der alles Schreiberhandwerk zu Schanden wird: dann würden sie dieses aufgeben, bevor sie die Lust anwandelte, frech zu werden! (F.868/72:12)

> For they [the music critics] ridicule the service my words render to Offenbach's rhythm by calling it a 'sincere and honest effort' ... If this pack had an inkling how much sheer poetry – poetry beyond the reach even of George, Hofmannsthal, and Rilke, not to speak of Werfel – is required to create a new and yet old harmony in triple linguistic bondage to the verse, to the text, and to the music, and to what extent even the problem of punctuation assumes an importance for the musical expression by comparison with which all routine writing is reduced to insignificance – if they knew any of this, they would give up writing before they felt any wish to become insolent.

He claimed that, because of the added, all-important factor of music, he found it harder to shorten Offenbach's texts than those of Shakespeare: 'Nun kann man ... weit eher Shakespeare kürzen als die Textautoren Offenbachs, die bloß die unentbehrlichen Vorbereiter seiner musikdramatischen Herrlichkeit sind' (F.845/6:15).

Kraus would not allow actors to extemporize within his Offenbach text, nor would he allow any word to be altered or left out. When, in 1931, the Berlin Staatsoper produced his version of *Perichole* and then considered cutting the text since the performance dragged, his lawyer sent an irate letter to the management. It read in part as follows:

> *Sollten Sie gleichwohl entschlossen sein, ohne Zustimmung des Autors [sic]*
> *die Weglassung auch nur eines einzigen seiner Sätze vorzunehmen,*
> *deren jeder für die musikdramatische Wirkung gewichtmäßig unentbehr-*
> *lich ist und ohne die diese Wirkung, auf welche es auch dem Textverfasser*
> *ausschließlich ankommt, schwer gefährdet wird, so würde der Autor*
> *sein durch Judikatur des Oberschiedsgerichts prinzipiell und durch seinen*
> *Vertrag mit dem Verleger speziell gesichertes Recht auf völlige Unver-*
> *sehrtheit des Textes mit allen juristischen Mitteln wahren und Sie für den*
> *ihm entstehenden ideellen und materiellen Schaden voll verantwortlich*
> *machen.* (F. 852/6:25–6)[16]

Should you nevertheless be determined to omit without the author's consent as much as a single one of his sentences, each of which is indispensable for the operatic effect and without which this effect, with which the writer of this text is exclusively concerned, is severely jeopardized, the author would defend his right to the complete inviolability of his text – a right guaranteed to him in principle by a decree of the court of appeal and in particular by his contract with the publisher – by every means the law puts at his disposal and would hold you fully responsible for the ideal [sic] and material damages accruing to him.

Reasoning that the text was 'the indispensable bridge to the splendour of Offenbach's musical drama' (ibid, p. 26), Kraus continued his dogmatic defence of the inviolability of his own versions of it. 'Die Offenbach-Renaissance wird stattfinden, wie ich sie textlich grundiert habe, oder sie wird nicht stattfinden! Streichungen, die eine Angelegenheit der geistigen Produktion sind, werde ich mir von keiner Theaterdirektion, die den Wunsch hat, Offenbach herauszubringen, diktieren oder ablisten lassen' (ibid, p. 26). [The Offenbach renaissance will take place on the basis of my texts, or it will not take place at all! Cuts affect the very spirit of a production, and I will not let the directors of any theatre wishing to stage Offenbach dictate cuts to me or trick me into permitting them.] From 1932 on, Kraus forbade any performances of his Offenbach texts.

Kraus's absolute demands for a pure and unabridged rendering of his version of the text could be met in his 'poetic theatre,' but could not possibly be fulfilled on the contemporary stage. In insisting on such textual perfection, he contradicted his earlier views on *Bühnendrama* and on the supremacy of the actor on stage and – as Hans Weigel has pointed out – made quite

unrealistic demands on producers. Recalling a performance of the Prague
production of *Madame l'Archiduc*, Weigel writes:

> *Wieder tritt die Diskrepanz zwischen seinen Anschauungen vom Theater*
> *und seiner Rigorosität in Erscheinung.*
>   *Ich war ... bei einer Aufführung von 'Madame l'Archiduc' im Prager*
> *Deutschen Theater. Es war eine musikalisch einwandfreie, aber eben*
> *operettenhafte Aufführung mit den üblichen Extratouren der komischen*
> *Darsteller, insbesondere des Buffos Erich Dörner. Und es war uns klar,*
> *daß Karl Kraus derlei nicht zulassen würde und daß eine Krise, wenn nicht*
> *Katastrophe in seinen Beziehungen zu dem Bühnenvertrieb bevorstand.*
> *Für ihn waren Texte, ob Goethes 'Pandora' oder Operetten-Dialoge,*
> *sakrosankt bis auf das letzte Komma. Derlei konnte er im Rundfunk als*
> *sein eigener Regisseur, äußerstenfalls bei der Erstaufführung in der*
> *Großstadt, keinesfalls aber im laufenden Repertoire mittlerer und kleiner*
> *Bühnen durchsetzen.*[17]

Again we can see the discrepancy between his views on the theatre and his
inflexibility [regarding the text].

  I attended a performance of *Madame l'Archiduc* at the Deutsches Theater
in Prague. It was a musically sound performance, but it was very much
in the style of the operetta, with the usual improvisations of the comic
performers, especially of the *buffo*, Erich Dörner. And it was clear to us
that Karl Kraus would not permit such goings-on, and that a crisis, if not a
catastrophe, in his relations with the theatre agents was imminent.
Texts, whether of Goethe's *Pandora* or of operetta dialogues, were sacro-
sanct for him down to the last comma. He could enforce this on the radio
when he was his own director or, at most, at a première in a large city, but
never in the daily repertoire of small and medium-sized theatres.

  Although Kraus insisted that operetta texts should not be published, he
himself published three Offenbach works and included some of the lyrics
in vol. ix of *Worte in Versen*. One of the songs to appear as a poem in that
collection was the letter aria from *Perichole*. Weigel points out that the
lyrics occasionally betray that they have been translated and gives two examples from this aria: 'Am Ende kriegt satt nur die Liebe,/Wer vergebens zu
essen begehrt.' [When all is said and done, you only become fed up with love
if you vainly crave to eat.] And, 'Ich fühl, wie dich schmerzt dieses Schreiben./
Was ich tue, ich kann nichts dafür.'[18] [I feel how this letter hurts you. I
cannot help what I am doing.] While acknowledging that Kraus deserved
praise for his work on these operettas and admitting that he had many
unforgettable memories of Kraus's readings of Offenbach, Weigel finds that
the adaptations display 'a certain brittleness and, with all due respect, [the

author's] lack of familiarity with the theatre ...'[19] That others, too, have
reached the conclusion that Kraus's Offenbach adaptations are not ideally
suited to the operetta stage is evident in the programme notes to a recent
(1972) production of *Perichole* in the Vienna Volksoper. In commenting
on why they did not use Kraus's text, the producers wrote:

> *Karl Kraus erschien uns allzusehr auf die Erfordernisse der späten*
> *zwanziger Jahre zugeschnitten. Wir hatten den Eindruck, sie würde*
> *unserer 'Perichole' nicht ganz gerecht. (Darüber hinaus fanden*
> *wir, daß ein sprachschöpferisches Genie wie Kraus nicht von einer*
> *Nebenseite gezeigt werden sollte, die nicht seine stärksten Leistungen*
> *beinhaltet.)*

> Karl Kraus's version seemed to us to be all too tailored to the demands
> of the late twenties. We had the impression that it would not do
> complete justice to our *Perichole*. (Moreover, we felt that, with a ling-
> uistically creative genius such as Kraus, we ought not to present a
> minor aspect of his work which does not show him at his best.)

Evidently, in the eyes of the authors of these programme notes, Kraus himself
had been unable to avoid the 'style of the times'!

In 1931, in his programme notes to his 600th lecture, Kraus announced
a 'flight from the times': he would no longer fight against the 'triumph of
stupidity and shabbiness' but would only sing of it.

> *Die Feier des 600. Abends würde dem Sinn des Vortragenden erst erfolgen,*
> *wenn er zum 601., dem seines geliebten* Vert-Vert, *ein ebenso vollzäh-*
> *liges Auditorium versammelt sähe. Sie wäre die Teilnahme an einer Zeit-*
> *flucht, die die wahre und letzte Beziehung zu der verpesteten Gegenwart*
> *bedeutet; sie wäre die Anerkennung der eigeneren Schriften des Autors*
> *und des Ranges, den der Vortragende des Theaters der Dichtung sich selbst*
> *streitig macht. Hingegen sei man endlich mit ihm überein, daß sich der*
> *Triumph der Dummheit und der Lumperei, denen wir alle mit Haut und*
> *Haar geopfert sind, nicht mehr bestreiten, sondern nur noch besingen*
> *läßt. (F.864/7:5)*

The celebration of the 600th evening of readings would only conform to
the wishes of the lecturer if he were to have just as many people in the
audience for his 601st evening, for his beloved *Vert-Vert*. Such a celebration would be a participation in a flight from the times that signified the
true, ultimate connection with the pestiferous present; it would be
recognition of those writings of the author that are more completely his
own, and of the rank for which the lecturer of the Theater der Dichtung
competes with himself. However, let us finally all agree with him that the

triumph of stupidity and shabbiness whose victims we all are from top
to toe can no longer be fought against, but only sung of.

This escape from the times is mirrored in Kraus's choice of operettas for his
repertoire from 1932. He avoided ones such as *Die Briganten*, where the satire
could too easily be applied to contemporary times, and chose instead those
which, through magic and fantasy (*Die Reise in den Mond*), vaudeville and
circus touches (*Vert-Vert, Die Prinzessin von Trapezunt*), or foreign and
exotic settings (*Die Kreolin*), could remove him from the cares and growing
horrors of Hitler's Europe to the 'never-never land' of Offenbach's works
and to the Viennese operetta style of the mid-nineteenth century. By 1935
Kraus even considered removing the last trace of any possibility of relating
the operettas to the contemporary world: he suggested that it might be advisable, in an era dominated by Hitler, in which satire was impossible and in
which even the contrast between Offenbach's world and Hitler's would throt-
tle laughter, to consider performing Offenbach's music without the text,
so that at least the joyfulness of the music could divert us.

> *Seit es Hitler gibt, kann es Offenbach ... nicht mehr geben, weil, was*
> *sich im Zeichen jenes abspielt ... das Lachen erdrosselt, wie es den*
> *Atem erstickt. Der Einlaß alltäglicher Narrheit aber, die vor dem*
> *Unsäglichen nicht verstummt ist, würde durch ihr geringeres Format*
> *die große Lücke noch fühlbarer machen ... Wäre sie [Offenbach's*
> *music] ohne textliche Grundierung und Überleitung möglich ... so empföhle*
> *sich – bei aller theatralischen Meisterlichkeit dieser Texte – in solcher Zeit*
> *die Isolierung der Musik ... Besser jedoch, von der Zeit durch Heiterkeit*
> *– und wenn deren tieferer Sinn ungefühlt bliebe – abzulenken, als durch*
> *diese an sie zu erinnern.* (F.909/11:25–6)

Since there is Hitler, Offenbach ... is no longer possible, because what is
happening under Hitler's rule ... strangulates laughter just as it chokes
our breath. But the addition of everyday folly that is not rendered speechless when confronted with the unspeakable would, by its lesser stature,
only make the great void more painfully evident ... If [Offenbach's music]
were possible without the foundation of the text and the transitions
provided by it ... it might be advisable – in spite of the theatrical brilliance
of these texts – to isolate the music in such times ... But even if the
deeper meaning of this serene art should remain unnoticed, it is better to
distract attention from the times by this serenity than to remind people
of the times by means of it.

Even in the case of Offenbach, then, Kraus had come to feel that words were
no longer adequate. In the end, his preoccupation with language and ethics
seems to have given way to a desire for the more purely aesthetic appeal of

music: art had become an escape for him, an ivory tower to which he could retreat before the horror of his times.

Kraus's turning to the past for his models of acting had been clearly evident throughout the 1900s. Almost without exception, the actors whom he admired had been associated with the Burgtheater. In the current period, his memories of Burgtheater performances from the 1880s and 1890s were reinforced (particularly in 1935) by the memoirs of actors, directors, and even critics from that era, which Kraus reprinted.[20] He even sought to trace the roots of the Burgtheater style of acting further back into the past by reprinting what he judged to be an exemplary piece of theatre criticism by the German revolutionary and American statesman Karl Schurz (F.885/7:21–30). Schurz wrote of the great impression that the French actress Rachel[21] had made on him when he had seen her perform in the tragedies of Racine and Corneille in Berlin in 1850. He was especially affected by the elemental power of Rachel – the same quality that Kraus had so admired in Baumeister, Matkowsky, and Mme Wolter. Schurz wrote:

> *Die elementaren Kräfte der Natur und alle Gefühle und Erregungen der menschlichen Seele schienen entfesselt in dieser Stimme, um darin ihre beredteste, ergreifendste, durchschauerndste Sprache zu finden.* (F.885/ 7:25)

> *Die Rachel war mir ein Dämon, ein übermenschliches Wesen, eine geheimnisvolle Kraft ...* (Ibid, p. 28)

The elemental forces of nature and all the feelings and emotions of the human soul seemed to be released in this voice, in order to find in it their most eloquent, moving, and thrilling expression.

For me, Rachel was a demon, a superhuman being, a mysterious force ...

Schurz's review substantiates Kraus's claim than an actor or actress of genius can have a formative influence on members of the audience. For Kraus, who had never seen Rachel (she had died in 1856), it was Charlotte Wolter who had had that kind of effect on him.

> *Das glaubt auch der, der in dem Maß der nachgebornen Welt den analogen Eindruck von einem Naturereignis der Wolter verdankt hat ... die Wolter, die von ihrer Zeit als ein jenseits allen Könnertums wirkendes Elementarwesen, als der Inbegriff tragischer Weibnatur empfunden wurde.* (Ibid, p. 21)

[What Schurz is saying] is given credence by a person who, on the reduced scale of later days, is indebted to the phenomenon of Charlotte

Wolter for a similar impression ... Wolter, who was felt by her time to be an elementary force beyond all technical ability, the epitome of the tragic woman.

This claim by Kraus must, of course, be taken with a grain of salt – one has only to read his critiques from 1892 to 1894 to realize that he had on occasion been quite critical of Mme Wolter. However, the details did not matter in 1935. For Kraus, Mme Wolter and her colleagues, as well as the books by or about them, were the mirror of their age (F.912/15:32). In writing about them, Kraus was escaping not just from the contemporary Burgtheater but from a whole era, to find refuge in a theatre in which ethical and aesthetic purposes seemed to complement each other. He reprinted some remarks by Lewinsky on the Burgtheater before 1888 that illustrate this point and show those actors' idealism and commitment to it:

Ein starkes und reizvolles Talent bedurfte ja immer einen Zusatz idealen Strebens und eines stolzen Bewußtseins, diesem Tempel der Kunst anzuge- hören und dadurch ein oberster Träger deutscher Kunst auf diesem Gebiete zu sein, um dem Drange nach Geldgewinn widerstehen zu können. Wer dies über sich vermochte, schloß sich inniger an diesen Gralstempel, dessen geistiges Wesen im ersten Drittel dieses Jahrhunderts Schrey- vogel gebildet hatte. Durch ihn wurde erfüllt, was Kaiser Josef beabsich- tigt hatte, eine Bildungsstätte höchster Art, eine Schatzkammer, in welcher sich die dichterischen Kostbarkeiten der führenden Nationen zusammen fanden ... Diese Idee und der familienhafte Sinn, der an der Scholle festhielt, machten das Burgtheater zu jener einzigen Erscheinung, die sich von allen anderen Theatern unterschied und nur im Théâtre français seinesgleichen hatte. (F.916:14–15)

An actor with a powerful and attractive talent always needed a touch of ideal ambition and proud awareness of belonging to this temple of art and thereby being one of the foremost champions of German art in this field in order to be able to resist the urge for financial gain. Whoever could do so formed an even closer alliance with this Temple of the Grail, whose spiritual character Schreyvogel had created in the first third of this century. He brought into being what Emperor Joseph had intended – a cultural institution of the noblest kind, a treasure-house in which the poetic trea- sures of the leading nations were gathered ... This idea and the sense of family which clung to the soil gave the Burgtheater that uniqueness which distinguished it from all other theatres and was only equalled in the Théâtre français.

Of the 'poetic treasures' in the custody of the Burgtheater that Lewinsky referred to, some of the most memorable for Kraus were Shakespeare's plays, as he remembered them from performances in that theatre during his youth. Kraus's criticism of contemporary performances of Shakespeare dramas is predictable. In the essay 'Lear im Burgtheater' (F.906/7:1–28), he attacked Röbbeling's 1935 Burgtheater production with Werner Krauß as guest performer in the title role. Kraus claimed that the production lacked all dimensions of greatness: the actors had scaled down and flattened Shakespeare's characters; most of them were unable to handle the language of the text;[22] the director was guilty of errors in both the staging and the editing.[23] Kraus again referred to the example of Sonnenthal as Lear in the 1889 Burgtheater production, a performance, while recognizing its faults, he now tended to idealize (ibid, p. 13). The implication of his criticism of the current Burgtheater production was that, with Sonnenthal gone and the theatre in the hands of untalented actors and directors, it was now he himself, with his adaptations and readings[24] of the dramas, who was best able to serve both Shakespeare and the old Burgtheater style of acting.

Perhaps Kraus's strangest return to the past was in an article entitled 'Die Handschrift des Magiers (Aus meinen Memoiren)' (F.912/15:34–62). The magician of the title was Reinhardt. *Der Magier* was one of Kraus's favourite terms for the by then world-famous director (another was *der Professor*, a sarcastic and perhaps envious reference to Reinhardt's honorary doctorate). 'Magician' was the catch word by means of which Kraus made fun of Reinhardt's 'magical' capabilities as a director: Reinhardt could put on huge spectacular shows which would dazzle audiences – he had, as Kraus put it, 'a flair for the effect on the masses' ('Sinn für Massenwirkung') (F.912/15:45); he seemed to be able to be everywhere (Hollywood, Paris, London, New York, Salzburg) at once; his rehearsals had an almost ritualistic quality; he seemed to have magic control over his actors, from whom he elicited a completely sycophantic response, and over audiences and the press, who treated him as a genius.

Kraus objected to Reinhardt's use of spectacle and his belief that 'real' scenery and props (such as real grass in *A Midsummer Night's Dream*) constituted 'genuine' theatre. Kraus's major grounds for artistic censure had been, and still were, that the 'play' was lost in the 'show' and that Reinhardt's concept of theatre did not proceed from concerns of language.

Oft nun, wenn ich Theaterleuten beizubringen suchte, wie aus dem Satzbau die Gestalt hervortritt ... war ich nicht nur vergebens bemüht, es zu erreichen, sondern auch zu erfahren, was 'der Professor' [Reinhardt] ... mit den Schauspielern anstelle, daß sie nicht sprechen können. (Ibid, p. 36)

Aber durch die Farbenfreude des Parvenüs, der blauen Dunst bevor-

zugt, des Dekorateurs, der an der 'Schau' der ärgsten Kunstgewerb-
lerzeit fortwirkt, zu einem Element des Spiels vorzudringen; durch die
Spielereien des Attrapisten zur Sprache und zur Sache zu gelangen, war
mir mein Lebtag nicht möglich. (Ibid, p. 37)

Often, when I tried to show theatre people how the form emerges from
the sentence structure ... I not only failed to do so, but I could not find out
what 'the professor' [Reinhardt] could be doing to the actors so that
they could not speak.

The play was impenetrably obscured by the gay colours of this parvenu
who prefers the foam to the beer, of this decorator who is still knitting away
on the 'show' of the worst era of amateur handicraft; not once have I
managed to reach the language and the message of the play through the
gadgetry of this mock-up artist.

In 'Die Handschrift des Magiers,' Kraus bolstered his argument for language
and against visual effects by quoting from an 1875 critique by Ludwig Speidel
and from a remark by Graf Schönborn to the actor Adolf Sonnenthal, both
of whom expressed sentiments similar to his own on this score (ibid, pp.
50–3).

As usual, Kraus made his readers aware that it was on ethical as well as
artistic grounds that he was criticizing Reinhardt. Reinhardt lived like a
prince, while his extras were paid starvation wages (ibid, p. 44). Hailed by the
critics as a genius, Reinhardt was making money in the Salzburg Festival,
whereas Mozart, the true genius of the festival, had died a pauper (ibid, pp.
43–4). The 'grovelling' of the press and the fans around Reinhardt was
morally reprehensible; in fact, Kraus stated, only the moral collapse of the
German nation presented a picture that was more undignified than the
'grovelling' in Reinhardt's palatial residence; 'Daß es, nächst dem Kopfsturz
der deutschen Nation, kein Bild eklerer Entwürdigung geben könnte als
die Kriecherei um Leopoldskron [Reinhardt's castle residence near Salzburg] ...'
(ibid, p. 43). This particular remark is typical of Kraus's ability to criticize
by insinuation. The two phrases 'Kopfsturz der deutschen Nation' and 'Kriecherei um Leopoldskron' have a common reference point: 'kein Bild eklerer
Entwürdigung.' For Kraus, Reinhardt had some of Hitler's sinister charis-
ma. In fact, in another passage, he is even more explicit. Commenting on
Reinhardt's dictatorial powers at rehearsals, where the actors seemed to
obey him blindly, he remarked that Reinhardt's rule 'bordered on the magical
essence of Hitler' (except that Reinhardt's magic was one of silence): 'dies
[Reinhardt's] wundertätige Walten ... grenzt an das thëurgische Wesen Hit-
lers, wovon es sich jedoch durch die völlige Schweigsamkeit der Regie

unterscheidet, welche eben den besondern Zauber ausmacht' (ibid, p. 35).
[(Reinhardt's) miraculous control ... borders on Hitler's theurgic nature,
from which it differs, however, by the complete silence of the direction, which
of course constitutes the special magic.] The comment is sarcastic and
meant perhaps half jokingly, but the equation is there nevertheless.

The remarks linking Reinhardt and Hitler's Germany are only a few of
the many instances in which Kraus tried to represent Reinhardt as typical of
all that was wrong with the times. Some of the characteristics of such a
type would be banality and a love for the decorative and superficial rather than
the essential, and an interest in business and a desire to make money.
According to Kraus, the shoe fit Reinhardt rather well, since here was a director who was interested in 'superficial' spectacle rather than 'essential'
language and whose cultural ventures were much closer to showbusiness than
to 'pure' theatre.

But Kraus had a very peculiar way of going about proving his case. He went
back to that disastrous performance of *Die Räuber* in 1893, in which he
had done so badly as Franz Moor. He reprinted the programme, which he
claimed had come into his hands in 1930 when it had been reprinted in
connection with the celebration of Reinhardt's twenty-five years as managing
director of the Deutsches Theater in Berlin. For the first time, Kraus's
readers discover that it was Max Reinhardt who had played Spiegelberg in that
production. The incident obviously still bothered Kraus. He did not fail to
mention that he had had no acting instruction, whereas Reinhardt was a
student actor. He admitted that Reinhardt 'doubtless made a more favourable impression' (ibid, p. 46), but laid part of the blame for his own failure
on his costume and wig, which were far too big for him, all the while asserting
that even at that time he was better able to represent an ensemble – as he
had done in his 1893 reading of *Die Weber* – than to play a single part: 'und
ich wäre, der schon damals besser ein Ensemble als eine Rolle darzustellen
vermochte, vielleicht auch dann durchgefallen, wenn mich nicht gleich beim
Aufgehn des Vorhangs ein zu weites Kostum [*sic*] nebst zu weiter Perücke
dem Gelächter der anwesenden Freunde preisgegeben hätte ...' (ibid, pp. 46–
7). From that time on, he now claimed, he had resolved to achieve 'dramatic
effects' without costume and make-up (ibid, p. 47).

Having established this early link with Reinhardt, Kraus went on to claim
that it was he who had started Reinhardt on his meteoric rise to fame and
fortune, since he had suggested his name to the Berlin naturalist director Otto
Brahm, who was in Vienna looking for talented actors for his troupes: 'Er
[Brahm] wurde von mir auf den Salzburger Charakterspieler [Reinhardt] ...
nachdrücklich aufmerksam gemacht' (ibid, p. 49). He then sketchily traced
Reinhardt's career in the theatre (ibid) and finally brought forward his evidence against him: a four-page letter written to him by Reinhardt in 1893,

which Kaus reproduced in facsimile (ibid, p. 54–7). In it Reinhardt thanked Kraus for his help and then went on to comment on the theatre. This private and casual letter, then more than forty years old, was Kraus's 'proof' of the bad qualities he had since discovered in Reinhardt and his contemporaries – and on the basis of the handwriting at that.

Nicht geistige Leere und Lücke der Bildung … sondern der untilgbare Charakter einer Schrift, deren perfektem Schönheitsdrang und ausschweifender Banalität jene Mängel wesentlich zugehören, macht das folgende Werk des Anfängers zu einem der fesselndsten Schaustücke des Meisters. (Ibid, p. 53)

Hier paart die kaufmännische Energie des Zugs mit dem Hang zum Dekorativen. (Ibid, p. 61)

It is not [his] emptiness of mind and bad education … but the indelible character of his handwriting, with whose absolute quest for beauty and excessive banality these defects shared the same essential nature, which makes the following work of the beginner one of the most fascinating revelations of [the character of] the master.

Here a businessman's energy is coupled with a love of the decorative.

The commercialism and the liking for empty pomp and circumstance displayed by Reinhardt's handwriting, Kraus asserted, were equally evident in the director's theatrical ventures, as was the banality displayed in the letter, which was marred by spelling mistakes, the use of abbreviations (some of them wrong), and a general lack of intellectual content.

Kraus then further projected the qualities shown in the letter into space and time and predicted that the dexterity of 'this sales clerk's script' would override the culture of Goethe and the 'purity' of the past:

Aber das Staunen, daß in demselben Jahrhundert die Züge, womit jene Feenhand das Goethewort schrieb, und diese Kommisschrift Raum hatten, weicht dem Grauen, daß eben deren Fertigkeit fortwirkt und daß die unbedankte Reinheit dessen, 'was gewesen ist', nicht Bestand hat vor dem Griff, der sich die Geisteswelt zueignet. Selbst die bange Frage, wie lange diese Illusionen noch vorhalten, bis sie zerstört sind mit allem Lebenswert, sie wird übertäubt von den Interessen, mit denen uns der tägliche Betrug die Zeit vertreibt. Daß wir zu lebenslänglichem Reinhardt verurteilt sind, ist gewiß. (Ibid, p. 62)

But one's astonishment that there was room in the same century for the magnificent handwriting in which Goethe's works were composed and for this sales clerk's calligraphy gives way to one's horror that it is the slickness of the latter which lasts, while the unrewarded purity of that 'which has been' cannot survive in the grip of those who now rule the cultural scene. Even one's anxious question as to how long these illusions can last before they are destroyed along with everything that is of value in life, even this question is silenced by the interests with which daily fraud kills time for us. That we are condemned for life to put up with Reinhardt is certain.

The essay ends on an apocalyptic note: 'Szenenwechsel: "Welch ein greuliches Entsetzen droht mir aus der finstern Welt!" Im Vordergrund Leopoldskron; im Hintergrund zwei wilde Völkerschaften, deren eine die Presse schont und von der andern mit Gas versorgt wird' (ibid). [Scene change: 'What dreadful horror threatens me from the dark world!' In the foreground Leopoldskron; in the background two savage tribes, one of which is coddled by the press but is supplied with [poison] gas by the other one.]

The reader may well be astonished at such a devastating reading of what even at second glance must seem to be an entirely harmless document. The article is true to Kraus's practice of proceeeding from the particular to the general in his evaluation and censure. But this case must seem like the reductio ad absurdum of such a method of criticism. Why would Kraus feel constrained at this point to unearth that old story about his failure as an actor in the *Räuber* performance? The ending of the essay would seem to indicate that he wanted us to take his analysis of the wording and handwriting of Reinhardt's letter seriously. Yet there is a disturbing discrepancy between the half-sarcastic, half-defensive personal aspect of the argument and the grave and frightening conclusions that he draws from the influence of the 'magician.' Kraus's own letters from 1893 (such as his letters to Schnitzler), although in a less florid script, were no less banal and superficial in content and style than those of Reinhardt. The article itself is disturbing in its own banality. There is a tragic irony in the fact that the man who had so eloquently expressed his opposition to Hitler in a ten-line poem and long months of silence should now, in the fall of 1935, devote twenty-eight pages to his own personal trivia.

BERTOLT BRECHT

Even when Kraus had been negatively disposed towards Brecht, he had always found occasion for an indirect compliment. Such was the case in 1927 in the essay 'Mein Vorurteil gegen Piscator' (*F.*759/65:69–71), in which he discussed Brecht's view that the material of some classics could be used to present an up-to-date message, while all those classical works which did not lend themselves to such a use should be left unperformed. Kraus criticized this view and defended the poetry and 'spirituality' (*Geistigkeit*) of the classical repertoire. He added, however, that in view of what the Berlin producers and directors had done to Shakespeare in the last few years, producing Brecht's plays instead might not be so unreasonable (*F.759/65:71*).

Caroline Kohn writes of an occasion in 1928 when Kraus and Heinrich Fischer attended a rehearsal of Brecht's *Dreigroschenoper*, at which they observed Brecht at work. Kraus was impressed with Brecht's theatrical talent:

> *Kraus wohnte 1928 in Fischers Begleitung einer Probe der 'Dreigro-schenoper' bei, bei der Erich Engel die Regie führte, aber Brecht vielfach zur Mitarbeit heranzog. Als Kraus den Dramaturgen und Regisseur Brecht einen Vormittag lang aus einer Loge bei der Arbeit beobachtet hatte, war er von dessen echter Theaterbegabung überzeugt, und bald kam es zur persönlichen Fühlungnahme und freundschaftlichen Annäherung der beiden gleichermaßen für das Theater begeisterten Männer.[25]*

In 1928, Kraus, accompanied by Fischer, attended a rehearsal of the *Threepenny Opera*, in which Erich Engel was the director but frequently asked for Brecht's co-operation. After watching Brecht at work as a dramatist and director all morning from one of the boxes of the theatre, Kraus was convinced of his genuine theatrical talent, and soon these two men who were so enthusiastic about the theatre established personal friendly contact.

Strangely, Kraus made no comment in *Die Fackel* about *Die Dreigroschen-oper*. However, in 1929 Alfred Kerr accused Brecht of plagiarism in that work. Brecht had indeed used some lines of K.L. Ammer's translation of the poetry of Villon. Kraus, who normally was opposed to plagiarism and who was critical both of Brecht's attitude towards the classics and of his Marxist sympathies, came to his aid against his old arch-enemy, Kerr:

> *Im kleinen Finger der Hand, mit der er fünfundzwanzig Verse der Am-merschen Übersetzung von Villon genommen hat, ist dieser Brecht origin-aler als der Kerr, der ihm dahintergekommen ist; und hat für mein Gefühl mit allem was ihn als Bekenner dem Piscatorwesen näher rückt als mir ... mehr Beziehung zu den lebendigen Dingen der Lyrik und der Szene als das furchtbare Geschlecht des Tages, das sich nun an seine Sohlen geheftet hat. (F.811/19:129)*

In the little finger of the hand which took the twenty-five lines from Am-mer's translation of Villon Brecht is more original than Kerr, who found him out. And for all that he is closer in my view to the practices of Piscator than to me, he has more relation to the living essence of poetry and theatre than those horrible ephemerals who now cling to his soles.

Similarly, in 1931 Kraus stated that Kerr's literary protégés could not measure up to Brecht: 'Doch alle zusammen können sie das Wasser ... nicht dem einen Brecht reichen, selbst wenn er sich als sein eigener Vampir mit Doktrinen das Blut abzapft: es bleibt immer noch so viel, um das Gedicht von Kranich und Wolke und die Gerichtssitzung in 'Mahagonny' hervorzubringen ...' (F.847/51:78). [But all of them together are not fit to hold a candle to one Brecht ... even though, like his own vampire, he sucks his blood away with doctrines: there will always be enough left to create the poem about the crane and the cloud and the court-room scene in *Mahagonny* ...] The works mentioned in this quotation were included in Kraus's *Theater der Dichtung*; in an introduction to a reading of them one year later, Kraus reaffirmed his support of Brecht.

> *Der Vortrag aus Bert Brecht, mit dem weder eine Übernahme seines Welt-bilds noch seines Begriffes vom Theater beabsichtigt ist, erfolgt aus mehr-fachen Gründen. Der maßgebendste dürfte wohl der sein, daß ich ihn für den einzigen deutschen Autor halte, der – trotz und mit allem, womit er bewußt seinem dichterischen Wert entgegenwirkt – heute in Betracht zu kommen hat ... (F.868/72:36)*

> Several reasons led to this reading from Bert Brecht, with whom I share neither world view nor theatrical concept. The most important reason is probably that I consider him to be the only German author whom one can take seriously today – and this in spite of and along with everything he does consciously to inhibit his worth as a poet ...

He hastened to add that it was the 'purely poetic value' of Brecht's works that he valued, the didacticism of which transcended Brecht's own didactic concept (ibid, p. 37).

Brecht's attitude towards Kraus can be discovered, at least in part, in his *Schriften zur Literatur und Kunst*. In 1926 he wrote:

> *Dieser Karl Kraus, der von der Allgemeinheit erstaunlich wenig geschätzt wird, kann sich doch nicht heute und nicht morgen die wirkliche Ach-tung der Besten erringen, da gerade der Geruch nach Vorzugsschüler auf gutem Niveau unangenehmer als der eines Unholdes ist. Kraus ist ein Beispiel dafür, daß aus der Antithese nichts herauskommt! Ein so aktives Gegenteil wie K. eines so schlechten Menschen, wie Kraus nicht ist, ist merkwürdiger- und beruhigenderweise noch keineswegs gut. Er legt immerfort ein anderes corpus non delicti auf den Tisch, der sich unter seiner Last schon biegt. Aber da es den Ansichten der Pessimisten zum Trotz so viele Verderbtheiten gibt, triumphiert er niemals ganz. Er wird einfach freigeschwiegen. Auch macht man ungern Aufhebens von Leuten, die durch Behebung eines Übelstandes überflüssig würden.[26]*

This Karl Kraus, who is astonishingly little regarded by the general public, is unable today and will remain unable tomorrow to gain the real esteem of the best people, since his aura of being an A student and the teacher's pet is more unpleasant than that of a rogue. Kraus is an example that nothing comes from an antithesis. Such an active opposite as K. to such a bad person as Kraus is not, is strangely and reassuringly not good. He keeps on putting another corpus non delicti on the table which is already groaning under its weight. But since, in spite of the views of the pessimists, there is so much corruption, he never triumphs completely. He is simply ignored and thus allowed to go his own way. Also, no one likes to make a fuss about people who would become superfluous if the abuse [they protest against] were to cease.

In a longer series of comments around 1934 ('Über Karl Kraus'), Brecht especially praised Kraus's technique of quoting without commentary in *Die Fackel*, as well as his criticism of language and his censure of the contemporary belief in progress. He asserted:

Lebend in einer Zeit, die unermüdlich fast unschilderbare Scheußlichkeiten hervorbringt, übt et eine Kritik von höchstem Standpunkt aus. Die Kräfte in diesem Kampf scheinen zunächst allzu ungleich. Aber nach einigem Nachdenken kann man erkennen, daß Kraus in drei bis vier Jahrzehnten viel erreicht hat: Es ist den finsteren Kräften zumindest nicht gelungen, die großen Bilder der Reinheit zu verwischen und die Begriffe der Sittlichkeit selber zu entfernen.[27]

Living in a time which tirelessly brings forth almost indescribable horrors, he practises a criticism of the highest standard. The forces in this struggle seem at first to be all too unequal. But after some reflection one can see that Kraus has accomplished very much in three to four decades: at least the forces of darkness have not succeeded in wiping out the great images of purity and in removing the concepts of morality.

In a poem written between October 1933 and July 1934 and entitled 'Über die Bedeutung des zehnzeiligen Gedichtes in der 888. Nummer der Fackel (Oktober 1933),'[28] Brecht showed his appreciation of the silence with which Kraus bore witness against the times. The following is the last stanza of the poem:

Als der Beredte sich entschuldigte
daß seine Stimme versage
trat das Schweigen vor den Richtertisch
nahm das Tuch vom Antlitz und
gab sich zu erkennen als Zeuge.[29]

When the eloquent man apologized for the fact that his voice was giving out, Silence stepped before the judge's bench, removed the veil from her face and declared herself a witness.

But after Kraus's long explanation of his silence (F. 890/905), Brecht wrote another poem about him, 'Über den schnellen Fall des guten Unwissenden,' which remained unpublished until 1961 and in which Kraus is represented as a person of good intentions, but one whose ignorance (presumably, his political naiveté) is such that he does more harm than good:

Als wir den Beredten seines Schweigens wegen entschuldigt hatten
verging zwischen der Niederschrift des Lobs und seiner Ankunft
eine kleine Zeit. In der sprach er.

Er zeugte aber gegen die, deren Mund verbunden war
und brach den Stab über die, welche getötet waren.
Er rühmte die Mörder. Er beschuldigte die Ermordeten.
Den Hungernden zählte er die Brotkrusten nach, die sie erbeutet hatten.
Den Frierenden erzählte er von der Arktis.
Denen, die mit den Stöcken der Pfaffen geprügelt wurden
drohte er mit den Stahlruten des Anstreichers.
So bewies er
wie wenig die Güte hilft, die sich nicht auskennt
und wie wenig der Wunsch vermag, die Wahrheit zu sagen
bei dem, der sie nicht weiß.
Der da auszog gegen die Unterdrückung, selber satt
wenn er zur Schlacht kommt, steht er
auf der seite der Unterdrücker.

Wie unsicher ist die Hilfe derer, die unwissend sind!
Der Augenschein täuscht sie. Dem Zufall anheimgegeben
steht ihr guter Wille auf schwankenden Beinen.

Welch eine Zeit, sagten wir schaudernd
wo der Gutwillige, aber Unwissende
noch nicht die kleine Zeit warten kann mit der Untat
bis das Lob seiner guten Tat ihn erreicht!
Sodaß der Ruhm, den Reinen suchend
schon niemand mehr findet über dem Schlamm
wenn er keuchend ankommt.[30]

When we had excused the eloquent man for his silence, a short time passed between the recording of this praise and its arrival. In that time he spoke.

He bore witness, however, against those whose mouth was gagged and condemned those who were killed. He praised the murderers. He blamed the murdered. He reproached the hungry for the crusts of bread they had grabbed. To the freezing he told stories of the Arctic. Those who were beaten by the sticks of the priests he threatened with the steel rods of the house-painter [Hitler].

In this way he proved how little goodness helps when it does not know what's what, and how little the wish to say the truth can do with a person who does not know the truth. He who set out to fight against oppression, well-fed himself – when he arrives at the battle, he stands on the side of the oppressors. How unsure is the help of those who are ignorant! Appearances fool them. Left to chance, their good will stands on shaky legs.

What a time, we said shuddering, when the goodwilled but ignorant person cannot wait that little time with his misdeed until the praise for his good deed has reached him! So that fame, seeking one who is pure, no longer finds anyone above the mud when, gasping, it arrives.

Krolop suggests that the basic theme of the two poems was developed further in Brecht's 'Fünf Schwierigkeiten beim Schreiben der Wahrheit,' as well as in his 'Pariser Rede' of 1935 and 'Madrider Rede' of 1937, in which Brecht tried to come to terms with the problems faced by an anti-Fascist writer in his fight against barbarism.[31] Jenaczek has many reservations about the second poem; why, he wonders, did Brecht not publish it? Why did he leave it in what is so obviously an unfinished state? What conclusions can be drawn from this about his attitude toward the poem? He also criticizes Krolop and some Marxist critics for what he considers to be a too biasedly Marxist and overly simplistic interpretation of Kraus and his motivations. For example, Jenaczek writes:

> Es ist ... einfach unrichtig, zu behaupten, Kraus sei 'dollfußfällig' geworden. Kraus bejaht in Dollfuß nur den entschlossenen 'Anschluß'-Gegner; darin zeigt er ihn der 'europäischen Staatsmannschaft' als das Vorbild, das den Galuben bestätige, 'Hitler-Sigasax' werde einer gemeinsamen militärischen Intervention aller europäischen Staaten weichen müssen. Innenpolitisch dagegen hat Kraus Dollfuß immer nur als das kleinere ubel bezeichnet – das kleinere, gemessen an dem von außen drohenden größeren, Hitler – und betont, daß keine andere Gemeinsamkeit zwischen seinem Denken und dem des Kanzlers bestehe ...[32]

It is simply not right to assert that Kraus had kow-towed to Dollfuß. Kraus affirmed in Dollfuß only his *determined* opposition to the annexation of Austria by Germany; *in this regard* he showed him to 'European statesmanship' as an example confirming the belief that 'Hitler-Sigasax' would have to give in to a common military intervention by all European states. In the field of *internal politics*, however, Kraus always merely called Dollfuß the lesser evil – lesser in comparison with the greater one threatening from outside, Hitler – and he insisted that [the opposition to Hitler] was all that his views had in common with those of Dollfuß ...

In failing to understand why Brecht decided not to publish his second poem about Kraus, Jenaczek displays a surprising degree of blindness towards the realities of the 1930s. Evidently, Brecht was motivated in writing the poem by a profound feeling of disappointment with Kraus's self-centred and repetitive apologia; to publish this poem, however, would have meant to attack an ally in the fight against Naziism and thus to commit a mistake of which Kraus himself was so often guilty.

⮌ Conclusion

There are three ways in which theatrical illusion functions: as make-believe, as revelation of reality, and as delusion. The creator of farces and operettas delights in make-believe, in creating a world as we might like it to be, without making any attempt to convince us that this is the way the world really is. The dramatist or performer of the second type uses illusion to illustrate moral truths. Finally, the playwright can pretend to use the magic of transformation to discover an enhanced reality while in fact only creating a dream world corresponding to his own wishes. In Kraus's case we can sense a natural development from one phase to the next. The motivating force behind this development is Kraus's obsession with power: Kraus the performer achieves a sense of power both from his ability to transform reality and from his ability to move or influence an audience.

A crude but perhaps useful way to illustrate this development is to compare Kraus's life with that of a magician who is caught up in the dynamics of his work. We begin with the magician who is content to astound his audience with the standard magician's trick of pulling rabbits out of a hat. He may then become tempted by an even more extraordinary possibility of theatrical transformation: he can pull not only rabbits out of that hat but great moral truths as well. If the magician is a humble man, he will realize that moral truths are complex – they are painted in mixtures of greys and pastels rather than in primary colours. But chances are that the magician is still principally interested in showing off his powers as a transformer and in impressing his audience. He will then distort these truths so that they have a striking dramatic quality. He will use sharp antitheses, and will present a vivid picture of a reality that is peopled by heroes and villains only.

But how is it possible for a hat to even *seem* to produce a moral truth? The answer is that in the theatre the magician has not only hats but words to play with. And it is the power of the word that enables him to assume the role of the preacher – not the true dispenser of wisdom, but the old-style evangelist who beats the drum and thunders hell-fire and brimstone.

What happens, however, when the moral truths no longer receive the applause of the audience and the house empties? The magician then easily falls prey to the temptations of the failed idealist. He may, for example, turn so far inward that he can convince himself that his power of illusion-making is the source of meaning itself, a rationalization which protects him from the fact that his illusions were not able to reveal reality. Or he may retreat completely into silence.

From what we have seen of Kraus's life and development, I think this schema is partially valid.

Kraus's delight in the theatre was evident very early in his life, as was the theatrical streak in his nature. His theatricality expressed itself primarily in his extravagantly dramatic way of presenting ideas in essays, critical reviews, and lectures. In the early 1890s, Kraus was also actively involved in the make-believe of theatre, either as theatre critic or, less often, as performer or reciter. And as a critic he was primarily interested in the performance of the actors or in the mechanics of the plays, and based his remarks for the most part on aesthetic criteria.

After 1899, with the beginning of the publication of Die Fackel, a strong moralistic streak in Kraus became increasingly evident. Purely artistic theatre or drama criticism now became rarer in his writing. All criticism had to serve and become subordinate to an ethical purpose: that of exposing and criticizing contemporary Austrian society. His information now came increasingly from newspapers rather than his own reading of plays or visits to the theatre, and a large part of his comments consisted of ridicule or censure of the writings of other critics. Artistic weaknesses, both in the critiques quoted from other newspapers and in the dramas or performances reported on, were now interpreted by Kraus as symptoms of ethical flaws, and artistic strength was often seen as evidence of strength of character. Faulty use of language by a dramatist or a drama critic was traced back by Kraus time and again to a shortcoming in the man's character, and an actor's great performance was attributed more to his fine personality than to his artistic skill. In the 1920s and 1930s a significant theme in his works was his moralistic adulation of the great Burgtheater actors he had seen in his youth. During the same period his negative criticism extended from individual plays or performers to the whole of society – the play or performer manifested (in Kraus's eyes) the surrounding corruption. This was particularly evident in his short essays of 1916 and 1917 on war plays. Another way he conducted his attacks was by using his readings of Shakespeare to underline the moral poverty of contemporary Viennese productions and his recitations of Nestroy to satirize Austrian society in general. During his lecture-recitations as well as in Die Fackel he often made direct references to contemporary figures such as Bekessy and Schober, references which actually amounted to full-scale campaigns of vituperation.

Kraus's growing reliance on ethical criteria in his evaluations often led him into untenable critical positions. In his treatment of Harden, he had tried to prove that stylistic weaknesses revealed ethical flaws in the writer. However, Kraus shifted the emphasis even further from artistic to ethical standards. By 1915 he was able to say that a poem was good until he found out who had written it: 'Ein Gedicht ist so lange gut, bis man weiß, von wem es ist' (F.406/12:131). Such a statement was the reverse of his previous view that a writer's style revealed his ethical flaws. In fact, the establishment of objective aesthetic criteria was rendered impossible by such a view and artistic criticism was made absurd.

Ironically, criticism which depended so heavily on ethical criteria or on an ethical interpretation often led Kraus to make unfair and, therefore, unethical judgments. This was evident in the case of Hofmannsthal, whom Kraus no longer judged on his artistic merits after 1899. Kraus even boasted about *not* having read a particular work of his. Thus, Hofmannsthal was damned because of his association with Bahr and Reinhardt and because of his work in the Ministry of War from 1914 to 1918.

Within the area of criticism to which this book is limited, we have seen that Kraus was sometimes quite wrong in his literary judgment. The reasons for such misjudgments were often of a personal nature, which he then rationalized as objective, rational criticism. It does not seem unfair to suggest that most of those who held up under Kraus's ethical scrutiny were either writers of undoubted merit who were no longer alive, such as Shakespeare, Goethe, Raimund, and Nestroy, or more recent writers who appealed to Kraus on ethical grounds and whose aesthetic merits he then tended to extol somewhat beyond reasonable proportions (in particular, Frank Wedekind).

We must not, however, exaggerate the analogy between Kraus and a megalomaniacal magician. No doubt, it is a matter for regret that Kraus, who was, after all, the contemporary of some very major writers and the eyewitness of much that has stood the test of time, found so much to object to and so little to praise in the first three decades after the founding of *Die Fackel*. There can, however, be no question that the ceaseless polemics he engaged in were motivated at least in part by a fine sense of justice, by a moral indignation that even in its quixotic aberrations compels one's respect and admiration. The failings and faulty judgments that we so frequently come across were not merely those of a theatrical virtuoso. They also sprang from an excess of zeal, from an ethical sensitivity that left him no choice but to speak out where he saw injustice done. It may well be argued that his need to pose as a prophet and cast himself in the role of the knight-in-shining-armour compelled him to seek out causes, to dwell on the sins of his contemporaries rather than their virtues. Such an argument, however, can quite easily be turned around, and it may well be fairer to claim that a man so thin-skinned where moral impropriety was concerned needed theatricality both to shield himself and to make himself heard. In any case, it cannot be doubted that the battles he staged on the pages of *Die Fackel* in his best years were waged to reveal a truth, and that the society he castigated so ceaselessly in his theatrical criticism as well as throughout his writings ultimately revealed its basic corruption by the almost total lack of resistance to the Nazis both before and after their take-over, and thus – if not in all details, at least in the overview – proved him right. It is all the more tragic that the prophet of doom lost his grip on reality when doom finally came.

When it did, the tragic ending of the magician in our schema has a biting relevance for Kraus. As the Nazi tide began to rise, Kraus's first reaction was silence. It was as if he had lost all faith in the power of theatre to ennoble the world, and he had excellent grounds for losing that faith since it was precisely the very theatricality of the Nazi movement that supplied its inexorable dynamic. He had even lost faith in the power of words. He took refuge in Offenbach's music, even to the extent of suggesting that words might not be necessary to Offenbach's 'supreme art' – the art of the totally escapist operetta. He had entered the garden of the aesthete and locked the gate behind him. Fortunately he died two years before the Storm Troopers arrived to smash down the gate and to put the torch to all the values that Kraus had stood for.

APPENDIX

～ A Chronology of *Die Fackel*

Die Fackel no.	Volume	Year	Number of issues published
1 –36	1	1899/1900	36
37 –72	2	1900/1901	36
73 –99	3	1901/1902	27
100–134	4	1902/1903	35
135–158	5	1903/1904	24
159–178	6	1904/1905	20
179–200	7	1905/1906	20
201–222	8	1906/1907	20
223–249	9	1907/1908	19
250–278	10	1908/1909	18
279–300	11	1909/1910	15
301–320	12	1910/1911	10
321–346	13	1911/1912	14
347–371	14	1912/1913	10
372–397	15	1913/1914	12
398–405	16	1914/1915	5
406–417	17	1915	2
418–453	18	1916/1917	7
454–473	19	1917	4
474–507	20	1918/1919	4
508–530	21	1919/1920	4
531–567	22	1920/1921	8
568–594	23	1921/1922	5
595–612	24	1922	3
613–648	25	1923/1924	4
649–685	26	1924/1925	5
686–723	27	1925/1926	6
724–756	28	1926/1927	7
757–777	29	1927/1928	5
778–805	30	1928/1929	5
806–833	31	1929/1930	5
834–851	32	1930/1931	4
852–872	33	1931/1932	4
873–887	34	1932	3
888	35	1933	1
889–905	36	1934	2
906–922	37	1935/1936	6

The volumes of *Die Fackel* begin in April.

❧ Notes

PREFACE

1 See my article 'Karl Kraus and the Problem of Illusion and Reality in Drama and the Theater,' *Modern Austrian Literature* 8 (1975) 48–60.
2 Schiller, 'Die Schaubühne als eine moralische Anstalt betrachtet,' *Ästhetische Schriften* (Paderborn 1961) 12–13
3 Büchner, *Leonce und Lena* (Stuttgart 1969) 58
4 I have used *Die Fackel* as the basis for my study. For the division into chapters, I have followed the pattern set by Friedrich Jenaczek in his *Zeittafeln zur 'Fackel'. Themen, Ziele, Probleme* (Munich 1965), but with three minor changes. First, whereas Jenaczek's major concern was obviously the criticism contained in *Die Fackel* (for example, his first chapter only covers the years 1899 to August 1902), I have included the early criticism in chapter 1, and then divided this chapter into two sections: the pre-*Fackel* period and the first two years of *Die Fackel*. Second, I have ended this chapter in June 1901, with the major break in publication of the periodical. The crisis which, at least in part, brought about the nervous exhaustion that necessitated this break was the Bahr/Bukovics case in early 1901, in which Kraus had his knuckles rapped publicly for the first time. After this incident, Kraus's style of criticism was somewhat less brash.

The third slight divergence from Jenaczek concerns the period from September 1909 to 1918, which Jenaczek has divided into two sections, since he considered the war years to require discussion in a separate chapter. As my own study is limited to a consideration of Kraus's theatricality and his theatre and drama criticism, I have devoted only one chapter to the years 1910–18, since I see his censorious comments on war plays in 1916 and 1917 as being the logical conclusion of the kind of criticism he made earlier in that decade.

CHAPTER 1

1 Paul Schick, *Karl Kraus in Selbstzeugnissen und Bilddokumenten* (Reinbek 1965) 23

2 Ibid, 29
3 Ibid, 30
4 *Die Fackel* (Vienna: Verlag 'Die Fackel,' 1899–1936) no. 912–15, p. 47. Future references to this periodical will be given in the text, stating the number of the issue and the page: (F.912/15:47).
5 See *Die Gesellschaft* 1893, no. 2, 234.
6 Ibid, 233
7 *Das Magazin für Litteratur* 1893, no. 26, 422
8 *Die Gesellschaft* 1892, no. 8, 1061–1. It is interesting to contrast this opinion with the views that Kraus held on this particular point from 1908, when he proclaimed, for example, that the Burgtheater had never been a literary stage, that it had 'always' been an actors' theatre, and that these actors were best served by Scribe and Sardou (see chapters 2 and 3)
9 Ibid, 1060
10 Ibid, no. 11, 1508
11 Ibid, 1894, no. 3, 384–5
12 'Aus vollkommenster Unkenntniß aller Tradition hat er sich bald eine Art seichter Modernität herausgeschlagen, die gleich mit aller Tradition es aufzunehmen erklärt, ein Litteraturinteresse, das beim "Heurigen" anfängt,' *Breslauer Zeitung* 1897, no. 58, 3
13 Ibid, no. 202, 3
14 Ibid
15 *Die Wage* 1898, no. 4, 74–5
16 Ibid, no. 43, 719
17 Ibid
18 *Die Gesellschaft* 1893, no. 2, 234–5
19 Ibid, 234
20 Ibid, 235
21 Ibid, 1892, no. 11, 1509
22 Ibid, 1893, no. 2, 233
23 Ibid, no. 5, 648
24 Ibid
25 Ibid, 1892, no. 8, 1063
26 'Sie werden an ihrer Schlichtheit Schaden nehmen, wenn sie in Schlichtheit "reifen", die Fühlung mit dem heimatlichen Boden verlieren und dafür die schlechten Manieren der Virtuosen erlernen. Man hüte sich, die immerhin merkwürdige und in der Geschichte des Theaters bedeutungsvolle Erscheinung agirender Bauern zur "Specialität" zu erniedrigen, von der zu der Orpheum-Pikanterie der "neunjährigen Soubrette" nur mehr ein Schritt ist' *Neue Freie Presse* 12 August 1894, 5
27 *Die Gesellschaft* 1893, no. 2, 234
28 *Wiener Rundschau* 1897, no. 13, 511
29 *Breslauer Zeitung* 1897, no. 340, 1

30 *Wiener Rundschau* 1897, no. 13, 512
31 'Herr Reicher soll fürder die Litteratur in Ruhe lassen und sich brav an den Svengali in "Trilby" halten,' *Breslauer Zeitung* 1897, no. 340, 1
32 Ibid, no. 714, 2
33 See pp. 8–9.
34 *Breslauer Zeitung* 1897, no. 202, 3
35 *Die Gesellschaft* 1892, no. 6, 800
36 *Wiener Literatur-Zeitung* 1892, no. 4, 19–20
37 Ibid
38 Ibid
39 *Das Magazin für Litteratur* 1893, no. 20, 324
40 *Breslauer Zeitung* 1897, no. 240, 2
41 Ibid
42 Ibid
43 Ibid
44 *Die Gesellschaft* 1893, no. 5, 650
45 Ibid, 649
46 Ibid
47 Reinhard Urbach, 'Karl Kraus und Arthur Schnitzler,' *Literatur und Kritik* 49 (1970) 514–15
48 *Das Magazin für Litteratur* 1893, no. 18, 294. See also *Die Gesellschaft* 1893, no. 1, 109–10.
49 Urbach, 'Karl Kraus,' 523
50 Ibid
51 Ibid
52 Karl Kraus, *Die demolirte Literatur* (Vienna 1897) 17. This pamphlet was first published in four instalments in *Wiener Rundschau* November 1896 to January 1897.
53 *Breslauer Zeitung* 1897, no. 271, 3
54 See p. 144.
55 *Die Gesellschaft* 1892, no. 6, 800
56 Ibid
57 *Breslauer Zeitung* 1897, no. 271, 3
58 *Die Gesellschaft* 1893, no. 5, 630
59 See note 52 (chapter 1)
60 '[Napoleon war] kein Held, sondern .. auch ein Mensch ... eine Erkenntnis, die wir uns mit einem Abend voll Langeweile erkaufen,' *Die Wage* 1898, no. 1, 17
61 *Wiener Rundschau* 1897, no. 9, 354
62 Ibid, no. 13, 513
63 Ibid, 514
64 I could find no evidence to support this statement by Kraus in the Munich papers of that period.
65 See also *F.*2:30.

66 See *F*.43:16–25 ('Vom Wechselgastspiel').

67 Kraus made no allowance for possible differences in aesthetic value of the plays by Holzer and Schnitzler. He admitted that he did not know Holzer's play, nor, from what he had seen of his previous work in the Raimund-Theater, was he tempted to become acquainted with it. But the question as to whether the Schnitzler play was good and merited defence by the critics did not even enter Kraus's purely ethical argument.

68 On the other hand, Kraus insisted that the six critics defending Schnitzler had been very personally motivated: 'Es ist zu auffallend, daß diese Gesellschaft [that is, the other critics] nur dann, wenn sie gerade mit dem Autor persönlich befreundet und mit dem Director gerade persönlich verfeindet ist, prinzipiell die Autoren-rechte wahrt ... Man hört ordentlich, wie die protestierenden Herren Bahr und Bauer bei der Nachricht von der definitiven Ablehnung des Schnitzler'schen Stückes erschreckt ausrufen: Was heute Schnitzlern passiert ist, das kann morgen auch uns passieren; das "erfüllt uns mit aufrichtiger Besorgnis" für uns und für die anderen heranwachsenden Talente ...' (*F*.53:4–5).

69 Kraus questioned whether Bahr had not also plagiarized Karl Bleibtreu when gathering material for his play *Josephine*. See *F*.67:22.

70 Presumably this referred to the caricature of Kraus.

71 Kraus's argument that changing styles are evidence of fraudulence is, of course, ludicrous. In that case, Picasso would have to be the most fraudulent of artists.

72 It is interesting to note that Kraus did not criticize Gerhart Hauptmann's use of detail in the stage directions and descriptions of setting in his naturalistic plays.

73 See Schick, *Karl Kraus*, 40.

74 The Christian-Socialist (anti-Semitic) press as yet escaped the brunt of his ire, probably because it was not so powerful. But in *Die Fackel* no. 57 (p. 25) he stated that the purging campaign the anti-Semitic press was waging in the Viennese theatre was only one of principle. In individual cases they were just as bad as the liberal press: 'Im Einzelfalle sind die Herren [der antisemitischen Tagespresse] mit den "verjudeten" Theatern zumeist geradeso versippt wie ihre liberalen Collegen.' Kraus lamented the fact that the anti-Semitic editors had reached such heights of objectivity 'von der aus sie mindestens das Wirken der schlechten und schädlichen Juden mit vorurtheilsloser Nachsicht betrachten können.' (Ibid, 27)

75 See p. 10.

76 He defended himself by stating that he at least had drawn the boundary lines for such 'art' – that is, it was to be practised on home ground only, and not sent off on trips and exposed to the world by impresarios.

77 Kraus again showed himself to be inconsistent in his criticism, for he had admired Hauptmann's dialect plays (such as *Die Weber* and *Der Biberpelz*) and had praised the naturalness of the dialogue.

78 Schreyvogl, *Das Burgtheater* (Vienna 1965) 67

79 Ibid, 106
80 Ibid, 67
81 Dingelstedt was director of the Burgtheater from 1871 to 1881. His productions depended heavily on spectacular theatrical effects.
82 Kraus gave no references for these quotations.
83 They were Franz Adamus's *Die Familie Wawroch* and Theodor Wolff's *Die Königin.*

CHAPTER 2

1 Bahr called Lewinsky's interpretation '(einen) ebenso läppischen als hämischen Einfall' (*F*.104:21–2). The occasion provided Kraus with the opportunity to show Bahr's stupidity as a critic (according to Kraus, the *Dovrealte* was played in the mask of Ibsen throughout Norway), and to praise Lewinsky's artistic integrity, seriousness, and honesty.
2 Lewinsky mentioned that he was unaccustomed to the recognition he had found in *Die Fackel* of 31 January 1905.
3 Koźmian was originally from Poland; by 1905, he had lived fifteen years in Vienna.
4 Sonnenthal had already been criticized by Kraus for accenting the word *Vater* in the line 'Dein Wunsch ist des Gedankens Vater, Heinrich' from *Henry IV*. This moved the spectators, but was rhetorically incorrect.
5 See p. 36.
6 Other critics, however, tended to stress the neo-romantic aspect of Kainz's style. See Herbert Ihering, *Von Josef Kainz bis Paula Wessely* (Heidelberg 1942) 7–15.
7 See his comments on Lewinsky and Matkowsky.
8 Kraus opened the article in *Die Fackel* no. 175 (p. 17) with a quotation from *Hamlet*, II.2. 'nun ist übrig,/Daß wir den Grund erspähn von dem Effekt,/Nein, richtiger, den Grund von dem Defekt;/Denn dieser Defektiv-Effekt hat Grund.' The lines are spoken by Polonius to the queen. The English version, including the lines immediately preceding, runs thus: 'Madam, I swear I use no art at all./That he [Hamlet] is mad, 'tis true; 'tis true 'tis pity;/And pity 'tis 'tis true: a foolish figure,/But farewell it, for I will use no art./Mad let us grant him, then; and now remains/That we find out the cause of this effect,/Or rather say, the cause of this defect,/For this effect defective comes by cause.' The opening line, 'I swear I use no art at all' (although not quoted by Kraus), has a particularly ironic effect if it is applied to the Berlin naturalistic style. That 'this defect' in the case of Hamlet was madness could also be considered a stab at Naturalism.
9 Kraus's conservatism is worth noting. In an article in *Die Fackel* no. 156 (pp. 1–6) he defended the royal family's right to forbid the performance of Hauptmann's *Rose Bernd* since it offended a royal princess. (The Hofburgtheater was, after all, a court theatre.) 'Der Freiheitspöbel möchte immer das Unvereinbare vereinen. Anstatt sich in seiner Art zu freuen, daß der Hof nicht hauptmannfähig ist,

greint er jetzt, weil Hauptmann nicht für hoffähig erklärt wurde ...' Kraus also
interpreted Nestroy in a very conservative, anti-liberal fashion (F.88:17 and
F.89:31–2). See also Jens Malte Fischer, *Karl Kraus. Studien zum 'Theater der
Dichtung' und Kulturkonservatismus* (Kronberg/Taunus 1973)

10 Kraus saw Girardi's leaving as a sign of the decay of the times; it was, in his eyes,
more of a cultural than a theatrical loss to Vienna. He began one aphorism
with the incredulous question 'Girardi in Berlin?' There were two aspects which
bothered Kraus. First, Vienna was so influenced by the Berlin naturalist style
that there was no room left for genuineness (that is, for a genuine talent and
personality such as Girardi's). Therefore, genuineness (*Echtheit*) had to go to
Berlin, where there was room for everything. Second, for Berliners, the Viennese
culture was ethnographically interesting, so that, in sending Girardi to Berlin,
Vienna had sent all that was characteristic of its culture to the world fair, to be seen
and admired by all (F.241:23–4). Kraus later referred to the complete indifference of the Viennese to losing Girardi as '(ein) kultureller Skandal, der nur zufällig
in der Theatersphäre spielt' (F.246/7:39). Viennese tradition and culture were
to be used by the machine age (Berlin), which had no tradition and culture of its
own, and in such an environment the genuineness of this culture would van-
ish, leaving only decorative effects. Girardi's fate would be akin to that of the
Schlierseer (see chapter 1), though on a higher level, since it was questionable
how long Girardi could remain 'genuine,' once cut off from his cultural roots.

11 The pun on *Buchbinder* is untranslatable: *Buchbinder* means bookbinder, but refers as well to the critic-playwright Bernard Buchbinder.

12 This notoriously inane snippet of blank verse is ascribed in Buchmann's *Geflügelte
Worte* to Hans Adolf von Thümmel.

13 These are roles in plays by Nestroy that Nestroy, who was very tall and thin, had
played himself.

14 This article was originally published in *Simplizissimus*.

15 He gave as an example a family of circus artists in Offenbach's *Prinzessin von
Trapezunt*, who unfortunately inherited a baronetcy. The father then had to
slip quietly into the kitchen in order to secretly eat fire and the son felt compelled to
jump over the table to sit down on a chair. Family life was threatening to
disintegrate – until they again stood together on the stage, *being* a family of
acrobats.

16 It may seem peculiar that he rescued such eminently 'theatrical' vehicles as the
operettas of Offenbach in his non-theatrical Theater der Dichtung. In this
article he did not distinguish between 'old' style operettas by Strauß or by Offenbach. However, in a previous article, 'Libretti' (F.172:6–10), he made a distinction between the libretti of Strauß's operettas, which gave the singer-actor
room to extemporize, and the texts of Offenbach operettas (by Meilhac, Cremieux, and Nuitter), which were wittier (*geistvoller*). This was basically the
same distinction as the one he made between stage drama and literary drama.

17 For an interesting comment on the importance of the feuilleton writer in Viennese bourgeois society at the turn of the century, see Carl E. Schorske, *Fin-de-Siècle Vienna. Politics and Culture* (New York 1980) 9.

18 See *F.*83:5–6. Kraus later used his two-column comparison technique to show the mediocrity of Lothar's play and to suggest the complicity of the *Neue Freie Presse* in the 'success' of the play. The *Neue Freie Presse* stated that the Munich performance of Lothar's *König Harlekin* had been a success, but offered no criticism and mentioned only the full house and the fact that the author had appeared on stage at the end of the performance. Kraus juxtaposed the critique of the play in the *Frankfurter Zeitung,* which stated that the play had not been well received. The fool (Harlekin) had merely posed as a man of the Renaissance, and the tragedy had turned into satire (*F.*85:21).

19 Ironically, at one point Kraus had to defend Buchbinder. After Buchbinder was forced to leave the *Neues Wiener Journal,* the other Viennese critics no longer feared him and so felt safe to reject his plays. Kraus considered all of Buchbinder's plays equally bad, but commented on the other critics' lack of morality. 'Etwas Scheußlicheres als diese Hetzjagd auf einen, der keinen Revolver hat, *bloß weil* er keinen mehr hat, etwas Elementareres als dies Geständnis, daß ausschließlich das geschäftliche Cliqueninteresse das öffentliche Urteil bestimmt, läßt sich nicht ersinnen.' (*F.*151:27)

20 Kraus still championed actors and actresses who were used and abused by theatre directors and critics alike (see *F.*148:4–9).

21 His attitude towards Schiller as a playwright was mixed. He protested against the pairing of Goethe and Schiller by literary critics, since neither could then stand as an individual. And he defended Schiller against Otto Weininger, who had linked Schiller and journalism. Kraus stated that this did not apply to everything by Schiller. In Schiller's defence, he cited two early poems. One, 'Der Venuswagen,' was worthy of Wedekind, in Kraus's opinion; the other was called 'Die Journalisten und Minos' (*F.*180/1:39–50). The choice, however, is more indicative of Kraus's penchant as a critic than of Schiller's literary or dramatic importance.

22 For example, Gelber's changes in *Troilus and Cressida,* mentioned in *Die Fackel* no. 93, 15–19

23 Kraus very much minimized any contact Nestroy had had with the stage in a professional capacity, as actor, director, or playwright.

24 To a lesser extent *Rose Bernd* was also an exception. See *Die Fackel* no. 155 (pp. 19–20) for Kraus's defence of this play against the critics.

25 It must be kept in mind that many Austrian writers at that time were proud to be called *Heimatkünstler* and that the term had more positive connotations than its English equivalent, 'regional artist.'

26 Kraus obviously admired Strindberg as a writer – much of the Swedish writer's prose was published in *Die Fackel.* However, he mentioned very little about Strindberg, the dramatist, in these years.

27 'Löscht' ich so der Seele Brand,/Lied es wird erschallen;/Schöpft des Dichters reine Hand,/Wasser wird sich ballen' (F.195:26). (Quoted from Goethe's *West-östlicher Divan.*)

28 See 'Maximilian Harden: Ein Nachruf' (F.242/3:26–7). Kraus insisted Wedekind's friendship with Harden was dependent on his *not* reading Harden's periodical *Die Zukunft.*

29 Kraus was also involved with cabaret theatre in 1906, when he was the director of a one-act sketch at the Cabaret zum Nachtlicht. He had never used *Die Fackel* to promote the cabaret and had thus, he felt, preserved his independence as a critic. However, the engagement met with disaster when Kraus was physically attacked by an actor, Herr Henry, for his criticism of Marya Delvard, an actress who was also associated with the cabaret. Kraus felt that his satirical exposé (F.201:26–8) of Marya Delvard's exaggerated idea of her own greatness was justified, since he did not criticize her until she had given an interview to the *Fremdenblatt* – that is, until she had entered his realm of the newspaper. (F.203:22)

30 This was evident in other articles from this period, which later appeared in the collection *Sittlichkeit und Kriminalität* (1908).

31 The pun on which the effect of the original passage depends – *Dirne* (prostitute) and *Dirndl* (which can mean both 'lass' and 'dirndl dress') – is lost in the translation.

32 Even in *Erdgeist* Lulu embodied for Wedekind, as for Kraus, an idea rather than a person – that is, the earth-spirit of woman's sexuality.

33 Even the alleged importance of the portrait must be questioned, for it does not appear in Act I at all, and it is not until Act III that the portrait becomes an integral rather than a decorative part of the play. In the final act not only does Lulu's former beauty contrast with her present extreme squalor, but, in rescuing the picture and smuggling it into London, Gräfin Geschwitz demonstrates her devotion to Lulu by a dramatic deed that we the audience can perceive and react to.

34 See chapter 6 of Aristotle's *Poetics.*

35 Goldmann had protested against perversity on the stage. Kraus countered that no one knew what Goldmann meant by perverse (F.217:23).

36 See F.226:13–14. Kraus reprinted Nordau's damning review in the *Neue Freie Presse* of Wilde's *Salome* (which had been produced in Paris). All of Nordau's criticism was on moral, not literary, grounds.

37 Presumably he could have seen the Berlin production with another actress in the title role.

38 Berger was an Austrian who later became director of the Burgtheater.

39 Kraus praised the 'ehrliche Lehrhaftigkeit' of *Helden der Feder* (F.102:17) and the 'didaktische Gewandung' of *Die Gerechtigkeit* (F.122:2).

40 In the case of the dramatist Antonie Baumberg, the critics' lack of scruples was violently attacked by Kraus. Kraus had already praised her as a promising

dramatic talent. However, her plays had never achieved success on stage, since neither the liberal nor the anti-Semitic press would support her. Finally in 1902, after three failures of what Kraus considered to be good plays, she committed suicide. Kraus blamed the press for this death. 'Eine begabte Frau, das erste außerhalb der Clique gewachsene dramatische Talent, hat sich aus der Welt fortgemacht, weil drei Einacter nach der zweiten Aufführung vom Repertoire des Deutschen Volkstheaters abgesetzt wurden' (F.100:11). '(Sie) wurde zwischen den Parteien zermalmt' (F.102:27).

41 That is from the middle of p. 3 to p. 13. Even most of p. 1 is taken up by a quotation from his criticism of Madjera's play in Die Fackel no. 102.

42 Kraus pointed out that the dramatic weakness of the work lay in the indecisiveness of the author's intention; Hawel swayed for four acts between the standpoint of the liberal phrasemonger and the uncle who despised politics. Not until Act v was his intent clear.

43 See F.162:24–8.

44 The Eulenberg and Moltke trials

45 See F.2:8 and F.69:23–5.

46 See also F.118:3 – 'Hier mußte wirklich "alles ruiniert" werden; denn jeder Versuch, die Tagespresse literarisch zu heben, würde der heillosen Schlechtigkeit ihrer ethischen Natur nur eine höhere Weihe geben.' In the same article, Kraus noted that he could probably ironically be blamed for the founding of a new Viennese newspaper, Die Zeit, which claimed to have a clear style. Kraus stated that this was only 'die Ablösung des blumigen Schmockstils der alten Blätter durch die nüchterne Mauschelweis der Herren Singer und Kanner [editors]' (ibid, 8).

47 Kraus had already taken exception to Harden's calling Wedekind's Frühlings Erwachen 'einen Lenzmimus' in which 'das Männern der Knaben und das Böckeln der Mädchen' is described.

48 In 'Maximilian Harden: Ein Nachruf' (F.242/3) Kraus was concerned with writers and intellectuals who had been taken in by Harden's legendary pose of revolutionary fighter (even though they might never have read a line of Harden), and who saw a parallel to the martyrdom of Oscar Wilde in the fact that Harden had had to spend a few months in jail for his accusations against Graf Moltke. Kraus showed a great distrust of their critical abilities vis-à-vis a 'literary personality.'

49 See F.251/2:15–18, F.254/5:41–8.

50 F.118:1 ff

51 F.232/3:44, F.244:23–4

52 For example, an essay in Die Fackel no. 292 (pp. 16–32) entitled 'Rhabarber'

CHAPTER 3

1 Kraus's praise of Nestroy's use of language was counterpointed in this period by his severe censure of Heine, whose wit Kraus considered to be shallow and in

whose (in his opinion) superficial use of language he claimed to see the origins of the twentieth-century phenomenon of *Feuilletonismus*. See Kraus's essay 'Heine und die Folgen,' which formed the highlight of his first public lecture in Vienna in May 1910, and which was subsequently printed both in pamphlet form and in *Die Fackel* no. 329/30 (September 1911).

2 In 1912 he wrote: 'Die letzten zwei Jahre ... habe ich fern einer Wiener Bühne verlebt ...' (F.343/4:20). Of the Burgtheater, he wrote in 1917: 'Jetzt gehe ich wieder erst in zehn Jahren ins Burgtheater' (F.445/53:62).

3 Here, a parallel can probably be drawn between Nestroy and Kraus. In the essay 'Der kleine Pan stinkt schon' (F.324/5:50–60), Kraus cited a criticism of his style made by Max Brod. Brod had stated: 'Ein mittelmäßiger Kopf dagegen, wie Karl Kraus, dessen Stil nur selten die beiden bösen Pole der Literatur, Pathos und Kalauer, vermeidet, sollte es nicht wagen dürfen, einen Dichter ... zu berühren' (ibid, 57). Kraus countered with the asurance that he *never* avoided the two opposite poles of pathos and pun: '(ich begnüge) mich damit ... ihn [Brod] mit der Versicherung zu verblüffen, daß mein Stil diese beiden bösen Pole nicht nur selten, sondern geradezu nie vermeidet. Ob es die höchste oder die niedrigste Literatur ist, den Gedanken zwischen Pathos und Kalauer so zu bewegen, daß er beides zugleich sein kann, daß er eine feindlich Mücke in die Leidenschaft mitreißt, um sie im nächsten Augenblick in einem Witz zu zertreten, darüber lasse ich mich mit keinem lebenden Deutschen in einen Wortwechsel ein.' (Ibid, 58)

4 Here, Kraus drew a parallel between Wedekind and Nestroy: 'Der Schauspieler hat eine Rolle für einen Dichter geschrieben, die der Dichter einem Schauspieler nicht anvertrauen würde. In Wedekind stellt sich ... ein Monologist vor uns, dem gleichfalls eine scheinbare Herkömmlichkeit und Beiläufigkeit der szenischen Form genügt, um das wahrhaft Neue und Wesentliche an ihr vorbeizusprechen und vorbeizusingen. Auf die Analogie im Tonfall witzig eingestellter Erkenntnisse hat einmal der verstorbene Kritiker Wilheim hingewiesen. Der Tonfall ist jene Äußerlichkeit, auf die es dem Gedanken hauptsächlich ankommt, und es muß irgendwo einen gemeinsamen Standpunkt der Weltbetrachtung geben, wenn Sätze gesprochen werden, die Nestroy so gut gesprochen haben konnte wie Wedekind,' (F.349/50:9). He went on to cite a sentence from Wedekind that could as well have been written by Nestroy, and two from a Nestroy play that displayed Wedekind traits. But his assertion that similarity of cadence or accent (*Tonfall*) was an indication of similarity of outlook is not convincing.

5 In fact, Kraus was even willing to admit that a critic (presumably himself) could have been misled by hatred of the Jewish liberal press into a temporary lack of appreciation for Sonnenthal: 'es war möglich, daß ein Ressentiment gegen eine jüdische Presse, die längst die Vertretung der Verfallszeit übernomen hatte, seinen ehrwürdigen Resten unrecht tat.' (Ibid, 36–7)

6 See pp. 46–7.

7 The one certain exception occurred in 1917, when he saw the Arno Holz produc-

tion of *King Lear* in which Wüllner and Reimers performed. Kraus wrote that this was his first visit to the Burgtheater in ten years (F.445/53:62). However, it is possible that he saw the production of *Richard III* in 1910, when Berger was managing director of the Burgtheater. See his comment in *Die Fackel* no. 311/12 (p. 4): 'ich habe mit Wehmut die welken Blätter betrachtet, die zur Totenklage der Königinnen in "Richard III." von den Soffitten fielen.' It is also possible, however, that he read about this piece of stage business in a newspaper critique of the play.

8 See Kraus's remark in 1907: 'Herr Reimers wird neuestens aus seiner dekorativen Tüchtigkeit, die für Herolde und ähnliche unbewegte Begleiter einer Staatsaktion langt, in eine gefahrvolle Natürlichkeit gelockt.' (F.239/40:30)

9 This last point was particularly accentuated in another, shorter article about the Burgtheater's Swiss tour entitled 'Es war einfach überwältigend.' Kraus first quoted from a newspaper: 'Das Wiener Burgtheater und somit die österreichische Kunst hatte *mitten* im Krieg einen *unblutigen* Kultursieg im neutralen Ausland errungen!' He then remarked: 'Verwundet wurde niemand. Aber ich bekenne offen und ehrlich und auf die Gefahr hin, daß ich bei meinem nächsten Versuch, das Burgtheater zu betreten, hofftentlich nicht hineingelassen werde: daß ich eine blutige Niederlage von Burgschauspielern in Zürich ... einem Weltkrieg vorgezogen hätte!' (F.457/61:77)

10 Friedrich Schreyvogl, *Das Burgtheater* (Vienna, 1965) 120

11 See p. 84.

12 See also F.326/8:59–63.

13 Schreyvogl, *Das Burgtheater* 113. Wüllner had played Lear in 1917 in the production of that play so criticized by Kraus. See F.484/98:88–91.

14 Schreyvogl, *Das Burgtheater* 113

15 F.445/53:60; F.454/6:8.

16 See F.445/53:62–3. See also the article entitled 'Ein Staatsverbrechen an Shakespeare und Jugend' (F.484/98:88 ff) in which he reprinted a lettter he had sent to the Ministry of Culture and Education, protesting against the performance of Lear which was given free of charge for high-school students and pointed out the inadequacies of the production. He asked for a list of all students given invitations to the Burgtheater performance, in order that he might invite them to his public reading of the play. His purpose was pedagogical: to restore the image of the poet's original intention to youth, which had been led astray. 'Hat ihn [Kraus himself] zu seiner ersten "Lear"-Vorlesung die Absicht bestimmt, die Spuren der Unkunst zu verwischen, und ist ihm dies ohne jeden Apparat theatralischer wie publizistischer Inszenierung ... gelungen, so liegt ihm nun umsomehr der Wunsch am Herzen, einer irregeführten Jugend das dichterische Urbild wieder herzustellen.'

17 That Kraus's concept of drama was more aural than visual is obvious in his *Theater der Dichtung*. See also F.150:1 – 'Aber mir ist's nicht vergönnt, Kunstwerke als Betrachter zu genießen; eine unselige Hellhörigkeit zwingt

mich, den Stimmen zu lauschen, die aus der Tiefe dringen ...' and *F.241:1* – 'Mein Gehör ermöglicht es mir, einen Schauspieler, den ich vor zwanzig Jahren in einer Dienerrolle auf einen Provinztheater und seit damals nicht gesehen habe als Don Carlos zu imitieren. Das ist ein wahrer Fluch. Ich höre jeden Menschen sprechen, den ich einmal gehört habe.'

18 See also *F.462/71:173.*

19 The title (lit., 'Limits of Mankind') is – ironically – borrowed from a Goethe poem.

20 *Der mährisch-schlesische Korrespondent* (22 October 1913)

21 This at least is the date given by Kraus in *Die Fackel*; unfortunately it has proved impossible to verify it.

22 For example, 'Worte zum Gedächtnis des Prinzen Eugen,' written at the end of 1914

23 *F.339/40:30–1*

24 *F.400/3:60*

25 See Martin Swales, *Arthur Schnitzler. A Critical Study* (Oxford 1971).

26 Kraus continually reminded his readers that he was one of the few in the camp of the enemy who took a stand against the lie. In his essay 'Weltgericht' (written at the end of October 1918) he wrote: 'daß die schmutzige Zumutung der Macht an den Geist: Lüge für Wahrheit, Unrecht für Recht, Tollwut für Vernunft zu halten, von mir tagtäglich mühelos abgewiesen wurde. Denn der bessere Mut war der meine, im eigenen Lager den Feind zu sehen!' (*F.499/500:2–3*)

CHAPTER 4

1 See Hans Weigel, *Karl Kraus oder Die Macht der Ohnmacht* (Vienna 1972) 250. 'Immer stärker trat das vorgelesene dramatische Wort gegenüber den "eigenen Schriften" in den Vordergrund. Immer kleiner wurden aber auch die Säle dieses Theaters der Dichtung. Die zunehmende Isolation ist aus dem Vorlesungskatalog zu ersehen, der immer häufiger den Festsaal des Architektenvereins nennt, dann den kleinen Saal, den Karl Kraus Offenbach-Saal nannte, schließlich den ganz abseitigen Ehrbar-Saal in der Mühlgasse 30.'

2 Helene Richter, *Josef Lewinsky. Fünfzig Jahre Wiener Kunst und Kultur* (Vienna, no date)

3 Rachel (1821–58), whose real name was Elisabeth Félix, was reputedly one of the greatest French tragediennes of the nineteenth century.

4 Wildgans later returned for a second term as managing director from July 1930 to the end of 1931.

5 See *F.640/8:167* ff.

6 Kraus did not censure all contemporary efforts at staging Nestroy. He commended Jarno's production of *Eine Wohnung zu vermieten* at the Lustspieltheater. In *Die Fackel* no. 676/8 (p. 31) he stated that the necessary theatrical, poetic, and metaphysical dimension would have been present in a performance of *Lumpaziva-*

gabundus by actors such as Kneidinger (who had performed in Jarno's production of *Eine Wohnung zu vermieten*) and Oskar Sachs (whose portrayal of Knieriem Kraus remembered from twenty years before – F.622/31:112). However, it must be noted that *Eine Wohnung zu vermieten*, which had not had any success during Nestroy's time, had been 'rescued from oblivion' by Kraus, who included it in the repertoire of his Theater der Dichtung, and that he had originally been asked to direct the production at the Lustspieltheater. As he himself, with little modesty, stated: 'Wohl der einzige Ertrag des Theaterfestes war die von mir ange-regte Aufführung von Nestroys "Eine Wohnung zu vermieten" ... jenem theatralischen Meisterstück, das von der zeitgenössischen Kritik totgetreten wurde und seit damals nicht auferstanden war. Die Verantwortung des Regisseurs (die ich ursprünglich nicht abgelehnt hatte) zu übernehmen, war mir im unverschuldet späten Zeitpunkt meiner Rückkehr nach Wien ... unmöglich ...' (F.668/75:64). Here, Kraus's subjectively biased criticism is apparent, for, along with his own readings of Nestroy in his Theater der Dichtung, this performance, in which he was an interested party, was the only one that received his approval.

7 *Im Burgtheater spielen s' den Nestroy und*
Man ist im Himmel, nämlich auf dem Hund.
Im Haus voll Würde und von stolzem Wuchs
Woll'n sie sich mit ihm machen einen Jux.
Und wenn s' den Z'riss'nen spiel'n in diesem Haus,
Kommt nur der Titel als a Ganzer 'raus.
Doch den Lumpazi bringen s' erst zu sich,
Denn den spiel'n s', wie sich's g'hört, ganz liederlich.
   Die Leut hab'n a Freud' beim Nestroy sein' Schaden:
   Der Leim der ist trocken und mit'n Zwirn hat's ein' Faden.
Beim Knieriem sein' Lied da wurde mir bang,
Bei dem Humor steht d' Welt auf kein' Fall mehr lang.
Doch ich hör' s' vor Begeisterung schrei'n –
Nein, die Welt fällt auf jeden Fall 'rein 'rein 'rein 'rein 'rein 'rein,
Die Welt fällt noch lang lang herein. (F.676/8:1)

8 Friedrich Jenaczek, *Zeittafeln zur "Fackel." Themen, Ziele, Probleme* (Munich 1965) 56.

9 See also F.676/8:57.

10 See F.717/23:106–7. The dialect was that of Darmstadt. Kraus indicated in the programme notes that he felt it to be his 'duty as an honest man' (*Ehrenpflicht*) to show that Karl [sic] Zuckmayer's *Der fröhliche Weinberg* was but a watered-down version of the Niebergall play.

11 Kraus had (unsuccessfully) invited the Burgtheater actors to his readings of Raimund's *Der Bauer als Millionär* – see F.668/75:53.

12 In the pages following, Kraus included his praise of Lewinsky's biography and reprinted some of that actor's letters to him.

13 The remark occurred in a conversation with Otto Kerry in Vienna on 30 May 1972.

14 See his comment on his readers in *Die Fackel* no. 546/50 (p. 71): 'Eine der unangenehmsten Begleiterscheinungen der Fackel sind ihre Leser.'

15 Weigel contends that in 1925 at least (during his campaign to drive Bekessy from Vienna) Kraus was more than a prophet, in that he tried to make the authorities act. 'Karl Kraus wollte einst vom Schreibtisch forteilen und in die Vorgänge draußen eingreifen. Diesmal tat er es. Er stellte eine präzise Forderung. Er sagte nicht nur, was zu sagen war, er zog eine Konsequenz. Er war nicht mehr jener Prophet, den die Existenz des Üblen bestätigt. Er ging dem Übel gerade an den Leib. Er wollte in unmittelbarer Relation Ursache einer Wirkung sein.' Weigel, *Karl Kraus* 287. That, however, the witness he bore as prophet could awaken strength in others is evidenced by the influence he had on many intellectuals in Israel during the Second World War. See the foreword by Elazar Benyoetz to the reprint of Paul Engelmann's *Dem Andenken an Karl Kraus* (Vienna 1967) 4: 'Daß zur Zeit der furchtbaren Vernichtung in Europa, als das Chaos sich vollzog, einige in Israel lebende, auf wunderbare Weise gerettete Juden sich weiter mit Kraus beschäftigen konnten, ist kein Mißverständnis des Mannes, dem zu Hitler nichts einfiel. Es zeigt vielmehr, daß sie eben nichts mechanisch übernommen, sondern in einer Weise von Kraus gelernt hatten, die ihnen mitten im Chaos einen Halt gab, der sich als Haltung im gelebten Leben bezeugen konnte.'

16 Kraus read plays or scenes from plays by Goethe, Raimund, Niebergall, Gogol, Hauptmann, and Wedekind, as well as his own plays.

17 Kraus's preoccupation with Nestroy was especially evident until 1925; after that, much of his critical and creative energy went into the 'discovery' of Offenbach and the reworking of Offenbach operettas.

18 Kraus continued his fight against the critics and literary historians who, beginning with Friedrich Hebbel, and with the exception of Ludwig Speidel, could not see or would not admit that Nestroy was a great writer and only saw in him an adapter of French farces or a comic who turned out 'vehicles' to show off his acting talent (see also *F*.608/12:45). As Kraus wrote in his short article 'Nestroy und die Literatur': 'Da kann ich mich auf den Kopf stellen, bei der Literatur setze ich Nestroy nicht durch' (*F*.595/600:53). Even a critic such as Egon Friedell, who was quite sympathetic towards Nestroy, did not get off without some criticism from Kraus, who accused him of superficiality in the book of Nestroy quotations that Friedell published (*F*.613/21:51–3). As for the press critics, who were paid to publish what Kraus considered to be worthless opinions, Kraus accused Löwy of factual inaccuracy (*F*.668/75:67 ff) and misquoting (*F*.622/31:109–10); Goldmann of inaccuracy, lack of proper respect, and lack of competence (*F*.640/8:81); and both Salten and Decsey of lack of critical judgment (*F*.622/31:110–11) – Salten, because he thought Nestroy's plays were dead, and Decsey because he did not share Kraus's prejudice against the quality of acting of the Burgtheater and judged

that theatre's performance of *Einen Jux will er sich machen* in 1923 to be 'genuinely Viennese.' Even newspaper critics who were Nestroy's contemporaries received their share of criticism from Kraus for disregarding the intrinsic value of the plays and contributing to their failure when Nestroy hit too close to home with his satire (see *F*.781/6:55–6).

19 See *F*.781/6:53. *Das Notwendige und das Überflüssige* was published in 1920. In 1925 Kraus published his version of *Der konfuse Zauberer* based on the play by that name, to which Kraus added lines from an unpublished Nestroy manuscript, *Der Tod am Hochzeitstag oder Mann, Frau, Kind* (which was, according to him, 'obviously' a sketch for *Der konfuse Zauberer* – see *F*.679/85:39–40). For Kraus, reworking these plays afforded relaxation from the polemical work, which he considered to be his duty (ibid, 40).

20 *Grundlosigkeit* can of course mean both 'unfathomable depth' and 'unreasonableness,' but the two meanings support each other in this passage: if we could subject life to rational analysis, it would not be unfathomable.

21 See *F*.349/50:23.

22 His allusions to 'der Spiegelmensch' (*F*.679/85:47), while obvious to anyone familiar with the Kraus/Werfel feud, would be lost to many reading Kraus's added verses in the 1980s.

23 For example, in Knieriem's 'Kometenlied' (*F*.608/12:46 ff)

24 See Jenaczek, *Zeittafeln* 34: 'Erst dank Karl Kraus wurde der hohe Rang und die Bedeutung der Kunst Nestroys erkannt, und anerkannt.' The most concrete evidence of renewed interest in Nestroy was the publication of the critical edition of his works by Fritz Brukner and Otto Rommel between 1924 and 1930.

25 See Schick, *Karl Kraus* 21.

26 There is, however, no proof that Kraus really saw this performance at the Carl-Theater.

27 Jenaczek, *Zeittafeln* 56

28 See Lotte Sternbach-Gärtner (Caroline Kohn), 'Karl Kraus und Offenbach' in *Der Monat* 96 (Berlin 1956) 57.

29 It is worth remembering that when Kraus himself was lampooned on the stage, he thought that this was improper and appealed to the authorities to protect him.

30 *F*.806/9:62–3. Reprinted from *Der Anbruch* (March 1929)

31 For example, with the exception of his readings before 1900

32 Karl Kraus, *Werke 11, Sittlichkeit und Kriminalität* (Munich 1963) 11

33 Karl Kraus, *Shakespeares Dramen* (Vienna 1934) Vol. I, xiii–xiv

34 In the 1930s Kraus often wrote about the problems he encountered in adapting Shakespeare. See *F*.908 and *F*.909/11:16–19.

35 *Erste Hexe.*   Wann kommen wir drei uns wieder entgegen,
             Im Blitz und Donner, oder im Regen?
    Zweite Hexe. Wenn der Wirrwarr stille schweigt,
             Wer der Sieger ist, sich zeigt.

Cf. Schiller's version:

> *Erste Hexe.*　Wann kommen wir drei uns wieder entgegen,
> In Donner, in Blitzen oder in Regen?
> *Zweite Hexe.*　Wann das Kriegsgetümmel schweigt,
> Wann die Schlacht den Sieger zeigt.

36 'Dazu aber bedarf der Nachdichter gar nicht der Kenntnis des Originals, sondern bloß des Vergleichs jener unzulänglichen Ergebnisse philologischer Bemühung.' Shak. I. ix.

37 For a negative view of Kraus as an adapter of Shakespeare, see Richard Flatter, *Karl Kraus als Nachdichter Shakespeares. Eine sprachkritische Untersuchung* (Vienna 1934).

38 The plays were performed in Berlin and Vienna (March and April 1924).

39 The example he gives of Hamlet in modern dress ('Hamlet im Smoking') was Jeßner's production of the play.

40 This affirmation occurs at the end of a long passage in which Kraus criticized the Berlin Expressionist directors for updating the classics in their productions. Kraus obviously allied himself with 'jene Epigonen': 'Det Janze [sic] aber mit der aus dem unvermeidlichen Untergang des Abendlandes bezogenen Sicherheit, daß alles, was die Zeit bietet und was im "Querschnitt" der Gehirne die Impotenz kubisch erhöht zeigt, nun mal auch auf das Theater gehört und daß schließlich nicht wir Regisseure für den Humbug verantwortlich sind, sondern die Zeit, deren Betonfestigkeit uns über alle Wortproblematik hinweghilft, deren amoralische, dynamoralische Tüchtigkeit unsere stärkste Hilfe ist gegen die Betriebsstörung durch jene Epigonen, die noch heute auf dem Schein bestehen, den sie für das Wesen in Kunst und Natur halten.' (F.676/8:32–3)

41 See Jens Malte Fischer, *Karl Kraus. Studien zum 'Theater der Dichtung' und Kulturkonservatismus* (Kronberg /Taunus 1973).

42 See F.668/75:90.

43 See Gröning & Kließ, *Friedrichs Theaterlexikon* (Hannover 1969) 346: 'Reinhardts Auffassung vom Theater als großem Fest, als letzten Endes unpolitische ... gesellschaftsverbindende und überhöhte Lebensäußerung erscheint sowohl als Nachfolge österreichisch-barocker Vorstellungen wie als Erfüllung des großbürgerlichen, luxuriösen Kunstbegriffs.'

44 See Weigel, *Karl Kraus* 280.

45 F.743/50:53–8

46 Kraus even (belatedly) praised Kainz for his performance of the Fool in *Lear*: 'unter den vielen (seiner Leistungen) schien mir sein Narr im "Lear" die Bühnengestalt nicht zu verkümmern' (F.622/31:121).

47 Kraus had satirized this 'musicality' in one of the topical verses that he composed for Offenbach's *Pariser Leben*:

> *Ich möchte gern zum Moissi gehn,*
> *Weil der Gesang zum Herzen dringt,*

> *Und das Chantant möcht' ich besehn,*
> *Wo abends er den Hamlet singt. (F.759/65:31)*

Ironically, in his book *Karl Kraus* (New York 1971) 101, Harry Zohn writes of Kraus's voice that 'in its musicality, vibrancy, and striking expressiveness ... was somewhat reminiscent of that of the actor Alexander Moissi ...' He does not, however, mention on whose authority he makes such a statement.

48 This ethical-aesthetic link between *Persönlichkeit* and art was even more striking when Kraus discussed some of Moissi's writings (F.743/50:57–8).

49 Originally, this essay was published in *Die Fackel* no. 182 (pp. 1–18). It was reprinted in the collection of essays entitled *Literatur und Lüge* (Vienna 1929).

50 Castiglioni was portrayed in Kraus's play *Die Unüberwindlichen* under the thin disguise of Camillioni. See Schick, *Karl Kraus* 112.

51 Hofmannsthal's play was performed in the cathedral in Salzburg.

52 See also *F.*613/21:8. Here Kraus made an equally unsavoury pun on the title *Der Unbestechliche*.

53 Kraus claimed to be quoting from an interview with Shaw printed (with photos of Shaw in swimming trunks) in a magazine called *Der Abend*. However, characteristically he gave no issue or page number.

54 Weigel, *Karl Kraus* 293

55 See p. 38.

56 See Jenaczek, *Zeittafeln* 49: 'Nach Ansicht von Karl Kraus ist das Drama nicht aufführbar (Brief vom 8. XII. 22 ...).'

57 Karl Kraus, *Die letzten Tage der Menschheit* (Munich 1964) I, 5

58 Weigel, *Karl Kraus* 201: 'Bei den Spielszenen sehnte man sich nach den Kraus-Vorlesungen zurück. Die Andeutung war mächtiger gewesen, als die Realisation sein konnte. Auch in den Vorlesungen Helmt Qualtingers und auf seinen Platten erstehen das Werk und sein Geist reiner und richtiger als in der Dreidimensionalität.'

59 Karl Kraus, *Werke* 14, *Dramen* (Munich 1967) 90

60 For example, his remarks on Wedekind and Nestroy noted in chapter 2

61 Quoted in H.H. Hahnl's dissertation 'Karl Kraus und das Theater' (Vienna 1947) 117

62 Weigel, *Karl Kraus* 237–8

63 See chapter 3, pp. 145 ff.

64 Kraus, *Dramen* 56–7

65 Ibid, 101

66 Ibid, 103

67 Ibid, 106–7

68 Ibid, 103

69 Ibid, 108

70 *Wolkenkuckucksheim* is the exception.

71 Hahnl notes that Kraus's drama is a kind of monologue: 'Das Drama Kraus', An-

griff, Vision oder Reflexion in der elastischen Formel des Aphoristen, ist ein schauspielerisch konzipierter Monolog.' Hahnl, 'Karl Kraus' 139.

72 Tom Prideaux in *Life*, 14 July 1972, 22

73 See Leopold Liegler, *Karl Kraus und sein Werk* (Vienna 1933) 378 ff.

74 See Weigel, *Karl Kraus* 225. See also Lotte Sternbach-Gärtner, 'Karl Kraus und das expressionistische Theater,' in *Worte und Werte*, eds G. Erdmann and A. Eichstaedt (Berlin 1961) 407–9.

75 Sternbach-Gärtner, ibid, 408–9. See also Lotte Sternbach-Gärtner, 'Die letzten Tage der Menschheit und das Theater von Bert Brecht,' in *Deutsche Rundschau* 9 (Baden-Baden 1958) 836 f.

76 The Berlin critics' reports were reprinted on pp. 2–51, and those of the Viennese critics on pp. 128–48.

77 Kraus, *Die letzten Tage der Menschheit* II, 264

78 Kraus did in fact use slides at some of his lectures during the war years. See F.400/3:46.

79 Weigel, *Karl Kraus* 234

80 Ibid, 237

81 Ibid, 238

82 It is interesting to note that Kraus hated all attempts (such as those by Piscator) at creating a 'revolutionary' theatre in Berlin.

83 His attack against Kerr at that time occurred in a series of articles, which incorporated the phrase 'der kleine Pan stinkt' – see F.324/5:50–60.

CHAPTER 5

1 Two further volumes of Shakespeare adaptations were promised but never appeared.

2 Kraus preferred actors, such as Peter Lorre and Helene Weigel, to singers for his Offenbach broadcasts.

3 It is a stunning illustration of Kraus's political blindness that he found nothing better to do with his time at this desperate stage in the history of Europe than to attack the moderate political Left.

4 Frank Field, *The Last Days of Mankind. Karl Kraus and His Vienna* (London 1967) 195–6

5 Paul Schick, *Karl Kraus in Selbstzeugnissen und Bilddokumenten* (Reinbek 1965, rowohlt) 129

6 Since 1914, Kraus had already read scenes and songs from Raimund's *Der Verschwender*, *Der Alpenkönig und der Menschenfeind*, and *Das Mädchen aus der Feenwelt oder Der Bauer als Millionär*.

7 In 1920 Kraus had mentioned Raimund's 'powerlessness in the presence of the spirit of the times' and, although admiring him, called him 'antiquated': 'Was insonderheit die Wirkung Raimunds anlangt, so bitte überzeugt zu sein, daß ich

mir seiner Ohnmacht vor dem Zeitgeist, dessen Opfern oder Bekennern, vollkommen bewußt bin und ihn für noch weit antiquierter halte als die Verehrer des
Alfred Kerr es tun. Und dennoch stehe ich lieber zu Raimunds "Jugend" als einer,
deren Erlebnis die Hysterie ist und deren Weltanschauung der Mangel an Ehrfurcht' (F.546/50:12–13). There is a terrible irony in this remark, for now it could
just as easily be applied to the Kraus of 1935–6. He, too, was 'powerless before
the spirit of the times' and was considered by many to be 'antiquated.'

8 In his programme notes to a reading of *Der Verschwender*, Kraus divulged that
around 1891 he had been a guest actor in a public performance of the play by a
school for actors. He had played Wolf in Act III. See F.909/11:51.

9 The article was originally published in the *Wiener Zeitung* 30 January 1936.

10 *Eisenbahnheiraten oder Wien, Neustadt, Brünn* had already been praised by
Kraus in 1901. See F.88.

11 2 March 1935

12 See F.847/51:43–4 regarding his one and a half year court battle (which he lost)
against the music critic of the *Arbeiterzeitung*.

13 Ibid, 41–3

14 This letter was first published in *Stimmen über Karl Kraus* (Vienna 1934), a
collection of articles and letters written in praise of Kraus on the occasion of his
sixtieth birthday.

15 These were: a programme of Offenbach excerpts under the title of *Der König ihres
Herzens*, in the Johann Strauß-Theater in Vienna in 1931, Reinhardt's productions of *Die schöne Helena* and *Hoffmanns Erzählungen*, Mehring's version of *Die
Großherzogin von Gerolstein*, and the 1932 Prague production of *Madame
l'Archiduc*.

16 It is again worth noting that Kraus is no longer in control of his language: in the
clause 'ohne die diese Wirkung …' In this passage, the relative pronoun 'die' has no
meaningful antecedent, and the reader has to guess the intended meaning.

17 Hans Weigel, *Karl Kraus oder Die Macht der Ohmacht* (Vienna 1972) 245–6

18 Ibid, 248

19 Ibid, 247

20 See especially F.912/15:21–33, F.916:11–16.

21 See also Zerline Gabillon's remarks about Rachel reprinted in 1926 in F.743/50.

22 'Die Bühne ist … besät mit den Sätzen, die sie [die Schauspieler] "fallen lassen,"
hauptsächlich Zitaten. Herr Werner Krauß unterscheidet sich von den anderen
wenigstens dadurch, daß er deutlicher macht, was er fallen läßt. Wenn er als
Lear "O Höll und Tod" oder gar "Pest, Rache, Tod, Verderben" sagt, so sind es
klare Feststellungen seiner Unzufriedenheit' (F.906/7:22). 'Das erhöhte Theater
verlangt die Fähigkeit, aus der Sprache zu gestalten. Heute aber entsteht
Charakteristik auf Kosten der Sprache oder es werden Verse von einem
verkleideten Herrn mit mehr oder minder richtiger Betonung aufgesagt.'
(Ibid, 23)

23 Not only had the director added lines (ibid, 5) but he had, in Kraus's opinion, cut the speeches in such a way as to simplify the thought and flatten both poetry and tragedy. When Kraus listened for the lines:

Gott, wer darf sagen: schlimmer kann's nicht werden?
's ist schlimmer nun als je.
Und kann noch schlimmer gehn; 's ist nicht das Schlimmste,
Solang' man sagen kann: dies ist das Schlimmste.

he heard only:

Gott, wer darf sagen: schlimmer kann's nicht werden?
's ist schlimmer nun als je. (Ibid, 4)

24 Kraus was not the only one in Vienna at the time who gave a one-man show of Shakespeare readings. Ernst Reinhold had received much critical acclaim for his dramatic recitations. They differed from those of Kraus in that Reinhold made use of lighting effects and a podium draped in purple. He did not use a text but recited whole plays by heart in English. In Kraus's opinion, this was sheer nonsense and gimmickry. 'Die freie Rede wie das Englisch wird mich zwar nicht beirren, aber ich vermute, daß es die andern Hörer beirrt, sowohl die, die es nicht verstehen, wie die, die es verstehen, und solche, denen bloß die Gedächtnisleistung imponiert. Mir ja nicht: der sie im Vorhinein für Unfug und für Manöver der Ablenkung hält' (*F*.857/63:92). For Kraus, it was indispensable to have the text in his hand, even though he insisted that he knew the plays by heart. It was as if the book formed the necessary barrier between him and his audience, which only the characters whom he brought to life could cross. 'Denn es kommt darauf an, das sichtbare Buch so unsichtbar zu machen, daß nur die Gestalten sichtbar werden, die daraus hervortreten ... Das Buch ist unerläßlich' (ibid). Nevertheless, the critical praise that Reinhold received for his performances rankled Kraus, especially when the newspapers claimed that Reinhold was the first to give such readings, completely ignoring Kraus's unique pioneering in that field (*F*.909/11:19 ff).

25 Caroline Kohn, *Karl Kraus* (Stuttgart 1966) 120

26 Bert Brecht, *Schriften zur Literatur und Kunst* ed. Werner Kraft (Tübingen 1967) I, 58–9

27 Ibid, III, 66–7

28 Quoted in Friedrich Jenaczek, *Zeittafeln zur "Fackel". Themen, Ziele, Probleme* (Munich 1965) 121–2

29 Ibid, 122

30 Quoted by Kurt Krolop in his article 'Bertolt Brecht und Karl Kraus,' *Philologica Pragensia* 4 (1961) 226–7

31 Ibid, 229–30

32 Jenaczek, *Zeittafeln* 137–8

✌ Selected Bibliography

A / BIBLIOGRAPHIES

Kerry, Otto *Karl-Kraus-Bibliographie* Munich 1970
– 'Nachtrag zur Karl-Kraus-Bibliographie' *Modern Austrian Literature* 8 (1975) 103–80
Scheichl, Sigurd Paul 'Kommentierte Auswahlbibliographie zu Karl Kraus' in: *Karl Kraus* Text + Kritik, Sonderband, ed. Heinz Ludwig Arnold, Munich 1975, 158–241

B / KARL KRAUS'S WORKS

Kraus, Karl *Die demolirte Literatur* Vienna 1897*
– ed. *Die Fackel* Vienna 1899–1936
– *Die letzten Tage der Menschheit* 2 vols Munich 1964
– *Shakespeares Dramen* Für Hörer und Leser bearbeitet, teilweise sprachlich erneuert von Karl Kraus. 2 vols Vienna 1934–5
– *Werke* 14 vols ed Heinrich Fischer, Munich 1954–67

C / WORKS ABOUT KARL KRAUS

Arntzen, Helmut 'Karl Kraus als Kritiker des Fin de Siècle,' in: *Fin de siècle: Zu Literatur und Kunst der Jahrhundertwende* ed Roger Bauer et al Frankfurt 1977, 112–24
– *Karl Kraus und die Presse* Munich 1975
Bohn, Volker *Satire und Kritik. Über Karl Kraus* Frankfurt 1974
Borries, Mechthild *Ein Angriff auf Heinrich Heine. Kritische Betrachtungen zu Karl Kraus* Stuttgart, Berlin, Cologne, Mainz 1971

* For the articles published by Kraus between 1892 and 1898 in *Wiener Literatur-Zeitung, Die Gesellschaft, Das Rendez-vous, Wiener Tagblatt, Liebelei, Montags-Revue, Wiener Rundschau, Breslauer Zeitung,* and *Die Wage* see Kerry's *Karl-Kraus-Bibliographie* listed above.

Brecht, Bertold *Schriften zur Literatur und Kunst* 3 vols ed. Werner Hecht, Tübingen 1967

Brock-Sulzer, Elisabeth 'Karl Kraus und das Theater' *Akzente* (December 1955) 503–9

Daviau, Donald G. 'Language and Morality in Karl Kraus' "Die letzten Tage der Menschheit" ' *Modern Language Quarterly* 22 (1961) 46–54

Deutsch, Otto Erich 'Offenbach, Kraus und die anderen (1931)' *Österreichische Musik-Zeitschrift* 18 (1963) 408–12

Dietze, Walter 'Dramaturgische Besonderheiten des Antikriegsschauspiels "Die letzten Tage der Menschheit" von Karl Kraus' *Philologica Pragensia* 5 (1962) 65–83

Disch, Andreas *Das gestaltete Wort. Die Idee der Dichtung im Werk von Karl Kraus* Zurich 1969

Dürrenmatt, Friedrich 'Die dritte Walpurgisnacht,' in Friedrich Dürrenmatt *Theater-Schriften und Reden* (Zurich 1966) 247–50

Engelmann, Paul *Dem Andenken an Karl Kraus* Vienna 1967

Field, Frank *The Last Days of Mankind. Karl Kraus and his Vienna* London, Melbourne, Toronto 1967

Fischer, Jens Malte *Karl Kraus* Stuttgart 1974

– *Karl Kraus. Studien zum 'Theater der Dichtung' und Kulturkonservatismus* Kronberg/Taunus 1973

Flatter, Richard *Karl Kraus als Nachdichter Shakespeares. Eine sprachkritische Untersuchung* Vienna 1934

Ginsberg, Ernst, 'Karl Kraus und die Schauspieler' *Forum* (August 1961) 229

Grimstad, Kari 'Karl Kraus and the Problem of Illusion and Reality in Drama and the Theater' *Modern Austrian Literature* 8 (1975) 48–60

Hahnl, Hans Heinz 'Karl Kraus und das Theater' Diss. Vienna 1947

– 'Karl Kraus und das Theater' *Wort in der Zeit* 2 (June 1956) 17–20

Hartl, Edwin, 'das Ja und Nein zu Karl Kraus' *Literatur und Kritik* 24 (May 1968) 247f

– 'Verblendete Hellseher und Schwarzseher' *Literatur und Kritik* 41 (1970) 3–14

Heller, Erich 'Karl Kraus: The last days of mankind' in Erich Heller, *The Disinherited Mind. Essays in modern German literature and thought* (Cambridge, 1952) 183–201

Himmel, Hellmuth 'Hugo von Hofmannsthal und Karl Kraus' *Österreich in Geschichte und Literatur* 10 (1966) 551–65

Iggers, Wilma A. *Karl Kraus: A Viennese Critic of the 20th Century* The Hague 1967

Jenaczek, Friedrich 'Protest' *Literatur und Kritik* 41 (1970) 14–21

– *Zeittafeln zur "Fackel". Themen, Ziele, Probleme* Munich 1965

Kars, Gustave 'L'esthétique de Karl Kraus' *Études germaniques* 8 (Oct./Dec. 1953) 252–61

Kohn, Caroline 'Bert Brecht, Karl Kraus et le "Kraus-Archiv" ' *Études germaniques* 11 (1956) 342–8

– *Karl Kraus* Stuttgart 1966

Kohn, Hans *Karl Kraus, Arthur Schnitzler, Otto Weininger. Aus dem jüdischen Wien der Jahrhundertwende* Tübingen 1962

Kosler, Hans Christian 'Karl Kraus und die Wiener Moderne' *Text und Kritik* Sonderband Karl Kraus (1975) 39–57

Kraft, Werner *Das Ja des Neinsagers. Karl Kraus und seine geistige Welt.* Munich, 1974

– 'Es war einmal ein Mann. Über die "Dritte Walpurgistnacht" von Karl Kraus' *Merkur* 22 (1968) 926–35

– *Karl Kraus. Beiträge zum Verständnis seines Werkes* Salzburg 1956

Krolop, Kurt 'Bertolt Brecht und Karl Kraus' *Philologica Pragensia* 4 (1961) 95–112 and 203–30

– 'Dichtung und Satire bei Karl Kraus' in Karl Kraus *Ausgewählte Werke* (Munich 1971) III, 651–91

Leschnitzer, Franz 'Ein zweites Gedicht Bertolt Brechts über Karl Kraus' *Neue Deutsche Literatur* 12 (1964) 212–15

Liegler, Leopold *Karl Kraus un sein Werk* Vienna 1933

Mautner, Franz H 'Karl Kraus. Die letzten Tage der Menschheit' in *Das deutsche Drama. Vom Barock bis zur Gegenwart. Interpretationen* 2 Benno von Wiese ed. (Düsseldorf 1964) 360–85

– 'Über Karl Kraus's Komödie *Wolkenkuckucksheim*: Aristophanes *Vögel* nach 2300 Jahren' in *Austriaca: Beiträge zur österreichischen Literatur: Festschrift für Heinz Politzer zum 65. Geburtstag* ed. Winfried Kudszus et al (Tübingen 1975) 315–28

Mayer, Hans 'Karl Kraus' in Mayer *Der Repräsentant und der Märtyrer. Konstellationen der Literatur* (Frankfurt/Main 1971) 45–64

Mühlher, Robert 'Karl Kraus und das Burgtheater vor 1890' *Österreich in Geschichte und Literatur* 10 (June 1966) 298–307

Muschg, Walter 'Karl Kraus; Die letzten Tage der Menschheit' in Muschg *Von Trakl zu Brecht. Dichter des Expressionismus* (Munich 1961) 174–97

Nachrichten aus dem Kösel-Verlag. Sonderheft zum 90. Geburtstag von Karl Kraus Munich 1964

Naumann, Michael *Der Abbau einer verkehrten Welt; Satire und politische Wirklichkeit im Werk von Karl Kraus* Munich 1969

Ögg, Franz *Personenregister zur Fackel von Karl Kraus Supplementband zum Reprint der Fackel* Munich 1977

Polacek, Josef 'Egon Erwin Kisch über Karl Kraus' *Literatur und Kritik* 41 (1970) 21–36

Politzer, Heinz 'Die letzten Tage der Schwierigen: Hofmannsthal, Karl Kraus und Schnitzler' *Merkur* 28 (1974) 214–38

Raddatz, Fritz J. 'Der blinde Seher. Überlegungen zu Karl Kraus' *Merkur* 22 (1968) 517–32

Rychner, Max *Karl Kraus* Vienna 1924

Schaukal, Richard *Karl Kraus. Versuch eines geistigen Bildnisses* Vienna 1933

Schick, Paul 'Karl Kraus: Der Satiriker und die Zeit' *Études germaniques* 12 (1957) 240–9

– *Karl Kraus in Selbstzeugnissen und Bilddokumenten* Reinbek 1965 (Rowohlt)

Schmid, Richard 'Die Fackel des Karl Kraus' *Merkur* 28 (1974) 1053–70
Snell, Mary 'Karl Kraus' "Die letzten Tage der Menschheit"' *Forum for Modern Language Studies* 4 (1968) 234–47
Stern, J.P. 'Karl Kraus' Vision of Language' *Modern Language Revue* 61 (1966) 81–4
Sternbach-Gärtner, Lotte [Caroline Kohn] '"Die letzten Tage der Menschheit" und das Theater von Bert Brecht' *Deutsche Rundschau* 84 (Sept. 1958) 836–42
– 'Karl Kraus und das expressionistische Theater' in *Worte und Werte. Festschrift für Bruno Markward zum 60. Geburtstag* ed. G. Erdmann and A. Eichstaedt (Berlin 1961) 398–409
– 'Karl Kraus und Offenbach' *Der Monat* 96 (1956) 55–61
Torberg, Friedrich 'Das Wort gegen die Bühne. Zur szenischen Uraufführung der "Letzten Tage der Menschheit" von Karl Kraus' *Forum* (Aug. 1964) 383–5
Urbach, Reinhard 'Karl Kraus und Arthur Schnitzler. Eine Dokumentation' *Literatur und Kritik* 49 (1970) 513–30
– 'Karl Kraus und Hugo von Hofmannsthal. Eine Dokumentation. I. 1892–1899. II. 1899–1935' in *Hofmannsthal Blätter* I Heft 6 (1971) 447–58. II Heft 12 (1974) 372–424
Wagenknecht, Christian *Das Wortspiel bei Karl Kraus* Göttingen 1965
Weigel, Hans *Karl Kraus oder Die Macht der Ohnmacht* Vienna 1972
Zohn, Harry *Karl Kraus* New York 1971

D GENERAL BACKGROUND

Aristotle *Poetics* trans. Leon Golden Englewood Cliffs 1968
Arntzen, Helmut *Literatur im Zeitalter der Information* Frankfurt/Main 1971
Basil, Otto *Johann Nestroy in Selbstzeugnissen und Bilddokumenten* Reinbek 1967 (rowohlt)
Catholy, Eckehard 'Schauspielertum als Lebensform' *Hebbel-Jahrbuch* 1951, 97–112
Gröning, K. und W. Kließ *Friedrichs Theaterlexikon* Velber bei Hannover 1969
Hadamowsky, Franz 'Die Commedia dell'arte in Österreich und ihre Wirkung auf das Wiener Volkstheater' *Maske und Kothurn* 3 (1957) 312–16
Harding, L.V. *The Dramatic Art of Ferdinand Raimund and Johann Nestroy* The Hague, Paris 1974
Hein Jürgen 'Nestroy-Forschung (1901–1966)' *Wirkendes Wort* 18 (1968) 232–45
Hofmannsthal, Hugo von/Leopold von Andrian *Briefwechsel* Frankfurt/Main 1968
Ihering, Herbert, *Von Josef Kainz bis Paula Wessely* Heidelberg 1942
– *Von Reinhardt bis Brecht. Vier Jahrzehnte Theater und Film* Berlin 1961
Irmer, Hans-Jochen 'Jacques Offenbachs Werke in Wien und Berlin' *Wissenschaftliche Zeitschrift der Universität Berlin. Gesellschafts- und Sprachwissenschaftliche Reihe* 18 (1969) 125–45
Jacob, P. Walter *Jacques Offenbach in Selbstzeugnissen und Bilddokumenten* Reinbek 1969 (rowohlt)

Kindermann, Heinz *Hermann Bahr. Ein Leben für das europäische Theater* Graz, Cologne 1954

Mautner, Franz H. *Nestroy* Heidelberg 1974

Nestroy, Johann *Werke* Munich 1968

Niederle, Bertha *Charlotte Wolter* Vienna 1948

Prohaska, D. *Raimund and Vienna* Cambridge 1970

Raimund, Ferdinand *Sämtliche Werke* Munich 1966

Reichert, Herbert W. 'Some causes of the Nestroy renaissance in Vienna,' *Monatshefte* 47 (1955) 221–30

Richter, Helene *Josef Lewinsky. Fünfzig Jahre Wiener Kunst und Kultur* Vienna, no date

Rommel, Otto *Die Alt-Wiener Volkskomödie* Vienna 1952

Rühle, Gunter *Theater für die Republik (1917–33). Im Spiegel der Kritiker* Frankfurt 1967

Schorske, Carl E. *Fin-de-siècle Vienna. Politics and Culture* New York 1980

Schreyvogl, Friedrich *Das Burgtheater* Vienna 1965

Shakespeare, Wm *Macbeth* New Haven 1954

– *Werke* 5 Darmstadt 1958

Swales, Martin *Arthur Schnitzler. A Critical Study* Oxford 1971

Volke, Werner *Hugo von Hofmannsthal in Selbstzeugnissen und Bilddokumenten* Reinbek 1967 (rowohlt)

Wedekind, Frank *Gesammelte Werke* Munich 1920

❧ Index

This book

was designed by

ANTJE LINGNER

and was printed by

University of

Toronto

Press